Rice Paddy Recon

ALSO BY ANDREW R. FINLAYSON

Killer Kane: A Marine Long-Range Recon Team Leader in Vietnam, 1967–1968 (McFarland, 2013)

Rice Paddy Recon

*A Marine Officer's Second Tour
in Vietnam, 1968–1970*

ANDREW R. FINLAYSON

McFarland & Company, Inc., Publishers
Jefferson, North Carolina

All photographs are from the author's collection. Maps by Becky Wilkes.

LIBRARY OF CONGRESS CATALOGUING-IN-PUBLICATION DATA

Finlayson, Andrew R.
Rice paddy recon : a Marine officer's second tour in Vietnam, 1968–1970 / Andrew R. Finlayson.
pages cm
Includes bibliographical references and index.

ISBN 978-0-7864-9623-5 (softcover : acid free paper) ∞
ISBN 978-1-4766-1818-0 (ebook)

1. Vietnam War, 1961–1975—Military intelligence—United States. 2. United States. Marine Corps—Officers—Biography. 3. Marines—United States—Biography. 4. United States. Central Intelligence Agency—Biography. 5. Vietnam War, 1961–1975—Campaigns—Vietnam—Tây Ninh (Province) 6. Vietnam War, 1961–1975—Personal narratives, American. I. Title. II. Title: Marine officer's second tour in Vietnam, 1968–1970.

DS559.8.M44F55 2014   959.704'345—dc23   [B]   2014040053

BRITISH LIBRARY CATALOGUING DATA ARE AVAILABLE

© 2014 Andrew R. Finlayson. All rights reserved

No part of this book may be reproduced or transmitted in any form or by any means, electronic or mechanical, including photocopying or recording, or by any information storage and retrieval system, without permission in writing from the publisher.

Front cover: silhouette (Dreamstime); background: the Song Thu Bon River (Author)

Manufactured in the United States of America

*McFarland & Company, Inc., Publishers
Box 611, Jefferson, North Carolina 28640
www.mcfarlandpub.com*

To the memory of Mr. Charles O. Stainback, a World War II Navy veteran who joined the Central Intelligence Agency in 1947 and served his country for thirty years doing some of the most dangerous and important work his country could ask him to perform. Like his colleagues in the CIA, he served silently and unsung. His fellow countrymen will never know the sacrifices he and his family endured in the service of our country, but I hope my humble effort to describe one small aspect of his career with the CIA during the Vietnam War will serve to remind America that we are kept safe because men and women like him chose to work in the shadows for us.

Table of Contents

List of Maps — viii
Acknowledgments — ix
Preface — 1
  1. Back to Vietnam and the War — 5
  2. Deja Vu — 10
  3. An Hoa—Patrols Redux — 41
  4. Base Area 112 — 67
  5. The Idylls of March — 76
  6. The Arizona Territory — 90
  7. Liberty Bridge — 105
  8. The Que Son Mountains — 114
  9. Hill 65 and the Palace Guard — 128
  10. Qua's Story: The Life of a Viet Cong Guerrilla — 148
  11. The House on Doan Cong Bu Street — 164
  12. The CIA Embassy House — 172
  13. First Impressions — 192
  14. Bad American Policy—A New Focus — 205
  15. London Interlude — 226
  16. America's Most Valuable Spy — 231
  17. The Pru Winter Offensive of 1969 — 246
  18. The Cambodian Invasion — 257
  19. My War Ends — 267
Epilogue — 281
Glossary — 297
Chapter Notes — 300
Bibliography — 303
Index — 306

List of Maps

1. South Vietnam — 6
2. Da Nang (detail of Map 1) — 18
3. Base Area 112 (detail of Map 1) — 30
4. Que Son Mountains, East of An Hoa — 32
5. Tay Ninh Province — 169
6. Ho Chi Minh Trail in Laos — 292

Acknowledgments

This book would not have been possible to write without the kind assistance of many people. I am particularly grateful to Lt. Col. George W.T. "Digger" O'Dell, USMC (Ret.); Col. Frederick J. Vogel, USMCR (Ret.); Col. John McKay, USMC (Ret.); Mr. Michael C. Henry; Mr. Bart Russell; Mr. Robert Garcia, Mr. Robert Buda; Mr. Rudy Enders; Mr. Andy Vaart; Mr. Ray Lau; Mr. James "Mac" McGee; Mr. Kevin J. Murphy; Mr. William Laurie; and Mr. Charles O. Stainback. These individuals provided both steadfast support and valuable firsthand information on the events discussed in this book. They also read portions of the book or the entire manuscript and offered many useful comments and suggestions.

I am grateful to Mr. Jim Downer, a former machine gunner in Company G, 2nd Battalion, 5th Marines, who provided his personal insights concerning the many fire fights he participated in during the summer of 1969. He also provided extracts from the daily diary of Sgt. John Ralston, which detailed both substantiating and amplifying information concerning the events that occurred during the period May 14 to August 22, 1969.

I was given many helpful leads and advice from Mr. Charles D. Melson and Mr. Kenneth H. Williamson of the U.S. Marine Corps History Division at Quantico, Virginia. These gentlemen allowed me to have complete access to the Marine Corps archives and pointed me in the right direction when I became lost in the files. Mr. Williamson also provided many valuable insights on publishing the combat memoir and provided a list of publishing companies that might have an interest in my book.

Before his death in 2010, I was privileged to have interviewed Col. Terence M. Allen, USMC (Ret.), who provided many details about the classified work done by the Provincial Reconnaissance Units (PRU). He was the senior U.S. military officer assigned to the PRU Program during the time period discussed in this book, and he had a high-level perspective on the role the PRU played in the Phoenix Program. He was able to fill in many holes in my knowledge about the PRU Program due to the compartmental and classified nature of this program.

Mr. Merle L. Pribbenow and Mr. Hal Meinheit provided unclassified information on "The Tay Ninh Source," drawn largely from North Vietnamese documents and articles, but also from recent interviews with former South Vietnamese intelligence officers with knowledge of this very valuable spy for the CIA. Since the CIA files on "The Tay Ninh Source" are still classified, their knowledge of this spy and the contribution he made to the American war effort was crucial in developing a fuller picture of the man behind the code name.

I am also grateful for the assistance of Dr. Jeffrey Race of Harvard University and Mr.

John D. Caldwell, for their assistance in understanding some of the underlying strategic failures of the Vietnam War, especially those involving the various pacification programs employed by the American and South Vietnamese governments.

Three good friends of mine assisted in the preparation of the text of this book, and I shall forever be grateful to them for their friendship and their technical advice. Mrs. Mary Davisson typed the manuscript and formatted it, Ms. Marla Markman proofread the manuscript, and Mrs. Becky Wilkes created the maps for the book. Without their expertise and help, this book would never have been published.

Although I have worked on the manuscript of this book for nearly four decades, the decision to finally publish it was made on the advice of Dr. Mark Moyer, a noted historian on the Vietnam War, who felt it was necessary to tell my story so historians and students of the Vietnam War might benefit from a firsthand account of that war at the rice paddy level.

Finally, I would like to thank my wife, Sarah, for putting up with the many hours of research and writing that this book demanded. Her patience, loyalty, love, and support played a major role in the creation of this book.

Preface

This book takes up the story of my experiences during the Vietnam War when I returned on my second tour of duty to that war-ravaged nation. My first tour of duty in South Vietnam is covered in my book, *Killer Kane: A Marine Long-Range Recon Team Leader in Vietnam, 1967–1968*. There are several reasons why I wrote the present work. Perhaps the most enduring one involved a question that has plagued me ever since 1975, when the communist forces of North Vietnam finally defeated the South Vietnamese. For forty years I have tried to answer the question of why we lost the Vietnam War. I realized I often changed my mind over time about many aspects of the war, including my appreciation of the complex variables that had an effect on the outcome, and this process caused me to hesitate to write with any degree of certainty about the reasons for the loss of that war. However, after many years of study and reflection, I think I have finally answered this question, at least in my own mind. In the last chapter of this book, the reader will find my answer to this question, an answer that is based upon both my study of the war and my own personal involvement. Along with my analysis of why we lost the war, the reader will find an alternate strategy that I feel would have been successful had it been adopted.

I also wanted to provide historians and others with a firsthand account of how one young Marine officer fought in that war. Most personal accounts of the war have been written by individuals who spent one year or less in Vietnam, often doing only one task in one geographical area of the country. Their perspective on the war, while important and interesting, often had little to do with the broader aspects of the war, since the experience of these veterans was narrowly focused on a single endeavor for only a short period of time. I spent thirty-two months in South Vietnam, doing three distinct combat jobs that allowed me to see the war in two different geographical areas and to do so during the most critical years of the war, 1967 to 1970. As a result, I saw how the war progressed during those thirty-two months and how different the war was in the coastal lowlands and mountains of I Corps in the north and the Cambodian–South Vietnam border areas in III Corps. As I relate my story, the reader will be taken along on long-range reconnaissance patrols in enemy-held territory, experience the terror and excitement of infantry firefights against Viet Cong (VC) and North Vietnamese (NVA) units, and learn how the U.S. Central Intelligence Agency (CIA) conducted special police operations against the enemy's political leadership in the hamlets and villages of rural South Vietnam. The reader will also learn about the most valuable spy the CIA had on its payroll during the war and the impact this spy had on the prosecution of the war. Some pseudonyms have been used to protect the identities of CIA case officers and Vietnamese who may be living in Vietnam and subject to retribution.

From these experiences in various geographical locales in South Vietnam over a three-year period, I gained a perspective that I suspect was far different from many of my comrades who served in that war, and I hope to convey this perspective to the reader. For instance, most of the American veterans of the Vietnam War were not engaged in combat, but served in support roles. Only one in five participants actually served in combat units. Also, most veterans of the Vietnam War served only one year in South Vietnam and in one geographic area of that country. Clearly, the impressions gained by an aviation mechanic repairing helicopters at Marble Mountain near Da Nang City in 1966 and those of a U.S. Army infantryman in the Central Highlands in 1970 would be vastly different. An American advisor with an ARVN airborne unit in 1965 would have a decidedly different outlook on the war from that of a supply sergeant working in a warehouse in Cam Rahn Bay in 1969. Similarly, a staff officer in the huge MACV headquarters at Long Binh near Saigon in 1968 would have an entirely different view of the war from that of a Navy Seal conducting special operations missions in the Mekong Delta in that same year. My point is this: The period of time when someone served in South Vietnam, where he served, and the job he performed could produce extremely varied impressions of the war, a fact that makes it difficult for historians and others to accurately assess the war based upon the impressions of the veterans of that war. I can only offer my rather unique perspective, based upon my thirty-two-month exposure to the war, in two geographic areas of strategic importance—I Corps and III Corps. I draw my conclusions about the conduct of the war based upon my personal involvement and my over forty years of study since I left South Vietnam. While it would be arrogant for me to assume that I have any special insight into the objective truths concerning the war, I hope that my story may provide some helpful information to those who seek to understand this very controversial and poorly understood war.

I had the greatest respect for many of the men and women I worked with or knew in South Vietnam during the war. Many Americans and South Vietnamese made a lasting, positive impression upon me, and I wanted to tell their story along with mine. I tell the story of U.S. Marines, South Vietnamese special police, CIA officers, a former VC, and several spies who penetrated the enemy's political leadership, and provided strategic and tactical intelligence of great value. My book is my way of remembering these people who often were quite ordinary but who accomplished extraordinary things during the war. This is especially true when I describe the South Vietnamese nationalists I lived and worked with who lost so much and deserved a better outcome to the war. As the reader will see, my view of the South Vietnamese does not match many of the stereotypes commonly found in other books. If I do not tell the story of these people, they and their remarkable deeds will be forgotten.

And finally, and perhaps most important, I wanted to write a book that explained why I volunteered to fight for my country and volunteered again to return to combat when I was not required to do so. The Vietnam War was the one great lyric passage of my existence; everything else I did in my life paled to insignificance when measured against that experience. I joined the military and served for twenty-five years in the Marine Corps because I wanted the people I knew and loved in my small town to respect and love me. I did not serve out of a great sense of patriotism or the pursuit of an adventurous life. While I loved and respected the Marines I served with, I did not fight because of my pride in the Marine Corps or a sense of obligation to the leaders of my country or its institutions. What motivated me was a need formed when I was a teenager to do something in my life that would make the people of Merchantville, New Jersey, proud of me.

Perhaps the best way to explain my love for my hometown is to quote a portion of a letter I received from a young woman shortly after I returned from Vietnam and she visited Merchantville with me. She wrote:

> On the drive to your hometown I must admit I was getting a bit bored with your recantations about how nice it was; and, yes, I was also getting a bit jealous since I am sure a great deal of those fond memories of your youth involved love interests. However, the moment we turned onto the main street of Merchantville, I knew immediately why you loved your hometown so much. I had the strangest sensation that I was driving through a Hollywood set for some movie about the quintessential American small town. The tree-lined streets, the small shops, the numerous churches, the quaint Victorian homes—I felt like we would soon encounter Jimmy Stewart or Mickey Rooney, and they would wave to us as we drove by. It all reminded me of the movie *It's a Wonderful Life,* and I had to admit to myself that what I thought was some eccentric attachment of yours was in fact a real appreciation for a lovely and unique place.

Of the failures in my life, the one that hurt the most was the realization that I never accomplished anything that merited the pride of my hometown residents in me. It was this vain attempt to win their praise that made me fight in the Vietnam War, and it was also the reason why I spent so many years in the Marine Corps trying to redeem myself for failing to win that war and to find some way to gain the respect and love of the citizens of my "lovely and unique" hometown of Merchantville, New Jersey.

Chapter 1

Back to Vietnam and the War

I was half asleep from the long flight from the United States when I was jolted into consciousness by the words of the pilot of our commercial airliner. His calm, professional voice announced we were approaching our destination, the city of Da Nang, South Vietnam, and he expected us to be on the ground in 20 minutes. He made a weak attempt at humor by telling us the weather was good with only intermittent rocket and mortar fire hitting the air base. None of the men sitting around me seemed to find his comment funny.

I had a window seat, so I looked out, searching for the first sign of land, a land that I had left only nine months before and had not really expected to see again so soon. It was pitch black outside my window; all I could see were some clouds as the plane began its descent. After a few minutes, I saw some lights in the distance and beyond them the dark peaks of the Annamite Mountain Range. Those mountains had been the place where my reconnaissance team, Killer Kane, had patrolled for ten months on my first tour of duty in South Vietnam, and they had a strange, almost spiritual attraction for me. Our team, one of the most successful long-range reconnaissance teams in the Marine Corps, had searched those mountains for units of the Second NVA Division and main force Viet Cong forces, often engaging them at very close range in desperate firefights or calling in artillery and air strikes on them. Killer Kane conducted over thirty long-range patrols, some of them as far away as the border regions near Laos, and several times we barely escaped death as the enemy attempted to track us down and use their superior numbers to surround and destroy us. In a very visceral sense, those mountains formed my opinion of how the war was being fought then, an opinion that was understandable but wrong. There was so much more to the war than just the mountains in a few provinces, but I did not see that when I was patrolling in those mountains. My perspective and my opinion on the war would change radically during the months ahead.

As the mountains loomed larger and larger in the night sky, I had an eerie feeling that I would soon be returning to them. Little did I realize then, but I would spend the next nineteen months in South Vietnam, all in combat assignments ranging from long-range reconnaissance, to infantry, and finally to special operations duties. These assignments would take me from the mountains and rice paddies of Quang Nam and Quang Tin provinces in the north of South Vietnam to the border province of Tay Ninh northwest of Saigon—and radically change my view on the war and how it was being fought.

As our plane began its final approach to the Da Nang Air Base's runway, I thought about the events that led up to my decision to volunteer to return to South Vietnam and

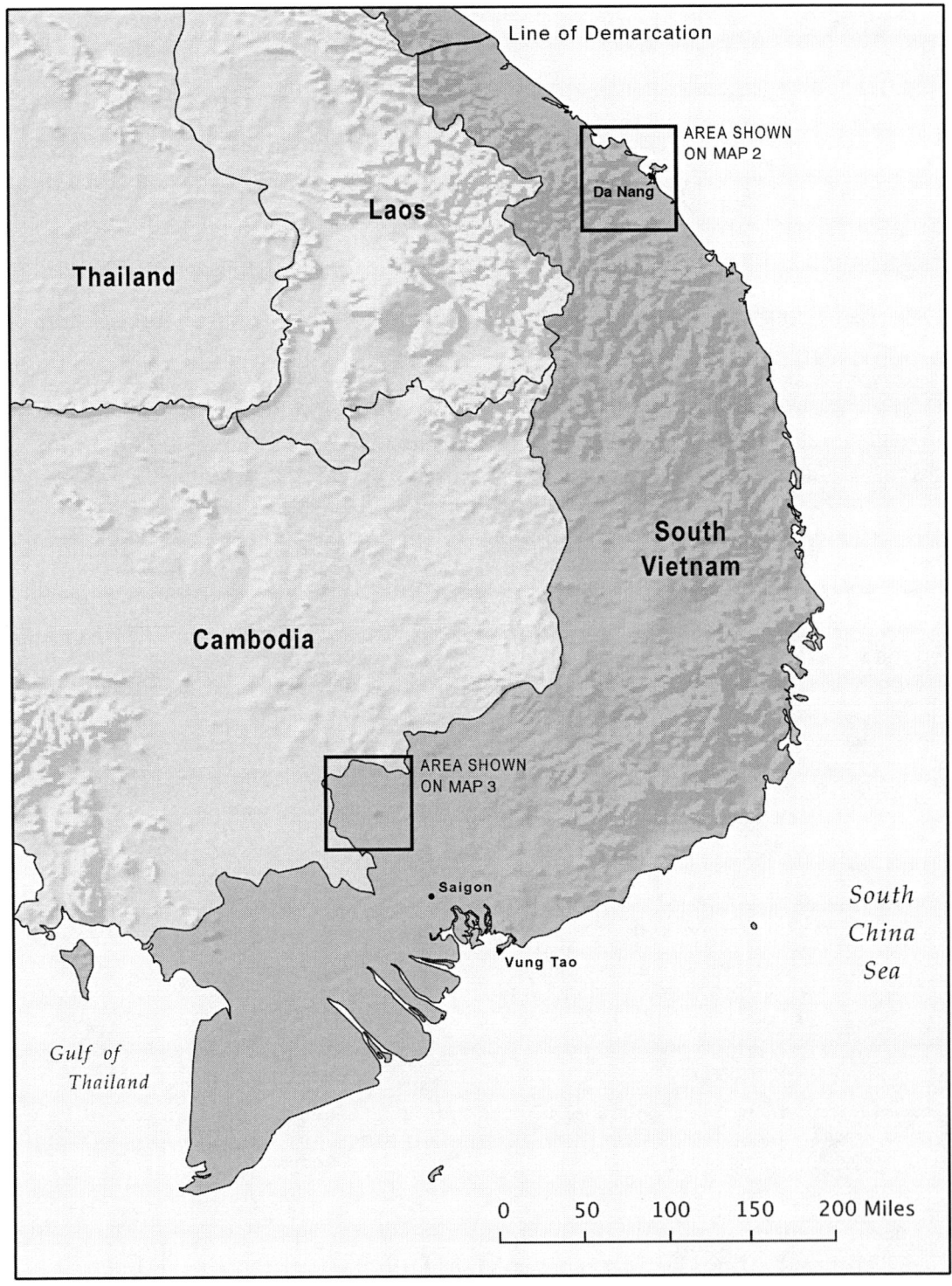

Map 1

the war. I had returned to the United States in March 1968 after spending thirteen months in South Vietnam. My stateside duty assignment was to the most prestigious post in the U.S. Marine Corps, the Marine Barracks in Washington, D.C., which normally would have been a dream assignment for any young Marine Corps officer. But the tragic events of that year, along with the news that my reconnaissance team had suffered heavy casualties in Hue City during the Tet Offensive of 1968, caused me to abandon the fascinating and attractive life of a ceremonial guard officer in our nation's capital and volunteer to return to the war. While a letter from my former commanding officer in South Vietnam, informing me of the heavy casualties sustained by my recon team, was the catalyst for my decision to return to the war, I began to have doubts about my decision to leave the war zone almost as soon as I arrived back from the war in my hometown of Merchantville, New Jersey. I began to regret my decision not to remain in South Vietnam and continue fighting. My first few months back in the United States were traumatic. It started with a homecoming marked by the warm embrace of my family, but marred by being ignored by the people in my small hometown. While I was on leave, none of my neighbors came by to welcome me home; no one even bothered to call me. I felt very isolated and rejected, especially when I saw how the veterans of World War II and the Korean War had been treated by my neighbors. My disappointment caused me to cut short my leave and to report early to my new duty station in Washington, D.C.

At my new duty station, I was given the plum assignment of ceremonial guard platoon commander, a job that called for precision in drill and ceremonies. Since my platoon participated in numerous state ceremonies throughout the nation's capital, I found myself involved with White House and Pentagon arrival ceremonies for visiting heads of state, military funerals at Arlington National Cemetery, evening parades at the Marine Barracks, and sunset parades at the Marine Corps Memorial in Arlington, Virginia. I also provided security for the presidential retreat at Camp David, Maryland. Since I was single and stationed at the Marine Barracks, I was also selected to serve as a White House social aide, assisting President Johnson's social secretary, Mrs. Bess Able. This latter duty allowed me to mingle in a social setting with many prominent Americans from all walks of life and to become friends with a few of the president's domestic policy staffers. For a young military officer, such a job was the epitome of both prestige and glamour, and I should have been blissfully satisfied that fortune had favored me in such a way. However, that was not the case.

Everything began to unravel on April 4 when Dr. Martin Luther King, Jr., was murdered in Memphis, Tennessee, and riots broke out in Washington, D.C. My pleasant routine of parades and ceremonies was abruptly brought to a halt as my platoon was called out, along with the rest of the Marines at the barracks, by President Johnson to assist law enforcement in restoring order and protecting the lives and property of the capital's citizens. What I saw and experienced during the riots and the week following them damaged my faith in the direction my country was taking and the ability of both national and local politicians to show either moral courage or effective leadership. I was also becoming increasingly angry at the national press, who I felt were misrepresenting events both in South Vietnam and the United States.

In what seemed like a crescendo of bad news, I received a letter from my former commanding officer in South Vietnam informing me of the deaths and injuries sustained by my recon team during the Battle of Hue. As a result, I found I was unable to live with myself while a war was going on and I was not fighting in it. I felt a Marine's place during a war was with a fighting unit, not one that was putting on parades and ceremonies for the public. It took a bit of persuasion, but my commanding officer at the Marine Barracks, Col. Joseph Fegan, agreed to let me return to South Vietnam, but only after I had completed the barracks' parade season and a suitable replacement could be found and assigned to take my place. In October, the parade season ended and a new officer replaced me. Col. Fegan made good on his promise, and I soon had orders to report to the 1st Marine Division, which was located in Quang Nam Province, South Vietnam. Despite the trauma my parents suffered as a result of my decision, I felt relieved that I was returning to combat.

When I arrived at Los Angeles International Airport on November 3, 1968, I took another plane to San Diego, collected my baggage, and went outside the terminal looking for a taxi to take me to Camp Pendleton. While I was waiting outside the terminal, a sharp-looking Marine colonel approached me, introduced himself as Col. Kelly, and asked me if I needed a ride to Camp Pendleton. I gladly accepted his kind offer, and the two of us drove to Camp Pendleton, where he dropped me off in front of the Staging Battalion headquarters. When I checked in, I assumed I would be immediately shipped out to Vietnam since I was a veteran of the war and had only recently returned to the United States. I did not think the Marine Corps would subject me to another three weeks of training in the Staging Battalion, but I was wrong.

The Marine Corps placed me in charge of 300 Marines slated for Vietnam, just as they had done on my first trip to Vietnam. This group of Marines was simply called Unit 4278. I reconciled myself to this assignment since I felt I would be able to gauge the value of the training better having already had a year of combat experience. I also thought I might give some personal advice to the Marines who were going over to fight for the first time. Unlike my earlier assignment to the Staging Battalion, I had a good number of returning veterans among the 300 Marines assigned to me, and these experienced men were extremely helpful with everything from troop handling to administration. I was also pleased that the training provided to the Marines, which was clearly better than the training I had experienced in 1967, was given by enlisted instructors with recent combat experience in South Vietnam.

Everything went smoothly until near the end of our training when we were assembled in the base theater to hear a lecture on race relations given by a Navy chaplain and a Marine major. I am sure these two men were well meaning, but their lecture seemed to provoke, rather than assuage, the racial tension that existed among our Marines, especially among the African American Marines who came from homes in the urban areas of our country. The psychological wounds inflicted on the national psyche, a result of the assassination of Martin Luther King, were still fresh, and this lecture only served to open them again. That evening, after the lecture, there were several fights between white and African American Marines in the barracks, requiring all the officers and SNCOs to spend the night in the enlisted barracks to avoid further violence and maintain discipline. Only a small fraction of the 300 enlisted Marines in my group were involved in the fighting, but this violent outburst put everyone on edge and distracted us from our main task—preparing these Marines for combat.

When our three weeks of training were completed, Unit 4278 boarded a commercial contract aircraft at El Toro Marine Corps Air Station late in the evening on November 25 for a 13-hour flight to Okinawa, Japan. No one came to see the plane leave; it was as if we were simply taking a flight to a place of no consequence. I read a book and slept for most of the flight, trying to ignore the beautiful young cabin attendants who made all of us painfully aware that feminine companionship of the "round eye" variety would be a distant memory soon.

After we arrived in Okinawa, we were given a host of shots by Navy corpsmen, required to fill out many administrative forms, attend briefings on what lay ahead of us in South Vietnam, and give blood for the wounded. It was all very mundane and boring. Once these administrative tasks were accomplished, we waited for the Marine Corps to tell us when we would make the last leg of our trip. We did not have to wait long; we were scheduled to depart for South Vietnam on the evening of November 29. However, unlike my previous flight to South Vietnam in 1967 aboard a slow, hot, crowded C-130 transport plane, this time we boarded a commercial contract jet airliner for the trip, a great improvement indeed.

Chapter 2

Deja Vu

While the flight to South Vietnam from Okinawa was far more comfortable than the one I had taken earlier, I could feel a certain tension in the air as we approached our destination. The Marines around me were silent, lost in their thoughts of what lay ahead for them. Unlike my first trip to South Vietnam when our plane arrived during daylight, this flight arrived just before sunrise, so I was unable to make out the mist-shrouded mountains, the harbor filled with ships and native fishing boats, or the emerald-green rice paddies inland; all I could see now was the dark shape of the mountains and the twinkling lights of the city set on a vast blanket of black. We touched down on the tarmac of Da Nang Air Base at 0400, debarked and walked to the transit building, which had been greatly improved since my departure, both in terms of the physical appearance and the efficiency and speed of the customs and administration process. Although I was tired and it was late, I felt an odd sense of relief and even exaltation at being back in-country. After nine months away from the war and South Vietnam, I finally felt at peace with myself and, in some strange way, happy to be back.

It was still dark when I boarded a two-and-a-half-ton truck for the short ride to the headquarters of the 1st Marine Division, which was located on the eastern slope of Hill 327, a few miles west of the Da Nang Air Base. I noticed the road from the air base to Hill 327 was no longer a dusty track of crushed stone, but a two-lane macadam road that made the trip far less bumpy and dusty than my previous trips along this road. The infamous village of Dogpatch, which hugged the road just outside of the air base, remained the same as I remembered it, with no visible signs of improvement; it was still a hodgepodge of ramshackle shacks, poorly constructed houses, and dirty storefronts. The early morning air did nothing to dispel the all too familiar smell of open sewage trenches that ran along Dogpatch's crowded alleyways. The trip from Dogpatch to the division headquarters took only 15 minutes, a ride that took me past the familiar sights of the Freedom Hill Post Exchange (PX) and the field hospital known as Charlie Med.

The first rays of morning light began to rise over the East China Sea as the truck entered the division parking lot and I debarked along with several other officers. We were told to take our baggage to the Officers' Transient Quarters, a collection of SEA huts near the Officers' Club, and wait until we were told to report to the G-1 office for our assignments. After checking in and each finding an empty cot to claim as our own, my fellow officers and I quickly found the headquarters mess hall and ate a hot breakfast of ham and eggs. We had hardly finished our breakfast when we were told to return to the Officers' Transient Quarters so the division's personnel officer could assign us to our units.

Dogpatch Village.

I did not have long to wait for my new assignment. Since I had been a reconnaissance platoon commander during my first tour of duty in South Vietnam and had never served in an infantry unit, I thought I would be assigned to one of the three infantry regiments in the division. I felt I needed this experience to be truly proficient in my Military Occupational Specialty (MOS) of Infantry, and so I requested such an assignment when I reported to the division's personnel officer. Evidently, the Marine Corps had other ideas, because the personnel officer informed me that "someone" had requested that I be assigned to my old unit, the First Force Reconnaissance Company, and that was where my orders said I was going. Since these orders were signed by the commanding general of the division, Major General (MajGen.) Ormond R. Simpson, I decided it would not be wise to challenge them. The personnel officer did not tell me who the "someone" was who asked for my reassignment to the 1st Force Reconnaissance Company, and I never found out. I had wanted to be assigned to a rifle company and reminded the personnel officer of my wishes, but he quickly disabused me of such an idea, informing me that my old company was short of officers and they needed an experienced reconnaissance officer for their operations officer since the company would soon be sent to An Hoa to participate in an upcoming operation called "Taylor Common." He told me this operation would be controlled by a newly formed separate command called "Task Force Yankee," under the command of Brigadier General (BGen.) Ross T. Dwyer, Jr.

I wanted to ask the personnel officer more about my new assignment and Operation "Taylor Common," but he cut short our conversation by informing me that Gen. Simpson wanted to see me, and it was now time to go to the general's office. I had an odd feeling of déjà vu since less than two years had elapsed since I had been ushered into the same office of the then-commanding general of the 1st Marine Division, MajGen. Herman Nickerson, for a "Welcome Aboard" talk. Then, I was a brand-new second lieutenant and Gen. Nickerson had been very firm in his guidance, informing me in the strongest terms that I was to avoid harming Vietnamese civilians, to avoid making stupid tactical mistakes that cost the lives of Marines, and to avoid situations where the Marines under my command might accidentally fire their weapons, causing injury to themselves or others. I wondered what guidance I would receive from Gen. Simpson, fully expecting a different set of instructions since nearly two years had passed since my previous conversation with Gen. Nickerson.

When I presented myself in front of Gen. Simpson's desk, I noticed he had a framed enemy flag mounted on the wall directly behind him. This flag, which was made of silk and was quite ornate, was a duplicate of the flag my old recon team, Killer Kane, had captured from the 402nd Sapper Battalion in Happy Valley in 1967. I say duplicate, because the flag mounted on the wall was not authentic, but a copy made by a seamstress in Da Nang. The bogus flag had been made because Gen. Don Robertson, who had succeeded Gen, Nickerson as the division's commanding general, had expressed a desire to present the flag to the Marine Corps History Division, a desire that was not shared by the men of Killer Kane who captured the flag and wanted to retain it. Gen. Robertson was unaware of this deception and had this false flag mounted for display in his office. The original enemy flag was maintained by the commanding officer of the 1st Force Reconnaissance Company. Given the circumstances surrounding the origin of the flag, I did not think it wise to mention it to Gen. Simpson.

The presentation of bogus enemy flags to General Robertson (center); the author is on the left, and Captain King Dixon on the right.

2. Deja Vu

Gen. Simpson was a tall, imposing figure of a man and a veteran of combat in both World War II and Korea. He greeted me by name and mentioned that he was familiar with the exploits of my old recon team, Killer Kane. He also told me that he had received a note from his old friend and my former CO at the Marine Barracks, Washington, D.C., Col. Joe Fegan, informing him that I was returning to Vietnam. He did not mention what Col. Fegan told him in the note.

I was invited to sit down, and Gen. Simpson asked me if I would like a cup of coffee. I declined and he poured a cup for himself. He began by telling me a lot had happened since I left Vietnam in January. During those intervening ten months, the Viet Cong had taken a terrible beating in the coastal lowlands of I Corps, and the NVA divisions had been pushed back into their base areas in the mountains or into Laos. He told me there had been great strides made in pacification, and the ARVN had greatly improved since the Tet Offensive. He had high praise for the 1st ARVN Division, informing me that it was nearly as good as a U.S. Marine division and could take on any NVA division it faced. He admitted that a lot of work had to be done to bring the other ARVN divisions up to the level of performance of the ARVN airborne and Marine divisions, but he had seen great progress during the time he had been in-country. On balance, his remarks about the situation in the division's tactical area of responsibility (TAOR) were upbeat and positive, but he also said a lot of hard fighting remained if we were to defeat the main force enemy units that threatened the coastal lowlands south of Da Nang. I asked him a few questions about the 2nd NVA Division and the 368th Artillery Regiment, two enemy units I knew from my previous tour of duty with the 1st Marine Division, and he responded that both of these mobile and highly professional units had been seriously damaged in the fighting after Tet, but he thought they would be back in force once they had received replacements and new weapons and equipment from their bases in Laos. This news bothered me, but I decided this was not the time to give voice to my anxiety.

After exchanging a few more pleasantries, Gen. Simpson repeated, almost verbatim, the same instructions I had received from Gen. Nickerson at the beginning of my first tour of duty in South Vietnam. When I heard these same instructions, I had an uneasy feeling. I could not help but think that nothing had changed since I left South Vietnam. It seemed the priorities were still the same, the enemy units were still the same, and the strategy was still the same. I hoped the strategic situation had changed, and Gen. Simpson and our other leaders had developed a strategy that would finally achieve a decisive result, but nothing I heard that morning indicated that was the case.

When I left Gen. Simpson's office at 0900, the cool monsoon winds were beginning to push the dark, heavy, moisture-laden clouds east over the East China Sea, and a bright sun appeared, bringing with it the beginning of another hot, humid, and uncomfortable tropical day. I was almost blinded by the sunlight when I exited the command bunker and made my way back down Hill 327 to the personnel officer's SEA hut to pick up my orders. When I arrived, the personnel officer was waiting for me, orders in hand. He told me to get my gear together while he called the 1st Force Reconnaissance Company to have someone come up to Division Headquarters and pick me up. Within a few minutes, a jeep driven by a lance corporal was in the parking lot, and a few minutes later I was standing in front of the desk of my new commanding officer, Major Roger Simmons.

I was immediately impressed by Maj. Simmons. He was tall, rugged-looking, and very

1st Force Recon Company area, Camp Reasoner.

muscular—what we called a "recruiting poster Marine." Despite the heat and humidity, his uniform was immaculate and his combat boots were highly shined. But more than his imposing physical presence, I was impressed with his obvious intelligence and calm, reasoned demeanor. He told me he had been waiting for me to arrive in-country, and he had heard many positive things about my performance as a recon team leader from some of the "old hands" in the company.

He said, "Andy, it is great to have 'Killer Kane' back with us again. We are going to be operating as a separate unit assigned to Task Force Yankee and move to the An Hoa combat base southwest of Da Nang. We will no longer be working for the 1st Reconnaissance Battalion here at Camp Reasoner, but for Brigadier General Dwyer's new task force, which will be headquartered at the An Hoa Combat Base. Our mission will be to screen the 5th Marines and elements of the 3rd Marines as they go after the 2nd NVA Division in areas south and west of An Hoa. It will be a difficult job and, since we are going to operate as a separate company, we will need an experienced operations officer who understands how to support such an independent operation. That is why you are here."

While I was appreciative of the value Maj. Simmons placed on my experience, and intrigued by the possibility of working with him on a mission where my knowledge of the area of operations would be helpful, I told him I would like to spend at least half of my second tour of duty in South Vietnam with an infantry company since I had an infantry MOS but no experience yet in that military specialty. He said he understood and would recommend I be transferred to the infantry after I had helped the company get established at An Hoa and Operation Taylor Common was nearing completion. I asked him how long that might be, and he told me he could not say for certain, but that he would not keep me

Camp Reasoner.

more than six months as his operations officer. He then told me to get settled in the officers' hootch and meet him again later that afternoon to go over the details of the move to An Hoa, as well as what he expected me to do in the few remaining days before we were to leave Camp Reasoner for An Hoa.

When I walked out of Maj. Simmons's office and along the narrow trail to the officers' SEA hut, I again had a strong sense of déjà vu. It was almost as if I had never left Camp Reasoner ten months ago. Everything was the same; nothing had changed. I entered my old hootch, half expecting to see the same faces I saw when I left. Only one officer remained from that time, Lt. Gene Meiners; the rest were all new to me.

One of these officers did not realize I had been to Vietnam before and attempted to make a foolish joke about the need for me to "go up to supply and get fitted for a body bag." I did not like his rude attempt at humor and told him so. This officer went on later to become a Marine general, so I guess his sense of humor did not irk others the way it irked me. I stowed my gear in a corner and took one of the empty cots for my own, noticing that my old hospital bed had somehow disappeared. The old familiar smells of diesel oil on the floor, dust from the helipad, and excrement burning from the nearby "four holer" head only added to my sense of déjà vu. I walked out on the back porch and looked out at the expanse before me—the rice paddies, the hamlet of Phuoc Ly, the city of Da Nang in the far distance, and the South China Sea beyond—and felt "at home" once again. I knew I would be leaving Camp Reasoner soon for An Hoa, but my return to Vietnam was made far more enjoyable by the familiar surroundings I found myself in now. After a stop at the supply shed to draw my field gear and weapons, I met Lt. Gene Meiners, our S-2, and Lt. Bob Hansen, the com-

Headquarters of 1st Force Recon Company at Camp Reasoner.

pany's communications officer, for lunch in the mess hall. I was pleased to note the quality of the cuisine had not diminished in my absence. After lunch I again went to Maj. Simmons's office for a longer conversation about what my new duties would entail.

I found Maj. Simmons sitting behind his desk signing papers, but he immediately stopped what he was doing and asked me to sit down. After inquiring about my duties in Washington, D.C., and the adequacy of the meal I had just had in the mess hall, he began to explain why my assignment to the company at this time was so important. He told me that he had no combat experience prior to coming to South Vietnam, but he had extensive experience with reconnaissance units during peacetime. He wanted me to be his operations officer because I had recent combat experience with the company, and I knew the area of operations from my previous tour of duty. Most of his experienced officers had left or were about to leave; a new crop of lieutenants would soon be joining the company, and they would need my advice. It was a critical time since the company would soon be detached from the 1st Reconnaissance Battalion and would operate independently at An Hoa, a situation that left little margin for error and was dangerous since there would be so many new and inexperienced officers in the company. He said he was particularly worried about patrols in the infamous Base Area 112 region west of the Ong Thu Slope, an area that had never been actively patrolled before and was suspected of harboring the headquarters of the 2nd NVA Division and one of its regiments. Of particular concern to him was the paucity of adequate helicopter landing zones in Base Area 112, a fact that made every landing there extremely dangerous since it allowed the enemy to concentrate their aggressive counter-reconnaissance teams on these few good LZs.

Da Nang City street scene.

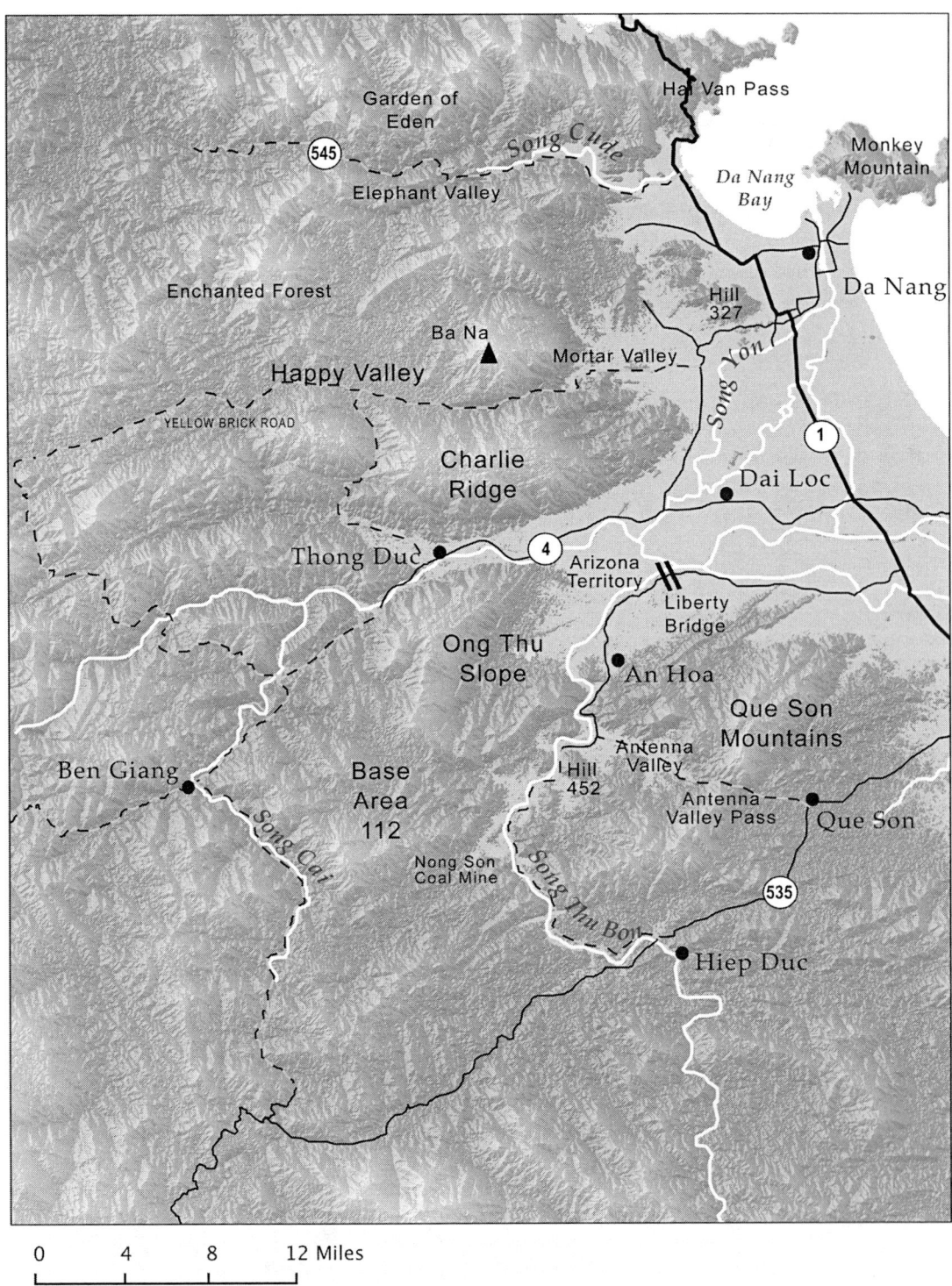

Map 2

I wrote down what Maj. Simmons told me in a small notebook I always kept in the carrying pocket of my jungle uniform, making sure to underline the information he told me about Base Area 112 so I would remember to research this area in the S-2 office later in the day. As Maj. Simmons began to end our conversation, he told me that he had recently attended a reconnaissance meeting at III MAF headquarters in Da Nang City. At this meeting, he heard of several insertion and extraction technologies that the U.S. Army's Studies and Observation Group (SOG) had used in Laos and Cambodia, where LZs were difficult to find or well-covered by NVA counter-reconnaissance teams. He suggested that one of my first tasks would be to visit the SOG's Forward Operating Base (FOB) 4 at Marble Mountain and gather as much information as possible on how SOG was able to overcome the problem of too few LZs. I told him I would arrange to visit the SOG facility as soon as possible.

After my meeting with Maj. Simmons, I spent the rest of the day in the S-3 and S-2 shops trying to get a grasp on what my duties would entail once our company was operating by itself at An Hoa. I observed the routine duties conducted by the battalion operations section, making sure I knew how to duplicate this work at An Hoa. I wrote down the duties of each member of the operations section so I understood how my own operations section would function. In the S-2 shop, I received a briefing on the enemy situation in the An Hoa Basin and the areas south and west of the combat base. I asked the S-2 for a map of all suitable LZs in Base Area 112 and, not surprisingly, the map indicated there were vast areas where no LZs existed. I began to see what Maj. Simmons was talking about when he said finding LZs for our teams there would be a major challenge. After a few hours of studying the maps and aerial photographs of the Ong Thu Slope and Base Area 112, it became apparent to me that I needed to visit SOG quickly, since the normal means of helicopter insertion and extraction would not work in the areas we would soon be required to patrol. I had the S-3 call SOG that afternoon and arrange a visit for me on December 6.

Although most of my time

Marble Mountain Air Base. Da Nang.

was spent preparing for the move to An Hoa, I did manage to see several of my Vietnamese friends from my previous tour. Mai Ly and Dien were still working as waitresses in the 1st Marine Division headquarters officers' club, and Mr. Smart was still plying his trade at his store near Camp Reasoner. Dien was visibly pregnant and told me she would soon take maternity leave. She and her husband, an Air Force sergeant, were very excited about the birth of their first child. Mai Ly told me she was soon to be married to a South Vietnamese Air Force lieutenant, and she hoped I would be able to attend her wedding. I could not tell her about the move to An Hoa for security reasons, so I told her I would very much like to attend the wedding, but work probably would make that impossible.

When I stopped by the small shop owned and operated by Mr. Smart, he greeted me with a surprised smile and told me he never expected to see me again after I left South Vietnam nearly a year ago. He was his usual gregarious self, but his mood turned serious when he told me the Tet Offensive was a real shock to everyone in Da Nang, and he was worried that the communists would launch another offensive during the upcoming Tet holiday. When I inquired about his family, his face clouded over as he told me his brother, a university professor in Hue, had been taken away by NVA troops when they occupied the city last February and his family did not know what happened to him. According to Mr. Smart, his brother was a member of the Dai Viet political party and a fervent nationalist, which was probably why he was abducted by the communists. Mr. Smart was the first Vietnamese to tell me that many VC have been captured and killed in Quang Nam Province since Tet, and he expressed pride in the way the ARVN soldiers and militia units had decisively defeated the VC units sent to attack Da Nang City.

On December 6, I took one of our parachute riggers with me to the SOG FOB 4 headquarters, where I met their operations officer and discussed with him the methods SOG had used to insert recon teams into the areas of Laos and Cambodia where there were few LZs. He was very helpful, taking me to see several items that SOG had used in the recent past. One was a large, spider-web-like contraption that could be carried beneath a heavy-lift helicopter and then placed on top of the jungle canopy. Recon men would then rappel down to the small platform on this contraption, and from there they would lower themselves via an electronic winch to the jungle floor. The spider-web-like, metal frame would remain on top of the jungle canopy until the patrol was finished with its mission, and then the recon team would use the winch to haul themselves up to the platform and await the arrival of an extract helicopter. The recon team and the platform would be retrieved by the helicopter and flown back to the SOG base.

We examined the device, but when we heard that it was no longer in use because of problems with its reliability, we decided not to take up their offer to borrow it. Instead, we settled on two other devices they had used that offered more reliability and were easier to employ. These two items were a large aluminum ladder and a device known as the Special Patrol Insertion and Extraction (SPIE) rig. My parachute rigger told me he was confident that he could construct duplicate SPIE rigs using our own heavy-duty sewing machines and materials in our parachute loft at Camp Reasoner. He said he would ask the SOG parachute riggers to show him how to rig the ladder to the Marine C-46 helicopter, which was our primary means of inserting recon teams. With this information, we signed for the ladder and arranged to pick it up the next day. We also took a SPIE rig the SOG S-3 gave us so we could make our own before we departed for An Hoa.

The next day, the ladder arrived at Camp Reasoner accompanied by a U.S. Army parachute rigger from SOG, who demonstrated to our parachute riggers how to install the ladder so it could be safely used over the back ramp of the helicopter. We had arranged with the 1st Marine Air Wing to send over a CH-46 Sea Knight helicopter from their base at Marble Mountain so our riggers could practice installing the ladder and the pilots could test fly the aircraft with the ladder fully extended. The helicopter made several takeoffs and landings without incident, but the pilots said the ladder made the helicopter more difficult to fly and they thought additional testing was needed before the ladder could be used operationally. They did, however, see the value of the ladder since it allowed an entire recon team to attach themselves to the ladder using snap links and to be inserted or extracted far more rapidly than the normal use of either rappelling one Marine at a time from the aircraft or using the even slower method of lowering or raising the "Jungle Penetrator" and winching the Marines up or down one at a time. Everyone agreed that the less time it took to insert or extract a recon team, the greater the safety of both the aircraft and the team, which meant we needed to seriously explore the use of the jungle ladder if we expected to insert and extract teams in areas such as Base Area 112. The SOG rigger also showed our parachute riggers how to anchor the SPIE rig lines to the deck of the helicopter, but he cautioned us that he thought the SPIE rig was better suited for use by a U.S. Army Huey helicopter than by a Marine Corps CH-46 helicopter. Despite some misgivings about employing new equipment without first fully testing it, I was satisfied by the end of the day that we had two new insertion-extraction systems we could use with great effect for our operations at An Hoa.

USS *New Jersey* firing in support of Marines on Go Noi Island.

On December 8, Maj. Simmons and I took a CH-46 Sea Knight helicopter on an aerial reconnaissance flight of the areas we would be sending our recon patrols into once we were established at An Hoa. On the way, we dropped off two naval gunfire liaison officers onto the deck of the USS *New Jersey*. We watched in awe as the huge battleship fired its 16-inch guns at targets on Go Noi Island in support of Operation Meade River, destroying everything in an impact area of 100 square meters. Even though we were high above the ship and at least a mile away, we could feel the helicopter shake each time a salvo was fired.

After leaving the USS *New Jersey,* we headed southwest toward An Hoa, skirting Go Noi Island to the north and then guiding on the Song Ky Lam River as it ran west to become the Song Thu Bon River and then the Song Thien Yen River near An Hoa. I directed the pilot to take us over the Hiep Duc area first since I was very familiar with this part of the TAOR. I pointed out to Maj. Simmons various places I had patrolled the previous year and areas we would need to patrol in order to screen for any Marine units operating south of An Hoa. I knew from recent intelligence that the 1st VC Regiment, a subordinate unit of the 2nd NVA Division, was currently held to be in the Hiep Duc area. I took a few photographs of key terrain features and then I told the pilots to head northwest across the Song Thien Yen River into the area known as the Arizona Territory, a flat area of rice paddies and tree lines bordered by the Song Thien Yen River to the east, the Song Vu Gia River to the north, and the high massif known as the Ong Thu Slope to the west. I told Maj. Simmons that the Arizona Territory was a highly contested area with no permanent Marine presence. Units from the ARVN and the 5th Marines would often conduct sweep operations there, but once

The Arizona Territory looking north with Charlie Ridge in the background.

these units left the area, the VC moved back in and took control again. I told Maj. Simmons that I had conducted several recon patrols in the hills bordering the southern edge of the Arizona Territory in 1967, and I had always seen enemy activity there.

Starting at the southern edge of the Arizona Territory, I had the pilots fly the entire length of the Ong Thu Slope, a huge jungle-covered massif that was rarely penetrated by either friendly recon or infantry units due to its height and lack of good LZs. I had never patrolled there before, so this strange jungle-covered plateau was as unknown to me as it was to Maj. Simmons. As we flew over this large, flat plateau, I noticed that a recent B-52 strike had created several large bomb craters that might serve as LZs for our teams, so I took pictures of these craters and a few other small openings in the jungle canopy that I thought might be big enough for a single CH-46 to land in. After flying north to the Song Thu Bon River, I had the pilots turn and fly south over the Ong Thu Slope one more time, again searching for any LZs I might have missed on the first run.

When we reached the southern edge of the Ong Thu Slope, I asked the pilots to fly west into the infamous Base Area 112. Base Area 112 ran north-south along the western side of the Ong Thu Slope for approximately five miles, and it stretched for nearly 10 miles to the west. It was a very good location for an enemy base area since the height of the Ong Thu Slope made artillery largely ineffective from firing positions to the east, and the dense jungle canopy made it very difficult for aerial observers to see anything below. It also had numerous streams with clear, clean water and fairly easy access to the rice-growing hamlets in the VC-controlled Arizona Territory and the alluvial plains beyond. Any NVA unit in Base Area 112 could easily obtain food and other needed supplies from the villages in the Arizona Territory or the An Hoa Basin.

Flying over this area I could easily see that conducting ground reconnaissance patrols would be both challenging and dangerous, especially since the base area was reputed to be the home of the 2nd NVA Division's headquarters and its 21st NVA Regiment. Special intelligence sources also reported that an enemy command and control unit called Group 44 was located somewhere in Base Area 112. This Group 44 had previously been known as the Quan Da Provincial Unit and was the political-military unit responsible for the control of the VC infrastructure in Quang Nam Province. It was even suggested to us that the enemy's Military Region (MR) 5 was located in Base Area 112. MR-5 was the enemy's command and control headquarters for all of I Corps south of Thua Thien Province.

Like most base areas used by the NVA, it was impossible to see any indication of human presence from the air. The thick, double and triple canopy of the jungle hid anything on the jungle floor from aerial view. For this reason, any base area looked exactly like any other piece of jungle terrain until someone got to ground level. Under the canopy there were numerous trails, often with steps built into them, with handrails on steep inclines, and 300-man rest areas every few miles along these trails. Elaborate, camouflaged bunker systems provided protection for the NVA troops and were invisible from only a few meters away. There were even garden plots and food storage areas under the jungle canopy, used to augment the food supplies provided by local VC cadres. The NVA never concentrated their forces in these base areas because they knew if they did they would make themselves vulnerable to attacks by aircraft or artillery. Instead, they spread their forces out over several square miles in platoon- or company-size bivouac areas. In most cases, these base areas were outside the range of U.S. or ARVN artillery, which meant recon teams patrolling near them had to rely on air strikes to attack enemy forces found in them. It also meant that a recon team discovered by the enemy had to try to escape as quickly as possible since the teams were not able to call in artillery to protect themselves from an attacking NVA unit.

Maj. Simmons and I both searched the area below us for good LZs as we passed over Base Area 112, but there were only a handful; most of the terrain was unbroken jungle canopy, thick, high, and foreboding with an almost primeval look to it. I took a few photographs of the LZs we did find and marked them on my map for future reference. I looked at Maj. Simmons and could see in his expression that he was deeply concerned by what he saw below us and was probably thinking the same thing I was thinking: How would we be able to effectively patrol in this area if there were so few LZs?

On the way back to Camp Reasoner's LZ Finch, I had the pilots take us over Charlie Ridge, the reputed base area for the 2nd NVA Division's 31st Regiment and elements of the 368B NVA Artillery (Rocket) Regiment. Although we did not expect to patrol Charlie Ridge while the company was located at An Hoa, I wanted to take some pictures of the southern slope of this massive ridgeline just in case the focus of our reconnaissance operations shifted to the north of An Hoa. As was often the case, Charlie Ridge's upper slopes were shrouded in thick, gray mist, but I managed to get a few good photographs of promising LZs at lower elevations.

On December 9, we began training the company on the use of the 40-foot aluminum ladder we had obtained from the SOG. All of our recon teams assembled at LZ Finch for several hours of training on this new device. We practiced rigging the ladder to a CH-46 helicopter from the 1st Marine Air Wing until we were able to do this in 20 minutes' time,

An aerial view of Camp Reasoner at Hill 327, showing Landing Zone Finch.

and then we had each team use snap links to attach themselves to the ladder for a short flight before landing again at LZ Finch and disengaging from the ladder. It soon became apparent that using the ladder required skillful flying by the CH-46 pilots, especially when the recon teams attached and detached themselves from the ladder. Only two men at a time could attach themselves, so the helicopter had to hover with most of the ladder on the deck while the first two men attached themselves. Once this was done, pilots would raise the hover height enough to allow two more men to attach themselves. This was repeated until eight men were securely snapped-linked to the ladder. The reverse process was employed when the team got off the ladder. All of this required precise cooperation between the crew chief looking over the rear ramp of the helicopter, the pilot flying the helicopter, and the team leader on the ground, who had to rely on hand and arm signals to tell the crew chief the status of his team. I made several flights on the ladder and found it thrilling to ride. While we all enjoyed this training, we knew that there was a compelling need for its use, and soon it would be tested in a combat environment—a very unforgiving environment, indeed. We all realized that using the ladder at LZ Finch was far less complicated and dangerous than using the ladder to penetrate high jungle canopy over enemy-controlled territory.

On December 10, the company began our journey to An Hoa Combat Base. We left a rear party at Camp Reasoner, consisting of the company executive officer, Captain Lingenfelter, and a dozen other administrative and supply men who would maintain our company rear area, and provide support to us from Da Nang. The bulk of our company, approximately 140 men, boarded a dozen trucks and several jeeps and left Camp Reasoner early in the morning for our drive south through the Quang Nam Province countryside. Our trip was without incident, and I was impressed with how tranquil the countryside seemed. We passed through several villages, making good speed on the hard surface roads, a marked improvement over the former dirt and gravel roads I encountered a year previously. I also noted that several houses in the villages had television antennae on their roofs, another feature I rarely saw in 1967 on my first tour of duty in South Vietnam. However, the most impressive aspect of our convoy ride south was the obvious progress made in the security of the countryside. All along our route I could see many newly constructed Regional Forces (RF) and Popular Forces (PF) defensive positions every few miles along the road. It was a very tangible indicator that security had improved since the Tet Offensive earlier in the year and the GVN now had a permanent presence in the villages and hamlets south of Da Nang City.

When we arrived at An Hoa, we drove to our future cantonment site on the south side of the base, an area that had been prepared for us by a Marine engineer platoon. The cantonment was 100 meters deep and 150 meters long, a perfect rectangle adjacent to the south side of the combat base's perimeter fence. The area had previously been used by Marine engineers for crushing rock to make gravel for roads and runway repairs, but now it would be our home. Triple concertina barbed wire had been strung along the perimeter of our cantonment, and on the east and south sides the engineers had constructed an earthen berm behind the barbed wire that could be used for defending the camp and preventing enemy direct-fire weapons from hitting the interior of the camp. Just inside the camp on the south side was a rock-crushing machine that stood over 20 feet tall. We immediately took charge of it and established a watchtower on top of it and a platform to practice our rappelling. A dozen hard-backed tents with wooden flooring had been erected for the Marines to live in, and several larger tents were erected for storage and maintenance purposes. The entire camp

An Hoa Combat Base and airfield.

was wired for electricity, and we used the combat base's electricity most of the time, but we also had our own generators as a backup.

There was only one solidly constructed structure in the camp, and it was nearing completion when we arrived. It was the Combat Operations Center (COC) bunker, a solidly built wooden bunker 20 feet wide and 40 feet long. This would be my workplace for my entire stay at An Hoa. During the next week, we busily strengthened this bunker by placing sandbags around its exterior and on its roof. We hoped that these sandbags would withstand any enemy mortar or rocket attack, events that often occurred at the combat base. We also began placing sandbags around the hard-backed tents and digging defensive positions into the berm and along the western side of the camp. Security was our primary concern, and the work was hot, tedious, and strenuous—but necessary. Unlike Camp Reasoner, where Marine reconnaissance units had their own mess hall, our company used the 5th Marines mess hall during our stay. We also availed ourselves of other services that the regiment provided, such as postal, PX, and secure communications.

It was the monsoon season, so rain was an almost daily occurrence. This turned the red clay soil around An Hoa into a soupy mud, making it difficult to walk without huge clods of thick, viscous mud clinging to our boots. However, the rock crusher provided us with a huge hill of crushed rock to use to build footpaths, something we considered a minor godsend since it kept us from sinking into the mud up to our ankles every time we had to walk around the camp. Just outside our perimeter wire to the south was the LZ we would use for recon missions. I asked if the LZ had a name yet and was told it had not been named, so I asked Maj. Simmons if we could name the LZ after my good friend, Capt. Eric Barnes, who had been killed on a recon patrol in 1967. Maj. Simmons agreed, and from then on we referred to the recon LZ at An Hoa as LZ Barnes.

The 1st Force Recon Company COC bunker at An Hoa Combat Base.

It only took us a few days to settle into the COC and prepare for our first missions from An Hoa Combat Base. I was fortunate to have a team of first-rate Marines working for me in the operations section. My operations section consisted of SSgt. Jack Mathis, Sgt. Ron Dorris, Sgt. James Killen, and Cpl. Shultz. Sharing office space with us in the COC bunker was our S-2, Lt. Meiners, and his clerk, along with three radio operators who monitored the recon frequencies for our teams in the field and the artillery and air frequencies needed for their support. Our bunker was large and well organized, with partitions for the S-3, S-2, and communications sections. Field desks, filing cabinets, typewriters, stencil machines, a mimeograph machine, safes, and chairs provided us with a spartan but adequate means to do our job.

One side of the bunker was devoted to the maps we used in our work. One was the operations map showing all of Quang Nam Province and the northern half of Quang Tin Province—the areas where we conducted patrols. This map identified all the NFZs for our recon teams currently on patrol and all the teams scheduled to be inserted, giving the dates of insertion and extraction for each patrol. SSgt. Mathis updated the operations map throughout the day, making sure we had the latest information on each patrol's location. The S-2 map had the latest enemy situation on it, as well as the LZs we knew existed in our area of operations. There was also a large status board giving the daily personnel strength of the company, the number of patrols in the field, the numbers and status of major equipment on hand, and other information that we needed to have readily available. For security reasons, we made curtains to cover the maps, using several Marine Corps issue blankets for this purpose. For the first week or two, we had to work in the stifling heat inside the bunker. However, we soon received a visit by a team of Marine combat engineers who installed two air conditioners in the bunker, a luxury for us, and one that made our work conditions as good as any in Vietnam.

Although the camp was not completely finished, we were able to begin inserting recon teams for Task Force Yankee on December 13, just four days after our arrival. In addition to the six platoons from our company, a platoon from the 3rd Reconnaissance Battalion was attached to us on December 11, giving us the capability to field fourteen recon teams. Since Task Force Yankee had elements of both the 5th and 3rd Marines, we coordinated with the S-3s of both of these Marine regiments, as well as the Task Force Yankee G-3. I felt a bit uncomfortable talking to these field-grade officers since I was only a first lieutenant and I had had no formal staff training, but after a few days I saw they valued the work our company was doing and they treated me and my staff as teammates. I was surprised by the amount of paperwork required by the units we were supporting, but my assistants were all very capable and produced the high volume of reports needed to satisfy our higher headquarters. Each day we forwarded—usually by hand delivery to make sure they reached their destination quickly—patrol orders for each recon team to be inserted, status reports on what the teams observed, frag orders to the 1st Marine Air Wing for helicopter support, and patrol reports within 12 hours of a team's return from the field. We also submitted a monthly command chronology detailing all of the significant events for the month with every patrol report attached. Unfortunately, we soon found that the burden of paperwork at An Hoa was made more difficult because we were forced to produce many standard administration and supply documents that normally would have been handled by the sections we had left at Camp Reasoner.

While I respected the officers I came in contact with in the intelligence and operations sections of the 5th and 3rd Marines and Task Force Yankee, it soon became apparent to me that these headquarters seemed to have a poor understanding of how to employ reconnaissance teams. Unlike my experience with the G-2 and G-3 sections of the 1st Marine Division, where these division staffs seemed to have concrete plans for the employment of reconnaissance patrols to gather information on the enemy, the Task Force Yankee and regimental staffs we supported at An Hoa seemed to be at a loss as to how to use the reconnaissance assets they now controlled. Both Maj. Simmons and I were concerned about this, since we received very little guidance or direction from the task force headquarters on how we were to help the task force's maneuver battalions. We found ourselves in a position where we were either left to develop our own concept for the employment of our recon teams or we had to specifically ask the task force staff what they wanted us to do. I found this very frustrating, and often got the impression they did not consider our work of any great value. Unfortunately, this problem continued during my entire stay at An Hoa, even though both Maj. Simmons and I attempted to resolve it on numerous occasions. From my perspective, I attributed this serious shortcoming not to malice or incompetence but to two factors we had little ability to change. The first was the obvious lack of reconnaissance experience, especially combat reconnaissance experience, by the commanding officers and staffs of the units we were supporting. These officers were experienced, conscientious, and well-trained Marine infantry officers, but none of them had ever served in a reconnaissance unit or, if they had, it had occurred so many years earlier in their careers that they had forgotten most of what they had learned. They simply had a fundamentally weak understanding of how to employ ground reconnaissance units to support operational plans.

The second problem was neither the 3rd nor the 5th Marines had any previous experience controlling reconnaissance assets, so they possessed no corporate memory for how to employ them. It was simply not part of their operational system to plan for the use of reconnaissance teams, since these teams were normally controlled at headquarters higher than the regiment. I was often perplexed whenever I discussed reconnaissance capabilities and employment techniques with my counterparts on the regimental staffs. They seemed incapable of suggesting feasible or effective employment plans for my company's teams. Sadly, the same applied to the more senior officers I dealt with on the Task Force Yankee staff. They seemed to think all I needed to do my job was to read the Essential Elements of Information (EEIs) they produced and I would miraculously come up with some means of using my recon teams to provide answers to their intelligence requirements. The end result, in my mind, was Task Force Yankee did not collect tactical intelligence properly to support the units assigned to it, and they did not employ their reconnaissance assets as efficiently as they should have.

One of the first patrols we inserted met with tragedy on December 15. I had told the Task Force Yankee G-2 that one of our first patrols should be inserted into Base Area 112 near Nui Ben, a mountain just a mile west of the Ong Thu Slope massif. I picked this site because I knew from my previous patrol experience that the NVA liked to hug the administrative boundaries of South Vietnam. They did this because they knew administrative entities, such as provinces and districts, were required to coordinate any military activity that took place close to these administrative boundaries. This made the use of supporting arms more complex and the maneuver of friendly units more difficult. The enemy could take advantage of this by moving their units along these boundaries and thus avoiding contact with Marine or ARVN units. The area around Nui Ben was on the border between the Duc Duc and Thuong Duc districts, and a major trail ran west to east along the southern portion of the mountain. My map analysis told me that we would find NVA in this area, and perhaps a major infiltration route. I was correct.

Team Pickwick Paper, a seven-man patrol led by 2nd Lt. John E. Slater, was inserted into one of the few good LZs near Nui Ben Mountain at 1030 on December 13. As was common in Base Area 112, this small, open area, which was just barely large enough to allow a CH-46 helicopter to land in it, posed a significant challenge for the pilots of the insertion helicopter carrying the team. To add to the difficulty, the LZ was surrounded by trees over 100 feet tall and contained very high elephant grass and bamboo, making it difficult for the helicopter pilots to land safely and for the team to rapidly move off the LZ once they were on the ground. Within an hour of landing, the team heard a single rifle shot in the distance, a clear sign that they had been observed landing and that an enemy trail-watching team was signaling to other enemy units that a Marine recon team had been inserted. The team spent the rest of the day moving slowly west and north, encountering several locations on the southern slope of Nui Hon Sai Mountain where the enemy had constructed fighting holes and sleeping shelters protected by punji stakes. Late in the day, after some very strenuous, cross-country movement in steep terrain, they also found a recently used trail connecting two well-hidden company-size bivouac areas. This trail was completely hidden from aerial observation due to the thick canopy above it.

Lt. Slater wanted to find the east-west trail that ran from the summit of Nui Ben Mountain west along the southern slope of Nui Hon Sai Mountain and then continued west for several miles to the Song Cai River and the old French road of QL 14, a road that was largely

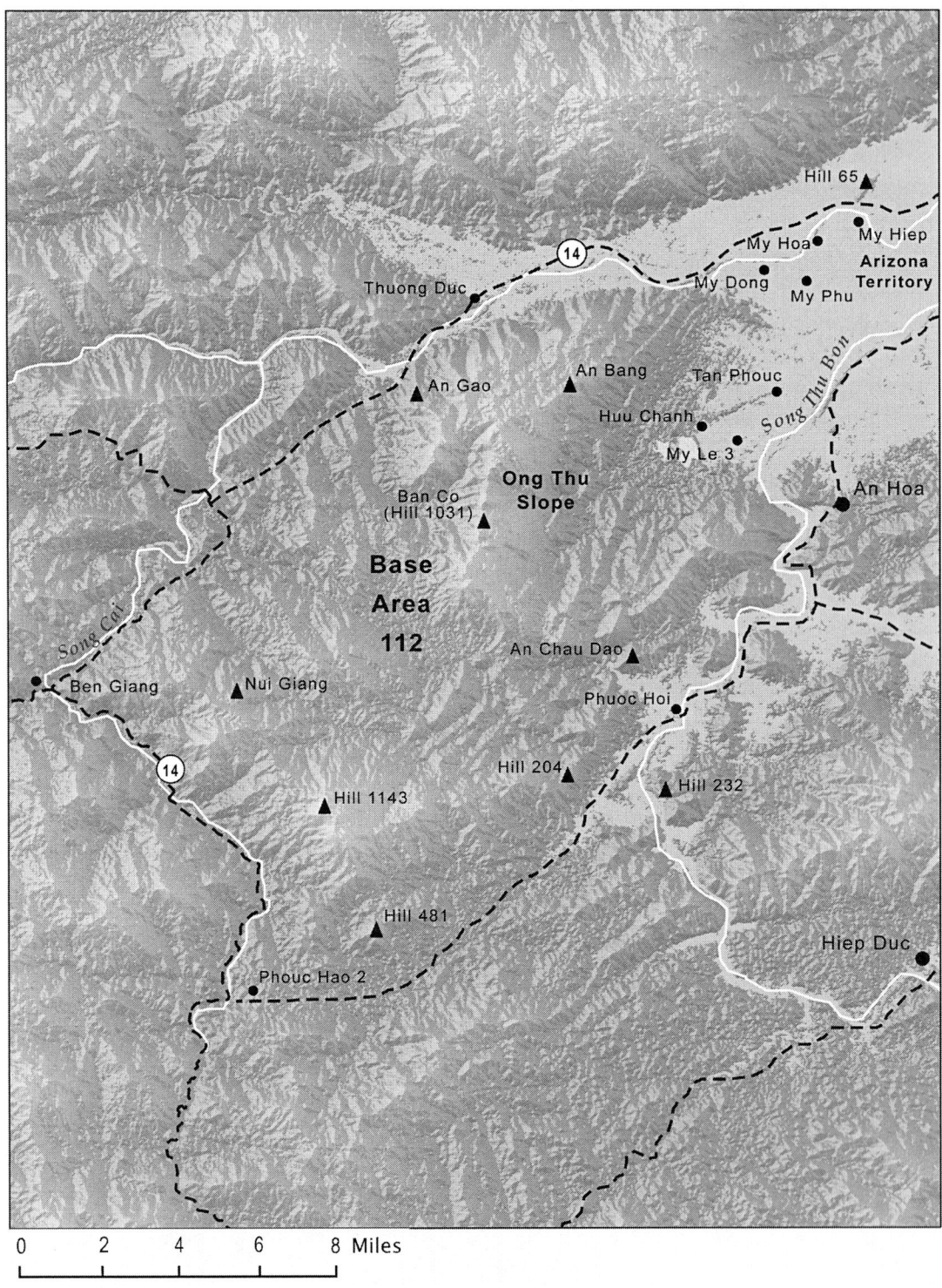

Map 3

destroyed and overgrown from lack of use. In most places it was little more than a footpath. This trail was marked on his map as having only an "approximate alignment," meaning the cartographers could not accurately determine the trace of the trail due to the high, dense jungle canopy above it. In other words, the trail marked on the map was the best guess of the cartographers who produced it.

In the last radio message the team sent that day, they reported there was no doubt that the area they had covered that day had been occupied recently by a sizeable enemy unit, but had been temporarily abandoned. As night approached, Lt. Slater and his men found thick brush to hide in. They would wait until morning to continue their patrol.

On December 14, Pickwick Paper continued to patrol northwest on the southern slope of Nui Hon Sai Mountain, attempting to reach the large east-west trail they suspected lay somewhere to their north and the trail I suspected was being used to infiltrate NVA units from Laos to the Ong Thu Slope. At 1030, they heard many Vietnamese voices talking within 40 meters of the patrol's position. The patrol requested air support, but the close proximity of the voices made it too dangerous to use bombs, especially since the team was under the jungle canopy and could not use any visible means of marking the enemy for the aerial observer to see. In the COC at An Hoa, I told the team that they were probably being followed by an NVA tracking team, and they should move out of the area in a 90-degree angle from their previous direction. I knew from my experience with such tracking teams that they would try to push the Marine recon team toward an ambush ahead of them. Lt. Slater whispered over the radio that he would move out immediately. An hour later, he reported that he thought the team had eluded their pursuers. He also reported that the team had found many well-used trails along their patrol route and several recently dug fighting holes. When he reported that they had also found a large, L-shaped bunker made of logs, covered by several feet of freshly dug earth, I became concerned that the team might be moving in the direction of a large enemy base camp, and I warned him to avoid the area if at all possible. A few minutes later, Lt. Slater radioed that the team had found a cultivated area 40 meters by 50 meters with evidence of recently eaten fruit near it.

Shortly after this radio transmission, the team reported that they had heard rifle shots coming from 10 meters north and south of their position, and they requested an emergency extraction. It sounded to me as if the NVA were "reconning by fire" in an effort to flush out the team or have the team give its position away by firing back. Fortunately, we had a helicopter package refueling at An Hoa, and they were immediately launched toward Pickwick Paper's position, arriving there at 1155. There were no LZs near the team, so it was decided to winch the team up to the helicopter using the helicopter's jungle penetrator hoist, a very slow and dangerous procedure, but the only one available given the circumstances. While the helicopter hovered 100 feet above the team, the penetrator was lowered through the trees. Two men attached themselves to the device on each trip and were slowly hoisted into the helicopter above. On the third trip, Lt. Slater and two other Marines got on the jungle penetrator despite the fact that the device was only designed to hoist two men at the maximum. Since the enemy was firing at the helicopter and they did not want to leave one man on the ground with the enemy closing in, they decided to load three men, instead of two. This was a serious mistake.

The helicopter lifted off, brushing the trees and nearly knocking the men off as it gained altitude and attempted to fly to a location where it could safely land so the three men riding

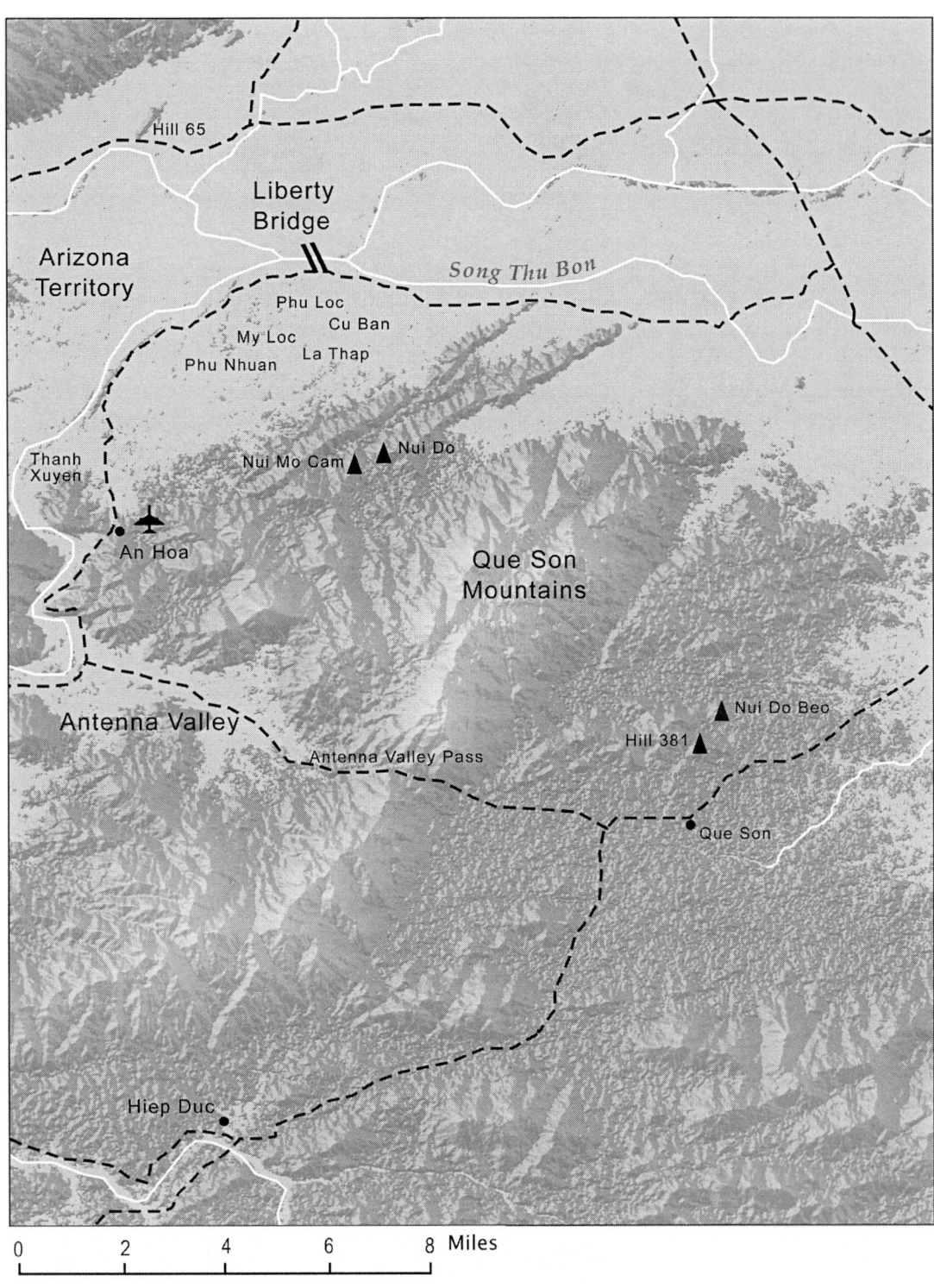

Map 4

the penetrator could get inside the helicopter. Lt. Slater was unable to use his snap link to secure himself to the jungle penetrator, which meant he had to hold on to the other two men until the helicopter could find a safe place to land. He was able to do this for a few minutes, but he soon became fatigued, and just as the helicopter approached a sand bank beside a small river, he fell 100 feet to his death. His body was recovered by his team and flown back to An Hoa. He was the first casualty for our company since we had left Da Nang, and his loss affected all of us profoundly. I had only known Lt. Slater a short time, but during those few weeks I had developed a very good opinion of this officer, and I expected him to be one of our best patrol leaders since he had so many of the attributes needed to succeed in this dangerous business. His death served to convince me that we must use both the aluminum ladder and the SPIE rig for future insertions and extractions in Base Area 112, since these two methods were far faster and safer than using a jungle penetrator.[1]

Our first month at An Hoa was a harbinger of things to come. During the period of December 13 to 30, our company and the attached platoon from 3rd Reconnaissance Battalion conducted a total of eighteen patrols with 581 enemy troops sighted, seventeen enemy killed, and two weapons captured. Unfortunately, we also suffered one Marine killed and one wounded. What was significant about these first few weeks was the increased number of patrols that were cancelled because of enemy activity. It was evident that the enemy was covering most of the suitable LZs and they were determined to thwart any insertion attempt. As a result, the majority of the insertion helicopters took ground fire as they attempted to land, often forcing the team to abort the insertion. We also had more emergency extractions than we would normally expect due to the aggressive actions of NVA counter-reconnaissance teams in Base Area 112. In most cases, whenever we landed in a good LZ, the enemy would attempt to follow the patrol and ambush it.

A few of these patrols were illustrative of the challenges our teams would be facing in the coming months. One of the most significant patrols was one conducted by Team Hunt Club, led by LCpl Jones. It was inserted on December 16 into the southern portion of Base Area 112 to observe a large, well-used trail that ran parallel to a stream, which ran east for several miles before it emptied into the Song Thu Bon River. We chose this area because we suspected the trail was being used to infiltrate NVA units into the An Hoa Basin. Team Hunt Club was only able to remain on the ground for less than seven hours due to enemy contact, but during this short patrol, they had two contacts with the enemy and killed three of them. Their first contact came at 1500 when the patrol sighted one NVA soldier walking west on the trail about a mile east of Hill 204. He was dressed in a green shirt and khaki shorts, wore a pistol and cartridge belt, and carried several chickens in a wicker cage. The NVA soldier saw the Marines and attempted to draw his pistol, but he was shot and killed before he could fire at the patrol. LCpl. Jones had his team drag the body off the trail, where it was searched for any items of intelligence value. They found several documents and a wallet containing South Vietnamese currency. Later, it was determined by Marine intelligence analysts that the NVA soldier the patrol had killed was an NVA lieutenant who commanded a reconnaissance platoon for the 368B Artillery Regiment, a unit supporting the 2nd NVA Division.

Twenty minutes after killing the NVA lieutenant, the patrol went back to the trail and encountered two NVA soldiers armed with AK-47 assault rifles searching the patrol's ambush site. The Marines opened fire on the NVA soldiers, killing both of them. The patrol retrieved one of the assault rifles and a pack containing personal items, including a bag of marijuana. Unfortunately, this second contact resulted in a very aggressive response from the NVA in the area. The patrol's radio frequency was jammed, and they were chased by a large group of NVA soldiers. The patrol managed to elude the enemy and to switch frequencies on their radio so they could call for an emergency extraction. I immediately approved the extraction, and the team was extracted under fire. Due to the rapid response to the patrol's request for an emergency extraction and the skill of the extraction helicopter pilots, the team escaped without suffering any casualties. This patrol confirmed the presence in Base Area 112 of at least one battalion of the NVA's 368B Artillery Regiment, a unit that often supported the 2nd NVA Division and was responsible for many of the rocket attacks on the Da Nang Air Base. The fact that the enemy encountered by the patrol were not carrying any heavy packs and were lightly dressed indicated they were based close to the area where the contacts occurred and the east-west trail was indeed a main avenue for NVA forces moving into the lowlands near An Hoa.[2]

Another significant patrol that occurred during our first month at An Hoa was one conducted by Team Steel Rim, led by LCpl. McDaniel. This eight-man patrol was inserted on December 17 into the southern edge of Base Area 112 with the mission of observing the junction of a trail running from the Ong Thu Slope south to the main east-west trail that ran for several miles from the Song Cai River east to the Song Thu Bon River near the village of Phuoc Hoi. LCpl. McDaniel's team spent 96 hours on the ground and observed 196 enemy soldiers moving along this trail. There were eleven separate sightings of groups ranging in size from a single NVA soldier to fifty-seven enemy troops. The patrol noted that these NVA soldiers were well dressed in clean uniforms, and many of them appeared to be carrying new, well-oiled AK-47 assault rifles and Type 56 carbines. A few of the enemy also carried the older French M1940-type submachine gun. Several of the NVA soldiers wore flak jackets and Soviet-style metal helmets.

What these enemy troops were carrying as they moved from the lowland area around Phuoc Hoi Village west into the mountains was particularly interesting. The patrol reported seeing many enemy soldiers carrying bags of rice, live pigs, caged chickens, and other foodstuffs in large quantities. One group was observed carrying what appeared to be three large mortar tubes and a radio. Several artillery fire missions were called by Team Steel Rim, but none of them produced any observable results, and the team deemed the artillery support "poor." This problem with inadequate artillery support for our teams in Base Area 112 continued throughout Operation Taylor Common until fire support bases on the Ong Thu Slope were established. These newly established fire support bases minimized the results of the masking effect of the Ong Thu Slope and increased the range of friendly artillery positions. Unfortunately for our teams operating in Base Area 112 in December 1968, the Marines did not establish these fire support bases until January. Team Steel Rim was able to employ air support using the services of an OV-10 aerial observer plane that came on station December 18 and used its machine gun to strafe a column of twenty-four NVA soldiers, killing one and scattering the rest. The team was extracted on December 20 without incident from a good LZ next to a stream bed not far from their insertion LZ. This patrol confirmed the presence of a large NVA force using the east-west trail near Phuoc Hoi Village and recommended a B-52 "Arc Light" bombing raid along the trail where the NVA were observed.[3]

Shortly before Christmas, I received a letter from the Sacred Heart Orphanage in Da

Nang City thanking me for my monthly $10 contribution to the orphanage and asking me if I would sponsor two orphans and increase my contribution to $20 a month. The letter was sent by Sister Marie Madeleine, a Filipina nun who had worked for many years in South Vietnam and was in charge of the orphanage. She asked to see me on my next trip to Da Nang so she could discuss with me which orphans I would like to support. I wrote back to her and gave my letter to the chaplain of the 5th Marines, who hand-carried it to Sister Marie the next day at the orphanage. A week later, on Christmas Eve, I was able to catch a helicopter flight to Da Nang to attend a meeting at Camp Reasoner, and I took this opportunity to borrow a jeep and drive over to the orphanage to visit with Sister Marie.

When I arrived, I met the diminutive nun at the door of the orphanage, and she invited me in to have some tea and discuss what orphans she thought would benefit most from my sponsorship. I soon found out that Sister Marie, although small in stature and quiet in speech, was no ordinary nun. She possessed a keen intellect and a charismatic personality; she was the kind of person who did not take no for answer and had an answer for everything. I have always held nuns in reverence and awe ever since my childhood when they instructed me in my catechism classes, so I was naturally inclined to agree with her; but no matter how I felt, it was soon obvious that I was no match for this middle-aged "Bride of Christ." She told me that most Marines always selected little girls to sponsor, but little boys needed sponsorship as well, and she thought I was the perfect person "to remedy this serious deficiency." She went on to tell me that a woman had come to the orphanage a year ago with her two sons and asked the sisters to accept them since her husband had been killed by the communists and she no longer had the means to support two small children. The sisters took the boys in and cared for them while the mother attempted to find some form of employment that would enable her to reclaim her children. In the meantime, the boys were enrolled in the orphanage's school.

Despite their best efforts, the woman could not make enough money as a domestic servant to care for her sons properly, so they remained at the orphanage. She told me that my previous monthly contributions had been used to feed and clothe the elder brother, but the younger brother was in need of help also. With a look of benign compassion and steely resolve, she firmly suggested I should sponsor both boys. It was obvious that Sister Marie knew how to close a deal, because she had the two boys brought in to see me before I even had a chance to reply.

The two boys, who were freshly scrubbed and dressed in immaculate white shirts, dark trousers, and plastic sandals, introduced themselves in English as Ngo Dung and Ngo Hue, ages eight and five, respectively. My fate was sealed since it was impossible to turn down a request to help these two young boys standing before me. Sister Madeleine smiled broadly when I accepted her offer to sponsor her young charges, and I could not help but get the feeling that this nun knew exactly how to tug on the hearts of visitors to her orphanage. I came away from this first meeting with Sister Madeleine telling myself that this tiny woman had powers of persuasion so strong she should be given the task of negotiating peace terms with the communists. I had no doubt she could convince them to surrender their arms, if given the chance. Thus began an association with Sister Marie Madeleine, an association that would last until the fall of Saigon in 1975, when she would be arrested, imprisoned, and later deported by the communist victors.

When I returned to An Hoa late in the day on Christmas Eve, the company held a

Orphan brothers Ngo Hue (left) and Ngo Dung.

Christmas religious service and I attended Mass. On Christmas Day, the 5th Marines mess hall served a traditional Christmas dinner with all the trimmings, but torrential rainfall turned the entire combat base into a sea of thick, viscous, red mud, taking the edge off any Christmas cheer this holy day normally would have produced. Added to this was a perfidious and violent act by the VC in Mau Chung (1) Village, just 500 meters outside of our perimeter wire. The VC took advantage of one of the insane "cease-fires" our politicians inflicted on us by entering the unprotected village on Christmas Day and murdering the village chief and his entire family, leaving their mutilated bodies on display in front of their house until a Marine patrol was able to recover them and give them a proper burial. The enemy routinely disregarded these "truces" and "cease fires," but that did not deter our political leaders from instituting them time and again. One would have thought the lesson of the Tet truce of 1968 would have been enough for these politicians to forego such lunacies, but that was not the case.

Team Steel Rim was again in the thick of it shortly after Christmas, when they found themselves in virtually the same area they had patrolled on their last patrol, the major east-west trail a mile west of the village of Phuoc Hoi. This time their mission was to observe any enemy movement along the trail near their previous sightings of NVA troops and, if possible, to secure a prisoner. The patrol was inserted on Christmas Eve and spent 47 hours patrolling their NFZ with most of that time occupying a very good OP site 100 meters north of the trail. From this excellent vantage point, they observed 122 enemy troops moving along the trail where it crossed a stream. It was obvious to the patrol that a large number of enemy soldiers were living somewhere close by because they only saw small groups of one to six soldiers walking along the trail at any one time, and these soldiers either had no packs or carried packs that appeared to be light. Several women were also seen accompanying the soldiers. A few of the male enemy were dressed in civilian clothes, while others wore the ubiquitous black pajamas of Vietnamese peasants. Several of the civilians carried pistols, a clear indicator that they were VC political cadres, although they were far from any habitation.

On December 26, Steel Rim attempted a prisoner snatch along the trail where it left the mountains and opened onto the flat lowlands on the west side of the Song Thu Bon River. In the early afternoon, the patrol saw two enemy soldiers dressed in black pajamas walking down the trail. They were armed with a Chinese carbine and a pistol and one of them carried a small pack. As was often the case in such a difficult operation, the enemy did not cooperate, and bolted back up the trail as soon as the Marines stepped into the trail to capture them. The Marines fired at the fleeing enemy, killing one and wounding the other. An emergency extraction was called, and the team was successfully extracted at 1430. The wounded enemy soldier died in the helicopter on the way to the Battalion Aid Station (BAS) at An Hoa, despite the heroic efforts of the team's corpsman, HN Estabrook, to keep him alive. The patrol captured two weapons, the pistol and the carbine, both of which I made sure were retained by the team. I still harbored some bad feelings from my first tour of duty in South Vietnam when I saw how high-value souvenirs would "disappear" once they were turned over to the intelligence staff of a higher headquarters.

The contents of the captured pack provided substantial information about the enemy soldier who had been carrying it. It contained four watches, blasting caps, a time fuse, and other items used in demolitions, as well as assorted documents indicating one of the enemy killed by the patrol had been a captain serving as the adjutant for the 2nd NVA Division.

This information was strong evidence that the headquarters of the 2nd NVA Division was located in Base Area 112 and probably not far from where the ambush occurred. The fact that these two NVA soldiers were wearing black pajamas and not regular NVA uniforms indicated that they had probably been returning from a visit to the Arizona Territory, where their civilian clothing would make it easier to blend in with the local peasant population while they gathered supplies or conducted reconnaissance.[4]

Late in the day on December 26, Team Crazy Bone landed in one of the few good LZs in Base Area 112, a fairly large open area that had once been cultivated by a Montagnard hill tribe but was now overgrown and abandoned. The LZ was situated in the long valley that ran for several miles from the Song Cai River in the west to the Song Thu Bon River in the east and served as the main enemy infiltration route that ran along the southern border of Base Area 112. Given the paucity of good LZs in Base Area 112, we decided we must take the chance of landing so near to a main enemy infiltration route. I took this into account when I arranged for several flights of Marine Corps F-4 Phantom jets to prep the LZ before we inserted the team and to maintain an aerial observer plane over the team for the first few hours they were on the ground.

The eight men of Team Crazy Bone had the mission of establishing a clandestine OP near a trail junction in a narrow valley approximately a mile north of their insertion LZ. We had received intelligence from a Hoi Chanh that this area, which was located a mile west of Hill 481, was being used as a bivouac area for infiltrating NVA units on their way south along a spur of the Ho Chi Minh Trail where it left the Song Cai River and turned east toward the coastal lowlands. A secondary mission for Team Crazy Bone was to map any additional trails they found inside their NFZ.

The team landed safely in their LZ and immediately moved north toward their objective, the trail junction. After a day of difficult movement in very steep terrain, which was made more difficult by a steady monsoon rain that turned the jungle hillsides into muddy and slippery obstacles, they finally came upon a stream that led north directly to their objective. Late in the day they found the trail junction and set up an OP only 100 feet from it. Their patrol lasted 60 hours, resulting in the sighting of 136 NVA soldiers and two contacts. The NVA were moving along the trail in groups ranging from a single soldier to as many as twenty-seven. One group had five women with it. The NVA troops all appeared to be well-equipped with new weapons and uniforms, flak jackets, helmets, radios, and large packs that were camouflaged with foliage.

Crazy Bone's first contact occurred at 1445 on the afternoon of December 27, when the patrol observed two NVA soldiers walking in a southwesterly direction on the trail, and one of the NVA soldiers suddenly stopped and pointed his rifle in the direction of the patrol. The patrol leader fired at the NVA soldier with unknown results, but there was no return fire from the enemy. The patrol leader assumed he had either killed the NVA soldiers or they had fled, but he decided it was too dangerous to move to the trail to search for them. Since the patrol was compromised by this contact, the team leader moved the team away from their OP and established a new OP close to the trail 200 meters to the south.

On December 29 at 1250, a single NVA soldier was observed walking along the trail. The patrol leader decided to attempt a prisoner grab, but the enemy soldier saw the team and began to flee back up the trail. The patrol opened fire on the enemy soldier, and he toppled over a steep cliff into dense brush. The patrol pursued the enemy by fire and found a large blood trail and a pack at the top of the cliff. Inside the pack they found three books about electronics and several documents indicating the NVA soldier was part of a communications platoon belonging to the 2nd NVA Division headquarters. An hour after this contact, the team was extracted by helicopter and returned to LZ Barnes at An Hoa.[5]

The last patrol of 1968 was conducted by Team Scandinavia, and it proved to be a short one, lasting just three hours. The insertion was delayed for most of the morning due to the thick mist covering the valleys in Base Area 112, but at 1100 the mist lifted long enough for a CH-46 helicopter to land on a sandbar along a stream close to the well-used trail that ran along the southern border of Base Area 112. The mission of the patrol was to investigate reports of an enemy base camp in the vicinity of Hill 232 on the south side of the valley and about one mile south of the insertion LZ. The patrol, which was led by Cpl. Murray, had moved only a short distance from the insertion LZ when they found sandal prints on a trail and an unoccupied enemy harbor site. As they skirted the harbor site, they spotted two NVA trail watchers following them and immediately took them under fire, killing one of the enemy soldiers. Within a minute, the team was taken under fire by an unknown size enemy force. They were forced to break contact and moved to a bomb crater, where they set up an all-around defense. A large and determined enemy force soon had the team pinned down in the bomb crater and was firing on them from three sides. The NVA were not eager to close in on the Marines, but they attempted to force the team to break from cover by throwing hand grenades near them. The team leader ordered his men not to fire their weapons at the enemy for fear of giving their position away. Instead he had the Marines throw hand grenades in the direction of the enemy fire. The team's radio operator called for air support since they were outside the artillery fan of friendly artillery units. Within minutes, Marine helicopter gunships arrived and began to fire rockets and machine guns at the enemy, forcing them to pull back from the beleaguered patrol. The monsoon cloud cover made flying difficult over Base Area 112, but fortunately for Team Scandinavia, the

The Song Cai River, Base Area 112.

weather broke shortly after a flight of CH-46 helicopters arrived over their position. Despite heavy ground fire and a misty rain, the extraction helicopters landed successfully and the team was able to scramble aboard and fly back to the safety of An Hoa. Unfortunately, one Marine was wounded by small arms fire during the extraction, but his wound was not serious.[6]

We had a few significant personnel changes at the end of 1968. Our S-2, Gene Meiners, rotated back to the States, and SSgt. Jack Mathis, my operations sergeant in the S-3 shop, was given Gene's job. SSgt. Mathis was an extremely intelligent and resourceful SNCO with a solid background in intelligence and reconnaissance operations, so he immediately began to make a positive impact on the way we prepared our teams for employment. He and I formed a strong bond of friendship since we had both been recon patrol leaders and both had a common understanding of the challenges that faced a small team of reconnaissance Marines patrolling in enemy territory and far from friendly lines. Together, we occupied the COC for 14 hours each day, making it easy for us to find the optimum ways to employ our reconnaissance teams and to assess their performance in the field. He and I would spend hours poring over intelligence reports from a variety of sources and studying the maps on the bulkheads of our offices in the COC in order to ascertain where we should insert teams to best effect. Jack Mathis possessed one of the most valuable traits an intelligence officer can possess: he had an uncanny sense for where the enemy was and what they were up to, a skill that he had acquired from his combat experience and his exhaustive study of every piece of intelligence available.

Replacing SSgt. Mathis as my operations sergeant was Gunnery Sergeant Bruce D. Trevathan, whom I had known from my previous tour of duty with the company at Camp Reasoner. Gunny Trevathan had extended his tour of duty in-country several times, and this gave him a keen insight into just about everything going on in the province. In addition to his experience as a patrol leader and platoon sergeant, he also possessed superior skills as an administrator. He understood how to organize the work being done in the S-3 shop, manage our enlisted watch standers, and produce high-quality reports and orders. In sum, he was one of the best Marine SNCOs I ever had the pleasure of working with, and I greatly respected him for his professionalism, sense of humor, work ethic, and attention to detail. To be honest, Gunny Trevathan could have done my job and his own with absolutely no effort at all. His ability to do the routine work in the S-3 shop made it possible for me to concentrate on planning future patrols, to coordinate with supported units, and to write papers and reports analyzing the tactical situation in southern Quang Nam Province.

As the New Year began, I felt we had a first-rate team working in the COC, and I never changed my opinion during the ensuing months of 1969.

CHAPTER 3

An Hoa—Patrols Redux

On New Year's Day 1969, Lt. Gene Meiners and I met with Maj. Simmons to review the events of our first month at An Hoa supporting Task Force Yankee. Gene was due to leave for the States in a few days, and we wanted to capture the lessons he had learned during his year-long tour of duty with our company. The three of us spent nearly four hours together going over a list of topics we thought Gene could help us with and reviewing the intelligence and patrol reports for the past year. We came to the conclusion that the recon patrols we were conducting at An Hoa were significantly different from the patrols the company had previously conducted in other areas of Quang Nam Province, especially in terms of the number of enemy troops observed on each patrol, the number of contacts with the enemy, and the number of emergency extractions necessitated by these contacts. It was also very obvious that Base Area 112 was heavily populated with NVA forces from the 2nd NVA Division and was being used as a major terminus for NVA replacements coming down the Ho Chi Minh Trail. I told Maj. Simmons that my previous experience patrolling in Quang Nam and Quang Tin provinces led me to believe that the 2nd NVA Division was continuing to use the same base areas they had used in 1967 and the efforts to stem the numbers of NVA infiltrating from North Vietnam had not been successful. Like most American military officers serving in South Vietnam, we knew the United States was using air power and covert special operations forces in Laos to reduce the flow of North Vietnamese troops and supplies moving south along the Ho Chi Minh Trail. We assumed these efforts in Laos were effective, but our analysis of what we were seeing in our patrol reports indicated these efforts were not having the desired effect. We could tell that, despite the severe enemy attrition as a result of their failed offensive during Tet 1968, especially the losses incurred by their locally recruited VC units, these gains were being offset by a steady flow of men and arms from North Vietnam. As proof of this, we only had to look at the interrogation reports of recently captured prisoners. For example, the 1st VC Regiment, a supposedly VC unit made up of southern communists, now consisted of 90 percent North Vietnamese troops, as were most of the other VC main force units in the five provinces of I Corps. Maj. Simmons shared Gene's and my assessment of the situation, and he decided this topic needed to be taken up with higher headquarters.

At this same meeting, I suggested that we begin to have a "lessons learned" meeting with all of the team leaders to share important knowledge of common benefit. Because so many of our team leaders were lance corporals and corporals, I thought they could increase their store of patrolling knowledge by listening to the views of those patrol leaders who had many patrols under their belts. When I listened to the patrol debriefings after each patrol, I noticed that some of the patrol leaders were making serious mistakes because of their lack of experience and that these patrol leaders could benefit from listening to the more experienced team leaders in a formal group setting. I suggested calling these meetings "Patrol Leader Seminars," and I told Maj. Simmons I would take notes at these meetings and forward them to division for incorporation in their monthly "lessons learned" reports to FMFPac. My final recommendation was to conduct more ambushes similar to those conducted by teams Steel Rim and Crazy Bone. These ambushes produced valuable and actionable intelligence on the 2nd NVA Division.

The New Year began on a successful note as Team Paddle Boat, led by Sgt. Norman Karkos, a naturalized citizen from France, made two contacts with the enemy while on patrol in Base Area 112 that resulted in four NVA soldiers killed and no Marine casualties. During the debriefing of this patrol, I was very impressed with Sgt. Karkos. He was older than most of his men, and he possessed a personality and approach to his job that engendered confidence and loyalty. What I found most impressive was the way he combined both aggressiveness with caution, a rare but valuable combination that made for a superior recon team leader. I considered him among the top two or three patrol leaders we had at that time. His leadership skills would be tested to the maximum in less than a month on a subsequent patrol.

The incessant monsoons during January 1969 continued to turn our base camp into a quagmire, and we began to see the first signs that this was adversely affecting our health. Dysentery and other waterborne diseases began to break out. I contracted dysentery but was able to keep working; however, many of our Marines suffered cases that required hospitalization. The bad weather also caused us to cancel several missions because the rain and cloud cover made helicopter insertions impossible. Despite this, we managed to improve our material condition by using the time we would normally have devoted to patrols to making small improvements around our camp. We built a small enlisted club from salvaged lumber where our Marines could drink beer and sodas, we strung new and better barbed wire around our perimeter, and we continued to pile sandbags around our tents and the COC bunker. I also had two exhaust fans installed in the COC bunker and had grating placed over the air vents so any enemy that penetrated our defenses would be unable to drop satchel charges down these vents. Every day saw progress in our efforts to make our small base camp more comfortable and secure.

On January 10, we were reinforced with the 2nd Platoon, Company E, 1st Reconnaissance Battalion from Camp Reasoner. This additional platoon, led by 1st Lieutenant Porpotage, allowed us to increase the number of teams we could field from fourteen to sixteen and to expand our span of operations further west into areas never previously patrolled by Marine reconnaissance units. Maj. Simmons wanted to send our teams to the border with Laos, since we continued to receive intelligence reports telling us that NVA units were using infiltration routes from the Ho Chi Minh Trail in Laos to Base Area 112, but no one was monitoring these infiltration routes. In the past, Special Forces teams and CIDG units patrolled the border areas near Laos, but most of these operations were no longer being conducted. The NVA aggressively protected their base areas along the Ho Chi Minh Trail, as well as the spurs that led from Laos into South Vietnam. Over the past two years, they had systematically destroyed the CIDG camps along the Laos–South Vietnam border in I Corps, including the vital CIDG Special Forces camps in the A Shau Valley and Kham Duc. Maj.

Simmons tried to convince Task Force Yankee and III MAF that our company should be conducting long-range reconnaissance patrols along the Laos–South Vietnam border, but his suggestions were not acted upon. The argument higher headquarters used to deny permission for the company to patrol to the Laos border was the logistics involved to support such long-range patrols was not worth the effort. They also said that the U.S. Army's SOG patrols in Laos and the A Shau Valley were suffering heavy casualties in terms of personnel and helicopters, making it highly likely that our patrols would suffer the same fate. Maj. Simmons did not give up his intention to conduct deeper reconnaissance patrols, but he decided it would be better to wait until a more opportune time to renew his efforts. Instead, we were instructed to continue to patrol south and west of An Hoa, placing special emphasis on Base Area 112. In retrospect, this was probably a wise decision on the part of III MAF, since any diversion of recon assets for patrols on the Laos–South Vietnam border would mean the Marine infantry units engaged in Operation Taylor Common would be left with fewer recon assets to screen their advances into Base Area 112 or locate the enemy's base camps there. Since plans for Operation Taylor Common called for two Marine regiments to penetrate to the far reaches of Base Area 112 and destroy the 2nd NVA Division and its base structure there, our company's reconnaissance patrols were most needed in Base Area 112.

On January 11, Team Forefather, led by Sgt. David Thompson, was given the mission of locating a suspected enemy supply station in the vicinity of a ford over the Song Cai River. One mile east of this ford loomed the very steep and high massif known as Yang Brai Mountain, which at a height of 1,143 meters dominated the western edge of Base Area 112. The

The Song Cai River, Base Area 112.

patrol was also given a secondary mission of monitoring enemy traffic on a trail on the west side of the Song Cai River, a trail that once was the old French road of QL 14 but now was little more than a footpath.

As was often the case when trying to insert a team into Base Area 112, there were no suitable LZs near the objectives of this patrol. As a result, the eight-man team had to rappel into a bomb crater in the valley east of the river ford between Hills 452 and 545. The team was able to rappel down 100 feet into the bomb crater with little difficulty, and soon they were left with only the sounds of the jungle as the insertion helicopter rose into the crachin and headed east toward Da Nang. After waiting 20 minutes to determine if they had been discovered and followed by the enemy, the team began to slowly move toward their objective of the suspected supply station. The patrol moved north 100 meters and came upon a trail that appeared to have been used recently since there were no cobwebs on it and the brush along its sides had been pushed back and broken. They stopped to observe the trail from a short distance away and then set up an ambush. Almost immediately they saw three NVA soldiers moving northwest along the trail. They let these soldiers pass, and 40 minutes later they saw two more enemy soldiers on the trail moving north. Five minutes after this group of enemy soldiers passed, the patrol made contact with six NVA soldiers following in the footsteps of the three NVA soldiers who had just passed the patrol. For some reason undetermined by the patrol, one of the NVA soldiers stopped only a few meters from the Marines. A second later the NVA soldiers initiated the contact using automatic weapons, but their fire was directed at a spot several meters away from where the Marines were hidden, making their element of surprise worthless and turning the initiative over to the Marines. Team Forefather returned fire, killing three of the enemy while two Marines sustained light wounds. The recon team broke contact using CS gas grenades to cover their movement and spent the next few minutes moving through dense jungle for a few hundred meters until they reached a small stream. They set up a 360-degree defensive position in some low ground near the stream, and they remained there hidden in thick brush until nightfall.

The next morning, January 12, the patrol decided to remain hidden and listen for any sign that the enemy was attempting to find them. Around noon, the patrol heard approximately twenty NVA soldiers searching for them nearby. The patrol waited until the enemy soldiers were within a few meters of the patrol's position, and then they opened fire, killing one NVA soldier. The patrol broke contact and moved 200 meters south, where they established a defensive perimeter and waited for the enemy to follow them. A few hours later, at 1700, the enemy launched an attack against the patrol, but their fire was ineffective since they did not know the patrol's exact location. The patrol returned fire, killing three more NVA soldiers, one of whom was distinctly larger than the others and was not dressed in the normal NVA light green field uniform. This enemy soldier was dressed in a camouflage uniform and wore a brown beret, a mode of dress we had never seen before, giving rise to the speculation that he might have been Chinese.

Since the team was outside the range of artillery, I dispatched an AO to the team's location, and soon the AO was calling in multiple flights of fixed-winged aircraft. Fifteen sorties of Marine and Air Force attack aircraft were called in to bomb and strafe the enemy, with some of the bombs landing less than 100 meters from the team and splintering the trees above their heads. The noise and concussion made by the bombs left several of the Marines deaf for hours afterward.

Because there were no LZs near the engaged recon team and they could not move from their current position, an attempt was made to extract the team using the jungle penetrator hoist of one of the extract helicopters. Unfortunately, this failed when ground fire damaged the CH-46's hydraulic lines as it hovered above the team. Meanwhile, back in the COC, I was running out of options for Team Forefather, so I decided to ask Maj. Simmons for permission to extract the team using the externally rigged aluminum ladder we had borrowed from SOG. In order to ensure that the extract was carried out properly, we had Sgt. Bob Buda, an extremely capable and experienced patrol leader and insert/extract NCO, rig the helicopter and accompany the CH-46 to the location of our beleaguered team. Maj. Simmons agreed, and soon we had a CH-46 Sea Knight helicopter on the ground at An Hoa, where Sgt. Buda quickly rigged the ladder and boarded it for the rescue attempt. As the helicopter lifted off of LZ Barnes, I noticed a large, dark bank of rain clouds forming over Base Area 112 and prayed that Sgt. Buda and the rescue helicopter would arrive in time before the cloud cover and rain made a rescue attempt impossible. In the meantime, Team Forefather was fighting for its life.

At 1800, Sgt. Buda had the helicopter's pilot, Captain Laurence Adams, hover his CH-46 over the last reported location of Team Forefather so the ladder could be lowered over the rear ramp and through a hole in the jungle canopy. It was a delicate operation since it required close coordination between the team on the ground, the helicopter pilot, the CH-46's crew chief, and Sgt. Buda, all working in perfect unison, to make the rescue successful. Despite heavy ground fire, Capt. Adams maintained his hover while five members of the recon team, using snap links, attached themselves to the ladder, leaving the remaining members of the team on the ground. Sgt. Buda informed Capt. Adams that there were three recon Marines still on the ground and requested he go back and retrieve them. Despite having sustained heavy damage to his helicopter and great difficulty in controlling it with a ladder and five men hanging onto it, Capt. Adams returned to recover the three remaining men. While this was being done, both Sgt. Buda and the helicopter crew chief were wounded by enemy small arms fire. Sgt. Buda was medevaced to Japan for treatment and earned his third Purple Heart. Capt. Adams was awarded the nation's second highest award for valor, the Navy Cross, for his actions during the rescue of Team Forefather. When the helicopter and Team Forefather returned to LZ Barnes at An Hoa, an inspection of the extraction helicopter found thirty-three bullet holes in its fuselage. Had it not been for the aluminum ladder, which we now called the "Simmons Rig" in honor of our commanding officer, and the bravery of Capt. Adams and Sgt. Buda, it is likely we would have lost the entire team.[1]

On January 12, Team Icebound, led by Sgt. Theodore "Ted" Ott, one of the best enlisted patrol leaders in our company, made several discoveries on the northern edge of Base Area 112 that caused Task Force Yankee to change the focus of our reconnaissance plan. In December we had sent most of our patrols into the central and southern parts of Base Area 112, but that would change after Sgt. Ott and his men finished their patrol.

The northern edge of Base Area 112 ran along the Song Cai River west from the Ong Thu Slope until it joined the Song Boung River, a distance of nearly 15 miles. When the French occupied South Vietnam, they had built a system of roads into the interior of the country, one of which was QL 14. This hard-surfaced road intersected with the main coastal highway, Route 1, south of Da Nang City, and ran west into the Annamite Mountains before it turned south to pass through the major towns of the Central Highlands and ultimately ended in Tay Ninh Province 70 kilometers northwest of Saigon. While portions of this road could still be used by vehicular traffic, the portion in Quang Nam Province was closed to traffic about a mile west of the U.S. Special Forces camp at Thuong Duc, where a bridge across the Song Cai River had been destroyed. The road was too susceptible to ambushes in the mountains west of Thuong Duc, so it was abandoned, and soon it was overgrown by jungle along much of its route. The enemy found this abandoned road convenient and used portions of it to move men and supplies via foot and bicycle into Base Area 112 and points south.

The Task Force Yankee G-2 directed us to insert a recon team in the vicinity of An Gao Mountain to attempt to locate what was believed to be the headquarters of the 2nd NVA Division. We were told that signals intelligence from the Marine Corps Radio Battalion had picked up radio transmissions indicating the enemy division headquarters was somewhere near this mountain. Sgt. Ott and his team were given the mission. They were inserted in a large LZ along the southern bank of the Song Cai River near the abandoned hamlet of Dai Hiep (4) and within a few hundred meters of the junction of two streams, the Khe Con and the Khe Houa, that ran north into the Song Cai River and flanked An Goa Mountain. On January 12, the patrol found a substantial supply cache on the south slope of the mountain. This cache, which was hidden in two straw and bamboo structures under a 100-foot high jungle canopy, contained five cases of 12.7 mm ammunition, several metal cases containing 7,500 rounds of 7.62 mm ammunition, 32 rounds of 82 mm mortar ammunition, and 12 rounds of 60 mm mortar ammunition. All of the ammunition was new and of Chinese communist manufacture. Sgt. Ott destroyed the ammunition cache with C-4 explosives and moved north up the slope of An Gao Mountain along a

Thuong Duc Special Forces Camp and district town.

trail that led from the cache to the mountain summit. At 1620, the patrol was approaching the summit of the mountain when they made contact with four NVA soldiers dressed in green uniforms and armed with AK-47 and SKS rifles. The enemy soldiers were tightly grouped in the trail in front of them and oblivious to the patrol's presence, since they were talking loudly and had their weapons at sling arms. Team Icebound opened fire on them, killing all four in seconds. The team did not have time to search the bodies since they heard movement to their north; plus, three of the bodies were off to the side of the trail and difficult for the team to reach without exposing themselves. They quickly searched the only body on the trail and retrieved a new SKS rifle made in China.

Team Icebound was able to evade the enemy and continue on their mission for another two days. During this time, they found enemy communications wire running in a north-south direction, but they decided not to follow it since they feared another confrontation with the enemy. NVA units relied heavily on the use of communications wire because they knew the Americans had excellent means of listening to and locating their radios. We were also able to decipher their codes. When I saw the report from Team Icebound informing us that they had found enemy communications wire, I informed Maj. Simmons, who directed the patrol to note the location of the communications wire so a subsequent patrol might be able to place a tap on it and record the enemy's communications.[2]

Captured documents and interrogation reports from NVA POWs often referred to the Ong Thu Slope as a major terminus for NVA forces infiltrating into Quang Nam Province from North Vietnam. These sources of intelligence were consistent in identifying this large, jungle-covered plateau overlooking the Arizona Territory as the final

Song Cai River in foreground and LZ with An Gao Mountain in background.

place these infiltration groups would reach before they would be parceled out to various NVA and VC units that needed replacements. The groups, which normally moved in 300-man increments, would begin their journey in North Vietnam, march west into Laos, travel down the western slopes of the Annamite Mountain Range using multiple trails, and then peel off and move east through the A Shau Valley before marching south along various trails until they reached the Ong Thu Slope. Marine intelligence was convinced there had to be major enemy camps on the Ong Thu Slope if the intelligence was correct. Unfortunately, the term "Ong Thu Slope" was used only by the enemy and not by local Vietnamese, so there was some doubt about its exact location. The local population called the massif west of the Arizona Territory the An Bang Plateau. Task Force Yankee wanted the 1st Force Reconnaissance Company and its attached units to locate the suspected enemy base camps so infantry units could destroy them. With this objective in mind, we decided to insert a recon team on the northern part of the plateau and have this team search for any signs that the enemy was using the plateau as the intelligence reports suggested. This would not be an easy task since there were very few suitable LZs on the plateau. Most of our insertions on the plateau would, by necessity, involve rappelling from a hovering helicopter, a difficult and dangerous method of insertion. For this patrol, SSgt. Mathis recommended Team Scandinavia since this team had extensive rappelling training and its leader, Sgt. Glenn, was a talented land navigator and skillful patrol leader.

On January 9, Team Scandinavia rappelled from the rear ramp of a CH-46 helicopter through 80-foot jungle canopy to the floor of the Ong Thu Slope. On three sides of them were extremely high cliffs that dropped off precipitously, making their rappel particularly

Recon team prepares for insertion aboard a CH-46 helicopter.

dangerous. Fortunately, the skills of the team and their insertion pilots resulted in a flawless rappel with everyone safely on the ground in a matter of minutes. Initially, they found the going very slow due to the thick vines and scrub growth under the canopy, which restricted their movement to only a hundred meters an hour. The rocky ground and the secondary growth were wet and slippery, and adding to the patrol's discomfort was an abundance of large leeches. Team Scandinavia was only on the ground for an hour when they observed a single NVA soldier attempting to locate them. He was dressed in the standard NVA light green uniform, but aside from an AK-47 rifle he carried no equipment or web gear. The patrol threw M-26 hand grenades at the soldier, and then they fled northwest. As they moved out, they heard voices and movement behind them. That night, as the team harbored in some thick brush, they saw three flashlights moving north to south in the jungle not far from their position. There was no doubt the enemy was on the Ong Thu Slope, but how many and where were questions the patrol did not have the answers to yet.

During the next two days, the team continued to move very slowly north, often stopping to listen if anyone was following them. On January 12, they were approaching their extraction location when they observed three NVA soldiers walking on a trail in front of them. These enemy soldiers were wearing khaki uniforms and the standard-issue NVA pith helmets. The patrol opened fire on the enemy soldiers, killing two of them while the third fell into the thick brush beside the trail. They searched the body of one of the dead enemy soldiers lying in the trail, retrieving his AK-47 assault rifle, three magazines of ammunition, and some documents. As they were doing this, another group of NVA soldiers came down the trail and began firing at the patrol. The patrol returned fire and broke contact, moving to a small opening in the jungle canopy where they waited until a helicopter could be dispatched to extract them using the jungle penetrator hoist. As the last man was being hoisted above the trees into the helicopter, the enemy opened fire and the helicopter sustained several hits from small arms fire. When Scandinavia returned to LZ Barnes and was debriefed, the documents they captured were turned over to the Task Force Yankee G-2, who told us the enemy unit that had made contact with the patrol was a security platoon assigned to Group 44, a political unit of the Lao Dong Party responsible for directing the war in Quang Nam Province. Further analysis of the captured documents led Marine intelligence to believe Group 44 might be located near Hill 1026, normally referred to as An Bang Mountain, on the Ong Thu Slope.[3]

It was during this time that Lt. Bob Hansen and I discussed the problem of maintaining good radio communications in Base Area 112. The high Ong Thu Slope plateau between us and Base Area 112 often made communications difficult. We made a map study of the terrain in Base Area 112 and decided that we might be able to solve this problem by establishing a clandestine radio relay site on Hill 1143, a very high mountain overlooking the Song Cai River on the western edge of the base area. On January 14, Bob and I took a visual aerial reconnaissance flight to Hill 1143 to see if putting a radio relay team on this mountain was feasible. As we flew over the primeval forests of Base Area 112, I was again struck by the high jungle canopy, the fast-moving streams and rivers, and the lack of open areas where a helicopter could land safely. As we flew towards the southwest corner of Base Area 112, we came upon the towering and forbidding Hill 1143, which also had the name of Yang Brai Mountain. We circled the mountain several times trying to find an LZ where we could land a recon team by helicopter, but neither we nor our pilots could find any close to the summit.

The summit was one of the most daunting pieces of terrain I had ever seen in South Vietnam. Nearly three miles east of the fast-flowing Song Cai River, it rose steeply to a narrow ridgeline far above the jungle floor below. On its western, northern, and southern sides there were dark, steep, rocky cliffs a thousand feet high. It was the highest point in the area, and it had an almost direct line of sight to An Hoa many miles to the east and to any patrols operating west of the Ong Thu Slope. In short, it was a perfect location for a radio relay site, but the mountain's near-vertical slopes and small summit posed some significant problems for any team using it. Despite our reservations, we decided we had to have a radio relay site there if we wanted to ensure continuous communications with our teams operating in Base Area 112. The survival of our teams depended upon their ability to rapidly communicate with us if they got into trouble, and the only way to ensure this was to have a radio relay team on Hill 1143.

Although we had only been sending patrols into the mountainous jungle west of the Ong Thu Slope for less than a month, it was fast becoming evident that the enemy was using the large, wide trail that ran 15 miles along the southern edge of Base Area 112. Starting at the ford that crossed the Song Cai River on the boundary between Quang Nam and Quang Tin provinces and running east until it reached the Song Thu Bon River at the village of Phuoc Hoi, this well-used trail was a logical avenue for the enemy to quickly move troops and supplies into and out of the base area. Just about every patrol inserted on or near this trail made contact with the enemy, and intelligence gained from these contacts told us that the NVA units using this trail were from the 2nd NVA Division and its supporting units. The trail ran along the southern edge of Base Area 112 in a narrow valley completely uninhabited by anyone other than the NVA; none of our patrols ever reported seeing civilians

The Song Thu Bon River looking west towards Base Area 112.

moving on the trail. The interrogation of a recently captured NVA supply officer indicated that the enemy had a way station and a supply point located at the western end of the trail on the eastern bank of the Song Cai River, where the river was fordable. We decided to insert a patrol a mile to the east of the suspected way station to determine if the NVA POW's information was correct or not. This mission fell to Team Crazy Bone, led by Cpl. Finkle.

On January 14, a CH-46 helicopter carrying Team Crazy Bone landed in a large, open area with six-foot-high elephant grass not far from the main east-west trail. Cpl. Finkle and five other Marines ran out the back ramp of the helicopter and disappeared into the dense jungle that bordered the LZ. This LZ had been used before, and I knew the dangers that frequent use of an LZ could produce. The NVA observed our pattern of inserting our recon teams, and if we used a LZ frequently, they were sure to employ a counter-reconnaissance team near it. I had spoken to Cpl. Finkle prior to his overflight the day before he was to be inserted and suggested he try to find another LZ for his insertion. When he returned from his overflight, he told me he had found a few other, less suitable LZs in the valley, but they were farther east, which would make it more difficult for his team to reach his objective near the Song Cai River ford. I reluctantly agreed with Cpl. Finkle to have his team inserted in the good LZ closest to his objective, but I made a mental note not to use this LZ again for at least 30 days.

After Cpl. Finkle and his team watched their insertion helicopters disappear into the clouds above them, the patrol moved 100 meters west, searching for the main east-west trail. It was beginning to get dark, so they decided to find a good harbor site and wait until morning to resume their movement west toward the suspected "way station."

The next day they found the trail and began to cautiously move west on it. Within a few minutes they came upon a hidden antiaircraft position that had been dug into the ground to a depth of 4 feet. It was the standard 12.7 mm heavy machine gun position built by the NVA—a round trench 6 feet in diameter with a raised mound in the center where a 12.7 mm machine gun could be mounted so it could traverse 360 degrees to fire at any airborne target. Team Crazy Bone was fortunate the position was not manned, or their fate might have ended with their helicopter being shot down. The NVA knew a good LZ when they saw one, and this prepared but unmanned heavy machine gun position was ideally located to take any Marine helicopters landing in this LZ under fire.

Two hours later, the patrol encountered five NVA soldiers walking down the trail. They wore green shirts and khaki shorts, and two of them were carrying six-foot-long pieces of lumber. The patrol opened fire on the enemy soldiers, killing two and capturing the other three, one of whom was wounded. The patrol captured two Chinese SKS rifles and several packs containing letters and other documents along with clothing. Crazy Bone called for an emergency extraction, and the team was safely extracted less than an hour after making contact. The prisoners and the captured documents were turned over to the Task Force Yankee G-2 for exploitation. It later turned out that the prisoners were part of a supply unit responsible for maintaining an infiltration way station capable of feeding and housing 300- to 500-man infiltration groups from Laos. As a result of the interrogation of these prisoners, a B-52 Arc Light bombing raid was ordered on the way station.[4]

While Team Crazy Bone was making contact with the NVA at the western extreme of Base Area 112, the staff officers of Task Force Yankee were mulling over what to do about the enemy communications wire Team Icebound had discovered near An Goa Mountain.

NVA soldier captured by Team Crazy Bone in Base Area 112.

They decided to send Icebound back to the site of the communications wire and attempt to tap into it and record the enemy's communications. SSgt. Mathis, our very conscientious and innovative intelligence officer, obtained the necessary equipment needed to tap into the communications wire and arranged for Sgt. Ott and two other Marines in his team to receive training on how to use the wire-tapping equipment they would be taking on patrol. We added another recon team, Forefather, to this mission so we could follow the wire in two directions to its source, which we suspected was the headquarters of the 2nd NVA Division, based upon signals intelligence.

On January 18, Team Icebound, consisting of six Marines, rappelled from a CH-46 helicopter onto a steep hillside a few hundred meters south of the summit of An Goa Mountain. Following them down the rappelling ropes was Team Forefather, led by Sgt. McDonough. After moving cautiously up the slope of An Goa Mountain, the two-team patrol was able to find the communications wire near the summit early on the morning of January 19. The NVA used a distinct communications wire that was colored robin's-egg blue, a color that was easily detected in the lush green of the jungle. U.S. communications wire was black and easier to hide. The wire ran east and west, crossing the trail that ran north-south, and

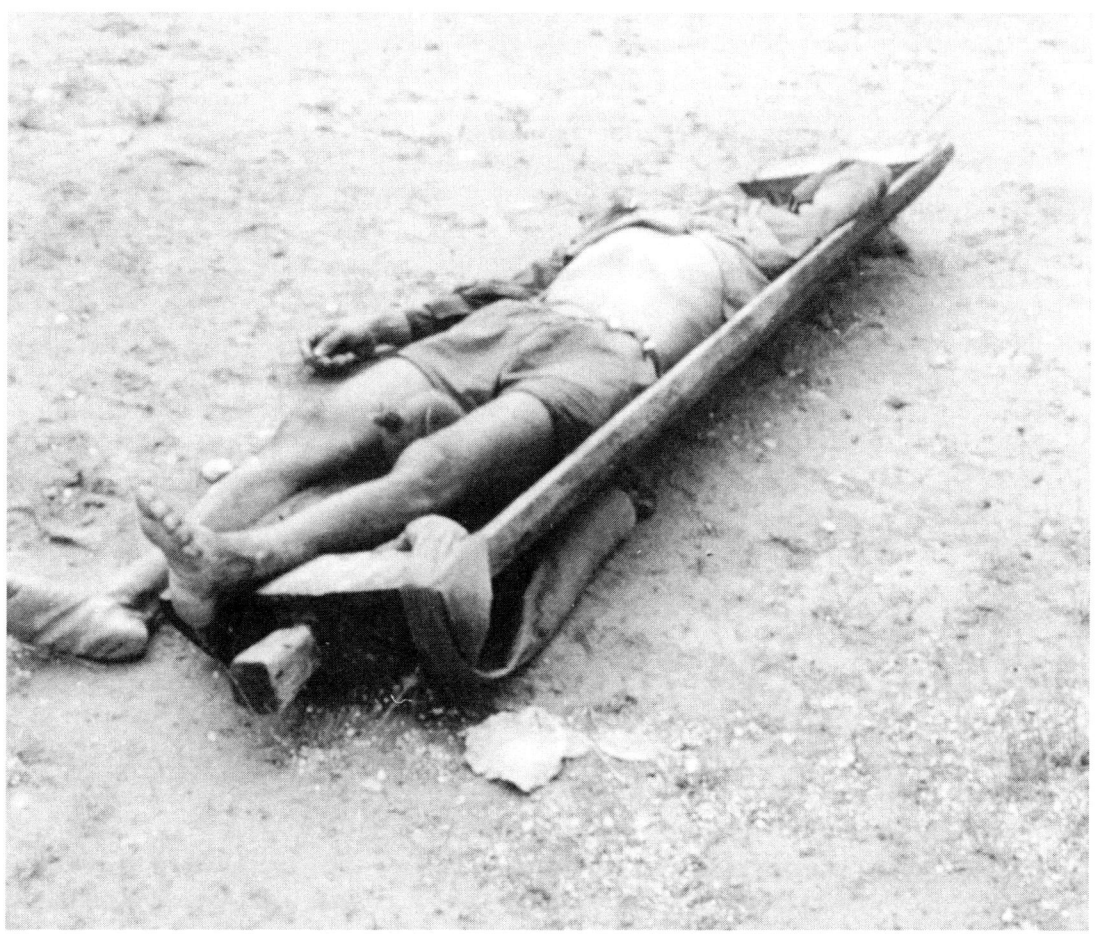

NVA soldier killed by Team Crazy Bone in Base Area 112.

leading up to the summit of the mountain. As the teams approached the wire, they sensed they were not alone and possibly had been detected. Still, they continued their mission, and Sgt. Ott began to splice the communications wire so he could attach the tapping equipment. Team Forefather provided security and prepared to move along the communications wire to the east toward the high cliffs of the Ong Thu Slope. However, just as Sgt. Ott finished his work, his team noticed five NVA soldiers preparing an ambush for the team near the trail the team had just left earlier. Icebound opened fire on the enemy soldiers, and the enemy returned fire. The patrol was unharmed, but due to dense foliage they were unable to observe whether or not they had inflicted any casualties on the enemy. The patrol broke contact and moved to the north side of the mountain's summit, leaving the phone-tapping equipment on the communications wire. When I heard this, I asked permission of Maj. Simmons to lead a reaction force to recover the phone-tapping equipment and link up with Team Icebound. He agreed, and we coordinated with Task Force Yankee for me to accompany a Marine rifle company, K/3/5, that would attempt to link up with the two recon teams at a predetermined location north of the summit of An Gao Mountain. Since our recon teams had made contact with NVA soldiers protecting the communications wire, we anticipated the enemy would put up a stiff fight to protect it and the enemy headquarters unit that was using it. Task Force Yankee also tasked another rifle company, B/1/3, which was operating in the central region of Base Area 112 as part of the ongoing Operation Taylor Common, to move north to link up with us near An Gao Mountain and to be prepared to engage any enemy troops attempting to escape south of the hill.

Within an hour, I boarded a CH-46 helicopter, along with the command element of K/3/5, and was on my way to a LZ 2,000 meters north of An Gao Mountain and only a few hundred meters south of the Song Cai River. The LZ was an overgrown rice paddy that was once part of the abandoned village of Dai Hiep. Once on the ground, I huddled with the commanding officer of the infantry company, a young 1st lieutenant like myself, and we quickly formed our plan. We had one of the radio operators with the infantry company make radio contact with Team Icebound and inform them that we were on our way up the trail that led to the summit of the mountain and to join up with us approximately 200 meters north of the summit. Sgt. Ott and Sgt. McDonough agreed and told us that they were going to set up an ambush at the site we had chosen for our linkup and cautioned me to be sure we maintained constant radio contact because they did not want to get caught between the enemy and K/3/5 in a firefight. With that, I told the CO of K/3/5 that I wanted to be the second man in his column behind his point as we walked up the trail and to have one of his radio operators on the recon team's frequency walking directly behind me. In this way, I could direct the point and advise him of how close the recon teams were and also advise the recon teams of the same information, thus precluding a chance of firing on each other.

From the rice paddy, we picked up the trail easily. Although there were no civilians within several miles of the trail, it appeared to be well-used. We crossed an old bridge across a stream and then began our ascent to the summit of An Gao Mountain. I did not rush the point man since I was keenly aware that the enemy, having already made contact with our recon teams, might have decided to establish an ambush north of the teams' location in an attempt to block any escape by the teams. I also knew that it was highly probable that the enemy had seen our helicopters land and assumed we were a reaction force, again leading them to establish an ambush along any potential route we might take. Radio communications

Air strikes prep the insertion LZ at the base of An Gao Mountain.

between teams Icebound and Forefather and our radio relay site on Hill 452 south of An Hoa was fairly good, but any artillery fire mission would require relaying the fire request through either the relay site or an aerial observer because of the masking effect of the Ong Thu Slope, which blocked any direct radio signals to An Hoa and the artillery batteries to the east of the teams.

It was nearly midnight when we finally wound our way up the steep jungle trail and found Sgt. McDonough waiting for us at the side of the trail. He told me Sgt. Ott and Team Icebound had set up an ambush site 100 meters farther south near the summit of the mountain. I decided to remain where we were for the night since I did not want to get too close to the communications wire or Sgt. Ott's ambush site in the dark. The ninety-two men of K/3/5 and I curled up on the trail and waited until dawn. It was a good thing we did, because shortly after first light, when we approached the enemy's communication wire near the summit, a squad of NVA blocked our way and attacked us. They poured fire into our lead element while simultaneously firing on our column from the ravine on our right flank. Because the trail we were on followed a narrow ridgeline to the summit, K/3/5 was able to get only a squad on line to assault the NVA soldiers firing at us from the summit. Despite great bravery and support from two machine gun teams, the Marine infantry were unable to advance and took several casualties. Throughout the day, K/3/5 attempted to drive the NVA from the summit, all to no avail. The company commander called in artillery fire, but again, the Ong Thu Slope thwarted our efforts. The only artillery with the range to reach us, the 175 mm guns at An Hoa, had a flat trajectory, which made them highly inaccurate at such a long-distance firing over the Ong Thu Slope. As a result, several rounds landed close to the Marines, causing additional casualties. An aerial observer came overhead and brought in helicopter gunships to strafe the enemy positions, and this had a better effect. The enemy fought tenaciously, determined to prevent us from reaching the communications wire or advancing any farther south where we might block their escape routes to the west. We paid a heavy price for that day's assault, with eight Marines killed and twenty-seven wounded. I helped to carry one dead Marine and several wounded Marines to a hastily built area on the trail 100 meters north of the contact, and then waited for an Army helicopter to hoist the dead and wounded out that evening and early the next day. One of the recon Marines with me was wounded in the leg by a sniper as we loaded a wounded Marine on the helicopter's hoist, so I placed him on the hoist as well, and he was medevaced along with the other wounded Marine. Throughout the night of January 20–21, we were sniped at continuously by NVA troops in the trees and the ravine to our west.

On January 21, the summit was finally taken with the help of B/1/3, which came up from the south and attacked from the enemy's rear. When I examined the area that the NVA soldiers had defended, it became obvious why we had been unable to dislodge them. They had built deep, well-fortified bunkers just off the trail near the summit, where they were safe from any artillery or air strike unless a direct hit was obtained. The summit of the mountain was a tangle of splintered and smoldering trees and fractured rocks, but the enemy and the communications wire were gone. Footprints told us that a large force, perhaps several hundred NVA, had moved from the Ong Thu Slope cliffs to our east along a trail just south of the summit and had then headed off to the west. The squad of NVA that had held us up for nearly two days had succeeded in their mission: they had prevented us from blocking the retreat of the headquarters of the 2nd NVA Division. It was a bitter disappointment, and I felt we had accomplished very little while paying a heavy price in killed and wounded. The men of K/3/5 had performed admirably and fought with great bravery and skill, but it was not enough to overcome a well-dug-in enemy determined to hold their ground. We found numerous blood trails, indicating the NVA had suffered many casualties also, but we could not ignore the fact that the main body of NVA had escaped. Along the western slope, we found an enemy bivouac area that consisted of a dozen well-constructed and neatly arranged huts that the enemy had hastily abandoned. Nearby we found a weapons cache of one hundred eight 82 mm mortar rounds, sixteen 60 mm mortar rounds, and over 90,000 7.62 mm rounds of AK-47 ammunition, which the enemy was forced to leave behind as they fled west.

On January 22, the small LZ from which we had hoisted our wounded and dead was expanded using demolitions. It was still too small for a Marine CH-46 to land in it, so U.S. Army Huey helicopters were requested, and they took out our two recon teams and K/3/5. The enemy made no attempt to harass the extraction, probably because they were no longer anywhere near us. I returned to An Hoa dejected over the failure of our mission and the loss of so many Marines in our vain attempt to capture the command element of the 2nd NVA Division. My dejection soon turned to abject sorrow within twenty-four hours of my return.[5]

The hasty LZ on An Gao Mountain.

On the day I was lifted out of the LZ near the summit of An Gao Mountain, Team Paddle Boat II was inserted into an area far to the south and west of my location. The patrol was led by a young second lieutenant whom I considered the best lieutenant in our company, Larry Beck, a native of Paoli, Oklahoma. Larry was new to South Vietnam and had only just begun to take out recon patrols as a team leader, but he possessed all the skills and attributes needed to succeed in this dangerous business. He was intelligent, cautious, observant, and meticulous, with a total dedication to his men and to the mission. His men had complete faith in him, as did everyone else who came in contact with him. It was because of his talents and abilities that his team was chosen to carry out a demanding and dangerous mission far beyond the range of friendly artillery. The mission of Team Paddle Boat II was to investigate the trail that led east from the abandoned hamlet of Zia Rong (2) on the eastern bank of the Song Cai River and follow the DeGhia stream in the steep valley north of Hill 551. An agent report told of an enemy bivouac site somewhere along this trail, and Maj. Simmons and the G-2 of Task Force Yankee wanted Team Paddle Boat II to attempt a prisoner grab to determine the validity of the information provided by the agent.

Due to the steep terrain in the team's NFZ and the complete lack of any LZs near their objective, Lt. Beck chose to have his team inserted on a sandbank on the eastern side of the Song Cai River two miles south of the trail near Hill 551. This LZ was clearly visible to anyone on the high ground on either side of the river. The old French road of QL 14 was only 100 meters away across the river. Sgt. Karkos, the team's assistant patrol leader, told Lt. Beck that he thought he had seen enemy soldiers as the insertion helicopter was coming in on its approach, but he was not sure what side of the river they were on. Lt. Beck decided to move east away from the river for several hundred meters, requiring the team to climb a hill that had a near 60-degree angle of ascent. After climbing the steep, slippery slope for two hours and struggling to keep their footing, Lt. Beck had the team move north toward their objective. The team traveled through 80-foot-high jungle canopy with thick secondary growth, making their movement slow and difficult. Lt. Beck halted the team several times to listen for any sign that the enemy was following them, but all they heard was the rush of the water in the river below them. As night approached, they harbored in thick underbrush before sending in a situation report via the clandestine radio relay site, which had just been established on Hill 1143 two miles to the east.

The next morning the team continued to move northeast toward Hill 1143 in an attempt to find terrain more suitable for cross-compartment movement. They were still far from their objective as they reached the base of the cliffs leading to the summit of this imposing massif. As they approached a small hill at the base of the cliffs, they encountered five NVA soldiers dressed in black pajamas and carrying AK-47s and large packs who appeared to be searching for them. Sgt. Karkos, who was walking point, opened fire on the NVA soldiers, hitting two of them. The three remaining enemy soldiers fled, taking one of their wounded comrades with them, but the other one lay wounded a few meters from the patrol. Lt. Beck and Sgt. Karkos attempted to capture the wounded NVA soldier, but he pulled a grenade from his cartridge belt, and it blew up in his hands, killing him instantly. The team retrieved the pack the enemy soldier was wearing and searched it for anything of intelligence value. They found numerous documents, articles of clothing, and several socks full of uncooked rice. They took the documents and left the other contents with the dead body. For the remainder of the day, the patrol moved downhill in a northwesterly direction in an attempt to reach the trail they had been given as an objective. The terrain made it very difficult to make any headway to the north, so the patrol continued toward lower ground near the Song Cai River in the hope of finding a less arduous approach to the trail. At sunset they harbored for the night and refilled their canteens in a fast-running stream. Lt. Beck put the entire team on alert for the first few hours of darkness since he suspected the enemy knew of their presence and would aggressively patrol to find them. The night passed quietly, with only the hum of mosquitoes and the sound of rushing water in the river below them.

On the morning of January 23, the patrol began searching for an easier approach to the

3. An Hoa—Patrols Redux

trail to the north. They were in a ravine and had just stopped to fill their canteens in a small stream when they were attacked by a force of approximately twenty NVA soldiers with automatic weapons. The enemy soldiers had obviously been following them and waited until the team was in a vulnerable position at the bottom of a steep ravine. Team Paddle Boat II was taken by surprise, and four members of the team were hit. Lt. Beck, PFC Rose, and the team's Navy corpsman, HN Pearce, were all killed, and Sgt. Karkos was wounded in the upper arm. Sgt. Karkos, although badly wounded and in pain, rallied the five remaining members of the patrol and had them return fire and throw CS gas grenades in an attempt to break contact and escape. After a few minutes of intense combat, the surviving Marines were able to climb out of the ravine and move along a ridgeline toward the Song Cai River valley. The enemy pursued them by fire but appeared reluctant to enter the ravine to chase them since the team now occupied high ground directly overlooking the ravine. Sgt. Karkos, who had removed the radio from PFC Rose's body, kept the relay site informed of the team's progress as they fled through the dense jungle growth toward the river and what they hoped would be a good LZ for an emergency extraction.

I had already planned on extracting the team soon after they made contact the previous day, but bad weather and fading daylight made it necessary to wait until the 23rd. I was briefing our insertion/extraction helicopter pilots in the COC at An Hoa when we received the urgent radio message from Sgt. Karkos that Paddle Boat II was in contact again, had casualties, and needed an emergency extraction immediately. We canceled our briefing and arranged for one of the CH-46 helicopters to be rigged with the aluminum ladder, now known as the Simmons Rig after our CO. The two Huey gunships that were part of our insertion/extraction package were immediately dispatched to Paddle Boat II's last reported location, and the relay site on Hill 1143 was told to inform the team help was on the way and to find an extract zone immediately. We also told them that the only known LZs were along the Song Cai River, a very dangerous location for an extraction with so many enemy in the area, and to be prepared to use the aluminum Simmons Rig ladder if they could not find an LZ. The gunships arrived over Paddle Boat II's position in 20 minutes, reported that there were no LZs within a thousand meters of the team, and advised that the team wanted to use the Simmons Rig as soon as we could get it to their location. Despite his wounds, the weight of the radio, and the high jungle canopy that prevented the gunships from seeing him and his team, Sgt. Karkos managed to direct the gunships so they were able to lay down a curtain of machine gun and rocket fire between Paddle Boat II and their pursuers. When the CH-46 helicopter with the Simmons Rig arrived, he directed them to his position and made sure that every member of his team was safely on the ladder before he finally attached himself and the ladder rose through the trees. His bravery and initiative in the face of great danger saved his team.

When we heard that Paddle Boat II had been safely extracted, Maj. Simmons and most of the company gathered at LZ Barnes to greet them. In the distance we saw the helicopter emerge from the clouds that shrouded the mountains to the west, at first a tiny speck in the sky but soon taking shape as it drew closer. Soon we could make out the ladder hanging behind it and affixed to the ladder were the six survivors of Paddle Boat II. As the helicopter hovered above us and lowered itself slowly so the Marines riding the ladder could detach themselves, we were filled with feelings of relief and joy that the team had escaped, but we also were filled with sorrow because we could not help but notice that three of their number were missing. Sgt. Karkos talked to BGen. Samuel S. Jaskilka, the new CG of Task Force Yankee, who had come out to the LZ shortly after the team returned, asking Sgt. Karkos about what had happened to his team. Sgt. Karkos could have gone immediately to the battalion aid station, but he stood by the side of the LZ calmly talking to us despite the bullet hole in his arm and the obvious pain it was causing him.

Finally, after a few minutes, we noticed that Sgt. Karkos was getting pale, so we insisted he be treated for his wounds. He started to argue with us and insisted he be allowed to go out immediately and attempt to retrieve the bodies of his dead comrades. Marines never leave their dead and wounded on the battlefield, and Sgt. Karkos felt guilty that his three friends were lying out in the mountainous jungle. He wanted to bring them back, but he was in no condition to do so. We dissuaded him of this and immediately arranged for a rifle company to be inserted near the site of the deadly encounter to recover the bodies of Lt. Beck, PFC Rose, and HN Pearce. After Sgt. Karkos went to the aid station, I went into the COC and started to write an award recommendation for this brave NCO. Maj. Simmons sat down in his tent and wrote award recommendations for the pilots of the extract helicopter and the Huey gunships. Sgt. Karkos told us that the gunships were the only thing that stood between them and certain death. That evening, as I sat down to dinner in the 5th Marines' mess hall at An Hoa, everyone around me was very somber and reflective. The normal jocular conversation among the lieutenants was absent. We were all saddened by the loss of our three friends from Team Paddle Boat II, and this somber mood stayed with us for many days after this tragic event. Lt. Beck, PFC Rose, and HN Pearce were three of the most popular and well-respected men in our company, and their deaths deeply hurt us. A week later we were finally able to retrieve their bodies and send them home.[6]

Marine Corps intelligence sources suspected that an enemy infiltration way station was located somewhere a mile west of An Chuo Dao Mountain in the southeastern edge of Base Area 112. Team Penny Wise, led by Sgt. Ulstad, was given the mission of searching for this suspected way station and calling in and adjusting artillery on any enemy they observed. As was the case in most areas in Base Area 112, there were few LZs in or near the team's NFZ, which forced the team to either rappel through high jungle canopy while their insertion helicopter hovered above the trees or to land in one of the few areas that allowed a helicopter to land. In this case, the team opted to land in a small area adjacent to the Khe Dienne stream, a narrow, fast-moving river that winds its way through a narrow valley two miles west of An Chuo Dao Mountain. This small LZ was one of only a handful of LZs within several miles of the team's NFZ. Due to bad weather in the mountains, the team was not inserted until early in the afternoon of January 25, when the cloud cover broke enough for helicopters to navigate toward Penny Wise's NFZ. They landed a hundred meters north of the fast-moving stream without incident, and soon they were moving northwest up a narrow and rain soaked ridgeline leading to the summit of Hill 406. The team hoped to find a north-south trail system marked on their maps and one they suspected might lead them to the way station intelligence reports alluded to. A steady rain restricted their visibility to only a few meters and made the ground difficult to traverse, but it also dampened any noise they might make moving through the thick secondary growth under the jungle canopy. As darkness approached, Sgt. Ulstad had his team stop and harbor for the night, but sleep was difficult for the team because of the steep terrain. The steepness of the ground they chose for their harbor site was so severe it forced the men to sleep on an uncomfortable angle using trees

A recon Marine crossing a stream in Base Area 112.

to prevent them from slipping downhill. They spent the night this way, huddled under their ponchos as a never-ending monsoon rain added to their misery.

    The next day, January 26, the team stopped climbing and started to move west and down toward the Khe Dienne stream again. When they reached the stream, they found a trail on the south side that appeared to have been recently cut and improved. Sgt. Ulstad and Sgt. Glenn left the team in a concealed position and went forward to examine the trail. They found that the trail was wide and recently used, and since it was far from the lowlands to the east, it was evident that the only people using this trail were NVA soldiers. Fearing enemy contact if they used the trail, Sgt. Ulstad decided to stop and set up a watch of the trail from a concealed position. They remained watching the trail for an hour until 1440 when a single NVA soldier was observed walking toward them along the trail. He was dressed in a gray shirt and khaki shorts, and he carried an SKS rifle. He appeared to be looking for them and probably was the point man for an NVA counter-reconnaissance team. The patrol opened fire from a distance of 20 meters, killing him. Sgt. Ulstad and two men moved onto the trail to search the body, but all they found was a blood trail and drag marks leading back up the trail. Within seconds they were taken under fire by a squad-sized enemy force, which resulted in PFC Rivera's being wounded. Sgt. Ulstad withdrew to where his team remained hidden, but soon the enemy located them and attempted to encircle them. A fierce firefight ensued in which another NVA soldier was killed. The team asked for an immediate emergency extraction through the recon relay station manned by Team Night Scholar on Hill 452. An aerial observer was in the area, and soon the team began to use the plane's machine guns and rockets to strafe the enemy positions. Marine Huey gunships were also sent to the team's aid, and their machine gun and rocket fire allowed the team to break contact and begin moving back to their insertion LZ. Since the only known LZ in the vicinity of the beleaguered team was their insertion zone—and it was several hundred meters away—I had the Simmons ladder rig attached to one of the extraction helicopters and told the patrol to be ready for a ladder extraction if they could not find a suitable LZ.

After spending nearly two hours running from the enemy, who were heard talking and moving behind them, the team reached a sandbank on the southwest side of the Khe Dienne stream, where the water was approximately 3 feet deep. Since the team was several hundred meters from their insertion LZ, the patrol asked to be extracted by ladder from the stream bank. With gunships providing covering fire, the helicopter with the ladder rigged below it approached the team on the sandbank and managed to maintain a hover long enough for six of the men to snap-link themselves onto the ladder. The helicopter attempted to gain altitude so the remainder of the team could get on the ladder, but it lost power for some reason, causing the ladder to be dragged eastward along the stream with several of the attached Marines underwater for nearly a minute. When the helicopter finally recovered and lifted off, two of the Marines were not on the ladder and were presumed lost. Another helicopter, despite the small size of the sandbank and enemy fire from both sides of the stream, was able to land and retrieve the remaining three members of the team. It was another bad day for our company and proved once again how dangerous patrolling in Base Area 112 was, given the paucity of adequate landing zones and the abundance of enemy troops.[7]

That evening, Sgt. Treseloni, who was in charge of our mess hall, baked a birthday cake for me and Lt. Hansen. Our birthdays were both on January 26, and he had decided to surprise us with the cake. The SNCOs and officers gathered in our mess tent to share the cake and drink some cans of warm beer, but the loss of two more of our comrades turned what would have been a happy occasion into one of sorrow. No one talked much, and few of us ate any cake. Maj. Simmons demonstrated his leadership by using the occasion to toast the Marines we had lost during January and to pay tribute to their sacrifice. He reminded us that our job was a difficult and dangerous one, but one that had to be done even if it meant we suffered the loss of good friends. I cannot remember his words, but I remember they had a soothing effect on us and steadied our nerve for the many patrols that lay ahead. He then vowed that we would recover our two lost Marines from the Khe Dienne stream, a promise that he made good two days later when our executive officer, Capt. Dell Williams, led a 25-man team back to the Khe Dienne stream and had scuba divers recover the bodies in 15 feet of water 100 meters downstream from where the ladder dragged them through the stream. The recovery operation lasted less than three hours and no enemy troops were sighted in the area by Cpt. Williams's recovery team.[8]

While most of our patrols were conducted west of An Hoa, we also inserted teams into the foothills and mountains south and east of An Hoa in support of the 5th Marines. Unlike Base Area 112, these were often near areas where civilians farmed, making it more difficult to tell friend from foe and to avoid contact with the VC. Due to attrition and the increased pacification efforts of the GVN, the number of VC in the coastal lowlands had significantly decreased since the Tet Offensive of 1968, but there were still areas in parts of Quang Nam Province's coastal plain where VC units could be found. Most of these VC units consisted of local guerrillas who were finding it increasingly difficult to remain in their home villages due to the Phoenix Program and the increased presence of GVN Regional and Popular Forces units. Almost all of the VC mobile units were destroyed or seriously depleted, and the enemy had to use NVA soldiers to fill the ranks of these units. One such unit, which had a long and famous history, was the 1st VC Regiment. At one time, the 1st VC was an independent regiment, but after the Tet Offensive over 90 percent of its troops were NVA soldiers, and it became one of the three regiments of the NVA 2nd Division. Marine intelligence held that the 1st VC Regiment was located in the Que Son Mountains southeast of An Hoa, along with several severely depleted local VC units that had been driven from their villages in the Hiep Duc and Que Son Valleys. The enemy called their base area in the Que Son Mountains Base Area 116. As January came to a close, one of our patrols into Base Area 116 proved to be highly successful and netted us an enemy POW.

SSgt. Mathis and his intelligence colleagues with the 5th Marines suspected that the trail network that ran north-south between Nui Mo Cam Mountain and Nui Do Mountain four miles east of An Hoa was a major transportation link used by the enemy to move forces from southern Quang Nam toward Da Nang City. Based upon their recommendation, we inserted Team Saddle Bag into the area on January 26, with the mission of conducting Stingray operations against any VC they observed. Unlike most recon patrols, this patrol was what we called a "walk in," since it started in a secure location, in this case the command

The lakes and lowlands east of An Hoa with Nui Mo Cam and Nui Do mountains where Team Saddle Bag patrolled, on the left.

post (CP) of Company C, 1st Battalion, 5th Marines, which was located 500 meters east of the village of Mau Chan (2). Team Saddle Bag, consisting of seven Marines, left the CP under cover of darkness on the 26th and began a long hike into the foothills toward Nui Mo Cam Mountain, where they hoped to establish several good OPs. The terrain in their NFZ was open with only grass and low scrub brush, making movement during daylight hours dangerous, so the patrol moved mostly at night from one OP location to another.

The highlight of this patrol occurred in the morning of January 29 near one of the team's OPs on the ridgeline called Nui Duong Thong. This OP was perfectly situated to observe any movement along the main trail to the south that ran through the cut between Nui Mo Cam Mountain and Nui Do Mountain. At around 0930, Team Saddle Bag observed ten NVA soldiers moving along the trail, and they called in an aerial observer (AO) who used the plane's rockets and machine guns to attack this enemy column. The terrain was open, so the enemy was unable to effectively hide from the AO, but the open terrain also made it necessary for the team to move from their OP position because they suspected the enemy had spotted them. The team moved a short distance when they encountered two NVA soldiers standing just a few meters in front of them. The patrol opened fire on the enemy soldiers, killing one and capturing the other. These enemy soldiers were wearing the standard light green NVA field uniforms under black pajamas, an obvious attempt to hide their true identities and making it appear that they were civilian farmers.

Back in the COC at An Hoa, I called for an immediate emergency extraction since the patrol had captured a prisoner and their position had been given away in fairly open terrain. Normally, when I suggested that a team should be extracted, no one questioned these decisions, but on this occasion, which was the first of several in the coming months, Task Force Yankee questioned whether or not the team should remain in place since it might be able to continue on with its mission. While I had the greatest respect for the Task Force Yankee staff, I was keenly aware that the officers making this suggestion had no experience as reconnaissance patrol members and some had no combat experience, which I felt made me and Maj. Simmons better suited to make a judgment on the wisdom of keeping a team in the field after they had made contact with the enemy. In fairness to them, they wanted to exploit the team's success in locating enemy units and calling in artillery and air strikes on them. Still, they did not have the field experience that would inform a wise decision concerning whether or not it was possible to keep a team in place once it was discovered by the enemy. I knew that once a team had been discovered by the enemy and had been attacked, it would spend the rest of any time remaining running from the enemy and not performing any useful purpose. It was also very dangerous to leave a team in the field once the enemy went after it, since the enemy had highly effective counter-reconnaissance teams that could hunt down and destroy a small recon team. Only stealth, supporting arms, and rapid extraction by helicopter could save a team operating far from friendly lines. After a few minutes of arguing, Task Force Yankee agreed with the decision to extract Team Saddle Bag, but I could tell they did not like having a 1st lieutenant arguing with them.

As if to make my point, Team Saddle Bag again made contact with the enemy while they waited for the decision on extraction. Another group of NVA soldiers moved up the hill from the south toward their position, reconning the patrol's position with small arms fire. The AO who remained on station after the first contact was called in, and he directed air strikes by Marine Corps F-4 Phantom fighter jets, killing three of the advancing NVA and forcing the others to flee south. At 1330, the team was safely extracted by helicopter and returned to LZ Barnes at An Hoa with their prisoner, who turned out to be a North Vietnamese soldier from the 1st VC Regiment. This prisoner provided valuable intelligence about where his parent unit was located in the Que Son Mountains, their plans for an upcoming offensive in February, and how he had infiltrated from North Vietnam to Quang Nam Province via the Ho Chi Minh Trail in Laos. He further stated that the headquarters of the 2nd NVA Division was located near the western cliffs of the Ong Thu Slope in exactly the area where signals intelligence predicted it was located, and only a mile or so from where Sgt. Ott's team Icebound had found the communications wire near An Gao Mountain.[9]

As January came to a close, I began to sense morale in the company was declining. At the time, I was not sure exactly why this was occurring, or if I was just imagining it, but I could not ignore some of the comments I heard during our second Patrol Leaders' Seminar in late January. Here, I began to hear complaints from some of the patrol leaders about their perception that their reports were either being ignored or disbelieved. They did not understand why their reports were not being acted upon by higher headquarters. They said they made recommendations after each patrol about what action should be taken, but they saw little or no evidence that any action was being taken, aside from scheduling a bombing raid now and then. They also told me that they did not see why we had to go back into Base Area 112 repeatedly since it was plain to them that the Marine Corps was not exploiting the intelligence their patrols produced. They also felt the focus of the Marine leadership was on the coastal lowlands, not Base Area 112. The more experienced our patrol leaders were, the more frustrated they seemed to be. They said that just about every patrol sent into Base Area 112 encountered significant numbers of well-equipped, aggressive, fresh NVA soldiers, and often these enemy troops employed highly aggressive counter-reconnaissance teams against them. It was apparent to our team leaders that we were suffering more casualties, especially deaths, than the entire 1st Reconnaissance Battalion at Camp Reasoner, and they attributed these losses to the fact that our company was patrolling primarily in Base Area 112. When I spoke to Maj. Simmons about my perception that morale was declining due to the casualties we had suffered in the first six weeks at An Hoa, he decided to talk to the assembled patrol leaders in our briefing tent about how our reporting was making a difference for the good. He used data provided by the Task Force Yankee staff concerning the results of Operation Taylor Common, which showed that the elements of the 5th and 3rd Marines had used the intelligence we had obtained on our patrols to conduct several successful sweeps of Base Area 112, all the way to the Song Cai River, killing over a thousand NVA soldiers and capturing large quantities of enemy weapons, ammunition, and supplies. His talk with the patrol leaders seemed to have the desired results, because we all sensed that the sacrifices made, while severe and hurtful, had not been in vain and that the intelligence we were gathering was being acted upon.

In late January, we began to see enemy propaganda leaflets turning up inside our camp. Some of these leaflets were delivered to us via mortar round, but others were simply placed near our perimeter wire at night. Most of us got a good laugh out of the rather amateurish and unsophisticated messages these leaflets conveyed, but a few of these leaflets carried a message that disturbed me since they contained quotes from American political leaders. These quotes caused some of our Marines to question why our political leaders would be saying such things. The quotes most often used were those attributed to Senator Gene

McCarthy and Senator William Fulbright, but there were also quotes from our former Secretary of Defense Robert McNamara.

One of the men who worked for me in the operations center, Sgt. Dorris, brought several of these leaflets to me one evening and asked me what I thought of them. I could tell he was angry, and he wanted to know if these American political leaders had actually said the things attributed to them on the leaflet. I told him I did not know, but that I doubted our political leaders would say anything that might aid the enemy and that, even if the words were correct, they were probably taken out of context. I told him that on my first tour of duty in South Vietnam I had never seen an enemy propaganda leaflet, although I assumed there were some. We had a rather lengthy discussion about how the war was being presented in the press at home and how the enemy's proselytizing organizations might be taking advantage of this. I spoke to him about the *Selected Works of Mao Tse-Tung*, which I had read as a midshipman at the U.S. Naval Academy. I explained to him how the Chinese communist system of civilian and military proselytizing was used to undermine the will of their opponents, and how the VC had taken a page from the Chinese communist playbook by using the same system in an attempt to break our morale. We both agreed that the communists had a good system of propaganda based upon years of experience against the Japanese, French, and South Vietnamese governments, but we must never allow that propaganda to influence us to the point where we failed to do our duty. Despite my explanation, I could tell my comments did not assuage Sgt. Dorris's anger over the antiwar quotes he had read on the propaganda leaflets. Unfortunately, I could not give him a good reason for why these American political leaders would say things that could be used in our enemy's propaganda campaign against us. I would see many more of these enemy leaflets in the days ahead.

CHAPTER 4

Base Area 112

When we first arrived at An Hoa, most of our team leaders were rather junior NCOs, but as February began, we saw the arrival of several much-needed young lieutenants. The deaths of Lt. Slater and Lt. Beck left us with very few officer patrol leaders or platoon commanders. With the influx of new lieutenants, we now had a solid cadre of officers leading our platoons and taking out patrols. They were an exceptionally gifted, intelligent, and motivated bunch, and their arrival had an immediate and positive effect on the efficiency of the company. These lieutenant platoon commanders were Lt. Wayne Rollings, Lt. Lynn Lowder, Lt. Rick Miller, Lt. Randy Champe, Lt. Jim Richie, and Lt. Ed Browder. Soon they would be leading patrols and providing the very highest level of scouting and patrolling leadership to our six platoons.

In February, our company, augmented with two battalion platoons, continued to support Operation Taylor Common by locating enemy infiltration trails, base camps, and supply depots inside Base Area 112. However, our teams saw a dramatic decrease in sightings of, and contacts with, the enemy. We attributed this to the aggressive actions of the 5th and 3rd Marines as they established artillery fire support bases on the tops of key terrain in the eastern portion of the base area and fought their way west, driving the NVA before them. As a result, we began to push our teams further west as we screened for the advancing infantry units clearing the base area. Surprisingly, we did not find much enemy activity on the western side of the Song Cai River. We had anticipated that the 2nd NVA Division would fall back along their supply lines to the west and attempt to defend the western side of the Song Cai River, but our patrols on that side of the river indicated that was not their intention.

On February 16, Team Beach Nut killed one NVA soldier in an ambush west of the Song Cai River, but that was the only real action we had on that side of the river. Our covert radio relay sight near the summit of Hill 1143 was critical for the safety of any team operating on the west side of the Song Cai River since it provided the only means of relaying radio messages from our teams back to An Hoa. Without this relay sight, our teams operating to the west would be unable to communicate. However, the continued use of this prominent terrain feature overlooking the Song Cai River was noted by the NVA, and they began to cover the few helicopter LZs near the summit, forcing several of our teams to abort their insertions or to constantly move to avoid making contact with NVA counter-reconnaissance teams. In addition, as Marine and South Vietnamese units moved west in pursuit of the 2nd NVA Division, these friendly units abandoned their artillery Fire Support Bases (FSB) on the Ong Thu Slope and in the eastern portion of Base Area 112, giving rise to a requirement

A Marine Fire Support Base in Base Area 112.

for our company to set up clandestine OPs near these FSBs. Task Force Yankee wanted to ascertain whether or not the enemy was moving into the abandoned FSBs, and they wanted recon teams to use artillery and air strikes against them if they did. As we moved our recon patrols farther west, we saw an increase in the number of rappel insertions and hoist extractions due to the lack of suitable places to land a helicopter.

After one of my early-morning briefings for our insertion/extraction helicopter crews, I asked one of the pilots, Capt. "Hot Rod" Hundley, about an area near the Laotian border that SSgt. Mathis and I were interested in as a potential site for a truly long-range reconnaissance operation. Based upon the interrogation of several NVA POWs, we suspected this area might be the main spur off the Ho Chi Minh Trail that led into Quang Nam Province. Capt. Hundley was famous for his bravery and flying expertise, making him the hands-down favorite helicopter pilot among our reconnaissance team leaders. When I told him about our suspicions and showed him the area on our map in the COC, he agreed to take us out to the area later in the day when he had finished making our insertions and extractions. In passing, he mentioned that he had been in this area before and had seen a wooden bridge over a river there. While we waited in the COC for Hot Rod to return, our fertile imaginations came up with the brilliant idea that we ought to bomb this bridge if we came across it during our recon flight with Capt. Hundley. Our "bombs" would be several M-26 fragmentation hand grenades inserted into empty beer cans that had their tops removed. We would pull the pins of the grenades and then drop the grenades from the "hell hole," a sort of bomb bay in the floor of the helicopter. The pins would not fall out until the beer cans reached the ground or the trees, thus delaying the explosion until the grenades were close enough to do any damage. The entire idea was foolish in the extreme, but we were young and foolish, considering this great fun despite the real possibility that such a contraption, if not employed properly, could blow the helicopter up and us along with it.

Around 1500 on February 14, we launched from LZ Barnes and flew west over the Ong Thu Slope, Base Area 112, the Song Cai River, and beyond toward the Laotian border. We had two Huey gunships with us flying escort. When we got over the area we wished to recon, we saw the bridge and asked Hot Rod if he would make a low pass over the bridge while we threw out the grenades. The beer can "bombs" dropped about 1,000 feet, and all of them went off, but not one of them hit the bridge or even came close. Since our "bombing run" had failed, we asked Hot Rod if we could use the 50 cal machine gun mounted on the left door of the helicopter to make a strafing run on the bridge. Again, Capt. Hundley agreed to our crazy scheme, and we banked sharply and descended until we were only a few hundred feet above the bridge, a narrow, crudely constructed footbridge made from bamboo and other local materials. This time we got some results, not all of which were good. We managed to hit the bridge with many rounds of 50 cal machine gun fire, but in the process we also succeeded in overheating the machine gun so one round actually fired through the side of the barrel, making the gun inoperable and causing great embarrassment and consternation for Capt. Hundley, who would have to explain this problem to his superior officers. The gunships followed up on our futile effort to drop the bridge, but they too were unable to succeed in destroying it. We flew home to An Hoa, and Capt. Hundley returned to Marble Mountain. A few days later, Capt. Hundley told us that he did not get into trouble for the damaged machine gun because he told his CO that our quick actions had probably saved his helicopter from being downed by enemy ground fire. When I asked him, "What ground fire?" he replied, "I am sure I heard shots fired at us and maybe even saw a tracer or two." He then winked, and we never discussed this incident again.[1]

On February 15, Team Screen Test found a large enemy way station, or base camp, a mile south of Nui Ro Mountain on the far western side of Base Area 112. The team reported that this way station was large enough to house several hundred men, and it appeared to have been occupied a week earlier and abandoned, probably because of friendly operations east of it. The way station, which was located on a hilltop under a dense jungle canopy, consisted of ten large huts, two mess halls, ten earthen bunkers, and twenty fighting holes with a latrine just outside its perimeter and a guard post at one entry point. The two mess halls, which were solidly constructed from finished lumber, were 16 feet by 40 feet and still contained several pots and other cooking implements. The team observed the base camp for two days but did not detect any enemy activity during their entire patrol.[2]

The description of this way station reminded me of several similar way stations I found in 1967 when my recon team, Killer Kane, conducted deep reconnaissance missions 20 miles north of where Team Screen Test found their way station. This triggered a conversation with SSgt. Jack Mathis about how the enemy was using these way stations and how we might benefit from keeping a record of their locations. Our thinking was based on our reading of various POW and Hoi Chanh interrogations that told of the infiltration system used by the enemy to move troops and supplies down the Ho Chi Minh Trail. We knew from these interrogations that the way stations were established approximately 15 miles apart, or a day's journey by foot. We also knew that the enemy often would maintain two infiltration routes, one for the movement of troops and the other for the movement and storage of supplies. SSgt. Mathis began to plot the known way stations we had uncovered during Operation Taylor Common, and I searched for the location of way stations I and other recon teams had discovered in 1967. A definite pattern began to emerge as we plotted these known way stations on our intelligence map in the COC. We began to see that the location of these way stations was not always in the most obvious places. For instance, Elephant Valley, west of Da Nang, was an obvious infiltration route for the enemy to use to move their troops into position to attack that city and its air base, but our plot of way stations indicated that the enemy was not using this logical approach. Instead, we found by connecting the known way station locations on our map that the actual infiltration route started south of the A Shau Valley in Thua Thien Province and ran south until it entered Quang Nam Province near the A Vuong River. Here, it split into two trails, with one branch continuing south and the other continuing east.

The southern branch of the infiltration route continued south along the A Vuong River until it reached the Song Boung River, then it turned east until it reached the abandoned village of Ben Giang on the Song Cai River. From there it continued south until it reached the ford a mile west of Hill 374. Once on the east bank of the Song Cai River, the route followed the main east-west trail on the southern edge of Base Area 112.

The eastern branch of the infiltration route stretched from the A Vuong River east for nearly 20 miles until it reached the Happy Valley on the border between the districts of Hieu Duc and Thuong Duc. It then made a sharp turn west of Tat Lay Mountain and continued south, following the Song Con River west of the village of Thuong Duc. After reaching the Song Cai River a few miles west of Thuong Duc, it crossed that river and ended in Base Area 112. The logic behind these two infiltration routes was easy to ascertain since both routes ended in base areas used by the 2nd NVA Division. The Happy Valley area was known to be the base area for one of the regiments of the 2nd NVA Division, the 31st Infantry Regiment, as well as elements of the 368B Artillery Regiment. The headquarters of the 2nd NVA Division and the 21st NVA Regiment, along with at least a battalion of the 368B Artillery Regiment were in Base Area 112. The third regiment of the 2nd NVA Division, the 1st VC Regiment, often operated south of Base Area 112 in the Quang Tin and Quang Ngai provinces, but it also moved into Base Area 116 north of the Que Son Valley on occasion. SSgt. Mathis and I decided that we would send patrols into the areas where we thought a way station should be and also schedule bombing raids on the way stations we had already discovered. Like most humans, the NVA were creatures of habit, and they seemed intent upon using the same way stations over and over again.

In what would be a continuing occurrence for teams establishing clandestine radio relay positions near Hill 1143, Team May Fly, led by Lt. Lowder, was probed by two NVA soldiers on February 21, resulting in the patrol's initiating contact with rifle fire and grenades. Both enemy soldiers fell and appeared to be dead, but Lt. Lowder decided not to check the bodies since he feared that more enemy were in the area and it would be best to move away quickly and establish another radio relay station farther south on the ridgeline overlooking the Song Cai River. This was a wise decision, because the team's primary mission was to provide a radio link for our recon teams operating west of the Ong Thu Slope, not to spend their time ambushing NVA patrols. It was critical for them to remain where they could provide FM radio communications to our recon teams, and that meant in the vicinity of Hill 1143. Had an emergency extraction of Screen Test been required, then several teams west of the Ong Thu Slope would have had to abort their missions, since they would have been without radio contact with our COC.[3]

We continued to receive credible intelligence from various sources that the enemy intended to launch another countrywide offense around Tet, similar to the one they had launched the previous year. Taking advantage of the bombing halt of North Vietnam and the numerous "truces" initiated by President Johnson, the NVA had reinforced and resupplied their forces in South Vietnam and were prepared for this event. Their leaders in Hanoi were determined to launch this offensive as a means of showing the incoming administration of President Nixon that they were prepared to fight, even if peace talks were going on in Paris. As a prelude to their offensive, the enemy spent much of January making periodic and largely ineffective mortar and rocket attacks on An Hoa. Just about all of these attacks came at night, with many of the incoming rounds falling harmlessly outside our wire. A few mortar rounds did fall inside our company's perimeter one night, but they did little more than shred a few tent roofs. Since the walls of the tents were protected with sandbags, none of the Marines sleeping in the tents were wounded. The response to these indirect fire attacks was swift and devastating, with Marine artillery returning fire on the enemy mortar positions.

Unlike 1968, the U.S. and South Vietnamese forces were prepared for this offensive. As part of the preparation, Operation Taylor Common had been launched to disrupt the infiltration of NVA units from Base Area 112 into the coastal lowlands south of Da Nang, a major target for the enemy's 1969 "Mini Tet" Offensive. We knew that the enemy would have to use staging areas in the lowlands as they moved to their attack positions near Da Nang, a process that would force them to transit from their base areas in the mountains along several trails we had discovered. As the suspected date for the start of this enemy offensive approached, tentatively given to us as between February 19 and 23, our company was sent on several missions to cover likely infiltration routes from the Ong Thu Slope and Base Area 112 into the lowlands.

One of these missions fell to Team Pony Team, led by Sgt. Pate. This six-man team was taking one of our new lieutenants, Wayne Rollings, along for one of his three "snap in" patrols. Their mission was to establish a clandestine OP on Hill 132 overlooking the intersection of two major trails and a ford over two streams that flowed east toward the Song Thu Bon River. This location was an obvious place for any NVA units to pass through as they infiltrated east along the southern edge of Base Area 112 on their way to the heavily populated coastal lowlands and Da Nang City. With this in mind, Pony Team was inserted at noon on February 20 by helicopter into an LZ just a few hundred meters southwest of Hill 132, in the valley that contained the two trails and the ford. They were on the ground less than two hours when they observed five NVA soldiers carrying AK-47 assault rifles and heavy packs walking along the wide, east-west trail in the valley. The patrol opened fire when the enemy came to within 15 meters of them, killing two of the enemy and causing the remainder to flee west along the trail. A few minutes later, the patrol again made contact with the enemy, and this time it was seven NVA soldiers dressed in green field uniforms and carrying AK-47s who came down the trail. Again, the patrol initiated contact with the enemy, killing one of the NVA soldiers and sending the rest fleeing to the north. Fifteen minutes after this contact, the patrol engaged three more enemy soldiers, killing one of them before the patrol broke contact and moved east. They had not moved 100 meters when they observed two more groups of NVA soldiers who were pursuing them. Helicopter gunships and fixed-wing aircraft were called in by the patrol, providing excellent coverage of these targets and beating back the enemy's attempts to attack the patrol. During the short time the team was on the ground, they observed twenty-three NVA soldiers and killed six of them with small arms fire before they were extracted under fire from the same LZ they had landed in two hours earlier. The results of this patrol led us to believe the area in the vicinity of Hill 132 was heavily populated by NVA soldiers who were either moving east along the main east-west trail or were occupying a way station nearby.[4]

February 20 was a busy day for our recon teams. Pony Team was not the only team to observe enemy movement on the approach routes toward An Hoa and the coastal lowlands. Team Off Spring also made contact with the enemy on that day shortly after it was inserted on the western edge of the Ong Thu Slope just south of Hill 1031, which was called Ban Co Mountain by the Vietnamese. Their point man saw two NVA soldiers walking toward them on the same trail the patrol was using. The enemy soldiers were carrying large transport packs and seemed to be oblivious to the Marines' presence, since they were talking loudly and carrying their rifles over their shoulders and not at the ready. The point man for Team Off Spring fired at the enemy soldiers at close range, killing one and wounding the other, who stumbled off the trail after dropping his pack. The team searched two packs left in the trail and found they both contained large quantities of rice, which had probably been picked up from the villages several miles to the east in the Arizona Territory. While the team was searching the packs, they came under fire from an unknown number of enemy troops to the east. The team moved 30 meters west off the trail to a position that afforded better protection from small arms fire and waited to see if the enemy came after them. A few minutes later, the team heard voices and then observed four NVA soldiers dressed in the standard light green field uniform of the NVA and wearing pith helmets. All of them carried AK-47 assault rifles, and they were moving cautiously eastward on the trail, searching for the team. The patrol fired on these NVA soldiers, killing one instantly. When the team attempted to reach the dead enemy soldier, they saw two NVA soldiers trying to drag the body away, and they fired on them, wounding one of them. The team called for an emergency extraction, and an hour later they were safely extracted using the Simmons Rig ladder after spending only six hours on the ground.[5]

The surge of sightings of enemy troops moving east throughout the 1st Marine Division TAOR, along with many intelligence reports, clearly indicated the impending Mini Tet Offensive was near. It was no surprise, then, when the long-awaited Mini Tet Offensive began on February 22. Unlike the 1968 Tet Offensive, this attack was much weaker and involved more attacks by fire using mortars and rockets and fewer ground attacks. It was also very much a North Vietnamese Army operation, since the VC units in Quang Nam Province were still recovering from their losses in 1968.

At An Hoa, we came under attack from mortars and 122 mm rockets, followed by a ground attack on the north side of the airfield, where a small number of elite NVA sappers managed to penetrate the defensive wire and blow up our ammo dump before being killed. On the south side of the airfield, we had two 82 mm mortar rounds land inside our compound, but the only damage done was to our supply tent and a jeep parked nearby. On the whole, the damage done was light, but four Marines were killed defending the northern side of the base before the fifteen-man NVA sapper unit was wiped out. A Combined Action Platoon (CAP) outpost near the village of Mau Chanh (1), east of An Hoa, was also hit that night, but again the enemy forces were beaten back and friendly forces suffered only minor casualties in the fighting. Throughout Quang Nam Province, the enemy attacks failed and the NVA units suffered heavy casualties, with little to show for their efforts. Some enemy units were ambushed before they even reached their targets, thanks to good intelligence and aggressive defensive measures.

However, American press reports made the attacks seem far worse than they actually were and made little mention of the heavy casualties suffered by the enemy. We attributed this to the absence of any American reporters in the field during these attacks. Most Americans back home believed the war was covered by American reporters who were with American forces in the field, but few actually were. Most American reporters stayed in Saigon and only ventured outside of Saigon when they were carefully and safely escorted by American public affairs teams. Few Americans knew that most reporting on the war was done by third country employees of the U.S. news organizations. In Quang Nam Province, I never saw an American film crew, but I did see Taiwanese and South Vietnamese film crews filming for U.S. news organizations. When American reporters did come to Da Nang, they stayed in the city or on the U.S. bases near the city, and did not venture outside the safety of these bases. They preferred instead to talk to rear-area personnel who tended to exaggerate the impact of enemy attacks and to place an inordinate emphasis on the sapper and rocket attacks that had a temporary effect on air operations. They never seemed interested in talking to the Marines or South Vietnamese forces that savaged the enemy in numerous ambushes or artillery missions on the approach routes taken by the NVA toward Da Nang City or the valiant local friendly forces, like the Popular Forces, who defended their villages and harassed the enemy troops moving through their districts. Had our American reporters spent more time in the field with those fighting the war and less time in the bars and brothels of Saigon, I think their reporting would have been more accurate and they would not have had to rely on foreigners and café politicians for their stories about the war.

Shortly after the end of the 1969 Mini Tet Offensive, I read an intelligence report that summarized information obtained from several prisoners captured during the offensive. This intelligence report explained the reasons for the failure of the enemy offensive. From this report, it was pretty clear that the North Vietnamese placed the blame squarely with the local VC political cadre in Quang Nam Province. Specifically, they felt the local VC provided inadequate logistical and intelligence support for the offensive—support they had promised but failed to deliver. Local VC had been tasked with stockpiling rice and other foodstuffs for the NVA units moving out of the mountains toward Da Nang City so these units could travel light, carrying only their weapons and ammunition. For some unknown reason, these food stockpiles were either not provided or were not of sufficient quantity for the number of transiting NVA soldiers. Also, local VC were given the mission of providing guides for NVA units moving from the mountains into the lowlands, but many of these guides did not show up or were incompetent, thus causing some NVA units to become lost or to launch their attacks too late or not at all. The NVA prisoners also said local VC cadres failed to provide porters to help them carry ammunition or to build adequate numbers of bunkers for the advancing NVA units to hide in during daylight hours. This caused several important units to be caught in the open during daylight and subjected to supporting arms fire or attacks from U.S. and South Vietnamese ground forces. Some prisoners even said the local population was not supportive of them and refused to provide any assistance at all. This attitude on the part of the local civilians ran counter to what the NVA soldiers were told to expect, and it had a negative effect on their morale.[6]

As the enemy offensive sputtered to an end, our company was given the mission of attempting to locate their retreating columns and to use supporting arms to attack them as they made their way back to their base areas in the mountains. One such mission involved Team Off Spring, a seven-man team led by Lt. Browder. Their mission was to conduct a clandestine reconnaissance of an east-west trail off the southern end of the Ong Thu Slope about a mile northwest of An Chau Dao Mountain (Hill 485) in an area of very steep, mountainous terrain with high jungle canopy and very thick secondary growth. The team was inserted in the afternoon of February 27, but they remained on the ground less than 24 hours due to their discovery by an exceptionally aggressive NVA counter-reconnaissance team, which pursued them as soon as they landed by helicopter. The team became prey of this enemy-tracking unit within minutes of landing. The rear point of the patrol spotted the NVA soldiers within minutes of the patrol leaving the insertion LZ, and he reported that the enemy had two dogs with them that were actively tracking the Marines. The team attempted to evade their pursuers and to call in artillery fire on them, but despite good coverage by the supporting artillery battery at An Hoa, the patrol made contact with this enemy force less than an hour after they first observed them. The recon team was moving northwest along the east-west trail toward the summit of Hill 375 when they were confronted by a force of sixteen NVA solders dressed in the standard NVA light green field uniforms and carrying AK-47 assault rifles. The patrol saw the enemy first and opened fire on them, killing one of the NVA soldiers. The stunned enemy did not react immediately, and this provided the patrol with enough time to break contact and move away to the east into thick brush.

As they broke contact, they heard dogs barking and several NVA soldiers shouting, but the enemy did not seem to be pursuing them any longer. Evidently, the NVA tracking team thought better of pursuing the Marines after they had seen one of their colleagues killed. The team continued to push through the thick brush and elephant grass for a few minutes, but Lt. Browder feared that the noise they were making as they moved through the dense foliage would allow the enemy to locate their direction of movement, so he decided to stop and harbor for the night.

Team Off Spring set up their security and radio watch for the night in thick undergrowth, and all seemed quiet until nearly 2100 that evening, when a Chinese hand grenade exploded a few meters away from their position. The team knew this was an attempt by the enemy to have the patrol fire their weapons and give away their position, a common trick of the NVA counter-reconnaissance teams. Lt. Browder told his men not to fire their weapons but to throw several hand grenades in the direction where they heard movement. A few minutes later, the patrol received erratic and inaccurate rifle fire which the enemy hoped would cause the patrol to return fire and give away its location. Lt. Browder and his men did not take the bait, remaining absolutely quiet so they would remain undetected. After a few tense moments, the team's radio operator was able to whisper a request for artillery and MC-130 gunship support. In the COC at An Hoa, I listened to the request and immediately contacted the 1st Marine Air Wing Liaison Officer at Task Force Yankee and relayed the request. Throughout the night, the artillery and "Spooky 13," the gunship, ringed the patrol with protective fires, causing two secondary explosions, indicating the supporting arms were having a telling effect on the enemy. The next morning, the patrol moved to a good LZ that an aerial observer pointed out to them. During the extraction, the helicopter received ground fire, but no one was injured.

An hour after the patrol returned from their mission, I listened to their patrol debrief in the S-2 briefing tent. At the end of their debrief, Lt. Browder and his men informed SSgt. Mathis that they thought there must be either a large concentration of the enemy near the southern edge of the Ong Thu Slope or something else the enemy did not want a recon team to discover because the enemy reacted very aggressively against the team as soon as it landed, and they continued to stay in contact with the patrol even after the enemy counter-reconnaissance team was subjected to devastating supporting arms fire.[7] A more ominous outcome of this patrol was the fact that it proved the enemy was still able to operate in Base Area 112, despite the extensive sweeping operations of the Marine infantry. The Marines had killed many of the enemy, captured a large amount of supplies, and driven the headquarters of the 2nd NVA Division west across the Song Cai River, but the enemy had not abandoned Base Area 112. On the contrary, they simply moved west and avoided any decisive engagement until the Marines left the base area and returned to the lowlands. As soon as the Marines departed, the 2nd NVA Division moved back into Base Area 112. I did not realize it at the time, but they would never abandon this vital base until 1975, when it would no longer be needed.

CHAPTER 5

The Idylls of March

March saw a change in both our status and the focus of our reconnaissance operations. On March 8, Operation Taylor Common was ended, and we no longer worked for Task Force Yankee. Instead, we were placed in direct support of the 5th Marines. Originally, our company was supposed to return to Camp Reasoner at Hill 327 outside of Da Nang City when Operation Taylor Common was finished, but this plan was changed when the 5th Marines began to conduct operations south of An Hoa near Hiep Duc and west of An Hoa in the Arizona Territory. Intelligence reports indicated the 1st VC Regiment was planning to contest the Hiep Duc Valley, and they had moved into their old base areas in the Que Son Mountains. As a consequence, we reduced the number of patrols conducted in the far reaches of Base Area 112 and increased our patrols in the mountains north of the Hiep Duc Valley. We also planned for several patrols in the foothills below the Ong Thu Slope so we could screen for the 5th Marines when they moved into the Arizona Territory.

In preparation for this new mission of supporting the 5th Marines, Team Trailer Park, a seven-man team led by Lt. J.D. Richie, was inserted on March 1 into an LZ on the northern slope of Nui Mat Rang Mountain (Hill 845) in the Que Son Mountains, with the mission of conducting a Bomb Damage Assessment (BDA) of an enemy base area that had been recently discovered by Marine infantry. A few hours after their insertion, the team located an abandoned enemy bivouac area hidden under the jungle canopy consisting of several huts, two wooden tables, and a latrine. From what they found, it appeared the enemy made a hasty departure, since they left several useful items behind, such as a steel Soviet-style helmet; two picks with 12-inch blades; spools of communications wire; and a large wire basket. After making a sketch of the bivouac area, Lt. Jim Richie moved his team 100 meters along a trail leading out of the bivouac area, where they took up a position from which they could observe movement on the trail. At 1845, the patrol made contact with a squad-size enemy force dressed in black pajamas and khaki uniforms moving down the trail. In the ensuing firefight, which lasted approximately 10 minutes, the patrol killed three enemy soldiers, and LCpl. Wallis was wounded by AK-47 rifle fire. The enemy broke contact and moved away from the team, dragging one of their dead with them. At 2045, a night helicopter medevac was made and LCpl. Wallis was safely taken to the aid station at An Hoa for treatment. Despite my request that the team be extracted at the same time as LCpl. Wallis, the team was required to stay in their NFZ and continue on their mission. As expected, the team did nothing during the next three days of their patrol but hide, reporting nothing of value. Since communications with the team was spotty, even when they were using their whip antenna, I made several additional requests to extract the team, but all of my requests were denied by the 5th Marines. Since I saw no compelling reason to keep the team in the field, I found the decision by the 5th Marines to be both dangerous and illogical, a view that was shared by Maj. Simmons and the rest of our company.[1]

During the first week of March several of our insertions were aborted due to enemy ground fire. Stung by their failure to achieve any appreciable success during their Mini Tet Offensive, the NVA units returned to Base Area 112 and were determined to keep our recon teams from entering their base areas again. Teams Report Card and Puppet Show had attempted to land in Base Area 112, but were unable to do so due to intense ground fire. In the case of Team Report Card, their helicopter received numerous hits from AK-47 rifle and 12.7 mm machine gun fire on March 2 as it attempted to land in an LZ near An Gao Mountain, the site of the ill-fated attempt to help Team Icebound tap into the communications wire they found near the summit of that hill. The ground fire was so intense, six of the nine recon Marines in the insertion helicopter were wounded and the helicopter barely made it back to An Hoa without crashing due to the loss of hydraulic fluid from the multiple holes in its fuselage.[2] The next day Team Puppet Show was also unable to land in their insertion LZ near the summit of Hill 734 in Base Area 112 due to heavy machine gun fire.[3] These failed attempts to insert our teams told us that, despite heavy losses during January and February, the 2nd NVA Division was far from defeated, and they had not been forced to abandon Base Area 112. Operation Taylor Common had lasted nearly three months and inflicted well over 1,000 deaths on the 2nd NVA Division, as well as the capture of large quantities of enemy weapons and ammunition, but it had failed to prevent the enemy from retaining its major base area in Quang Nam Province. The infiltration of NVA forces from Laos continued unabated, allowing the 2nd NVA Division to reinforce and resupply for future operations in the lowlands.

As if to make my point, on the morning of March 7, the NVA threw everything but the kitchen sink at the An Hoa airfield. Over 100 rounds of 82 mm mortar, 120 mm mortar, 75 mm recoilless rifle, and 122 mm rocket fire struck inside of the base's perimeter. Seven of these rounds landed inside our company's perimeter, wounding two of our Marines, one of whom had an unexploded 82 mm mortar round penetrate the bunker he was in and break his leg. We took the wounded into the COC, which was the most secure structure in the company's perimeter, and our corpsmen tended to them until they could be medevaced to Charlie Med at Hill 327. Most of this enemy artillery and mortar fire came from across the Song Thu Bong River in the Arizona Territory, and for once the NVA seemed to have done their homework, since most of their rounds landed inside the airfield's defensive perimeter. Still, damage was light and few Marines were seriously hurt. Marine artillery on the base was effective in silencing the enemy after a short period, and the next day Marine infantry units swept the area where the enemy fire originated and found several dead NVA, killed by the counterbattery fire.

Although the local VC never stopped committing atrocities in southern Quang Nam Province during Operation Taylor Common, they outdid themselves in early March with a particularly vicious and egregious example of the kind of terror they were capable of inflicting on civilians. In a refugee camp 10 miles south of An Hoa, the VC came into the camp after dark, taking advantage of the absence of the South Vietnamese forces who would normally have provided security for the camp. The VC burned down thirty-one houses and murdered nine adults and twenty-two children. As they left, they warned the refugees that unless they returned to their farms in VC-controlled areas, they would return and kill all of them. Such acts, while not always on the same scale, were routine in areas where the local VC held sway in the province and provoked a profound fear among the population. In some areas of Quang Nam Province, the Phoenix Program was having a very telling effect on the enemy's local political cadre and assassination teams, but those successes were primarily concentrated closer to Da Nang City and the coastal districts. Although severely depleted during the months after the 1968 Tet Offensive, local VC still were a force to contend with in southern Quang Nam Province near An Hoa.[4]

It was about this time that I began to see a pattern in the enemy's actions, and I intended to take advantage of it. During 1967, I had conducted many patrols in the mountains south of An Hoa in the districts of Duc Duc, Hiep Duc, and Que Son, and had built up a store of personal knowledge about how the enemy operated in these three districts. Each day, I would see intelligence and patrol reports that gave me a sense of déjà vu since it appeared the enemy was using the same trails and the same base camps they had used in 1967. I began to develop a plan to insert recon teams into the same areas I had patrolled in two years previously in the hope that the enemy was continuing to operate in these areas. As I will explain later on, this plan worked better than I expected. However, despite the efficacy of this plan to use recon patrols in areas known to me to have a high probability of enemy activity, no real strategic advantage was obtained. Allow me to explain.

The U.S. Marines had by this time been operating in Quang Nam Province for four years, but it seemed as if many of our commanders were oblivious to these patterns of enemy activity and did not know how to prevent the enemy from repeating them. This was probably due to the policy of having Marines serve thirteen-month tours of duty in South Vietnam and commanders normally serving only six months in command of their units. This policy did not allow Marine officers to develop a strong understanding of their tactical environment. By the time they had a good working knowledge of the terrain, the local population and the methods of the enemy, they either changed jobs or returned to the United States. This resulted in a general lack of tactical sophistication and an overreliance upon intuition and training and not on practical knowledge gained from experience. We continued to mount fruitless operations, fighting over the same ground, inflicting heavy casualties on the enemy, but failing to achieve any decisive results. We deluded ourselves by thinking we were winning every battle, so we must be winning the war. Over and over again, the enemy would suffer defeats as our infantry units conducted search-and-destroy missions in our province, but since no one was effectively preventing them from sending more troops and supplies down the Ho Chi Minh Trail, the tactical situation in Quang Nam Province remained relatively the same year after year with the enemy, not us, dictating the tempo of operations. Many of our Marine leaders at the time realized this, but they were powerless to do anything about it since both the war strategy and the personnel policies were dictated by our civilian leaders, and none of our military leaders thought it appropriate to challenge the authority of the president or Congress. I often heard these Marine officers lament a war strategy that was attrition-based (i.e., the body-count, numbers-oriented approach of Secretary McNamara, and the graduated response approach favored by our civilian national security team in Washington, D.C.). Many of these military officers lamented the fact that the enemy seemed to be using Laos and Cambodia with impunity, but our government never allowed them to mount operations against the enemy's bases in these two countries. Far too many officers, however, clung to the belief that if we could just inflict enough dead and wounded on the NVA in South Vietnam, Hanoi would tire of the war and sue for peace on terms favorable to the United States.[5]

The first patrol I recommended based upon my patrol experience during 1967 was inserted on March 18 into the Antenna Valley area, with the mission of establishing a clandestine OP from which enemy activity could be observed in the area around the village of Ap Bon (4) on the southern side of the valley. Antenna Valley ran from the Song Thu Bon River east toward the Que Son Pass. I had patrolled the hills overlooking this valley, and I always found enemy units using it, often moving in squad-size units. In this case, the mission was assigned to the eight-man team of Crazy Bone, and I briefed the patrol leader in detail about what I had seen before in the valley and where he should be looking to find the enemy. As I suspected, the enemy had not changed their pattern of behavior, and within hours after being inserted, Crazy Bone was reporting sightings of small groups of enemy soldiers moving along a trail a few hundred meters north of the hamlet of Ap Ba (3) on the south side of the valley. During March 18 and 19, the team reported eight separate sightings of a total of thirty-three enemy soldiers, all using the trail mentioned above. They were dressed in a variety of uniforms, indicating a possible mix of local VC and main force NVA. Several of them carried very large packs, which the patrol suspected contained rice or other foodstuffs that the enemy was transporting from the valley into the mountains north or east of the hamlet. Late in the day on March 19, the team moved down to the trail and encountered four NVA soldiers walking toward them. The team opened fire on the group of NVA soldiers and wounded one of them while the others fled west. The team captured the wounded enemy soldier and called for an emergency extraction, which was successfully completed at 1700. When the team returned to An Hoa, the prisoner was interrogated, and he revealed that he was an NVA soldier from the 1st VC Regiment.[6]

In March 1967, my recon team, Killer Kane, conducted several successful ambushes along the narrow path that winded its way through the pass between Antenna Valley and the Que Son Valley. These ambushes were made to avenge the deaths of two members of the 1st Force Reconnaissance Company, Capt. Eric Barnes and Sgt. Godfred Blankenship, who died near Deo Le Mountain when an enemy land mine exploded. The Killer Kane ambushes were triggered in the pass between Geo Coc Mountain and Deo Le Mountain that linked Antenna Valley with the Que Son Valley. I decided to insert a recon patrol in the same area because I suspected the enemy continued to use this pass to transit from the Song Thu Bon River to the Que Son Valley. Since the valley was steep and narrow with jungle growth hiding much of the trail running through it, I thought it offered many places where a successful ambush or prisoner grab could be accomplished. With this in mind, I gave Team Off Spring, led by Lt. Browder, the mission of conducting a prisoner grab along the trail a few hundred meters north of Hill 350, if the situation presented itself.

On March 23, Lt. Browder and his eight men landed in a good helicopter LZ on the western slopes of Deo Le Mountain on the north side of the pass, from which they moved south to an OP site that afforded excellent observation of the trail running east and west below them. They did not observe any enemy troops using the trail on the 23rd, but on the 24th, they made three separate sightings of a total of sixteen enemy soldiers on the trail. The last sighting was made when the team left their OP and went down to the trail to attempt a prisoner grab. At 1430, a group of four NVA soldiers approached the ambush site from the west. They were wearing gray uniforms, web gear, and pith helmets. Lt. Browder had prepared for this prisoner grab by creating a command-detonated explosive device containing both C-4 plastic explosive and CS gas that he hoped would shock and disable an enemy soldier and afford the team enough time to capture him. When the lead NVA soldier entered the team's ambush zone, Lt. Browder triggered the device, but the blast proved to be too strong. It killed the lead NVA soldier and stunned the others. One of the enemy soldiers attempted to throw a grenade at the patrol, but he was killed along with another who attempted to flee. The patrol found one wounded enemy soldier in the blast area, whom they captured. Lt. Browder requested an immediate emergency extraction, and the team and their prisoner were safely extracted one hour after the ambush was sprung. The prisoner, along with several weapons and packs, was turned over to the 5th Marines, S-2 Section, for exploitation.[7] The day after the patrol returned to An Hoa, we learned that the captured prisoner was a scout for a reconnaissance company of the 2nd NVA Division who had been escorting a political officer to a meeting in the Que Son Valley.

I planned another patrol based upon my patrolling experience from 1967, and I assigned this patrol to Team Report Card, which was led by Lt. Wayne Rollings. I made several patrols in 1967 in the area south of our radio relay station on Hill 452, during which Killer Kane sighted numerous enemy moving along the trail that ran from Thach Bich hamlet on the eastern bank of the Song Thu Bong River north to the Antenna Valley. I had also successfully ambushed the enemy on this trail near the hamlet of Ninh Long (2), and I felt confident the enemy would continue to use this trail since no friendly units were located near it and it was a natural infiltration route for any enemy force moving north from Hiep Duc to An Hoa. I knew there were many very good ambush sites along this trail where a successful prisoner grab could be carried out. Although Lt. Rollings was a newly arrived officer to our company, I chose him for this mission because he was a very mature individual who had been an enlisted Marine SNCO for several years before gaining his commission. I also knew he possessed the cunning, bravery, intelligence, and aggressiveness needed to carry out the difficult mission of a prisoner grab. All of our lieutenant patrol leaders were outstanding, but Wayne was clearly the most aggressive, possessing what I would term a "killer instinct" that manifested itself in a keen desire to inflict maximum damage on the enemy. These traits would make him one of the most formidable and famous recon team leaders of the war. It would also start him on the path to becoming a major general.

On March 26, Lt. Rollings and his team of seven Marines and a Navy corpsman landed by helicopter in a large abandoned rice paddy a few hundred meters east of the trail mentioned above. They spent the rest of the first day moving west toward the trail along a small stream until they harbored for the night. On March 27, the team continued to move slowly through thick undergrowth until they came to the trail and established an ambush site close to it. This spot allowed them both to observe traffic on the trail and to ambush any enemy that might prove vulnerable to a prisoner grab. The morning hours passed uneventfully, but at 1300, the team saw what appeared to be a supply column of NVA soldiers and civilian porters carrying large packs. The team counted thirty-one individuals passing their position as the group moved south toward Thach Bich hamlet on the Song Thu Bong River. The team was too close to the group to call in artillery, so they let it pass. Thirty minutes later, the men of Team Report Card spotted a lone NVA soldier walking down the trail carrying an AK-47 assault rifle and a large pack. The team triggered an ambush, killing the NVA soldier. However, when they began to move onto the trail to search the body, a group of fifteen NVA soldiers moving north on the trail appeared and began firing on the patrol and throwing grenades. In the ensuing firefight, Lt. Rollings and his team killed five of the enemy before breaking contact and moving to an emergency helicopter LZ a few hundred meters west of the trail. As they moved to this LZ, the enemy pursued the team and Lt. Rollings personally killed six more of the enemy as he took over the duties of rear point. His leadership, bravery, and marksmanship were instrumental in his team's safe extraction without suffering a single casualty.[8] For his bravery during this patrol, he was awarded the Navy Cross, our nation's second highest award for valor.

A good example of the enemy's tendency to return to base areas they had used for years in Quang Nam Province occurred when Team Third Round "A," a seven-man team led by Cpl. Eddy, was inserted into an NFZ on the south side of Antenna Valley. This patrol took place March 24 to 28 in the foothills north of Hill 344 and very near the hamlet of Ap Ba (2), an area that afforded several good OP sites from which the valley and east-west trail to the north could be observed. On previous patrols in 1967, I had observed considerable enemy traffic in Antenna Valley at this location, and I thought it would be a good idea to send Cpl. Eddy and his men back into this area, especially in view of recent intelligence reports that indicated there was a large enemy base camp nearby.

Both my experience and the intelligence reports proved to be valid. During just one 24-hour period from 1600 on March 24 to 1600 on the 25th, the team observed 138 NVA soldiers moving north along a trail running east of the hamlet of Ap Ba (2). The team called in several artillery fire missions on the enemy columns but was unable to observe any results.[9]

This patrol and others proved the futility of the war strategy employed by the United States in Quang Nam Province. Marine units had conducted numerous sweeps in Antenna Valley and would continue to do so, often inflicting very high numbers of casualties on the local and main force units in the valley, but after each successful operation, the enemy simply withdrew to their base areas, hid from the Marines and South Vietnamese forces, and reinforced their depleted forces with NVA soldiers infiltrating down the Ho Chi Minh Trail. This process led to the destruction of most of the local communist units, but that did not matter since these units were reformed using North Vietnamese soldiers until the local main force units, like the 1st VC Regiment, were made up entirely of northerners. Unless some effective means of cutting off the enemy's ability to reinforce and resupply their units in Quang Nam Province could be found, the war could drag on indefinitely.

Around the end of March, I began discussing my eventual departure from 1st Force Reconnaissance Company with Maj. Simmons. I had promised him that I would stay with the company until the completion of Operation Taylor Common and then request a transfer to an infantry unit. He supported my decision to spend the second half of my tour of duty in-country with an infantry unit because he knew I needed to gain some practical experience in my MOS. He realized I had missed this experience during my previous tour of duty in South Vietnam, which was a deficiency I needed to correct if I planned on making the Marine Corps a career. We both agreed that early May would be the best time to make this change, since we expected the company to leave An Hoa around that time, and it gave Maj. Simmons enough time to find a suitable replacement for me. Col. James B. Ord, the CO of the 5th Marines, had spoken to me earlier about serving under his command, promising me that he would place me in command of one of the infantry companies in his regiment. When Col. Ord was relieved by Col. William Zaro on March 23, he spoke to Col. Zaro about my desire to join the 5th Marines, and Col. Zaro expressed his willingness to have me assigned to his command whenever I was ready. Since I saw Col. Zaro frequently during my many trips to the 5th Marines COC, I was able to arrange for my transfer to his regiment easily and to discuss with him what he expected from his officers and how he intended to employ his battalions against the enemy in the An Hoa Basin. It was during one of these conversations that he told me that I knew more about the mountainous areas of Quang Nam Province than anyone he had met. I was able to tell him about likely ambush sites and enemy base areas because I had actually covered the terrain in 1967, and I knew from recent experience that the enemy was likely to be found in the same areas that they had used two years earlier. I was flattered that such a senior officer took an interest in my comments and seemed willing to use my knowledge of the enemy. The more I talked to Col. Zaro, the more eager I became to join his regiment.

As March came to an end, I received a large "care package" from the Dowd family that contained food luxuries I had almost forgotten existed. Mr. and Mrs. Dowd were the parents of a very good friend of mine, Lt. Tom Dowd, who was killed in action in March 1967 while serving with the 1st Marines. Ever since Tom's death I remained in contact with Tom's family and wrote to them often. Tom's father managed several large department stores on Long Island, New York, and I noticed the address on this care package was from one of these department stores. In this particular package, I found an abundance of Belgian chocolates, tinned rum cakes, dried fruit, European cheeses, gourmet canned bacon, and other exotic delights otherwise not available to a Marine far from home. The best items in the package were several cans of alcoholic drinks that had somehow escaped the attention of the customs inspectors. This package was the first of several the Dowd family sent to me, and each time I received one I was filled with gratitude for their thoughtfulness. The Dowd care packages and those I received from my parents allowed me to vary my diet and not rely solely on C-rations and the rather bland menu items served in the 5th Marines mess hall.

The end of March also marked the departure of SSgt. Mathis, who was given a field promotion to second lieutenant and transferred back to Camp Reasoner. Lt. Bob Hansen, our very able communications officer, replaced him as our S-2. Hansen was one of those very versatile and capable people who could do any job assigned to them—and do it well. I cannot say enough about how capable Hansen had been as our communications officer since his job was key to the very survival of our teams. Our small teams, often as few as six men, operated in enemy-controlled territory, far from friendly lines. The success of these teams depended upon their rapid reporting of information they gathered on the enemy, and this was done using their PRC-25 radios. Their survival depended upon their ability to use their radios to call in artillery and air strikes on any enemy force pursuing them and to request an emergency extraction when the situation dictated. Without good and continuous communications via radio, they were at a distinct disadvantage when they encountered the enemy. Bob Hansen always made sure we had good and continuous communications, from using field expedient antennae he designed and built to selecting the best locations for clandestine radio relay sites. Like Lt. Mike Henry, our communications officer in 1967, Bob performed miracles when it came to maintaining communications with our teams. His work often meant the difference between success and failure for our reconnaissance mission and life or death for our teams. Neither of these superior officers ever let us down.

On March 4, I drove to Da Nang to deliver $310 to the Catholic orphanage on Rue Yen Bay, home of the two orphans I supported. I gave the money to Sister Marie Madeleine and told her it came from contributions collected from the Marines of my company. She was delighted and thanked me profusely. I also spent a few moments with Ngo Hue and Ngo Dung and had their picture taken in the courtyard of the orphanage with Sister Marie Madeleine. They told me that they were doing well in school and that they prayed for my safety every night and at Mass on Sundays.

Later in the day, I went to visit my Vietnamese friends, Mr. Smart and Mai Ly. Mai Ly told me she had recently married, and her new husband, a lieutenant in the South Vietnamese Air Force, was in Okinawa, Japan, for helicopter training. She invited me to have lunch with her and her sister in their small, three-room house in Phouc Toung Village near the air base. During a Spartan lunch of rice, nuoc mam, steamed vegetables, and warm tea, she told me she hoped to buy a small plot of farmland soon for

Mai Ly.

her family but was waiting to see if the security situation near Hoi An improved. Hoi An was the capital of Quang Nam Province, and the area around it was protected by South Korean Marines. She said the VC had been beaten badly during the months following the 1968 Tet Offensive, but it was too early to tell if they might make a comeback. Her family had owned farmland before, and the VC had taken it away from them, so she did not want a repeat of this family tragedy. She and her husband wanted to make sure the security situation where they wanted to purchase a farm was stable before making such an investment. After lunch, I stopped by Camp Reasoner to drop off some paperwork, and then I got in my jeep and drove back to An Hoa, noticing how peaceful and beautiful the countryside was along the road south. It was hard to believe the country was at war.

As April began, the company worked to screen the 5th Marines by conducting patrols in the Ong Thu Slope area and the Que Son Mountains. The enemy was becoming far more aggressive when we attempted to insert teams near their habitual base areas, and as a result, several of our patrols were aborted because they were unable to land in their assigned LZs. Team Recline made three attempts to land in their LZ on the eastern side of the Ong Thu Slope, but on each attempt ground fire prevented their helicopter from landing. After several heavy air strikes by Marine fixed-wing jets, they were finally able to land, but they spent the next 92 hours running from the enemy in the vicinity of an abandoned Marine FSB that was used during Operation Taylor Common. They had two contacts with the enemy, resulting in two enemy KIAs and the capture of some documents, a wallet, and a large pack containing rice.[10]

Team Hireling, a six-man team led by Sgt. Pate, suffered the same fate as Team Recline a few days later when they attempted to land near the infamous Hill 1026 on the western edge of the Ong Thu Slope. They landed under fire in their LZ, but the enemy was determined to prevent the patrol from moving off the insertion LZ. As soon as the team attempted to move off the LZ and begin their patrol, they were attacked by a squad of NVA soldiers armed with AK-47 and SKS rifles and dressed in the standard NVA field uniform. During the running gun battle that ensued, four enemy soldiers were killed and Sgt. Pate was wounded by Chinese grenade fragments. The team was extracted under fire from the same LZ they were inserted in just two hours earlier.[11]

An unusual and sad patrol was conducted on April 4 by Lt. Browder's Team Impressive. A rifle company, M/3/5, requested that we assist them in the recovery of three Marine KIAs that had been left behind when M/3/5 had been involved in heavy fighting with an NVA force during Operation Taylor Common. The CO of M/3/5, Captain Burns, and two enlisted Marines from that rifle company were attached to Lt. Browder's five-man team for the body recovery operation. The team's means of insertion would be the Simmons Rig ladder, the first time this system was used for an insertion. With all eight men affixed to the ladder, the insert helicopter lifted off LZ Barnes at 1030 and flew west into Base Area 112 to an area near Hill 332 where Capt. Burns believed the bodies were located. The team landed 200 meters from their objective, but moved quickly to it through high jungle canopy and thick bamboo. When they arrived at the objective, they found all three bodies of the missing Marines. However, as they were preparing to move the bodies to an extraction zone, they observed two unarmed NVA soldiers walking along a trail leading uphill to the patrol's position. The patrol opened fire with unknown results and continued toward their extraction LZ, a large bomb crater, where they were extracted along with the dead Marines at 1230 by the Simmons Rig ladder.[12] This mission finally proved the efficacy of the Simmons Rig in areas where there was an absence of suitable helicopter LZs and the use of rappelling was not practical. While the system was dangerous to use and required skillful flying by the helicopter pilots, it was the best means of inserting and extracting a team quickly when there was nowhere for a helicopter to land.

During April, the 5th Marines launched Operation "Muskogee Meadow," in which we were tasked with the mission of locating elements of the 2nd NVA Division south and west of An Hoa. Our job was to find the enemy so the 5th Marines could engage them and drive them out of the coastal lowlands and back into the mountains to the west. We inserted several teams north and south of the Que Son Valley with some of the teams reporting large numbers of enemy troops. Team Crazy Bone saw 105 NVA soldiers moving in the valley during April 6 and 7, and Team Serviceman II observed fifty enemy soldiers moving in small groups in the southern part of the valley during April 5 through 7. Both teams called in artillery and air strikes on these enemy formations and relayed the enemy activity to the 5th Marines.[13]

Serviceman II was in the thick of it again just a week later when they were inserted into an LZ on a high ridgeline overlooking a bend in the Song Thu Bong River at the western extreme of Antenna Valley north of Thach Bich Village. Their NFZ was only a mile west of where Lt. Rollings had had his significant contact with a large body of enemy troops a month earlier. Since I was due to take a five-day R&R in Taiwan and would not be in the COC while Serviceman II was in the field, I brought in the patrol leader, Sgt. Crouch, and briefed him on the likelihood of encountering the enemy in his NFZ. I told him that both Lt. Rollings and I had made contact along the trail running from Thach Bich Village north through the pass at the abandoned hamlet of Ninh Long (2), so he should expect the same. I warned him that my experience patrolling in this area told me this trail was a major infiltration and transport route for the enemy, so he and his patrol should expect the enemy to defend it. We both worried about the absence of any large trees on the hills west of the trail, a situation that would make hiding difficult and daylight movement dangerous. Events were to prove our concerns to be correct. On the day I departed to begin my R&R, I mentioned to my operations chief, Gunny Trevathan, that I had a bad feeling about Serviceman II's patrol. He promised to keep an eye on them in my absence.

Late in the day on April 13, Sgt. Crouch and his seven-man team attempted to land at their primary LZ, but ground fire forced the pilot of their helicopter to land in an alternate LZ 200 meters further east, which was a large, open area with a sheer cliff on its south side. Unfortunately, this LZ was easily observed by the population of a small hamlet called Tu Pho (5), a mile west on the eastern bank of the Song Thu Bon River. Since the LZ was fairly open and offered little in the way of concealment, Sgt. Crouch moved the team as rapidly as possible into an area of thick, head-high brush and waited until nightfall to move again. With nightfall, he moved his team 100 meters to an area thick with waist-high brush where he thought it was safe to harbor his team. That night the patrol was awakened around 2000 by shouts in English coming from several different directions west and south of their harbor site. The voices yelled "Recon go home" and "Recon dies" in perfect English. These unnerving taunts persisted for nearly an hour until they abruptly ceased. Later that night, the team observed ten bright lights moving through the hills 1,000 meters to their north, so they called in an artillery fire mission on the lights, and they went out. Sgt. Crouch, an experienced team leader, suspected the yelling and the lights were attempts by the enemy to locate the team's position or force it to leave the vicinity. In any event, such actions by the enemy were rare and indicated the VC had a fairly good fix on the patrol's location.

The next day, on April 14, Serviceman II observed thirty-two enemy soldiers moving southwest along the main trail leading into Thach Bich Village. This group consisted of two uniformed NVA soldiers carrying rifles at the head and tail of the enemy column, with the others in between dressed in black pajamas and carrying large packs on their backs. The patrol called in an artillery fire mission on the enemy with excellent coverage, resulting in five of the enemy killed. From the description of this group, it was evident it was a supply column transporting rice from the paddy fields south of Hill 452 to enemy units west of the Song Thu Bong River. Shortly after this first observation, the team spotted another fourteen enemy soldiers moving southwest along the same trail where it paralleled a small stream. This group was dressed in black pajamas and carried AK-47 assault rifles and packs. The enemy stopped on the trail when they found the body of one of the enemy killed earlier and attempted to drag it away with them. The patrol called in another fire mission using the same artillery concentration, and this time they killed another enemy soldier. The rest of the enemy moved away into a tree line to the east and disappeared. While the patrol occupied an excellent OP from which to observe the trail below them, Sgt. Crouch worried about the absence of any vegetation that could allow the patrol to remain covert, so he again moved the team into some thick brush and hid for the rest of the day. That evening, at around 2000, the patrol again heard voices yelling taunts to the Marines, similar to the ones they had heard the previous night. In addition, they observed a brush fire on the ridgeline where they had been inserted and approximately thirty enemy soldiers moving about searching the area. The team called for "Spooky," the U.S. Air Force MC-130 gunship, and within an hour the gunship was pouring a steady stream of red tracers down from the sky onto the enemy. The patrol heard screams of pain coming from the impact area that "Spooky" had fired upon.

Sgt. Crouch called for an emergency extraction that night based upon his belief that the open terrain in the area and the number of enemy searching for the team made it impossible to continue with his mission. In the COC, Maj. Simmons and Gunny Trevathan listened to Sgt. Crouch's request for a night emergency extraction, but somehow the request was not granted. I was never sure why the request was not granted, but it probably had to do with the dangers attendant to a night extraction by helicopter. Since the recommendation was turned down and the team was told to continue on their mission, all anyone could do was hope for the best. Gunny Trevathan told me later that he had a very uneasy feeling about the decision to keep the team in the field, so he spent the entire night listening to the radio in the COC. Fortunately, the night passed quietly, and those who had made the decision to keep the team in the field felt justified with their decision. On April 15, the team remained hidden in high elephant grass and sent in only a few whispered position reports. Gunny Trevathan listened to these whispered radio transmissions in the COC at An Hoa and noticed that each position report was the same, indicating the team was hiding in the same position they had occupied during the night. Trevathan thought this was dangerous, so he asked Sgt. Crouch if he thought the team could move. Sgt. Crouch replied that he was afraid to move the team during daylight, since they were in open terrain and he feared the enemy would see them moving. He knew it was highly dangerous for a recon team to stay in one place for more than 24 hours, but he saw no safe alternative. Everyone in the COC hoped that the patrol would remain hidden until the 16th, when it was scheduled to be extracted.

Their hopes were dashed during the night of April 15 when several hand grenades landed in the patrol's harbor site and a vicious and prolonged firefight developed. Using their claymore mines, M-26 fragmentation grenades, M-79 grenade launcher, and M-16 rifles, the patrol fought back against the larger enemy force. The team called for an immediate emergency night extraction, and this time it was approved. While the extraction helicopters launched from Marble Mountain, an MC-130 "Spooky" gunship flying near the team was directed to the patrol's position and given the team's frequency so they could coordinate the use of the plane's devastating firepower. It arrived over the team in minutes, and its lethal Gatling guns were used with good effect on the enemy who now surrounded the team. "Spooky's" highly accurate fire from its Gatling guns saved the team from being overrun by creating a veritable wall of fire around the team's position. After a 30-minute flight from Marble Mountain, the extraction helicopters found the patrol's location in the dark and miraculously managed to land in complete darkness and take the team to safety. This close-range firefight resulted in seven enemy KIAs, but the team suffered very heavy casualties: PFCs Jarnolinski and Gell were killed, and all but one of the remaining members of the team wounded, including the team leader, Sgt. Crouch.[14]

This tragic event had a devastating effect on the company's morale. When I returned from my R&R, several team leaders came to me and demanded to know why a team that was obviously compromised and had little chance of finding a safe haven was allowed to stay in the field. I could not give them an explanation since I was not there when the decision was made and I had no idea what factors were taken into consideration. I simply told them that often the decision to keep a team in the field was made at a higher level than our company, but generally we always recommended a team be pulled if they requested it and they had made contact with the enemy. This event, along with several others that involved keeping teams in the field after they had been compromised, added to a growing disenchantment among some of our officers and men. I even had one lieutenant come into my COC and ask my advice about whether or not he should request mast with the CG of the 1st Marine Division so this subject could be brought to a senior officer's attention. I advised him that it would not be a good idea to jump the chain of command and bypass Maj. Simmons and the CO of the 1st Reconnaissance Battalion since they were the ones who should be taking this matter into advisement. Gunny Trevathan echoed my sentiments and helped the lieutenant write up the administrative action form requesting mast with Maj. Simmons. I am not sure if the lieutenant ever submitted the request for a mast interview with Maj. Simmons, but I took the matter up myself with Maj. Simmons later that evening. During that meeting, I stressed to him the need to take any request for an emergency extraction very seriously and always give the patrol leader the benefit of the doubt. I told him it was impossible for anyone sitting in a COC to understand what it was like to be far from friendly lines with the enemy in pursuit, unless that person had actual combat experience. I said that, based on my experience, it was always wise to extract a team after they had made close contact with the enemy. I explained that contact with the enemy had a psychological effect on the team members that drastically changed their perspective. Instead of focusing on their mission, their fear of being surrounded and killed caused a team to only want to hide, and to move as little as possible. This made it impossible to accomplish anything worthwhile. We both agreed that Task Force Yankee and the 5th Marines were really not in a position to make sound judgments concerning a decision involving the emergency extraction of a recon team. These decisions should be left to us, unless there was some very compelling tactical reason to do otherwise.

When I returned from R&R, I was informed that my request for transfer to the 5th Marines had been approved, and I would report for duty with them on May 1. This meant I had about two weeks to close out my affairs with the 1st Force Reconnaissance Company and to prepare myself for my new duties with a Marine infantry regiment. Each day I worked feverishly in the COC to complete several projects that had to be completed before I left the company. I wrote a new standard operating procedures (SOP) for our operations section, a training records SOP, and an after action report (AAR) for Operation Taylor Common. I also finished a reconnaissance training course that included twenty-one lesson plans and had been a project of mine ever since I arrived at An Hoa.[15]

Much to my surprise and delight, I also received a letter from one of the Pan Am airline flight attendants I had met in Taiwan. Her name was Carol, and she had been one of the crew on the plane I took to Taiwan. When I arrived at my hotel in Taipei, I found Carol in the lobby checking in, and we struck up a conversation as we waited. We chatted again for a few minutes later in the lobby, and she introduced me to another flight attendant who was talking with an Australian Army sergeant, John O'Connor. John was also in Taipei on R&R. We decided to all meet again that evening for drinks and dinner at a restaurant the girls recommended. During the next five days, the four of us went on several tours of local tourist attractions and shopping expeditions. Each evening we would go to a different restaurant, followed by a trip to a movie theater or local club to see a floor show. The highlight for me was a trip to Whu Lai, a mountain resort whose rustic beauty reminded me of some Chinese watercolor painting or the mythical Shangri-La. We went during a weekday so we pretty much had the place to ourselves. For some reason, Whu Lai's beauty and serenity seemed to soothe my spirit and make me forget the war. Sgt. Connor later told me he felt the same way, as if the place had a medicinal effect on his psyche. I wrote back to Carol, who was based in Hawaii, but I never heard from her again. Alas, I guess I did not make much of an impression on her.[16]

One thing that dawned on me during my last week with the company was that I would not be able to take all the gear I had accumulated during my first five months in-country. In the infantry, everything one used was carried on one's back, so I had to significantly lighten my load. I could store a footlocker and duffel bag in the rear with the 5th Marines, but nothing more. This meant I had to give away several books my parents had sent to me and cull through my other gear to make sure I only retained those items essential for my new job. I retained only two Vietnamese language books and a two-volume history of East Asia, but I gave away the remainder of my books, at least a dozen, to Marines who expressed an interest in reading them. The four books I retained were purchased from the Charles B. Tuttle Publishing Company's office in Tokyo, and I would order several more books from them during the next year. I also started a subscription to the *Far Eastern Economic Review*, since I found the information in this publication concerning events in Asia to be accurate, comprehensive, and unbiased. I would keep this subscription current until the magazine went out of business many years later.

On April 27, I went to Da Nang to take care of some last-minute administrative work at Camp Reasoner, and I used this opportunity to once again visit the orphanage and my Vietnamese friends. This trip was marred somewhat by a massive explosion at the ammunition supply point (ASP) near the Da Nang Airfield, which caused a huge pyrotechnic display and considerable damage to the ASP and the surrounding civilian community. As I drove up to Da Nang, I saw the huge column of smoke from this conflagration and thought the enemy must be attacking the airfield, but this costly event was actually caused by accident and not enemy action.

One of my Vietnamese friends was directly and tragically affected by this catastrophe. Ly Thi Lan and her family lived in a small house near the southern end of the airfield, and I found her and her family sitting beside the charred embers of what had been her home only hours before. Lan was the sole source of income for her family, and her job working for the Marine Corps at various facilities around Da Nang paid well. She spoke excellent English and was employed as an interpreter when I first met her in 1967. Her father, who had been paralyzed from the waist down from a VC bullet, sat in his wheelchair with a stunned look on his face, as if to say, "What else bad can happen to me?" When I spoke to Lan, she told me that they had lost everything in the

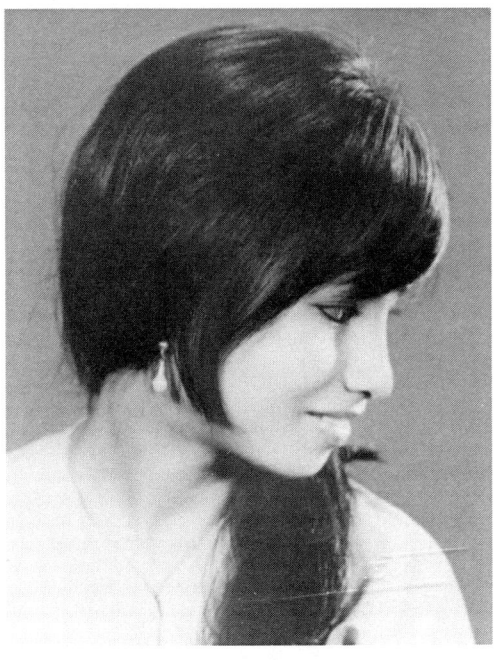

Ly Thi Lan. Her family suffered many hardships during the war.

Mr. Ly in the ruins of his home near Da Nang.

house, even their power saw, which was the family's primary source of income. Despite the family's plight, they offered me a cold soft drink from the only thing to survive the fire: an ice chest they used to sell cold drinks from. I was almost moved to tears seeing how bravely they accepted their fate. On my way back to An Hoa that afternoon, I bought two cases of soft drinks from the PX and dropped them off so Lan and her family could restock their ice chest. Her father thanked me profusely, but I knew my meager contribution to the family's welfare would not go far in making up for the catastrophic loss of their home. As I left, I saw Mr. Ly sifting through the rubble that had been his home and having difficulty moving about in his wheelchair. I helped him move to a flat piece of ground in his front yard and then turned to leave. But before I did, I told Mr. Ly that I hoped things would get better for him and his family soon. He only smiled and said, "Maybe in 100 years."[17]

A year later, on another trip to Da Nang, I stopped by to see how the Ly family was doing, and I was pleasantly surprised to see that they had rebuilt their home, obtained another power saw, opened a drink shop stand, and planted a small vegetable garden in their tiny backyard. On this trip, Lan proudly and happily told me she had just been married, and she introduced me to her new husband, a handsome young ARVN sergeant she had known since she was a child. They invited me to attend Mass with them at the small Catholic church a short walk from their new home, and I eagerly accepted. As I stood at the back of the roughly built little church and looked around at the devout and stoic faces in attendance, I knew the cause I was fighting for was worth it. The strength of this family and their neighbors in the face of adversity greatly impressed me and reinforced my positive feelings for the Vietnamese people.

Chapter 6

The Arizona Territory

On the first day of May, I loaded my footlocker and duffel bag onto a dusty and battered jeep and climbed in to take a very short ride to the command post (CP) of the 5th Marines, which was located only 200 meters away inside the An Hoa Combat Base perimeter. There I presented my orders to the adjutant, and he told me I would be temporarily assigned to Company F, 2nd Battalion, 5th Marines. He assured me the assignment would only last a few weeks and then I would be permanently assigned to another company in the 2nd Battalion. I was taken in to see Col. Zaro, who spoke to me about the importance of my temporary assignment, which he described as "over the shoulder training." He said he wanted me to spend two weeks under the tutelage of his most experienced company commander, learning how to be a company commander in the field. Since I had never served in an infantry billet before and needed to see how his rifle companies operated, I thought this was a good idea and a great opportunity to study under a man who obviously enjoyed the confidence of Col. Zaro. He then told me that once I had served my two weeks with Company F, he would give me command of another company in the 2nd Battalion as soon as one became available, and the battalion commander agreed. As he ended the interview, he told me to stow my gear in the 2/5 supply shed, draw my weapons and web gear, and be prepared to leave at noon on a helicopter that would take me from An Hoa to the 2/5 CP in the Arizona Territory. The 5th Marines did not waste any time getting their warriors into the fight.

The helicopter that carried me from An Hoa to the CP of 2/5 took only a few minutes to lift off, head west across the Song Thu Bon River, and land near the village of Huu Chanh (1) in the southern part of the Arizona Territory. A low ridgeline ran from Huu Chanh (1) northeast for 3,000 meters to the village of Tan Phuoc (1). This ridgeline was one of the few pieces of key terrain for miles since it provided good observation over the rice paddy fields and tree lines to the north and south. Palm trees, bamboo groves, and clusters of peasant huts dotted the ridgeline to the left and right of a wide trail that ran the entire length of the ridgeline. The CP of 2/5 was collocated with one of its four rifle companies on this ridgeline, while the other three rifle companies occupied defensive positions a few hundred meters to the north and east. After the helicopter landed in a cloud of red dust and offloaded a supply of water and rations, I walked over to the perimeter of the rifle company guarding the CP and asked where I could find the CO of 2/5. A young Marine dressed in ripped camouflage trousers, worn and dirty jungle boots, faded green T-shirt, shredded flak jacket, and a helmet covered with graffiti smiled and volunteered to show me the way. He carried an M-16 rifle with a sling made of parachute cord and a bandolier of M-16 ammunition slung over one shoulder. His weapon was immaculately clean, but everything else about him was covered in dust and grime.

After a short walk, my Marine escort pointed to a group of Marines sitting around a small fire under some palm trees and told me that was where I would find the CO. I walked over and found the CO, Lt. Col. James H. Higgins, and his operations officer, Maj. A.L. Vallese, sitting by the fire and looking over a map. I introduced myself to both officers, and they greeted me warmly, asking me to sit with them by the fire, which I noticed was fed with discarded C-ration boxes and grenade canisters, in addition to an assortment of local vegetation.

Lt. Col. Higgins was known as "The Arizona Kid" because he and his battalion had been in this notorious piece of real estate for several months, and he looked the part. He was a lean, wiry man with a ruddy complexion, chiseled features, and a steely look in his eyes that brought to my mind the vision of a cowboy sheriff of the Old West. He was wearing camouflage utility trousers, a green T-shirt, a shoulder holster with his 45 cal. pistol in it, and a bright red checkered bandana around his sunburned neck. He looked every bit the Marine infantry battalion commander, and within minutes I would find he took his job very seriously and expected the same of me. He told me in no uncertain terms there were three things he wanted me to keep in mind always. First, I was not to make stupid tactical mistakes that got my Marines killed; second, I was never to allow anyone under my command to mistreat any of the civilians they encountered, even if they suspected they were VC; and finally, and most important, if he assigned my company an objective and it failed to take it, he expected me to be either killed or wounded, otherwise I would be relieved of my command. These forceful words from my new CO made a strong impression on me and served to focus my attention clearly on my new duties.

He went on to tell me that he knew I had nineteen months of combat experience but that

Lt. Col. J.E. Higgins, CO of 2/5 at Liberty Bridge.

none of it was with the infantry, and for this reason he wanted me to spend two weeks learning how to be an infantry company commander before he assigned me to take over one of his companies. I would be assigned to Company F, led by his most experienced company commander, Capt. Robert Kingrey, who would give me the benefit of his nearly two years of combat experience with the infantry. Before that, I would spend two days with the 2/5 command group, getting to know his staff and having them brief me on what I would need to know if I was to be given command of a rifle company.

While Lt. Col. Higgins had started our relationship in a rather stern and cautionary manner, he spent the next hour or so graciously asking about my family, my previous combat experience, and what I knew about Quang Nam Province, setting me completely at ease and even sharing with me some personal information about his career and the officers he had served with prior to coming to South Vietnam. As I sat beside him sharing a cup of C-ration coffee in his canteen cup, I came away from this first meeting with a keen appreciation and solid respect for this seasoned and highly professional combat leader. Over the next five months that appreciation and respect would grow even more.

During the next two days, I spoke with all of the 2/5 staff officers, picking their brains for vital bits of information that might help me in the coming months. I was pleased that in the course of my conversations the staff officers of the battalion asked me to explain to them details about the enemy and Quang Nam Province. I was also disappointed that they seemed unfamiliar with any of the intelligence my reconnaissance company had developed during Operation Taylor Common. For some odd reason, this vital information on the enemy did not find its way to 2/5, or at least it was not widely disseminated. The more I talked to them, the more interested they became in my knowledge of the enemy, especially the trail systems leading from Base Area 112 and the Ong Thu Slope and the locations in the Arizona Territory where I had observed enemy movement or learned of it from my recon patrols.

Maj. Vallese, the S-3, was particularly interested and took many notes on where I suspected enemy movement was likely to occur. He told me that I had far more knowledge of Quang Nam Province than anyone else in the battalion, including the battalion intelligence officer. I learned a great deal from Maj. Vallese during my first few days with the battalion. Even though he was quite busy with the day-to-day operations of 2/5, which often caused our conversations to be interrupted so he could respond to some emergency or important report from the line companies, he always took the time to answer any question I had and to pass on any information about how his operations staff worked in the field. I took notes feverishly as he explained what he needed in the way of reporting from the battalion's rifle companies and how to format these reports properly.

On May 4, a squad of Marines from Company F took me from the 2/5 CP to the company's location at Phu Loi (2) hamlet two miles to the north. While the distance traveled was only two miles, the squad took a rather circuitous route so our little "walk in the sun" took well over an hour. The pace of our march was extremely fast, too fast in my mind for safety, and strenuous, especially in view of the time of day and the 100-degree-plus temperature. As we progressed, I had the distinct feeling I was being "tested" by this squad leader to see if I was up to the physical demands of serving with Company F. By the end of our journey, I was breathing heavily and sweating profusely, but I was determined not to ask the squad to stop and rest or to indicate in any way I was feeling stressed. I knew I only had one chance to make a good first impression, so I simply followed along at their rapid pace as we raced along paddy dikes, through tree lines, and over bamboo fences in the sweltering heat and humidity. When we reached Phu Loi (2) hamlet, I saw the company's defensive position nestled among several civilian huts on a low-lying hill. Capt. Kingrey greeted me and said, "What took you so long?" I smiled and only said, "You better ask your squad leader; he led the way." I would later find out from the company gunny that this entire "show" was the idea of Capt. Kingrey, who wanted to see how I reacted to having one of his squads "push" me on my first day under his command. I didn't like it, but I decided it would be best to simply ignore this trivial attempt to test my endurance.

Although my introduction to Company F and Capt. Kingrey was not as auspicious as I might have desired, I soon grew to value my association with Bob Kingrey because he was an exceptionally good company commander and he went the extra mile giving me the benefit of his experience and knowledge. Capt. Kingrey was a bit of a character and much beloved by his Marines. He had a deep Southern drawl, a homespun vocabulary, and a nonregulation handlebar mustache that was often mentioned by Lt. Col. Higgins as "not to my liking" every time Bob showed up at the 2/5 CP. My training was "over the shoulder" and "on the job," with each day devoted to watching everything Bob did as he commanded his company with great efficiency. In addition to showing me how to develop and report daytime and nighttime activities, such as patrol routes, killer team assignments, ambush sites, and listening posts, he also gave me valuable insights into how to move the company in the open terrain of the Arizona Territory and where to set up the company's defensive position so as to maximize its effectiveness. For example, he said it was always wise to ensure that civilian houses were inside the company perimeter since the VC would not attack their own hamlets for fear of alienating the local populace. He said the NVA were not so particular about attacking villages full of innocent civilians, but at least the local guerrillas and the main force VC units were not likely to attack a Marine defensive perimeter if it included civilian homes. He also told me that it was always a good idea to pay "rent" for using the ground around these farm homes, either with a small amount of GVN currency or excess food. This benefited the farmers and often led to their providing valuable information on the location of booby traps and other enemy activities. Everything Bob Kingrey told me during my two weeks with him proved to be both accurate and helpful to me when I took command of my own rifle company.

I did not have to wait long for my first taste of combat with the infantry. On the night of May 5, Company F was told to move north to establish a blocking position two miles northeast near Phu Bac Village. When I took out my map to plot the company's route to Phu Bac, I noticed the village lay astride the boundary between Dai Loc District and Duc Duc District. I mentioned to Bob that it was common for the enemy to move their units along these boundaries since it complicated the coordination of supporting arms. American and ARVN units had to receive permission to use artillery and air strikes from two different district headquarters before a mission could be cleared. This always doubled the time to obtain clearance, which was enough time for the enemy to escape. He asked me if I thought the enemy would be using the district boundaries that bisected Phu Bac Village and I said it was highly likely, since the boundary ran from the northern edge of Base Area 112 east all the way to the Song Thu Bon river on the east side of the Arizona Territory. It seemed obvious to me that the enemy would use this route to infiltrate their forces into the coastal lowlands. When Bob gave his operation order to his platoon commanders, I was pleased to note that he included the information I had given him on the likelihood of the enemy's using the district boundary to facilitate their movement toward the Song Thu Bon River.

As soon as it was dark, we moved out of our company position and began our march northeast. At first we moved in column along a trail, but Bob considered this too risky, so he had the company shift 200 meters to the east so we could walk parallel to the trail in the rice paddies. Most of the time we were able to walk on the paddy dikes, but often we found ourselves in the paddies and up to our ankles in thick, viscous mud. The movement was slow as front and flank security elements cleared nearby tree lines or took up covering positions near farm huts. Hordes of mosquitoes followed us, feasting on our blood and distracting us as the column slowly snaked its way to our objective.

Bob did not like the exposed, flat area around Phu Bac Village, so he decided to move further north to find better terrain to establish a blocking position. He made a quick map study, covered by his poncho so the light from his flashlight could not be seen by any enemy in the area, and then he called over his artillery forward observer and his platoon commanders to give them his instructions. He explained to them that the original position for a blocking position was too exposed, and he showed them on the map a new location that he thought would offer better cover and concealment for his rifle company. The new location was on the western side of Phu Phong (3) hamlet, where two trails intersected. Once the platoon commanders had returned to their platoons to issue new instructions to their men, Bob instructed the artillery forward observer to plot several artillery concentrations near the location of the new blocking position in case we needed them. That decision would prove to be a good one.

As we approached the south side of Phu Phong (3) hamlet around 0130, we were taken under fire by a few VC snipers as we crossed a small stream. The VC who fired on us did not want to stand and fight with a U.S. Marine infantry company, so they ran back into the hamlet. Some villagers appeared out of the darkness from their homes and told us there were fifteen VC in the group that fired on us, and they had moved off to the southeast. The 1st platoon gave chase, and Capt. Kingrey called in 81 mm mortar fire on the retreating VC, but a search of the area at first light produced only one dead VC and the capture of one AK-47 rifle.[1] Capt. Kingrey called back his 1st platoon, since he feared the VC were attempting to lead them into an ambush. Since our mission was compromised, the battalion ordered us to move back to the village of Ham An (5) and remain there until 0830 on May 6. On the 6th, we moved back to our old defensive position in Phu Loi (2) hamlet, where we began digging deeper foxholes, clearing better fields of fire, and registering more artillery and mortar missions.

A few days later, acting on intelligence that a large enemy force was located in the northeast corner of the Arizona Territory and was planning an attack on Liberty Bridge, Company F was ordered to again make a night march north and establish a blocking position near the village of My Dong on the southern shore of the Song Vu Gia River. Lt. Col. Higgins wanted the enemy to believe the battalion was preparing to leave the Arizona Territory, so he sent several false voice radio messages in the clear indicating the battalion was preparing to move east to a ford on the Song Thu Bon River. To give added credence to his ruse, he even moved some attached tanks and amtracs to the ford as a deception measure. Then he took his remaining rifle companies and swept north in an arc toward Company F. The ploy worked initially, but not all of the enemy were caught in Lt. Col. Higgins's trap.

As dawn approached and the first fingers of sunlight rose in the east, our company approached our objective of My Dong village. Our point squad observed a large group of enemy soldiers running west and into the hills near the village of Minh Tan (1). Had we closed our blocking position before first light, we would have caught several hundred NVA between our blocking position and the rifle companies advancing north. Like many things in war, an hour meant the difference between life and death for the NVA troops who fled west. Capt. Kingrey called in several artillery missions on the fleeing enemy, but since our mission was to establish a blocking position anchored on the Song Vu Gia River, we did not pursue the retreating enemy. Later in the day, shortly after noon, three NVA soldiers approached our defensive position, oblivious of our presence and speaking loudly to each other. Our first platoon took them under fire, killing all three and capturing their weapons. The next day, a patrol from the company found an additional dead NVA soldier near the spot where we had seen the enemy fleeing the previous day.[2] Although Company F's blocking position had not closed off the escape route of several hundred NVA, the three rifle companies maneuvering toward our position still killed nearly 200 of the enemy and captured several POWs, who identified their unit as a battalion of the 90th NVA Regiment. They also revealed their battalion was preparing to attack Marine positions on Hill 65 on the north side of the Song Vu Gia River. Lt. Col. Higgins's innovative plan and the battalion's aggressive attack broke up this enemy plan and drove them out of the Arizona Territory, at least temporarily.

During my two weeks with Company F, I was impressed with the morale and abilities of the individual Marines who, despite poor living conditions, intense heat, numerous skin and intestinal maladies, and very little sleep, performed their difficult and dangerous duties with a cheerfulness and élan that was truly inspiring. For my part, I found duty with an infantry company new and interesting, although it took me quite a while to get used to wearing a flak jacket and helmet most of the time. These items were never worn in a recon company; we often simply dressed in our khaki swimming trunks and green T-shirts inside our compounds when we were not on patrol. Any Marine who served in the infantry knows what I mean when I say a flak jacket has a distinctive smell to it—a mixture of dirt, oil, and sweat that initially is unpleasant but is hardly noticed after spending a few

The author in the Arizona Territory.

days in the field without washing. In fact, an infantry company has in the aggregate a distinctive, pungent smell that sets it apart from everything else around it and often makes it easy for the enemy to smell the arrival of Marines before they see them. This is easy to understand when one takes into consideration that 2/5 had been in the field continuously for over 80 days when I arrived and had not benefited from even a cold shower during this entire time. I soon found that I sorely missed the hot chow and showers I took for granted when I was with a reconnaissance company. Life in an infantry company was neither easy nor pleasant, but the work was exciting and the comradeship of one's fellow Marines a pleasure to experience.

On May 13, Lt. Col. Higgins told me to take command of Company G because their CO, Capt. Robert. W. Poolaw, had been wounded and medevaced. The next day I joined Company G at their defensive position on a small hill at Dai Khung (7) hamlet in the southern Arizona Territory. I hardly had time to meet my platoon commanders when we were directed to move to a new position a mile southwest near the hamlet of My Le (3), a hamlet I had often observed on several recon patrols in 1967 and one that I knew was very close to a main infiltration route the enemy used. I expected to encounter the enemy in this area, and I was not mistaken.

We spent the day of the 13th digging foxholes and organizing our new defensive position. That night we received small arms fire from the hamlet of My Le (3), and we returned fire with small arms and 60 mm mortars. A search of the area at first light on the 14th by the second platoon found two dead NVA soldiers, several bloody bandages, and numerous blood trails. We searched the bodies of the dead NVA soldiers and retrieved two bags of rice, an AK-47 rifle, several magazines of ammunition, and some documents that were forwarded to the battalion S-2.

The next day, an old woman and a young girl approached our lines asking for medical assistance. The girl, who was around 10 years old, had small shrapnel wounds in her arm. Our corpsman cleaned and bandaged her wounds and gave her some antibiotics. While this was going on, our Kit Carson Scout interviewed the old woman, who volunteered information on the enemy who attacked us. She told us that there was a company of NVA troops in My Le (3), and they were digging in when she left there. She also said they were guided by two local VC who demanded rice from the villagers to feed the NVA company. I relayed this information to battalion and told my platoon commanders to prepare for an attack that night. Company G had suffered heavy casualties in the previous weeks and only had a "foxhole" strength of ninety-three men when I took over on the 14th, so we were manned at less than half of our authorized strength. In order to make up for our small numbers, I had our artillery forward observer (FO), Lt. Kevin Murphy, surround our position with artillery and mortar concentrations so we could respond rapidly with massive firepower if we were attacked.

That night one of our listening posts on the south side of our perimeter radioed to tell us they heard movement near them. I told them to move back into our perimeter as quickly and as quietly as possible, and I alerted the two platoons on the south side of the perimeter to allow the listening post team to enter their lines. I also alerted everyone to the impending attack and told Lt. Murphy to be ready to fire his artillery and mortar concentrations. A few minutes after midnight, I heard the sound of an M-26 hand grenade exploding, followed by a burst of small arms fire on the south side of our perimeter. Soon the entire south side was firing their weapons at the enemy and throwing hand grenades. As the battalion's 81 mm mortar platoon began firing illumination rounds above our position, elements of the 40th NVA Regiment began firing small arms, B-40 rocket grenades, and mortar rounds into our position. Throughout the night they continued to probe our lines and harass us with sniper fire, but they never were able to penetrate the perimeter. We continued to call in numerous artillery and 81 mm mortar missions on them, often hearing screams and moans coming from the impact areas. We suffered five wounded that night.

Early the next morning, on the 15th, the second platoon found three dead NVA soldiers in front of our lines along with a number of bloody bandages, an AK-47 assault rifle, an RPG launcher, an RPD light machine gun, eight Chinese hand grenades, two packs, and some medical equipment. Later that morning, a squad from our company left the company perimeter with the mission of conducting a reconnaissance of the hamlet of Ben Dau (3), which lay a few hundred meters east of My Le (3). Shortly after leaving our lines, the patrol received enemy small arms, B-40, and machine gun fire from a tree line on the north side of My Le (3). They assaulted the tree line, killing two NVA soldiers and capturing an RPG-2 launcher; an RPD machine gun; eleven B-40 rounds; six Chinese hand grenades; and several packs containing rice, cans of fish, and personal items. They also found some documents belonging to a company from the 40th NVA Regiment.

Later that morning, I had Lt. Murphy call in over 500 rounds of artillery on My Le (3) and the likely routes leading into the village from the south and west. Just minutes after we ceased firing the artillery, we were still taking some sniper rounds from the village despite the massive bombardment directed on the hamlet. For some reason, the enemy was determined to keep us pinned down and out of My Le (3). When the enemy sniper fire increased, despite the terrific pounding inflicted by Lt. Murphy's artillery barrages, I decided we would attack the hamlet and clear it of the enemy.

I called my platoon commanders up to my command post and issued them an attack order. While my platoon commanders issued their attack orders to their platoons, I personally directed ten flights of fixed-wing aircraft as they dropped 500-pound fragmentation bombs and canisters of napalm on the hamlet. I wanted to make sure we had softened up the enemy positions before I launched the infantry attack. My plan called for two of my platoons to assault the hamlet from the east, driving deep in behind the village and then pivoting to the west and north so any enemy in the hamlet would be caught between the two maneuver platoons and the remaining dug-in platoon north of My Le (3). I left an escape route to the west open for the NVA, but I had Lt. Murphy pre-register several artillery concentrations along this escape route. After all these preparations had been made and I had given the attack order to my platoon commanders, I moved with the two maneuver platoons to an attack position 200 meters from the edge of the western side of My Le (3). There I had the two platoons get on line behind a paddy dike, and once this was done, I had Lt. Murphy shift his artillery preparation fires away from us to the western side of the hamlet.

At 1630, the two maneuver platoons stood up and charged across the paddy field toward the hamlet. We took a few sniper rounds, but no one was hit as we rapidly closed to the tree line that marked the eastern edge of the hamlet and we began to clear a trench line just inside of the tree line. We saw several NVA soldiers running away through the hamlet, and we took them under fire, hitting several of them. We threw grenades into all of the enemy foxholes and bunkers we found, and then we began to pivot to the north. As we did this, we came under murderous small arms fire from a group of NVA soldiers who had taken refuge in a small pagoda and some bunkers directly in front of us. While Lt. Dennis Storm took his platoon and began chasing the enemy fleeing to the west, the other platoon assaulted the pagoda. As I moved with this second platoon toward the pagoda, we began to take casualties. The NVA in the bunkers near the pagoda were well protected and the assaulting Marines were exposed to their fire. Despite exceptional bravery on the part of the Marines, the under-strength platoon of just twenty-three men was unable to reach the bunkers. My radio operator was shot in the head and killed instantly, and another Marine kneeling to my left was also killed. I saw that it was fruitless to continue to assault the well-protected NVA near the pagoda, so I pulled the platoon back behind an earthen wall 50 meters from the pagoda and told Lt. Storm to bring his platoon back to our position so we could use supporting arms to destroy the bunkers. During this time, Lt. Murphy demonstrated great bravery as he ran forward during the firefight and carried back two wounded Marines to the safety of the earthen wall. Since my radio operator was dead, I took the radio and began calling for air support and telling the platoon we left behind to be watchful for any NVA moving toward them and to get down in their foxholes when I brought in air strikes. Lt. Storm organized our defense, redistributed ammunition, and directed the fire of the two platoons behind the earthen wall. My lead corpsman told me we had suffered significant casualties with eight dead and many wounded, two of whom would die if they were not medevaced immediately. I radioed battalion and informed them of our situation, requesting an immediate medevac of our seriously

Lt. John Thomas (right) and Lt. Kevin Murphy.

wounded. Lt. Col. Higgins and Maj. Vallese told me to hold my present position, consolidate my company, and secure an LZ for the medevac helicopter, which they said was on the way. I informed them that one of my platoons was between me and the NVA, so it would be impossible to consolidate all of my platoons at my location.

At the same time as we were assaulting My Le (3), Company E also encountered a strong NVA force dug in a few hundred meters to our east near the hamlet of My Le (1). They lost six killed and fourteen wounded from small arms and mortar fire as they attacked the enemy position. It was evident that both of our companies had run into at least an NVA battalion, which had infiltrated into the hamlets of An Bang (1), My Le (3) and My Le (1) in preparation for an attack against either our battalion or some target across the Song Thu Bon River near An Hoa. It was also apparent that they intended to defend their positions tenaciously.

Throughout the remaining daylight of the 15th, Company G called in artillery and air strikes against the NVA, who had us pinned down behind the earthen wall. Several medevac helicopters attempted to land, but the enemy ground fire was so intense each medevac mission had to be aborted. Since the condition of our wounded was deteriorating, I asked for an emergency night medevac but was told the 1st Marine Air Wing at Da Nang thought the perimeter we occupied was too small and the enemy ground fire too intense for any helicopter to land safely and pick up our wounded. I did not know it at the time, but the Air Wing asked for pilots to volunteer for the mission since it was so dangerous. The squadron commander of the "Purple Foxes" of HMM-364, Lt. Col. Eugene R. Brady, volunteered. As darkness fell around our small perimeter, we continued to receive small arms and RPG fire from NVA soldiers to our north, west, and south, wounding several more Marines. The NVA soldiers in the pagoda would pick off any Marine who dared expose himself above the earthen wall for more than a second or two. The enemy pressed closer and closer to us, and I feared we would soon be overrun, especially when I learned that our ammunition was running dangerously low. I had thrown both of the hand grenades I carried at the pagoda and emptied all but one magazine for my M-16 rifle. SSgt. Robert C. Pace, our acting company gunny, reported that we were out of machine gun ammunition and very low on ammunition for our rifles and M-79 grenade launchers.

Things were looking rather bleak when, at approximately 2300, Lt. Col. Brady came up on our company radio frequency and informed me that he was nearing our position to pick up our wounded and to drop off several boxes of machine gun ammunition. I told him we had a very small perimeter—only 50 meters across—and it was exposed to enemy fire from three sides. I told him I would understand if he decided it was too risky to attempt a landing, but he told me to mark the LZ and he would land in it, regardless of the enemy fire. It was pitch black, and I could not see his helicopter, but I could hear its rotors off in the distance, and the sound was getting closer.

In an act of incredible bravery, Lt. Storm took a strobe light and placed it in his helmet and then stood in the middle of the LZ so Lt. Col. Brady could guide on the light and find our LZ. As the helicopter made its approach into the LZ, enemy green tracer rounds arched through the sky and into its fuselage. With only Lt. Storm's strobe light to guide him in the darkness, Lt. Col. Brady maneuvered his helicopter into the small vegetable garden that served as our LZ. As he did so, several RPGs and mortar rounds landed near the helicopter. Our Marines on the perimeter attempted to suppress the enemy fire, but the disciplined

NVA soldiers fought back ferociously in an attempt to bring the helicopter down and inflict more casualties on our depleted rifle company. Lt. Storm and several others carried the wounded onto the CH-46, using ponchos as litters for those who could not walk. One of the men carrying the wounded was himself wounded in the leg as he climbed up the rear ramp of the helicopter. He simply stumbled aboard and was lifted out of the LZ along with the other wounded. As the helicopter rose out of the LZ, it was hit numerous times with enemy small arms fire, and I thought surely it would be brought down. Miraculously, Lt. Col. Brady flew his helicopter above the trees and into the night as green tracer rounds lit up the sky around him.

After the medevac was completed, the enemy persisted in their attempt to overrun us, but thanks to the bravery of a flight of Marine Huey gunships and an Air Force "Spooky" gunship, we were able to beat off these attacks. The heroism of the pilot of one of the Marine gunships, Maj. "Rip" Miller, was far beyond the call of duty. Several times, he placed his helicopter in a hover directly over our position and fired his guns and rockets in a 360-degree arc. It was truly awe inspiring to see him hover in the darkness above us as the enemy fired at him. I told him to leave several times, but he refused and continued to stand his ground, firing at the enemy's muzzle blasts until they were silenced. There was no doubt in my mind that we would have been overrun by the enemy if it had not been for the heroism of Maj. Miller.[3]

The next day we medevaced our eight dead and then left our small perimeter and moved north to join the platoon we had left at our old position. On the way, we found the bodies of two NVA soldiers we had killed during the night, several blood trails, and some abandoned enemy equipment. We also examined the pagoda that had caused us so much harm and found out why it had been so difficult to overcome the enemy near it. We saw that the enemy had dug a tunnel under the pagoda with two camouflaged spider holes on each side so they could pop up and fire at the Marines and then drop down and crawl under the pagoda's foundation when grenades, artillery, or other ordnance were used against them. The pagoda was a mass of rubble, but the tunnel underneath it was intact and undamaged. We found no blood trails in or near the spider holes, so we assumed the enemy had escaped unharmed during the night after they had had enough of the constant pounding from Maj. Miller's Huey gunship.

We spent the 16th back at our original perimeter north of My Le (3), improving our defenses and receiving a much-needed resupply of water, C-rations, and ammunition. In the afternoon, we were visited by BGen. Samuel Jaskilka and Col. Zaro. I briefed both officers on our attack on My Le (3) and then they spent some time talking to me about the battle Company E had fought nearby against what they thought was the same outfit we had run into. After talking to a few individual Marines about the role they played during the fight and going over my defensive plan for the night, they went outside of our perimeter to look at four dead NVA soldiers lying in front of our lines. As they were preparing to leave, they told me that we would be receiving replacements for our killed and wounded soon. I also told them of the heroism of the Marines in the company and especially Lt. Murphy and Lt. Storm, as well as the extreme bravery exhibited by Lt. Col. Brady and Maj. Miller. They both agreed with my recommendation that these four men deserved personal awards for valor, and they asked me to begin the paperwork needed immediately. That afternoon and the next day I spent several hours writing award recommendations: Navy Crosses for Lt. Murphy and Lt. Storm, and Medals of Honor for Lt. Col. Brady and Maj. Miller. The awards were downgraded at division to Silver Stars for Lt. Murphy, Lt. Storm and Maj. Miller, and a Navy Cross for Lt. Col. Brady. I do not know why these awards were downgraded, but this action once again eroded my faith in the Marine Corps award system. In my mind, and I think in the minds of my men, these brave Marines were deserving of the medals I had recommended for them.

On May 17, we moved a mile east to a new position near the hamlet of Ben Dau (3) on the banks of the Song Thu Bon River in preparation for leaving the Arizona Territory. We had no contact with the enemy, but on a routine patrol near Ben Dau (3) one of our platoons detected the strong odor of decaying human flesh and found the bodies of eleven dead NVA soldiers in a trench line. They were fully dressed and had their weapons and equipment with them.[4] Lt. Murphy retrieved a pistol from one of the dead NVA soldiers and several other Marines took a pistol and two SKS rifles as souvenirs. These captured weapons were not reported, since everyone knew they would be conveniently "lost" if sent to the rear.

My company spent several days at Ben Dau (3) guarding the river crossing there and preparing covering positions so the main body of 2/5 could pass through our lines and begin to move across the river to An Hoa. During this time, Father G.E. Powell, the battalion chaplain, visited us every day to say Mass and to talk to the Marines. He was very popular with everyone in the battalion and seemed utterly fearless, often walking from one company position to another with only his assistant as a bodyguard. I enjoyed talking to him whenever he traveled with my company and I attended each Mass he held in the field, as did most of the men in my company. In my mind, he was the perfect chaplain for a rifle company in combat: friendly, humorous, compassionate, comforting, and pious in the most endearing, selfless way. Throughout my time with 2/5 he was the battalion chaplain, and never once did I see him fail to inspire and console a member of his flock. I considered him a saint in a camouflage uniform and helmet.

After spending ninety-five straight days in the field without a break, the battalion was finally ordered to cross the Song Thu Bon River and leave the Arizona Territory. The entire battalion was tired and dirty but proud of their accomplishments. Just in May alone, during my first month with the battalion, they had killed 259 NVA and VC. Sadly, this accomplishment came at a high price for us, since we lost twenty-five valiant Marines during that month. We spent May 21 to 22 covering the movement of the battalion command group and three rifle companies, and then we crossed the river on the 23rd, turning over our perimeter at Ben Dau (3) to Company C, 1st Battalion, 5th Marines. Company G left the Arizona Territory and crossed the Song Thu Bon River with only eighty-nine men, far from the 214 men that is the standard T/O strength of a Marine rifle company. I was told the company entered the Arizona Territory with a "foxhole strength" of 168 Marines, but three months of constant fighting and medical problems had depleted its ranks significantly. We linked up with Company F on the east side of the river, where we waited for trucks that would drive us the rest of the way to An Hoa.

While we were securing the east side of the river and waiting for our trucks, I set up my CP in the refugee camp called Thanh Xuyen (3). I was struck by how beautiful and well-organized this refugee village was in comparison to many other villages I had seen around An Hoa and in the Arizona Territory. Its fields were well-tended and full of rice; its houses well-constructed and clean; its children happy, well-clothed, and clean; its population healthy and well-fed; its pathways neat, cool, and well-shaded by tall trees—in short, this village

Father E.G. Powell saying Catholic Mass for Company G.

looked like the kind of peaceful village the majority of Vietnamese longed to live in but were unable to do so due to the war. Unlike the sullen and unfriendly peasants we encountered in most of the Arizona Territory, the inhabitants of Thanh Xuyen (3) greeted us with smiles and offers of cold water and tea. During my four hours in the village, I bought several coconuts and pineapples from a farmer and passed them out to my CP group. The fresh fruit tasted delightful after so many days of eating only C-rations.[5]

Back at the 5th Marines base camp at An Hoa, our company rested for two days, ate some welcome hot food, took showers, and did some remedial training. We also received some much-needed replacements, some of whom were returning to South Vietnam for their second tour of duty, giving us some added combat experience in several leadership positions. As we were preparing to move the company to China Beach near Da Nang for a few days of in-country R&R, I became very sick with a fever, diarrhea, and nausea. I was attending to some company administration in my SEA hut office when I passed out from the fever and I woke up in the battalion aid station a few minutes later. I was medevaced to the 1st Medical Battalion near Hill 327 and spent the next week there recovering. Initially the doctors thought I had malaria, but after what seemed like an unending number of blood tests, they decided they did not know what caused my fever, so they decided to treat it with a massive dose of antibiotics. This proved successful, and I was discharged from the hospital on June 10.

On the day I was discharged from the hospital, I borrowed a jeep from 1st Reconnaissance Battalion at Camp Reasoner and spent a few hours driving around the Da Nang area. Since my helicopter flight back to An Hoa was not due to leave until the late afternoon, I had most of the day to drive around my old haunts. I stopped off at Hill 34 to visit my old outfit, 1st Force Reconnaissance Company, and talk to Maj. Simmons about his new camp and the company's new mission of supporting III MAF, instead of the 1st Marine Division. I was impressed with how much more comfortable the living conditions were at Hill 34 compared to the ones we formerly occupied at An Hoa. I also stopped at Lan's house and saw that she and her family had recovered from the devastation that befell them when the ammunition dump blew up the previous month.

The author at Thanh Xuyen (2) hamlet.

They had framed a new, even larger house, and had the roof built with newly acquired tin roofing sheets provided by the local government. I also noticed they were doing a brisk business selling soft drinks and beer from the cooler in front of their home.

On my way back to Camp Reasoner to catch my flight to An Hoa, I stopped off at the Freedom Hill PX to buy some film for my camera and a set of captain's rank insignia, since I expected to be promoted soon. There I encountered my first, but not my last, situation involving racial tension in South Vietnam and how corrosive this tension was to military discipline. As I approached the entrance of the PX, I noticed a group of sullen-looking African American Marines standing to one side studiously ignoring any officers who passed by and giving the clenched fist "Black Power" salute to each other and any other African American serviceman they saw. When I passed, they looked the other way so they would not be forced to salute me. I entered the PX, purchased my items, and left about 30 minutes later. On my way out, I saw there was a commotion of some sort taking place near the entrance. A white Marine SNCO had seen the Afro-American Marines fail to salute an officer and had tried to correct this breach of military discipline. Instead of responding as Marines normally would when corrected by a Marine SNCO, the African American Marines threatened the SNCO, and one of them raised his rifle and pointed it at him. I was only a few feet away when I heard the African American Marine shout, "I don't have to listen to your shit, motherfucker!" I saw that this SNCO was alone among five or six angry African American Marines, so I went over to see if I could help him and defuse the situation. I did not even get a word out of my mouth when several of these African American Marines began to shout expletives at me and threaten me. This was the first time I had encountered Marines who did not show the proper respect for an officer or SNCO, and for a moment I thought about drawing my pistol to protect myself. Fortunately for both me and the SNCO, several MPs approached us and told the African American Marines to put their weapons on the ground. The MPs then asked to see the ID cards of the African American Marines, and they found that several of them were in an unauthorized absence (UA) status and had been missing from their units for over a week. These were arrested by the MPs, and the others were ordered to leave the PX area. The MP sergeant in charge told me that incidents like this were becoming rather common now and MPs routinely patrolled the PX looking for UA Marines. He also told me that most, if not all, of the troublemakers came from support units in the rear and not from combat units.

Chapter 7

Liberty Bridge

At 1600, I left LZ Finch at Camp Reasoner on my flight back to An Hoa. There I found my company preparing to leave by truck for Henderson Hill, a strong defensive position a few miles northeast of An Hoa Combat Base. Our mission was to relieve Capt. McClung's Company E and take over their responsibilities. We left in a cloud of dust and sped up the road leading from An Hoa north to Liberty Bridge, passing through several villages on the way, scattering chickens and other farm animals wandering around the road unattended. Our trip went without incident, and within 30 minutes we were offloading at Henderson Hill, which was about one mile south of Liberty Bridge and the new site for our battalion CP.

My company had received several replacements in my absence. Two extremely competent and seasoned platoon commanders, Lt. Dennis Storm and Lt. Robert Conti, had been transferred to new positions in the battalion, but I still retained Lt. John R. Thomas, a battle-wise veteran, leading one of our platoons, and he would soon be joined by a newly arrived lieutenant from the States, Philip N. Huth. Fortunately, the company had strong continuity in the form of its platoon sergeants, the men who provided our platoon commanders with the advice and leadership that can only be gained from years of training and leading enlisted Marines. These valuable noncommissioned officers were SSgt. Robert C. Pace, Sgt. M.T. Bisaha, Sgt. John Ralston and SSgt. Travis Harper. As any Marine will tell you, the most important enlisted Marine for an infantry company is the company gunnery sergeant, and I was truly blessed with the one I had in Company G. His name was GySgt. John T. Coffer, a fair but no-nonsense leader who looked after the men of Company G like the father of a large family of very tough kids. I would come to rely on his wise counsel and caring friendship in the coming months. Lt. Kevin Murphy, my artillery FO, had been replaced by Lt. Pelham, who impressed me with his knowledge of supporting arms and his eager approach to his job. One of my company radio operators, PFC Mackerel, remained with the company, and he was joined by Cpl. G.L. Shoemake, giving me two very capable communicators in the company command group. I was glad to see that my Kit Carson Scout, Tran Van Qua, was still with the company; his value would be proved time and time again over the next few months. While I missed the very competent and brave lieutenants who had left, I felt very comfortable with the new officers and SNCOs who joined the company.

June was largely an uneventful month for us, although the term "uneventful" does not really do justice to the level of violence we experienced that month. It only seemed uneventful because we did not have any large firefights with NVA units. We spent the majority of our time occupying fire-team-size OPs along the road from Liberty Bridge south to the hamlet of Phu Nhuan (4) and conducting squad and platoon patrols during the day. At night we would put out two squad-size ambushes and several five-man "Killer Teams," which were mobile teams assigned a grid square to patrol. All of our activities had the objective of protecting the road from Liberty Bridge to An Hoa from local VC efforts to emplace mines and booby traps. There was only one road between An Hoa and Da Nang, so it was critical to keep this road open so supply convoys could travel safely and regularly. This was a never-ending battle, as evidenced by the large number of mines and booby traps that patrols from 2/5 discovered near the road during the month of June. Forty-three of these devices were found, ranging in size from 500-pound bombs and 105 mm artillery shells to Chinese grenades and locally fabricated tomato can mines. Most of the explosives used in these booby traps and mines came from unexploded or captured U.S. munitions, a fact that made all of us acutely aware of the need for ammunition security and the proper policing of any battle site.

Gunnery Sergeant John T. Coffer, USMC.

In an effort to reduce the availability of unexploded ordnance or other sources for the explosive materials used in these deadly devices, monetary rewards were given to any Vietnamese who turned them in to U.S. forces. Several times during the month of June, Vietnamese peasants, usually young boys, approached our lines or our patrols to turn in ammunition they had found. On a few occasions, villagers would point out the location of mines to our Marines so the mines could be destroyed. All of these villagers and children were given rewards in Vietnamese currency from a battalion cash account I maintained for this purpose. This system of rewarding local villagers for turning in ammunition or identifying the location of booby traps and mines saved many Marine lives and clearly angered the VC who seemed unable or unwilling to stop it.

We also had several VC approach our patrols to surrender, bringing their weapons with them. The VC who rallied to the GVN were called Hoi Chanhs, and they provided valuable intelligence on the condition of local VC units and the hardships they and their comrades were experiencing due to aggressive U.S. and South Vietnamese actions. Of particular value was the information they provided about the fear the local VC political cadre had for the "Phoenix agents" who were increasingly active in Quang Nam Province, making it impossible for these VC political cadres to carry out their duties or even to live in their homes. My Kit Carson Scout, Qua, who was a former VC and had rallied to the GVN a year earlier, interviewed each of these Hoi Chanhs before they were sent to battalion, and he provided me with a verbal report on each one he spoke to. He also helped assuage their fear, since he could tell them from his own personal experience that life with the GVN was far better than life with the VC.

One day in June, while I was visiting the battalion CP at Liberty Bridge, I had the opportunity to attend a meeting between our battalion commander, Lt. Col. Higgins, and the U.S. district advisor for Duy Xuyen District and the Vietnamese district chief. The purpose of their meeting was to coordinate the planning for a "New Life Hamlet" that would be built near Liberty Bridge. This was an example of civic action that dwarfed the civic action program I had helped with in the village of Phuoc Ly in 1967. The U.S. advisor, a U.S. Army captain, and the Vietnamese district chief presented detailed plans for this "New Life Hamlet" that included everything from a list of building materials needed for each house in the hamlet to where each water well was to be drilled and the location for the new hamlet primary school. The district chief had a list of 200 families who had requested resettlement inside the New Life Hamlet, informing Lt. Col. Higgins that these farm families owned small plots of land in the district, but were willing to move to new homes in the New Life Hamlet because they were tired of being harassed and taxed by the VC and subject to Marine artillery fire at night. The district chief, a young man with a ready smile and a great deal of enthusiasm, told Lt. Col. Higgins that the prime motivation of the volunteer inhabitants of the New Life Hamlet was their belief that they and their valuable livestock would be much safer living in the New Life Hamlet than in a hamlet where the VC could enter at night. The plan called for these farmers to toil in their fields during the day, but to return to the safety of the New Life Hamlet each night, where they would be protected by a platoon of Popular Forces (PF) recruited from the families living in the hamlet. Completely surrounding the New Life Hamlet would be a barbed wire fence and earthen berm. The district chief said it was a hardship for these families to leave the land they had worked for generations, but they were willing to trade their old homes for ones in the New Life Hamlet because they were not safe in their old homes. He said they also wanted to benefit from the medical clinic and school that would be available to them in their new homes. The district chief ended the meeting by asking Lt. Col. Higgins to provide security for the people constructing the New Life Hamlet and to provide Marines to escort the farmers to and from their farmland. Lt. Col. Higgins agreed and promised to do everything in his power to assist the district chief with this new project. While I knew Lt. Col. Higgins was sincere, I also knew his promise was one that could not be met. Our battalion, like every other Marine battalion in South Vietnam, was a mobile force, and that meant we were always on call to move to where the enemy was threatening. It was rare when any Marine battalion spent more than a month or two in one location.

While June was rather quiet for Company G, we did have a few significant contacts with the enemy that month. On June 15, one of our patrols observed two VC near the hamlet of Thu Bon (3) and gave chase. The VC ran away through a hedgerow, followed close behind by the patrol. The two VC were the bait for an ambush that had been set for the Marines. When the Marines approached the hedgerow, a command-detonated mine exploded, wounding five of the Marines. The Marines were also taken under fire by a group of VC on the other side of the hedgerow; however, the patrol rallied rapidly, gained fire superiority, and maneuvered to the flank of the ambush, cutting off the enemy's route of retreat. As the VC ran from cover, the Marines cut three of them down and took their weapons off their bodies. The remainder of the VC fled west toward the Song Thu Bon River.[1]

On June 19, a platoon from our company was conducting a patrol two miles southeast of Liberty Bridge near the hamlet of La Thap (1) when a villager pointed out a bunker to them and told the newly arrived platoon commander, Lt. Michael C. Urenovich, there were VC hiding in it. Lt. Urenovich was new to his job and to South Vietnam, but he was naturally aggressive and decisive, so he quickly deployed his platoon to surround the bunker and ordered its occupants to come out and surrender. After a short standoff, four local VC guerrillas came out of the bunker with their hands raised. They were all armed with captured U.S. military weapons and equipment, including an M-14 rifle, a Marine Corps haversack, several U.S.-made battle dressings, and a red air panel. The prisoners were turned over to the battalion S-2 for interrogation.[2]

Another platoon patrol from Company G made contact with the enemy on the eastern edge of the hamlet of My Loc (4) on June 21. They spotted a large group of approximately fifty VC moving east across an open rice paddy. Using small arms fire and artillery, the platoon killed three VC. This enemy force fled east, but 30 minutes later sniper teams from the battalion command group killed nine more of this same group as it attempted to escape in the direction of La Thap Village. That evening, at 2030, one of our ambush teams near the hamlet of Cu Ban (2) observed twenty-five VC moving toward them along a paddy dike, and the Marine squad triggered their ambush. Despite the numerical superiority of the enemy force, the Marine squad killed two of the enemy and captured two more, without sustaining a single casualty. The rest of the enemy fled east toward the hamlet of Cu Bon (2).[3]

On June 26, our company saw a vivid and disturbing example of the brutality and ruthlessness of the local VC political cadres. In a letter home to my parents, I described this event:

> A rallier to the Vietnamese government from the VC ranks brought his 25-year-old-wife [to our company position] for medical treatment. While he was away at Dai Loc district headquarters, the VC came to his home looking for him. Instead, they found his wife and small child. They shot the baby in the head, killing it instantly, and then they gave his wife the worst beating I have ever seen inflicted on a human being. Her face looked like a meat grinder had been used on it. She had half of her teeth knocked out by these "liberators" and several bones in her face were broken. This is not an isolated incident—things like this happen all the time and the VC call it "selective terrorism." It is just plain gutless savagery to me.[4]

As June came to an end, our OPs and patrols began to find enemy propaganda leaflets near the main road to An Hoa where Marines could easily find them. These leaflets were brought to me by our patrols, and I was disturbed by their contents. Unlike the enemy propaganda leaflets I had seen previously in South Vietnam, these were highly professional propaganda leaflets, using offset printing and often containing pictures of antiwar demonstrations in the United States. Most of these leaflets also contained antiwar quotes from some U.S. political leaders. The most often-quoted politicians on these leaflets were Senators William

Fulbright and the late Robert Kennedy, but there were also quotes attributed to the Rev. Martin Luther King, Jr., and Communist political activist Angela Davis. While these leaflets had no discernible effect on the officers and SNCOs in the company, they did have some effect on a few of the junior enlisted Marines, who would ask if the quotes were accurate or not. In one case, I felt it necessary to hold a meeting with my leaders so they could give a unified and informed answer to such questions. I also found it necessary to remind my leaders that it was against the law to say anything negative about an elected U.S. official, no matter how badly they felt about what those officials had said.[5]

July found Company G located at Liberty Bridge along with the rest of the battalion. We had left Henderson Hill on June 16, and now the entire battalion was devoted to protecting the newly finished bridge spanning the Song Thu Bon River at My Loc (6). The enemy considered this bridge a primary target, since it was the only bridge across the river that cut the province into the north and south, aside from the old railroad bridge across the river that was located several miles to the east. The VC's Quang Da Unit, which represented the VC political organization for the province, bragged that it would destroy Liberty Bridge, and they had tried to make good on their threats several times during the bridge's construction, but in every case they had failed. Our battalion's mission was to keep road traffic between the north and south of the province flowing over this new bridge uninterrupted. While life at Liberty Bridge could not be remotely described as easy or comfortable, we did enjoy a field kitchen that provided two hot meals a day and access to a beach along the river where our Marines could hold swim call and soak up some sun when they were not on patrol or busy with working parties.

My "office" at Liberty Bridge was a CP tent that I shared with my radio operators. Surrounding the tent to a height of 4 feet were sandbags. Inside, I had only a cot and a desk that the Company Gunny, GySgt. Coffer, built for me out of old ammunition boxes and wooden pallets used to ship artillery ammunition. My "chair" was an empty 60 mm mortar ammunition box. From this office, my radio operators and I controlled the movements of our platoons as they conducted day and night activities on the south side of the river.

It was strangely quiet during the first two weeks of July, as if the enemy had decided to avoid contact with our patrols. However, we did have one significant contact with the enemy on July 5 that turned out to be more important than we originally suspected. That night, around midnight, a squad from Lt. Urenovich's platoon was lying in ambush near the hamlet of Phu Nhuan (7) when they saw a group of ten enemy soldiers walking toward them on a trail. It was pitch dark and a thick mist hung close to the ground, so the squad waited until they had positively identified the people approaching their ambush site as enemy before opening fire and throwing hand grenades. They killed three of the enemy and sent the rest running back toward the south. They waited until daylight to search the killing zone since visibility was poor and they were not sure that the surviving enemy had actually fled the area. When they searched the killing zone, they found they had killed several officers from the command group of the 3rd Sapper Battalion, an elite NVA battalion with the mission of destroying Liberty Bridge. This enemy command group was on its way to conduct a reconnaissance of Liberty Bridge in preparation for an attack they had planned for the night of July 10. Among the three dead was the commanding officer of the battalion and his executive officer. Captured were two AK-47 rifles, two Chinese 9 mm pistols, and three packs. In the packs were a pair of binoculars, two flashlights, a hammock, a poncho, a pound of loose tobacco, several pounds of rice, three wallets containing South Vietnamese currency, pictures, pens, books, and many miscellaneous documents, including a detailed map of the defenses around Liberty Bridge and its approaches. This intelligence bonanza was turned over to the S-2 for analysis.[6]

Although the enemy's 3rd Sapper Battalion had suffered the loss of its two most senior leaders in our ambush on July 5, we did not discount the possibility that an attack on the bridge would still be mounted. We increased our patrols around the bridge, hoping to find any enemy force intent upon attacking it. One of these patrols was led by SSgt. Henry E. Sparks, an SNCO on his second tour of duty in South Vietnam, who had joined the company less than two months previously. He was a skilled and experienced infantryman, so he was placed in charge of a squad-size night ambush that we placed along one of the approach routes marked on the captured 3rd Sapper Battalion map. SSgt. Sparks left the company perimeter with a squad from his 2nd Platoon shortly after 2100 on July 10 and moved south to his ambush site just north of the hamlet of Phu Lac (3). At 2225 that evening, as the patrol was approaching their ambush position, they heard movement behind them, and a minute later, they were attacked at close range with small arms, B-40 rocket grenades, claymore mines, and Chinese hand grenades. A ferocious firefight ensued between the Marines and the enemy, and in this encounter SSgt. Sparks and PFC David D. Peppin were killed. SSgt. Sparks was killed as he went to help PFC Peppin, who lay wounded in an exposed position. As SSgt. Sparks attempted to pick up PFC Peppin and carry him to safety, the enemy fired a B-40 rocket grenade that landed beside the two men, killing both of them instantly. Our intelligence officer surmised that SSgt. Sparks's ambush patrol had left the perimeter later than our other patrols, and enemy scouts incorrectly assumed that no more patrols would be near the bridge, making it safe for them to take up attack positions near Hill 31 along SSgt. Sparks's patrol route. They were surprised by SSgt. Sparks's patrol moving through their attack position, and thinking they had been discovered, attacked the patrol as it passed them in the dark and the heavy rain. SSgt. Sparks and his squad probably caused the enemy to abandon their planned attack on Liberty Bridge that night, but the price was very high for our company, and the loss of SSgt. Sparks and PFC Peppin saddened all of us.[7]

Hoping to break up any more planned sapper attacks against Liberty Bridge, my entire company began a sweep on the hamlets of Phu Nhuan (1), (2), and (3) on July 11. We found ten booby traps without sustaining a single casualty. However, as the sweep was ending on the morning of July 12, I received a radio call from Lt. Philip Huth, the platoon commander of the 3rd platoon, that he was not sure of his location on our left flank and was worried that his platoon might become separated from the rest of the company, which was passing through My Loc (2). I told him to take his compass to obtain two back azimuth readings on some prominent mountains and use them to locate his exact position. For some reason, his view of the mountains was obscured, so he told me he wanted to get to some higher ground so he could get a better view of the mountains to the south and west. A few minutes later, I heard his radio operator tell my radio operator that Lt. Huth had detonated an enemy box mine and was severely wounded. Two other Marines standing near him were also wounded. I grabbed the radio and told the 3rd platoon's radio operator that I was requesting an emergency medevac and I needed the grid coordinates of where Lt. Huth was located so the helicopter could pick him up. I spoke to the radio operator and to the platoon's corpsman for a few minutes, telling them to do their best for Lt. Huth, but before the medevac helicopter could reach the small hill where he was to be picked up, Lt. Huth died. His last words were to ask about the condition of the two other wounded Marines.

I had known Lt. Huth for only a few months. He had been in-country only four months when he died, but during that time I had come to respect him for his warm personality, his devotion to his Marines, and his conscientious and reasoned approach to his job. Like me, he was a Roman Catholic and he was always at any Mass we held in the field. His faith was strong, and it showed in every aspect of his life as a Marine officer. Several men in his platoon were crying when they returned to the company perimeter that day and I asked Chaplain Powell to hold a special memorial Mass for him, SSgt. Sparks, and PFC Peppin on July 14. Every man in our company attended that Mass.[8]

On July 13, our company went looking for the VC who planted the box mine that killed Lt. Huth. We swept south from Liberty Bridge, following the western edge of Liberty Road, the road that lead north to Da Nang and south to An Hoa. After following the road for a few miles we pivoted and headed west toward Hill 31, the area where Lt. Huth had been killed. Around noon, we took up a defensive position on a hill called "The Dog Bone," which was located about two miles south of Phu Lac (6). While we were there, the local children brought us all kinds of explosives and ammunition, which I paid 1400 Vietnamese piasters for—a cheap price to pay, since these items could all be turned into deadly booby traps. A few women brought their sick children to us, and our Navy corpsmen held an impromptu MEDCAP for them. Most of their ills were related to skin problems and sores, but one little girl had a badly burned arm that had become infected, so we had the girl and her mother transported to Liberty Bridge, where our battalion surgeon could attend to her. Both the mother and daughter were later sent to Da Nang City for further treatment.

After we had treated their children for some very nasty sores, two young mothers offered valuable intelligence to us. They told us that the VC planting the mines and booby traps along Liberty Road did not live in the area, but actually lived in the hills several miles to the south in Duc Duc District. The women said these VC only came into their village at night when everyone in the village was in their family bunkers. They also told us that the VC often had NVA soldiers with them when they came down from the hills. Two items of information they provided proved to be highly accurate and were acted upon by our battalion: the frequency of these VC visits to their village and the routes they took to enter the village. I was a bit skeptical of the women at first, but my Kit Carson Scout, Qua, said he believed they were truthful. I asked him how he determined this, and he told me that he had asked them a few "test questions" to determine their veracity, and they had passed. Qua added that the women had told him the local villagers were normally informed by the VC of the location of the mines and booby traps so the villagers could avoid them, but this was not always the case, and several villagers had been killed and wounded in the past year because they did not know where the mines and booby traps had been emplaced. He also told me that the villagers did not like the NVA soldiers and resented the heavy rice tax the northerners insisted on collecting.

On July 14, a USO show came to Liberty Bridge, the first such USO show that had ever come to the 5th Marines TAOR. Previously, the area around the An Hoa Combat Base was considered too dangerous for USO entertainers to visit. I did not attend the USO show, choosing instead to remain in my tent working on paperwork and monitoring my company radio traffic. I never attended a single USO show during my entire thirty-two months in

South Vietnam; for some reason, such entertainments struck me as out of place and not something combat troops needed or wanted. In retrospect, I was probably wrong, since many Marines have told me they enjoyed the rare USO show that came their way. But for me, they were a distraction. While the USO show went on, I stayed in my tent and wrote letters to the families of SSgt. Sparks, Lt. Huth, and PFC Peppin.

For the rest of July, the company remained at Liberty Bridge, and most of our time was spent conducting small unit patrols and night ambushes south of the bridge. During many of our patrols, we found booby traps and mines that the enemy had emplaced during the hours of darkness. Friendly villagers often told us of the location of these insidious devices before they could do any harm to either the Marines or local farmers. Normally, we would just destroy them in place using sympathetic detonation from C-4 explosives or M-26 fragmentation hand grenades. Many of these devices had hidden tripwires or dual detonation devices that made attempts to deactivate them extremely dangerous for the Explosive Ordnance Disposal (EOD) personnel attached to our company or the combat engineers who often accompanied our road patrols.

Unfortunately, sometimes we were unable to detect them or have them pointed out to us by the villagers, and in these cases, we suffered casualties. Such a case occurred on July 17 when Lt. Thomas and his platoon were returning from a night patrol near Phu Lac (4), a mile south of the bridge. They saw an opening in a hedge and suspected it was mined, so they moved several meters away from the opening. As their point man and Lt. Thomas pushed their way through the thick hedge, there was an explosion near the opening, showering Lt. Thomas with shrapnel from a booby-trapped M-26 hand grenade. Fortunately for Lt. Thomas, the explosion was several meters away and the hedge absorbed much of the shrapnel, so his wounds were not serious. A medevac was called for Lt. Thomas, but as the platoon was establishing a secure LZ for the medevac helicopter, another Marine tripped a second explosive device, in this case an 81 mm mortar canister filled with C-4 explosive. Both Marines were medevaced when the helicopter landed.

After the medevac helicopter departed, an investigation of the hedge showed the enemy had anticipated the Marines' avoiding the opening in the hedge and had strung their tripwires on both sides of the opening for a distance of 30 feet so anyone pushing through the hedge would trip the wires. They had also hidden several other booby traps inside the hedge where they thought the Marines might try to go to avoid the more obvious opening. This event, and many others like it, taught me several lessons about how ingenious the enemy could be when planting improvised explosive devices (IED). One lesson we learned from our experiences with the enemy's IEDs and the interrogation of VC POWs was how the enemy used the habits of Marines to emplace their deadly devices so they would have the maximum effect. They often planted IEDs where Marines might gather in a group, such as a narrow opening in a hedge, the top of a prominent terrain feature like a hill, or an obvious place where Marines might set up an ambush or OP. As a result, I always found myself harping on the need to keep at least five meters between individual Marines when we were moving outside of our perimeter and to avoid gathering in groups in the open or elevated terrain.

Another lesson I learned was that fatigue caused many Marines to disregard normal safety procedures or to fail to pay attention to their surroundings, making them vulnerable to IEDs. This was particularly true when Marines were returning from night activities or had been on sweep operations all day and had had little sleep. Tired Marines were more likely to trigger these explosive devices than ones who were fresh and alert. Unfortunately, the tempo of operations for a Marine infantry unit often precluded any possibility of rest or sleep. We were lucky if we ever got more than four hours of sleep a day. When added to the extreme tension of combat in a hostile environment and the debilitating effects of the hot and humid weather conditions in South Vietnam, this lack of sleep often produced an indifferent approach to danger. For this reason, I struggled every day to find ways to allow my men to find some extra hours of rest.

Perhaps the most important lesson we learned was how necessary it was to have constant surveillance over one's operating area—especially at night—so the enemy teams implanting IEDs could be observed in the act and killed. This meant saturating our AO with small patrols and ambushes near likely spots for the enemy to emplace explosive devices. Of course, having indigenous people providing intelligence on the location of the devices also was of great value, but this could only be obtained if the villagers were rewarded for doing so and protected from retribution by the enemy. Unfortunately, most Marine units did not stay in one place long enough to develop the kind of relationship needed with local villagers to obtain this valuable intelligence or to provide adequate protection for villagers who cooperated with us. In this regard, Combined Action Platoons (CAP) and South Vietnamese Popular Forces (PF), which were permanently located in the villages they protected, were far more effective in dealing with the problem of IEDs.

Chapter 8

The Que Son Mountains

As July came to an end, we began to hear that we would soon be participating in a new operation in the Que Son Mountains called "Durham Peak." This operation would use just two of the four rifle companies in our battalion, since Company E was required for security of the airfield at An Hoa, and Company H was needed to provide security for two artillery batteries at Fire Support Base (FSB) "Pony." The enemy's main force units had been driven out of Quang Nam Province's lowlands, at least temporarily, so it was decided to pursue them into their base areas in the mountains and disrupt their efforts to rest and resupply for another round of fighting. These lulls in fighting had occurred many times before, but this time the 1st Marine Division decided to run the enemy to ground during this lull and destroy him. We were told to be ready to launch our assault into the Que Son Mountains as early as the first day of August. Since Lt. Col. Higgins knew I had patrolled the Que Son Mountains extensively as a reconnaissance team leader in 1967, he asked me several questions about the area and where I thought we would find the enemy base camps. I was able to provide him with many details that he would use in formulating his plan for the operation. I spent several hours with both Lt. Col. Higgins and our operations officer, Maj. Vallese, showing them on a map of the Que Son Mountains where I had seen enemy troops in 1967, areas that I suspected would be used again by the enemy in 1969.

It was a bright, very hot day on July 31 when the first helicopter load of Company G's Marines landed in an LZ on the summit of Nui Da Beo Mountain overlooking the Que Son Valley to the south. Operation Durham Peak had begun. The enemy referred to this part of the Que Son Mountains as Base Area 116, and it had been used as a base by the Viet Minh when they fought the French and later by the VC as they fought the GVN and the United States. Normally, we would be transported by medium helicopters, like the CH-46 Sea Knight, but the high elevation of Nui Da Mountain restricted the combat load of these helicopters to as few as ten men; so on this occasion, the heavier CH-54 Sea Stallion helicopter was used since it could carry as many as thirty Marines and their combat gear to the top of the mountain. I landed in the first helicopter into the LZ, along with my CP group and a squad from the 3rd Platoon. The battalion CP group and Company F had landed an hour ahead of us and had already taken up defensive positions 100 meters from us across a deep ravine.

As soon as we landed, I moved the company to a narrow, jungle-covered ridgeline that ran east-west and afforded us a perfect view of the Que Son Valley 2,000 feet below. Gunny Coffer and I dug a foxhole on the western side of our perimeter and spent the rest of the day checking our lines to make sure every avenue of approach into our position was well covered with our machine guns and every dead space was covered with mortar and artillery concentrations. I was particularly proud of the efficiency and proficiency of my 60 mm mortar section, and they more than justified my pride with the way they quickly dug pits for their three mortars, leveled their weapons, unpacked their ammunition, and prepared their range cards. As I looked at their handiwork, I knew they were true professionals, men who would never let the company down no matter how difficult a situation we found ourselves in. We also made sure the two trails that led up to the summit were covered by two M-60 machine guns each and that good fields of fire were cut close to the ground so the machine guns could fire at ground level along the length of these trails for at least 50 meters. Claymore mines were emplaced along likely avenues of approach, and trip flares were also put out so any enemy approaching our position at night would give themselves away. Finally, I spoke with Lt. Pelham, our artillery FO, and we went over his defensive fire plan for our position, outlining the respective concentrations he had registered for our 60 mm mortars, the battalion's 81 mm mortars, and the 105 mm howitzers and 155 mm howitzers firing in direct support of the battalion from a FSB north of us. When all of our defensive measures had been taken care of, I drew up my defensive plan and had it delivered by a runner to the battalion CP. All of these procedures were routine for our company; but, nonetheless, I made sure every aspect of our defense plan was actually implemented. I remembered a piece of helpful advice I had received in a letter from Capt. (later BGen.) Marvin Hopgood, a colleague of mine at the Marine Barracks at 8th and I Streets, who had combat experience with a rifle company in Vietnam. He wrote, "Always supervise, never take anything for granted—check everything again and again to make sure it is being done and done correctly." His advice was priceless and probably saved the lives of several of my Marines.

As evening set in and the shadows crept across the ravines and ridgelines of the Que Son Mountains, Gunny Coffer and I settled into our foxhole and talked while we took in the expansive and beautiful view below us. My radio operators occupied another foxhole to our right, and in the gathering dusk I could hear their voices as they sent in our nightly position report and situation report that I had drafted minutes before. After they had sent in the reports, I took the handset of the company tactical net and spoke to my platoon commanders, reminding them again, ad nauseum I am sure, to have their Marines remain silent during the night and to speak softly and infrequently during the daylight. I was obsessive about several things and noise discipline was one of them. Marines in the infantry made too much noise, and I had to constantly remind everyone that the human voice travels far in the mountains. I would tell them the best way to get killed in the mountains was to simply talk in a normal tone of voice so everyone within a mile could hear you. I kept stressing that one usually never saw one's enemy in the jungle, but a voice was like a bullet magnet, and the more one talked, the more likely the enemy would pick you out as a target.

While I was looking at the sun setting, Gunny Coffer passed me his canteen cup, which contained an inch or two of dark brandy. The Gunny always took a canteen filled with brandy with him to the field, and I chose to ignore this since it did not seem to affect him in any way and he was always careful to imbibe only a small amount at night when he was out of the sight of his Marines. The Gunny was a solidly built African American from Georgia who was on his second tour of duty in South Vietnam. He cared deeply for the men in our company, and they loved him for it. He provided wise counsel and a wealth of professional

Lt. Pelham (left) and the author plotting defensive artillery fire on Nui Da Bao Mountain, Operation Durham Peak.

knowledge to me, always maintaining a friendly and positive attitude and rigorously carrying out my orders. In short, he was my right-hand man. As I took a welcome sip of brandy and handed the canteen cup back to him, he spoke softly to me about what I thought lay ahead of us. For some reason, I began to talk about how dispirited I was over the loss of Lt. Huth, SSgt. Sparks, and PFC Peppin. He heard me out, and then he gave me a bit of advice that jolted me. He spoke with that distinctive African American drawl that revealed his rural Georgia roots. For the first time since we met, he spoke to me more like a brother than a Marine SNCO. He said:

> Skipper, you can't afford to think that way. We all feel bad about the death of our friends, but we can't allow that to get in the way of doing our jobs. This company needs to have you thinking about getting us out of this war alive, and that means you have to think about your job 24 hours a day and not think about anything else. We need you to do the things we can't do. You have to lead us and make the right decisions—that is what we expect from an officer. You know I am right. Remember, we are all going to die one day. We don't know when it will be, but we know for sure we are going to die. We are all here under a sentence of death; we just don't know the date for the execution.

The soft-spoken words of John Coffer could not have had a more dramatic effect on me had they been spoken by some wise philosopher or cleric. Immediately, I saw that my despair over the deaths of the men in my company was a self-indulgence that the living men in my company could not afford. I was letting my men down by allowing such thoughts to get in the way of doing my job. As I stared out into the gathering darkness, I resolved to take the Gunny's advice.

We spent a few days perched on top of Nui Da Beo Mountain, sending out patrols in every direction. One such patrol found an enemy harbor site that could accommodate 400 men and showed signs that it had been occupied recently. Fresh feces were found in a latrine and some empty cans of fish were strewn about, indicating that the enemy had made a hasty departure, probably on the day the battalion landed on the mountain. The harbor site was concealed from the air by high jungle canopy and included over thirty caves dug into and around some large rocks and boulders, which afforded a fair degree of protection from artillery fire and air strikes. Since most of the patrols sent out were not finding much enemy activity on the high slopes of the mountain, Lt. Col. Higgins decided he would send our company down to the valley floor to scout out several locations where I had sighted enemy activity two years previously. When I gave my movement order to my platoon commanders, I mentioned I knew the area we were going into fairly well and we could expect to find enemy activity in the valley south of Hill 381, since a main trail ran through the valley less than a mile south of the summit of that hill. That trail led to the main east-west trail that ran through Antenna Valley pass, a main avenue for the enemy whenever they threatened the Que Son Valley.

We left our position before dawn on August 2 and wound our way along a finger south toward Hill 381, which was called Nui Khuc Son. We picked up a trail that paralleled a small stream until we reached the northern slope of Nui Khuc Son Mountain. There we found a split in the trail, with one branch leading south to Nui Khuc Son and the other heading west up a steep ridgeline. My point man reported that the branch leading west had several Ho Chi Minh sandal tracks on it that appeared to be recently made, perhaps only an hour old. I went forward to examine his findings and decided we would follow this trail and see if we could catch up to this enemy force. I told the point man to use the two-man point system we used in recon so one man was always covering the other as they "leap frogged" forward. I also had one of my machine gun teams move up behind the point so we would have superior firepower immediately if we ran into the rear of the enemy column. I was afraid we might be led into an ambush, especially since we were moving on a trail and the direction was uphill, so I cautioned the point team to be very careful and to keep their weapons on their shoulders and aimed so they could immediately return fire if ambushed. As we began to follow the trail, we heard voices speaking Vietnamese ahead of us. A few minutes later, our point man found a wounded NVA soldier hidden among some rocks just off the trail. His comrades had been carrying him in a litter made out of parachute silk and two bamboo poles, but abandoned him when we approached. Our Kit Carson Scout interrogated the wounded prisoner, who told us that he was one of forty wounded NVA soldiers from the 38th NVA Regiment who were being transported to a jungle hospital somewhere nearby and that his regiment had only 200 effective soldiers left alive. We called in a medevac helicopter to take the prisoner to An Hoa, and he was hoisted through the trees to the helicopter using the helicopter's jungle penetrator hoist. I will never forget the terrified look on the wounded NVA soldier's face as he as lifted 100 feet above us to the helicopter.

A few minutes after the wounded NVA soldier had been medevaced, our point security squad was ambushed by a squad of NVA soldiers. The Marines assaulted the enemy, driving them back up the trail. Unfortunately, two Marines were wounded in the initial burst of fire from the enemy ambush. The wounds were not serious, but both men were medevaced, again by helicopter hoist. The Marines of the point squad were confident that they had hit several of the enemy, but a search of the immediate area produced only one small blood trail. Since our position was now compromised and the enemy could ambush us again if we tried to follow them, I decided it was too dangerous to continue using the trail. I felt it was wiser to abandon the chase and instead take the company down to the valley floor, where I knew several well-used trails were located.

We followed the trail toward Hill 381 and found that it turned sharply at the hill's base eastward through a narrow, uninhabited valley. We had moved in column along this trail for only 200 meters when our point man observed five NVA soldiers in camouflage uniforms, carrying AK-47 rifles and B-40 rocket grenade launchers, moving away from him on the same trail. The lead platoon fired on the enemy soldiers and they fled into very thick brush. A search of the area produced no evidence that any of the enemy had been hit. Two hours later, around 1430, as we continued to move east along the trail, our lead platoon, 1st Platoon, encountered twenty NVA soldiers moving away from them toward the east and took them under fire at a range of 100 meters. As the Marines of 1st Platoon maneuvered to attack, an AO flying above us mistook them for the enemy, and without clearance from me, began to fire rockets at them as well as the fleeing enemy. This stopped our attack dead in its tracks. I radioed the battalion forward air controller (FAC) to call off this AO immediately and moved forward with the rest of the company to secure an LZ so the four Marines who had been wounded by "friendly fire" from the AO's rockets could be medevaced. Fortunately for us, the wounds were not life threatening and the enemy did not attempt to hinder our medevac helicopter when it landed in the LZ. I was boiling mad at the AO for firing his rockets at us without first attempting to contact us and obtain clearance to fire. His thoughtless aggressiveness cost us four wounded Marines and allowed the enemy force to

Wounded NVA soldier captured by Company G, August 2, 1969.

Medical evacuation of wounded NVA soldier using the jungle penetrator.

escape. All I could do was call in several artillery missions on likely avenues of escape for the enemy.

Since it was getting late in the day, Lt. Col. Higgins ordered us to return to our original defensive position on Nui Da Beo Mountain. I felt frustrated since I was sure the enemy was nearby and I wanted to remain in the valley and continue to search for the NVA units that had eluded us that day. I reluctantly had the company move north up the steep slope toward Niu Da Beo Mountain, a climb through thick jungle with no trails to make the climb easier. We had climbed for an hour when we came across a double strand of NVA communications wire running east and west along the southern slope of the mountain. We followed the wire with its distinctive robin's-egg-blue color until we found a large group of rocks with several bamboo platforms built between them. This site was obviously an NVA OP since it afforded a panoramic view of the entire Que Son Valley for miles in any direction. Using this site, the enemy would be able to observe any movement by Marine or ARVN units in the valley below and report it to other NVA units using either radio or landline telephone. The construction of the bamboo platforms included an ingenious system for capturing fresh rainwater in two large plastic basins under one of the platforms. This system used bamboo pipes that caught the rainwater as it dripped off the surrounding tree leaves and transported it, using gravity, to the plastic basins under the platform. We could tell the site had been recently abandoned because there were sheets of paper on the platforms that were dry, and it had rained the previous night. I suspected the enemy had seen us start up the mountain and decided to temporarily move to another location to avoid capture. I asked permission from Lt. Col Higgins to continue to follow the communications wire in both directions, but for some reason my request was denied. Later, I was to find out that the battalion radio operator had misunderstood my radio message and had failed to tell Lt. Col. Higgins of the communications wire. My mistake was not insisting on speaking with Lt. Col. Higgins personally and assuming the radio operator understood what I was saying. Had I been able to follow the communications wire to its source, we might have found the headquarters of the 38th NVA Regiment or one of the other NVA regiments rumored to be in the vicinity. Instead, I had the platforms destroyed and the communications wire cut before we continued our arduous climb back up the mountain to our old position.[1]

Due to the steepness of the climb and the heat, which was in the high 90s, we were unable to make it back to our old defensive position before dark. I had the company form platoon defensive positions along a finger leading up the mountain, but we did not have time to adequately dig in since it was dark within minutes of halting our column. During the night, we saw a dozen flashlights moving in a column along a ridgeline parallel to ours. As this column came within several hundred meters of us, I called in 81 mm mortar and artillery fire on it, extinguishing the lights. I later called in a night air strike on the ridgeline, but due to the darkness, we could not observe the results.[2]

The next day, we finally reached our old position. We were very tired and dehydrated, but Lt. Col. Higgins radioed me as soon as we arrived and told me to walk over to the battalion CP immediately. I had just crawled into my old foxhole anticipating some welcome rest after clawing my way through thick jungle undergrowth for two days, so I was not happy about the prospect of a long, hot walk so soon. But I told him I would be there in a few minutes. Taking a fire team with me for security, I descended into a small but deep ravine and then climbed up the other side to reach the battalion's perimeter on another spur of the mountain. When I arrived at the CP, Maj. Vallese and Lt. Col. Higgins expressed surprise when I told them about finding the NVA communications wire. They asked me why I had not told them about it. I explained that I had radioed this information to them and that I had specifically requested to follow it. Needless to say, both officers were not happy that a golden opportunity to find an enemy headquarters had been squandered because their radio operator did not understand the significance of my report. They asked me if I could find the wire again, and I said I could. They then instructed me to take my company down the mountain again toward Hill 381, and this time follow the wire until I found out where it was leading. Since my men and I were both very tired from our climb, I requested we rest for one night before descending the mountain again, and Lt. Col. Higgins reluctantly agreed.

That afternoon, we received a resupply of water and C-rations, and I briefed my platoon commanders on the mission we would undertake the next day at first light. I could tell from the look in their eyes that they were wondering why we were going right back where we came from so soon, but they were tactful enough not to ask me. After finishing talking to them, Gunny Coffer brought over my mail that had come in with the resupply helicopters. There were a few letters from my parents with interesting tidbits of local and family news, including some newspaper clippings about people I knew in my hometown of Merchantville. The Gunny was also carrying a large package, about the size of a small suitcase, which he ceremoniously placed at my feet and announced, "Looks like we will eat well tonight, sir." I did not even need to look at the return address to know that this was the latest "care package" sent to me from Mr. John Dowd and his family, filled with exotic and delicious items from the Gertz department stores on Long Island, New York. I eagerly opened the package and found cans of Danish ham and bacon, imported mandarin oranges, salted peanuts and cashews, English soups, and American chicken à la king, along with several small half-bottles of French wine packed in bubble wrap. There were also several packets of gourmet instant coffee from Germany and two boxes of assorted European candies. My command group hovered around me like buzzards around a carcass, waiting for me to pass out these "goodies," knowing full well that such a heavy load was impossible for even two men to carry in their packs, and there was no way I could haul such a largesse on my person alone. I gave everything away, except for one can of Danish bacon and two small bottles of French wine, both of which were welcome additions to my C-ration meal of crackers and cheddar cheese I had planned for my evening meal. That evening, Gunny Coffer and I took a large, empty C-ration can and flattened it into a grill, and then we placed the homemade grill on top of our small C-ration can stove, cooking the pound of bacon strips until they were crispy and brown. The smell of the bacon, wine, and cheese was intoxicating, and we both said that no meal ever tasted so good. After eating this rare and sumptuous feast, I prayed for the Dowd family and asked God's blessing on them for their kindness to me and my men.

Around 0400 on the morning of August 4, Company G began its second descent down the mountain toward Hill 381. This time we took a different route since we wanted to avoid any ambushes similar to the one we encountered earlier. We made good time along a ridgeline just east of the trail we had used previously. Soon we reached the junction of a trail and a stream on the southwest side of Hill 381. I sent in my CP group along the stream among some large rocks and placed my three rifle platoons above the stream on the ridgelines 50 meters to our west, north, and east. I noticed that the streambed near us formed a perfect place to hold "swim call" for my tired and hot Marines, so I allowed each platoon to send down a squad at a time to take a dip in the cool, clean waters of this natural swimming pool. Several of the Marines washed their clothes in the running stream and sunned themselves after taking a refreshing dip, a welcome way to deal with the prickly heat and other skin problems that plagued us. I had to warn each squad that sound traveled well to the high ground above us, so I insisted they refrain from talking, or I would cancel their swim call. I did not want the enemy to hear us and attack while any of my men were swimming and washing their clothes. We stayed in this position for two days, sending out patrols in every direction, including a few as far south as the village of Lanh An (3) and the well-used trail that ran along the north side of the valley floor between the hamlets of Thanh Hai (1) and Nhgi Thuong (1). Despite extensive patrolling, none of our patrols found the enemy's communication wire, which we suspected had been removed once the enemy knew we had discovered it.

On August 5, a patrol from the 1st Platoon saw several enemy firing at a medevac helicopter that was attempting to land near our CP, and they assaulted the enemy, causing them to flee south toward the abandoned hamlet of Thon Ba (2). The patrol followed the fleeing enemy, calling in mortar and artillery missions on them. When the patrol searched the area where they last saw the enemy, they found an NVA soldier hiding behind a rock, and they killed him with rifle fire. They retrieved an SKS rifle from the dead soldier, which was disassembled and retained as a souvenir. As was often the case, the capture of this weapon was not reported. Later that day, another patrol found three caves on the south side of Hill 381 that had been used recently as a harbor site by the enemy. The patrol searched the caves and found several abandoned items of NVA equipment and clothing, including three AK-47 rifle magazines, two NVA green field uniform shirts, and some assorted medical supplies. The next day, a similar enemy harbor site was found by a patrol from Company E in an area south of where we had made contact with the enemy two days earlier just before we were hit by friendly rockets from one of our own AOs. They found ten huts and several caves containing uniform items and medical supplies that had been abandoned. I had recommended this area to Lt. Col. Higgins at the start of Operation Durham Peak as a likely site for an enemy base camp, and Company E's discovery proved again that the enemy was a creature of habit and tended to use the same base camps over and over again.[3]

On the morning of August 6, I was told to move my company farther south and establish a blocking position near the abandoned hamlet of Lanh An (3), which was located a few hundred meters north of a small grassy hill that had a PF platoon's defensive position on it. We cleared fields of fire, positioned our crew-served weapons, and dug deep foxholes into the soft earth. The location chosen for the blocking position was an ideal spot because it was on high ground that dominated the valley floor near the main trail. I had one of my platoon commanders coordinate our defensive fires with the PF platoon and then I sent out security patrols to the southwest to cut off the trails leading down from Hon Nui Tau Mountain, which loomed above us to the northwest. Once we were in our blocking position, the battalion began to sweep down the southeastern slope of the mountain toward us, hoping to push any enemy forces on the mountain into our blocking position. While we were there, we heard that Company E had found an enemy harbor site and many bloody bandages close to where we had found the wounded NVA soldier on August 2. This led me to believe that our subsequent firefight on the trail that day had produced some additional enemy casualties.

NVA soldiers killed by Company G in the Que Son Mountains.

The rifle companies of 2/5 swept down the slopes of Hon Nui Tau Mountain, making sporadic contacts with the enemy, who seemed to have little heart for a fight, choosing instead to flee in front of the advancing Marines, often abandoning their equipment and supplies in the process. In one case, they even abandoned twelve rifles, a pistol, and numerous packs filled with ammunition and food, along with a valuable Chinese field radio. Abandoning such equipment was rare for NVA units, and it reflected how demoralized and weak these units had become.[4]

On August 8, I had Lt. Urenovich's 1st Platoon leave our company defensive position shortly after dark and move to an ambush site where three trails coming off Hon Nui Tau Mountain converged. I thought it likely that the enemy would try to move off the mountain at night so as not to be caught in the daylight by the other Marine rifle companies descending toward the valley. It proved to be a good choice, because at 2015 the platoon heard a group of enemy soldiers moving down the trail off the mountain and into the killing zone of their ambush. Lt. Urenovich initiated the ambush with a burst from his M-16 rifle, and the rest of the platoon followed suit with rifle fire and hand grenades. A search of the ambush site produced two NVA killed, three captured rifles, and a field pack containing personal items and documents.

The next day the platoon captured an NVA-enlisted courier and an NVA lieutenant. The prisoners were brought to me for interrogation before being sent to battalion. Using my Kit Carson Scout Qua and a Marine corporal who spoke fluent Vietnamese, I found out that the NVA unit these prisoners belonged to had nearly been wiped out by air strikes and artillery a few weeks previously, and had tried to escape to their base camp in the Que Son Mountains. Their unit, which normally had 350 men, had been reduced to seventy-one men, most of whom were sick and starving. Shortly after arriving in their base camp on Hon Nui Tau Mountain, they were told to turn over all but fourteen of their weapons to another unit because that unit had lost their weapons in a battle near Da Nang. When I asked them what they were doing just before they were captured, they told me they had been attempting to acquire rice from the local villagers. It was obvious that both prisoners were suffering from a high fever, which my corpsman diagnosed as the likely result of a very severe case of malaria. At times, they were nearly incoherent because of the fever and their hunger. We fed them some C-rations and water and then had them medevaced.

The prisoners we captured during Operation Durham Peak all told the same story: their units had been savagely depleted during the "Mini Tet" in February and the subsequent Marine and ARVN search-and-destroy operations that followed. These operations reduced many NVA units to less than half their normal strength and totally wiped out some local VC units. One NVA prisoner from the NVA 36th Regiment told us that there was no escape for his unit—in the mountain base camps they died from malaria, bombs and ambushes; and in the lowlands, they died from artillery, air strikes, and search-and-destroy operations. There were no safe places for them to rest and hide, even in the base areas that formerly had been safe and secure for them.

During the period of August 9 to 12, the company continued to occupy blocking positions in the valley while the rest of the battalion swept toward us from Hon Nui Tau Mountain. We sent out both daylight and nightly patrols and set up ambushes on trails leading off the mountain. Lt. Pelham also called in numerous artillery fire missions into the base of the mountain. We captured several more POWs, all of whom were in poor physical condition due to malaria and other fevers. On August 10, while we were moving to a new blocking position on a grassy hill that dominated the terrain for several miles, we came upon the body of an NVA soldier who had obviously been killed by an air strike or artillery. There was little left of his body, only the trunk, which was being voraciously consumed by a blanket of black flies. Had we not seen his intestines strewn about and the shreds of his field uniform, we would not have known it was a human body. A few feet away we found his severed hand in a bush. The stench was terrible and we did not have time to bury him, so my CP group left his carcass to the flies and moved on. As the battalion swept down the mountain slopes toward our blocking positions, Company F found a very large abandoned base camp and spent nearly two days destroying it.

An unusual and disappointing event occurred in the afternoon of August 11. On that day our battalion concentrated on the valley floor in preparation for our movement by helicopter back to An Hoa the next day. The rifle companies of 2/5 occupied individual company defensive positions on some low hills at the base of Hon Nui Tau Mountain, all within a few hundred meters of the battalion CP. We had a squad of combat engineers attached to us that day, and I told GySgt. Coffer to have these combat engineers take up positions on the company perimeter and to start digging foxholes like the rest of our company. Soon thereafter, the Gunny came back to me and said the combat engineers were refusing to take up any positions on the perimeter or to dig any foxholes. At first I was incredulous, having never heard of such a breach of discipline by Marines when given a direct order to help with a unit's defense. Gunny Coffer assured me that this breach of discipline was real, and it reflected the attitude of the engineer squad leader, whom the Gunny described in terms that

Charlie Ridge.

only a Marine gunnery sergeant could use. Fearing that the Gunny was close to rearranging this squad leader's dental records, I decided to talk to the corporal in charge of the engineer squad to see why his squad was refusing my order to help with the defense of the company. I walked over to where the corporal and his men were sitting on the ground, and I asked them who was in charge of their squad. They pointed to a Marine smoking a cigarette a few feet away. I approached the corporal, who remained sitting when I spoke to him and asked him if I could speak to him in private. I suspected the corporal thought I was about to attack him because he picked up an entrenching tool and gave me a look that was anything from assuring. After a few tense seconds, he rose and told me his name. I took the corporal aside and out of the hearing of anyone but the Gunny, and I asked him why he felt his squad should not dig foxholes and man them on the perimeter. I was astounded by his reply. He said in a rather aloof and belligerent tone, "It's not our job; we don't do that shit. That's the infantry's job." Containing my anger, I asked the corporal if he understood the concept of "Every Marine is a rifleman," and he replied that he was a combat engineer and he was not going to have his men stand watch on the perimeter. I then asked the corporal if he understood what a lawful order was, and he replied, "Yes, and what you are asking me and my men to do is not legal, and we are not going to do it." This was the second time during my second tour of duty that I had encountered such an example of a breakdown in military discipline, the first being the incident at the Freedom Hill PX a few months earlier. I was now having some difficulty controlling my anger, and I could see the Gunny had also picked up an entrenching tool, expecting violence and readying himself for it. Before the Gunny could do anything, I asked the corporal to give me his weapon and to come with me. The corporal was surprised by my request for his weapon, and for a moment I thought he might resist, but evidently he thought better of it and so he surrendered his rifle to me. I then took him over to the battalion CP, which was a short five-minute walk away, where I found Lt. Col. Higgins and the battalion sergeant major having a canteen cup of C-ration coffee. I was steaming mad at this point. As I approached Lt. Col. Higgins, I threw the corporal's rifle on the ground and said, "Sir, this sorry excuse for a Marine and the shit maggots he has with him refuse to help defend our defensive position. They feel they are too good to stand watch on the perimeter or dig foxholes. I don't want them anywhere near my company. I suggest you take these shit maggots and send them back where they came from with a charge sheet for willfully disobeying a lawful order." I then returned to my company position and told the combat engineer squad to collect their gear and get out of my position. They asked me where they were to go, and I replied, "Ask that shithead of a squad leader you have—he's over at battalion now." The next time I saw the squad of combat engineers they were busy digging a slit trench latrine near the battalion CP under the careful supervision of the battalion sergeant major. Gunny Coffer watched with satisfaction as the combat engineers sweated away digging the latrine.

CHAPTER 9

Hill 65 and the Palace Guard

On August 12, Operation Durham Peak ended, and our company was transported by helicopter back to the An Hoa Combat Base. We only had time to drink some cold beer and hold mail call before we were loaded on trucks again and driven north over Liberty Bridge to Hill 65, which would be our new home for the next month. Hill 65, which had previously been occupied by Company I, 3rd Battalion, 7th Marine Regiment, was a dominating terrain feature that was situated between Charlie Ridge to the north and the Song Vu Gia River to the south. As such, it controlled all east-west movement along the north side of the river.[1] An old French road, Route 4, ran between Thuong Duc Special Forces Camp 16 kilometers to the west and Route 1, which was 18 kilometers to the east. Hill 65 sat astride this strategically important road, and thus served to control the main approach to the coastal plain south of Da Nang City. Across the Song Vu Gia River to the south of Hill 65 was the infamous VC-infested Arizona Territory, an area our battalion was all too familiar with and one we did not look forward to visiting again.

A few hundred meters west of Hill 65 and hugging the north shore of the Song Vu Gia River was the refugee camp of Tam Hoa. My company's first job after arriving at Hill 65 was to provide security for the refugee village and its 5,000 inhabitants. I established my CP in an abandoned Buddhist shrine not far from a Roman Catholic Church that was pockmarked with numerous bullet holes, evidence that the refugee camp was not on the list of the VC's favorite places in Dai Loc District. My platoons set up their positions in an arc on the western, northern, and eastern sides of the refugee camp, and sent out patrols to the north until they reached the foothills of Charlie Ridge. The area around the refugee camp was fairly secure, and we did not make contact with any enemy while we were protecting it. The other companies in the battalion, operating farther west toward Thuong Duc, made only light contact with small groups of VC who fled rather than fight. Several enemy soldiers surrendered to our sister companies, and these prisoners all told stories of their units being seriously depleted due to their inability to elude Marine and South Vietnamese forces. In many cases, these POWs reported starvation and disease as contributing factors in their decision to surrender. Several of these POWs told harrowing stories about how malaria had ravaged their units ever since they began their long trek from North Vietnam down the Ho Chi Minh Trail to Quang Nam Province. A few of these captured enemy soldiers contended that their units suffered more deaths from malaria and other diseases than from combat.

While I sat in my Buddhist shrine CP and listened to my company and battalion radios and went about the normal day's activities, I began to notice that the tranquility and serenity that we found ourselves in was beginning to affect the alertness of individual Marines. My platoon commanders had to constantly remind their Marines to wear their flak jackets and helmets at all times and to remain alert to any signs of the enemy. I knew we were under constant surveillance by the enemy from their OPs on Charlie Ridge and by their local spies in the surrounding villages, so I did not want the enemy to take advantage of any lax in security on our part.

Because we were now in an area of greater security, we benefited from the availability of local merchants who could reach us and sell us cold drinks, ice, and other comfort items we normally would not have access to at An Hoa or the Que Son Mountains. While the area around us was rural, it was more densely populated than the more contested areas we normally operated in, such as the An Hoa Basin and the Arizona Territory. I used my Kit Carson Scouts to control access to our positions, but it was often difficult to keep children, water buffalo, and local entrepreneurs from getting close to our perimeter.

We had not been in our new positions near Hill 65 very long when I began to notice that many of my Marines were surprisingly eager to have their hair cut in a barbershop at the base of Hill 65. Normally, haircuts were not a high priority for my Marines, even though they were free and given by Gunny Coffer and Mr. Qua, the Kit Carson Scout. I began to wonder why so many Marines were asking to avail themselves of the services at this barbershop, so I walked over to it one day. Inside of the humble hut made out of flattened beer and Coke cans, chicken wire, and tin roofing, I saw why so many of my men were eager to pay for a haircut. Inside, busily cutting hair, were two of the most beautiful girls I had ever seen in my life. They were sisters, 19 and 16 years old, who lived in the refugee camp with their mother and had been recruited by the male owner of the barbershop who astutely knew their presence would bring in Marines in large numbers. The girls were half–French and half–Vietnamese, a combination that seemed to always produce an individual with the most pleasing characteristics of both nationalities. As I entered the dusty shop, the dozen or so Marines waiting for their haircuts rose and rather sheepishly looked back and forth between me and the girls who continued to cut hair. I would have needed a chainsaw to cut the collective lust in that room. Needless to say, there were few takers in my company for one of Gunny Coffer's free haircuts, but it seemed everyone had the need for a good "high and tight" haircut at the Hill 65 barbershop. I often wonder what happened to those barbershop girls. They could easily have been movie stars under different circumstances.

Since the tempo of operations was rather low for our company during our first two weeks in August, I had an opportunity to spend many hours talking to my two Kit Carson Scouts about their lives prior to rallying to the GVN. Tran Van Qua, my senior Kit Carson Scout, who had been with me ever since I took command of the company, provided many hours of conversation and gave me an insight into the life of a VC fighter that I could never have learned in any book. His story is so compelling and illustrative, I have devoted an entire chapter to it.

Also, about this time, I began to think seriously about extending my thirteen-month tour in South Vietnam for an additional six months since I still felt there was nothing gained by me going home. Like all the Marines in the 1st Marine Division, I had heard about the redeployment of the Marines from South Vietnam and the likelihood that most U.S. ground forces would be leaving South Vietnam soon. President Nixon's "Vietnamization" policy, which would turn over the fighting to the South Vietnamese, was beginning to take effect.

I could see that we were beginning to transition to a more defensive mode in Quang Nam Province in anticipation of eventually leaving the country. I had discussed the possibility of extending my tour six months with Lt. Col. Higgins, and he told me that it was unlikely that I would be allowed to retain my command of my rifle company after I had been in command for six months. Instead, he said I would probably be assigned to the battalion's operations section if I remained in the battalion. If I did not want to stay in the battalion, he thought it likely I would be assigned to a staff position at either regiment or division. Since none of these prospects appealed to me and would take me out of the fight, I began to look for a job that would allow me to put my combat experience to good use and possibly allow me to continue to participate in combat operations. I wrote letters to some of my friends at division headquarters and asked them if they had any leads on interesting jobs.

On August 17, a day when many young Americans were enjoying drugs, sex, and rock and roll at the Woodstock Festival in White Lake, New York, I was accompanying a patrol by the 2nd Platoon a few miles northwest of Hill 65. During a short rest stop in the shadow of Charlie Ridge, I received a radio message from the battalion to report to the CP and to bring my rifle company with me. I quickly assembled my company and began the short march to Hill 65, all the while wondering what new mission awaited me and Golf Company. As it turned out, we were to take over perimeter security for our CP and the artillery battery on the hill from one of the other companies in the battalion. When I arrived, Lt. Col. Higgins informed me that my promotion orders had come in, and I was now a Marine captain, effective July 1, 1969. We held a company formation on the hill, and Lt. Col. Higgins pinned my captain's insignia on my jungle utility uniform after the battalion adjutant read my appointment order. The entire ceremony lasted less than five minutes. I sent one of my lieutenants in the company Jeep to the Freedom Hill PX to buy twelve cases of beer and soda for my men, and we celebrated that evening in the company area just before dark.

The next day, Lt. Col. Higgins relinquished his command and departed South Vietnam for a new assignment at the Marine Corps Base at Quantico, Virginia. Again, my company formed up on the hill, but this time we had a proper ceremony for the change of command. The 1st Marine Division Band and the Commanding General, MGen Simpson, showed up, and Lt. Col. Higgins was shown off in grand style, although there was not enough room on the hill for a "pass in review." For some odd reason, someone had invited a dozen young American Red Cross women to the change of command, flying them in with Gen. Simpson. While the sight of these attractive young women in their distinctive uniforms stimulated the interest of the Marines at the ceremony, I felt it was both dangerous and inappropriate to have them at such an event. It was the first time since I began my second tour of duty in South Vietnam nine months ago that I saw these Red Cross volunteers, and I wondered what earthly reason had been given for inviting them, since it was obvious they had no role to play in the change of command ceremony.

I was sorry to see Lt. Col. Higgins leave. I considered him a tactical genius and one of the most professional and competent officers I ever encountered during my career as a Marine officer. I was confident in his abilities, as were my men. We all knew we would miss "The Arizona Kid" with his distinctive red-checkered bandana and locally made walking stick, leading us from one hot spot to another, raining death and destruction on the enemy. His replacement was Lt. Col. J.T. Bowen, another very capable commander, who quickly took charge after Lt. Col. Higgins's departure, making for a smooth transition. On Lt. Col. Bowen's

The Change of Command Ceremony for Lt. Col. Higgins on Hill 65.

The Red Cross volunteers at the 2/5 change of command ceremony on Hill 65.

first day he spent nearly an hour talking to me, asking me questions about the battalion, my company, and the general situation around Hill 65. I felt important and valued when he told me that he had heard from Lt. Col. Higgins and our battalion executive officer, Maj. Robert E. Loehe, that I was one of the most experienced officers in the battalion and had an extensive knowledge of Quang Nam Province from my previous tour as a recon team leader.

He asked me what I thought of the idea of holding a "county fair" in the villages west of Hill 65, and I told him I did not think it would be wise to do so. He seemed surprised by my answer, but I explained to him that the concept of the "county fair" may have been applicable in the early stages of the war, but now such operations would only irritate the villagers and not produce any positive results. He listened intently to my explanation as to why I thought "county fair" operations were no longer applicable in the province, especially in areas that were relatively secure. A "county fair" was a counterinsurgency technique where a battalion or two would surround a village, search the village for VC and contraband, and then try to "win the hearts and minds" of the villagers by feeding them and holding a MEDCAP to treat their minor ailments or showing cartoons and GVN propaganda movies. I told Lt. Col. Bowen I thought the concept was outdated and likely to be counterproductive. I explained that the villages near us on the north side of the river were controlled by the GVN and few, if any, VC were able to live in these villages. I told him that ever since the 1968 Tet Offensive, the VC had been dramatically weakened in the province, and it was now almost impossible for any VC to live in the villages north of the Song Vu Gia River. I pointed to the massive Charlie Ridge above Hill 65 and told him, "Sir, if you want to find the enemy now, you have to go into the mountains. Sure, VC can be found by our patrols and ambush teams, but that is when they are trying to enter the villages, not because they live there. These local people want to be left alone to tend their farms and to be protected from the VC and the NVA who are taking their rice and sons away. If you interrupt their farming and fishing routines for something like a 'county fair,' you will only succeed in making them hate you. I strongly recommend you ask the U.S. district advisor if he thinks it is a good idea before you decide to do it." I could tell he did not like my answer, but I was pleased later when I found out he had taken my advice and abandoned his plan for a "county fair" in Dai Loc District.

I was sitting in the bunker on Hill 65 that served as my CP and sleeping quarters on the afternoon of August 20 when Maj. Vallese poked his head into the bunker to tell me that I would be taking my company on a reconnaissance in force mission into the Arizona Territory the next day, and I would be taking some "special people" with me. He took out his operations map and showed me the intended route my company would take. The route for this night movement would take my company two miles southeast of Hill 65 to a ford that crossed the Song Vu Gia River, where we would wait until just before first light to cross the river. Once on the other side, the company would then sweep west parallel to the river for two miles, passing through the hamlets of My Hiep (1), My Hiep (4), My Phu, and My Hoa (2) before crossing the river again in local fishing boats near the hamlet of My Hoa (3). He said the operation would last two or three days, depending upon what we found and whether or not we made contact with the enemy as we swept west. The reach of the government of South Vietnam did not extend into the Arizona Territory, so I fully expected we would encounter the enemy during our travels, and I wondered why the battalion had decided to send a single rifle company into this very dangerous and contested area. Maj. Vallese anticipated my question and told me we were not going into the Arizona Territory alone: Company E would also be crossing the river to conduct a similar reconnaissance in force operation a few miles west of us near the hamlets of My Dong and My Hoa (1). As an aside, he said our company had a secondary mission of providing protection and cover for the "special people" going with us. I asked him who these "special people" were, and he simply held his finger up to his lips and said, "I will let you know when they get here."

That evening, after I had given my operation order to my platoon commanders for our river crossing into the Arizona Territory, a dozen very tough-looking South Vietnamese clad in black pajamas came out of the dark and approached my bunker. They were armed with AK-47 assault rifles and an M-60 machine gun. They looked exactly like the VC to me and my men. With them were two Americans, also dressed in black pajamas, armed with M-16 rifles. Their faces were camouflaged with black and green face paint.

One of these Americans looked very familiar. As he got closer I saw him smile and say, "Hi, Andy, funny we should meet like this!" It was my old friend, Capt. Fred Vogel, whom I had taken on his first recon patrol in December 1967. His American companion was GySgt. Richard Hendrickson. After a short introduction, Fred, the Gunny, and I sat down to go over the reconnaissance in force operation scheduled to begin in a few hours with our night march from Hill 65 to the river crossing site. Fred explained to me that the tough-looking South Vietnamese with him were members of the Quang Nam Provincial Reconnaissance Unit (PRU), and he commanded this force of approximately 300 PRU soldiers. He explained that their mission was to destroy the VC political leadership in the villages of the province by capturing them, killing them, or convincing them to rally to the government. I had only heard rumors about this unit, and I was fascinated by the tales Fred told me about how his small group of highly trained and highly motivated PRU soldiers were systematically destroying the political infrastructure of the communist Lao Dong Party in the towns and villages of the province. He went on to tell me that he had a former VC with him who had rallied to the GVN, and this Hoi Chanh was going to go back into his home village in the Arizona Territory so he could identify any remaining VC political cadre who might still be there. Our job was to provide protection for

Captain Fred Vogel, USMC, with Vietnamese frogmen.

the PRU and this Hoi Chanh while they searched the village looking for any VC political cadres. Fred warned me that these enemy political operatives were armed, and they seldom traveled alone. We could expect a firefight with them and the guerrillas who provided security for them.

Shortly after 0300 on August 21, my company and the contingent of PRU soldiers left the perimeter wire on Hill 65 and began our night movement to the fording spot two miles southeast of the hill. We did not have far to travel, but I wanted to take it very slow since I feared we might be ambushed. I had the company move in two columns approximately 200 meters apart so each column could support the other if we were hit. Each column had point, flank, and rear security, so we covered a fairly large area as we moved toward the ford. We reached the ford without incident and set up security while I sent a squad across the river to make sure we could ford it safely and there were no enemy on the other side. Around 0500, the squad leader, who had been a reconnaissance team leader on a previous tour with the 3rd Marine Division in Quang Tri Province, radioed back that the far bank of the river was secure, but we needed to be careful because the river was deep close to the far bank and moving swiftly. I warned my platoon leaders to make sure the men carrying radios, crew-served weapons, and other heavy loads knew about the deep water and swift current, and then I had a fire team take a 200-foot climbing rope across so the squad on the other side could use it to pull any Marine caught in the current to safety. I also told the recon squad leader to post security 100 meters to each side of the crossing site and to put four of his best swimmers in the river near the deep water in case any of my men had difficulty crossing. After every preparation had been made, I moved with the first platoon across the river. The point where we crossed was approximately 200 meters wide. On the near side it was quite shallow, perhaps only 2 feet deep, and it remained rather shallow until we were less than 50 meters from the far side, where it dropped off to around 5 feet. The current was quite swift near the far shore, and we all had difficulty keeping our footing. Thankfully, the four swimmers we had in the water near the far shore were able to assist those of us who had difficulty. Everyone got across the river safely, although we had a few close calls with the men carrying our mortars and machine guns. It was getting light as the last man crossed, so I had the company take up defensive positions in an arc of 180 degrees, fearing the enemy might attack us once they knew we were in their backyard. Our fording site took us to the eastern edge of the hamlet of My Hiep (1), a hamlet that clearly showed the ravages of war. Many of the houses were abandoned, while others were pockmarked with bullet holes or reduced to rubble by bombs and artillery. From a distance, the hamlet looked serene and peaceful, but up close one could tell this was not like the hamlets on the other side of the river. This was "Indian Country," an area that had either been controlled by the VC for years or contested recently. There were no friendly CAP or PF platoons in the Arizona Territory, no local GVN officials, no GVN schools, no medical services—nothing but sullen and silent villagers, mostly women and young children. We were not welcome in this hamlet and all of us knew it.

I began our sweep to the west along the river, placing two platoons forward on a frontage of 100 meters each, followed by my CP group, the mortar squad, and the PRU, with one platoon behind me acting as rear security. Like a living, amoeba-like organism, Company G moved elastically, ebbing and flowing in and around tree lines, paddy dikes, and clusters of huts as it moved west with its right flank anchored on the river.

The previous night Lt. Pelham and I had spent an hour going over our fire plan for the use of our organic 60 mm mortars, the battalion's 81 mm mortars, and the 105 mm howitzers of the artillery battery firing in direct support of our battalion. With meticulous care, we plotted on our maps the various mortar and artillery concentrations along the route we intended to take. Now, as we moved west, Lt. Pelham and I coordinated with each other so he knew exactly where I was taking the company and what concentrations should be fired if we ran into the enemy and needed fire support. I had also plotted phase lines for our sweep and provided them as part of my frag order to the battalion operations officer. This would allow me to keep him informed by radio of my exact location without using the grid coordinates on my map. The use of phase lines and coded checkpoints prevented any enemy radio intercept operators from determining our position.

I had an eerie feeling that we were being watched by the enemy as we moved west through My Hiep (1) and into a large area of rice paddies on the other side. I felt as if some malignant animal was crouching in wait for us to make a mistake or show some lapse in security. The villagers working in the rice paddies avoided eye contact with us as we passed them, and I could not help but notice that there were no young men to be seen. We entered the hamlet of My Hiep (4), which had the same war-ravaged look about it as its sister hamlet of My Hiep (1). This hamlet had been the home of the Hoi Chanh with our PRU contingent, and the PRU soldiers set him to work immediately after we entered the hamlet. Here, one of our platoons apprehended a 40-year-old male who was carrying a pack with rice and clothing in it. A quick field interrogation of him by Mr. Qua and the PRU team leader could not determine whether or not he was a VC, so it was decided to keep him with us and take him back to battalion for further interrogation.

An hour later, the Hoi Chanh and the PRU brought a young woman to us whom they identified as a VC nurse. Fred Vogel and Gunny Hendrickson interviewed the VC nurse but she was not cooperative, refusing to respond to even the simplest of their questions. The PRU soldiers were none too pleased with this woman's intransigence and were frustrated that they had not captured any significant VCI in the hamlet. In order to avoid the potential of violence, Fred decided it would be best to send her and the man we had detained to the interrogation facility at An Hoa, where they could be interrogated by Marine counterintelligence (CI) personnel. We tied both prisoners' hands behind their backs and then waited for our resupply helicopter to drop the prisoners off at An Hoa.

As we waited for this resupply helicopter, Fred asked me if I had ever considered working as an advisor with the Vietnamese. I told him I had, but the opportunity had never presented itself. He said I should consider taking over his job when he left in a few months. With only a few more months to go on my thirteen-month tour, I didn't think there was enough time left in my tour to make it worthwhile, but Fred had an answer for that. He suggested I extend my tour six months so I would have enough time. I was intrigued by the kind of work Fred was doing and the mystery surrounding the activities of his PRU team. His secretiveness about who he was actually working for made the prospect of working with the PRU even more enticing. I knew I would soon be sent to a staff job, and I did not want to do that. I wanted to be near the action where I could use my knowledge of the province and the enemy to help win the war. I told Fred I would extend my tour of duty six months, and he said he would talk to his "boss" about me. As the helicopter with our water and food came in, I shook hands with Fred and told him to let me know as soon as his "boss" accepted my "application" for work with the PRU. Fred and his PRU team went along with the prisoners to An Hoa to make sure the prisoners were delivered safely, and that was the last time I saw Fred until years later in Washington, D.C.

Shortly after the resupply helicopter departed, I received a radio call from Company E's CO, Captain J.L. McClung, that his company had been in contact with the enemy earlier in the day near My Dong hamlet. They had killed several of the enemy and captured five. He warned me that this enemy force was made up of NVA regulars, not local VC guerrillas, and they were headed in my direction. I thanked him for the information and informed my platoon commanders of what I had just heard. Later that evening, as I sat in my foxhole on the western side of My Hiep (1) listening to the battalion tactical net radio, I heard Capt. McClung inform the battalion that he was receiving sporadic sniper fire in his night position. He said one of his patrols had made contact with the enemy resulting in one enemy, killed and one Marine killed. We could hear the small arms fire in the direction of Company E, and we looked into the darkness fully expecting the enemy to also hit us during the night.[2]

Staring into the darkness and leaning forward in our foxholes, we could hear sporadic small arms fire coming from Company E's defensive position near the hamlet of My Dong, as well as the distant and distinctive sound of mortar and artillery rounds exploding around their position. Despite our fears, the enemy did not attack our position, but we all sensed they were in the vicinity and our turn might be coming soon. We did not have long to wait!

The morning of August 22, we left the hamlet of My Hiep (4) and approached the next hamlet 300 meters to our west, My Hiep (2). I suspected that the enemy who had been attacking Company E's night defensive position may have withdrawn east into My Hiep (2), so I approached this hamlet with care. I remembered the problems we had had in May when we attacked a fortified village in the southern Arizona Territory, and I did not want to repeat that costly form of attack. Instead, I sent one of my platoons around to the south of the hamlet so as to cut off any escape attempt in that direction, and I informed Capt. McClung that my company was advancing toward his company and to be alert to any enemy troops we might push toward them. Since there were civilians in My Hiep (2), I decided not to prep the hamlet with artillery, but instead had mortar and artillery concentrations preregistered in two open areas north and south of the hamlet so they could be adjusted quickly if we took fire from the hamlet. Finally, I sent a single squad across the 100 meters between my company and the eastern edge of the hamlet to conduct a reconnaissance of the near edge of the hamlet. The rest of the company took up overwatch positions so they could provide covering fire for the squad as they moved rapidly across the open rice paddy toward the trees in the hamlet. A few minutes after the squad disappeared into the trees, the squad reported back that they saw no sign of the enemy and that several old bunkers inside the tree line were empty. I then ordered one platoon to cross the rice paddy and join the squad on the other side while they were covered by my remaining platoon. My CP group then crossed the rice paddy, followed by my last platoon. The platoon that I had sent south of the hamlet reported they did not see any unusual activity. While everything appeared to be peaceful in My Hiep (2), I noticed the hamlet seemed empty, except for a few old women looking out of the doors of their huts. It was too quiet and too empty, not at all like the bustle of activity one would normally find in a South Vietnamese hamlet shortly after dawn. I was even more concerned when my Kit Carson Scouts told me that there were no cooking fires in any of the peasants' huts, a clear sign that the normal routine of morning food preparation was being abandoned and the villagers were expecting trouble.

We moved west through the hamlet, passing a Buddhist temple that lay in ruins. I remembered the trouble we had with a Buddhist shrine in My Ly (3) in May, so I had a squad search it thoroughly for any hidden bunkers before we passed by. I moved the company slowly, stopping frequently to search huts and bunkers for the enemy. As we passed the Buddhist temple and approached the center of the hamlet near some large trees and scattered huts, one of my platoon commanders radioed to me that he thought his men had spotted a single NVA soldier following his platoon about 200 meters away. I was talking to this platoon commander on the radio and standing under a tall tree when we began to take fire from two sides. One platoon was fired upon from a group of huts on the western side of the hamlet, while our CP group and the other platoon received small arms and B-40 rocket grenade fire from a tree line to our east, a tree line we had just cleared only minutes earlier. Both platoons returned fire and Lt. Pelham and I began to call in artillery fire on both enemy targets. As I was talking on the radio to the battalion, a B-40 rocket grenade was fired at the tree I was standing under, wounding me and three of the Marines in my command group. I felt a white-hot burning sensation in my upper back and head where shrapnel hit me. I had taken off my helmet to use the radio, but thankfully, I had my flak jacket on or I would have been more seriously hurt. I sunk to my knees and told my radio operator that I was hit, and he immediately yelled, "Corpsman up." Within seconds one of my corpsmen was beside me asking me where I was hit as he opened his Unit 1 and began taking out a field dressing. I was bleeding from the minor head wound I received, which was obvious, but I told him I also felt some pain in my upper back under the collar of my flak jacket. The pieces of shrapnel that hit me hurt more due to their heat than any damage they had done, and soon the pain subsided. I told the corpsman I was all right and he should see to the wounds of the other Marines in the CP group. While one Marine was wounded badly enough to require a medical evacuation from the field, the rest of us were treated in the field and remained with the company. Nine years later, in 1978, I was taking a shower when I noticed I was bleeding from a hole in my upper back, and on the floor of the shower I found two pieces of B-40 rocket grenade shrapnel that had somehow worked their way to the surface of my skin and fallen out. For several years after being wounded, I noticed a small lump in my back, but I had always thought it was a benign cyst instead of the remnants of the shrapnel that hit me on May 22 in the hamlet of My Hiep (2).

Since we were in a good defensive position in My Hiep (2) and we had a clear view of the open terrain between us and the enemy firing at us, I used our 60 mm and 81 mm mortars to hit back at the enemy while we remained under cover behind some paddy dikes and trees. Marine helicopter gunships also provided suppressive fire with their miniguns and rockets. In less than 30 minutes, the enemy fire ceased, and we were able to safely medevac the only wounded Marine needing medical attention in the rear. We continued to sweep west, but we did not see any more enemy. Unfortunately, twice during the day we had Marines wounded from M-26 hand grenades that had been rigged to go off when a Marine hit a tripwire attached to the grenade. These grenade booby traps were set within a few meters of occupied huts, but the villagers did not warn the Marines that the booby traps were present, despite their obvious knowledge of the booby trap locations. Because of this, I instructed my men to burn the huts of anyone near the booby traps and to have my Kit Carson Scouts tell them why I was doing it. Unlike the villagers we had encountered near Liberty Bridge or on the north side of the Song Vu Gia River, these villagers were definitely VC sympathizers, if not VC themselves. They needed to know that there was a price to pay for allowing the VC to plant mines and booby traps near their homes.[3]

An incident occurred on August 23 that was indicative of the kind of problem that could occur when a poorly disciplined Marine is unable to control his urges. As we were establishing a new night defensive position near the hamlet of My Phu, a lance corporal returning from a patrol brought two detainees with him: a badly beaten middle aged man and a teenage girl. The lance corporal had taken his fire team on a short patrol in front of our lines and had "captured" the two detainees, whom he described as VC. I asked how the man had been beaten, and the lance corporal said the man had jumped him from behind for no reason, so the lance corporal had reacted by defending himself. I was immediately suspicious of this story because my experience with Vietnamese peasants, even those sympathetic to the VC, told me it was highly unlikely for one of them to physically assault an American nearly twice his size and weight. Upon further investigation, we found out that the lance corporal had touched the girl inappropriately while he searched her. When he did this, the man, who was her father, went to her defense, and that was how he was beaten. When I found out the truth, I had the man untied and I apologized to him, telling him I would punish the Marine for the liberties he took with his daughter. On the advice of my Kit Carson Scout, Qua, I gave the peasant ten dollars in Vietnamese piasters, all that I had remaining in my possession, along with some cigarettes. I had one of our corpsmen treat his injuries, which were not serious, and then I released him and his daughter to return to their homes. When I interviewed the lance corporal later, I could tell he was sincerely remorseful, but I needed to make an example of him or others might think it was all right to molest Vietnamese women. I had him dig foxholes and latrines all the next day, and then I sent him to the rear to be placed under the supervision of 1st Sergeant Rooney, who was very adept at dealing with troublesome Marines. I also administered nonjudicial punishment a few days later when the lance corporal returned to the field. In a company formation, I reduced his rank to private, fined him, and warned everyone in the company that I would not tolerate any mistreatment of civilians, whether they were VC or not. I explained why it was important for us to act professionally at all times, and I warned them that I would punish severely anyone caught abusing civilians.

On August 24, we ended our sweep of the northern Arizona Territory. Using fishing boats sent to us from the refugee camp across the Song Vu Gia River, we moved the entire company across the river in an hour. After a short boat ride, my command group landed on the north shore and we joined the company and waited for the last platoon to cross the river and join us. Once everyone was on the north shore, we marched back to Hill 65. As our company marched through the hamlets on the way to Hill 65, I was struck by how different the hamlets looked and the people acted on this side of the river. The differences between the hamlets on the north shore and those in the Arizona Territory were stark. The hamlets around Hill 65 looked prosperous, clean, and untouched by war, with many small shops and vegetable stands doing a brisk business. Some of these homes even had television antennas on their roofs, a sure indication that prosperity could be found inside. I wondered if this juxtaposition was noticed by the Vietnamese civilians living in the Arizona Territory.

After returning to Hill 65, our company settled into our new role as the battalion reserve, a job that meant many working parties during the day repairing and strengthening the bunkers on the hill's perimeter and many long hours of duty manning those bunkers at night. We also sent out a few daylight patrols into the fields around the Tam Hoa Refugee Camp to protect the farmers working in their fields and to prevent the VC from taking rice from them. On one such patrol on August 26, several children approached the patrol and informed the platoon commander that two VC from the Arizona Territory wanted to surrender and rally to the GVN. The children took the platoon to the edge of the Song Vu Gia River and told them to wait for the VC to cross the river toward them. An hour later, two VC walked across the river and surrendered. They told the platoon commander they had been in contact with the Marines a few days previously and their local VC squad had been completely wiped out by a mortar barrage. They also told us that very few VC were left alive in the Arizona Territory and those who were still alive were in no condition to fight. We asked them about any NVA units near their hamlet, and they told us the NVA lived in the Ong Thu Slope area and only came down from that plateau to take rice from the villagers and plant mines and booby traps. They added that the NVA were all suffering from malaria, but fresh NVA groups of approximately 300 men arrived in the Ong Thu Slope every month or so. When we asked them why they wanted to surrender, they simply said they were tired of running from one place to another, hiding from the Marines and the GVN soldiers and police. They were sent to the Cheiu Hoi Center in Da Nang for further interrogation and processing.[4]

Near the end of August, Lt. Col. Bowen told me that Company G would be detached from the battalion to provide security for the 1st Marine Division Command Post at Hill 327, Quan Hoa Vang District, starting on September 1. The division command post had come under a rocket and sapper attack, and they needed a rifle company that could serve as a reaction force if the enemy tried to hit the division headquarters again. I gathered the entire company together and told them what our new mission would be and how our company had been chosen for this important mission by the battalion commander because he knew we were capable of independent operations. I also warned them that the hamlets and villagers around Da Nang were different from those we encountered near An Hoa or in the Arizona Territory. We would find a far more pro–GVN population there, and it was necessary for every man in the company to realize this. We must treat every villager we encountered as our friend and not a potential enemy. I also told them that when we traveled to Da Nang, we must look like the professional Marine infantry line company we were, which meant our uniforms must be clean, our hair cut to regulation length, our flak jackets and helmets worn at all times, and our weapons clean and at the ready. I stressed the division staff would judge the entire 5th Marine Regiment by how we looked and how we performed our duties, and we needed to keep that in mind during our entire time at Hill 327.

On September 1, we departed Hill 65 aboard trucks and were convoyed to the 1st Marine Division CP. When we arrived at Hill 327 two hours later, I had the company dismount and fall in at the bottom of the hill directly in front of the division CP. I went into the headquarters bunker on the hill and reported to a major from the Division G-3, informing him that my company was standing by for his instructions. He briefed me on the recent attack on the CP and directed me to take my company and conduct a sweep of the area lying south of Hill 327 and to establish a patrol base in the hamlet of Ap Phuoc Thuan. I left the division CP, issued a frag order to my platoon commanders, and then I had the company climb up to the ridgeline that ran from Hill 244 to Hill 327. There, we moved along the ridgeline, dropping off a squad at intervals of 200 meters. After a short rest on the ridgeline, I had the squads move down the steep slopes toward the valley below, searching the jungle for any signs of enemy activity, past or present. We found nothing and finally reached the valley floor as it was beginning to get dark. We did not have much daylight left to find and prepare a defensive position, but fortunately we did manage to find a low hill surrounded by a rice paddy that afforded a measure of observation and protection. We dug in, completing this task just as the sun set and darkness enveloped us. I had each platoon send out a listening post while I sent in a situation report to the division G-3. We were about 1,000 meters east of the hamlet of Ap Phuoc Thuan, and we could see the lights in the houses in the hamlet, as well as the lights in other houses in other hamlets to our west and south. I think all of us thought about how different the hamlets around Da Nang were from those we found in the contested areas to the south in Quang Nam Province. Here people and vehicles could be seen walking about at night, and there was a peaceful, even serene feeling to these hamlets. Despite this feeling of tranquility and safety, I insisted we maintain the same level of security we had always employed previously in the less secure areas of the province. I knew that it was always a mistake to let one's guard down and assume all was well—the enemy would take advantage of such an attitude, and the results would not be pleasant.

The next day, the company began to sweep west toward the hamlet of Ap Phuoc Thuan. A Marine rifle company on-line and maneuvering is a beautiful sight to behold. I watched in awe and wonder as my rifle company moved like some living organism across the dark green rice paddies, ebbing and flowing with the terrain. Squads providing flank security moved swiftly from one covered position to another on the north and south, while two squads moved in tandem to our front. Each pair of Marines maintained a distance of at least five meters between each other while they provided cover for their advancing comrades. Our radio operators had their tape antennas tied down so it was not easy to see they were carrying a radio, and our platoon commanders did nothing to indicate their rank, like taking their maps out to look at or using their lensatic compasses to fix their position. None of the men bunched up, and all of them had their weapons in their hands ready to use them. I felt confident that my rifle company could go anywhere it wanted to go, and no force on earth could stop it. As Company G moved out that day, I thanked God that he had given me the opportunity to be with such magnificent warriors. I also knew from watching many NVA and VC units that the good ones moved like professionals, and I wanted any NVA or VC scouts who were watching us to know that we were good—really good. I wanted them to know that if they chose to fight us, we would fight them like a pit bull, never letting go and always pressing the attack. Marines are always trained to attack aggressively, something that is ingrained into their psyche from their first days of basic training. It is the result of the Marine Corps' experience during World War II, when U.S. Marines needed to be trained to attack heavily fortified Japanese islands in the Pacific. This experience became part of the doctrine and training of the U.S. Marine Corps that has been in use ever since. In fact, I often found it difficult to hold back my Marines once the first shots were fired—they had this reflex action to immediately maneuver to attack, to close with, and destroy the enemy. There was never any hesitation or any attempt to stop and call in supporting arms, just a collective will to attack and kill the enemy. This aggressive, assault-minded ideology produced Marine casualties, but it also often made for very heavy casualties for the enemy. We knew from talking to prisoners that they feared this aggressive response from the Marines, and these prisoners often spoke of how disastrous it was to have a meeting engagement with a Marine unit, since the Marines always pressed their attacks and maneuvered to cut off avenues of retreat.

Company G spent the first week of September inside the hamlet of Ap Phuoc Thuan, a beautiful and well-tended hamlet. I set up my CP beside a villager's house, paying him "rent" in piasters and C-rations for the space I used. The village chief lived nearby, and I made it a point to visit the chief each day and keep him informed of what my company was doing on his turf. I also took this opportunity to ask him if any of my Marines were doing anything that might cause him or the other villagers a problem. The chief was a relatively young man for a village chief, probably no older than his late 30s, but he was capable and wise, two attributes that made for a good village chief. He told me that it was rare for a Marine unit to stay in his hamlet since the area was quite secure and no enemy forces had been in the area for nearly two years. A local PF platoon provided security for the hamlet, and the village chief said this local militia unit kept any VCI cadres out of his hamlet or the nearby villages. He did say that VC and NVA sapper units managed to infiltrate into the area once in a while to fire rockets at the air base and the division headquarters, but these attacks had been quite rare after the 1968 Tet Offensive. He took me over to the PF platoon's triangular fort and introduced me to the hamlet security chief, who was also the PF platoon commander. I was pleased when the security chief volunteered to send his men out with my Marines on patrols and night ambushes.

During our week-long stay in Ap Phuoc Thuan hamlet, we encountered no enemy activity whatsoever. I sent out daylight patrols in all directions, often using the PF militia as guides and interpreters, but all we saw were tranquil, rural scenes of rice farmers in their fields and women tending to their homes while school children in their white and blue school uniforms walked to and from the small primary school nearby. The only "incident" we had was when the hamlet chief informed me that a South Vietnamese man on a motorcycle was attempting to bring a prostitute into the village, intending to capitalize on the new business opportunity Company G's presence in the village offered. Gunny Coffer and I accompanied the village chief to where this individual was talking to several of my Marines and introducing them to a heavily made-up teenaged girl. When I approached the man, the Marines walked away and the man began to get on his motorcycle with the girl astride the bike behind him. We stopped the man, and I told him that I did not want to see him near the village again, and if I did, I would arrest him and turn him over to the National Police. He and his prostitute left in a cloud of dust, but I later found out that either he or some other pimp had been successful in getting prostitutes and Marines together because near the end of our stay, my company corpsman reported that several of my men had come down with venereal diseases. While life near Da Nang was far more peaceful and pleasant for Company G than it was in the south of the province, we soon found that drugs, primarily marijuana, and prostitutes could become a problem near Da Nang and its environs. Sadly, my officers and SNCOs found that they had to worry more about drug dealers and prostitutes around Ap Phuoc Thuan hamlet than the VC. I was glad when I was called to the division headquarters to receive a new mission that would take me away from the peaceful hamlet of Ap Phuoc Thuan.

The major from the division G-3, who met me the first day our company arrived at Hill 327, visited our position after a week of fruitless patrols and told me it was pretty obvious that there were no enemy forces near our current location. He decided it would be better if we moved to a new location, one where the enemy had recently launched several rockets at the division headquarters. According to the major, the enemy had launched the rockets from the eastern slope of Hill 244. He pointed to his map and gave me the grid coordinates where he wanted me to place my rifle company. At first I was incredulous when he gave me the coordinates of this new location because it was on a very steep slope and not a very likely place for the enemy to set up their rockets. I questioned the information he gave me and asked him how he arrived at the idea that this steep slope was the origin of the enemy rockets. He immediately became defensive and simply stated, "Captain, that is not important for you to know. All we want you to do is take your company and secure those grid coordinates so the enemy does not use that place again for a rocket attack." I knew the major meant well, but I felt immediately that whoever gave him the location he was pointing to on his map was wrong. I only asked him if there was any potential that the grid coordinates had been misread or the numbers reversed, but this only seemed to anger him more. Our conversation ended with his telling me, "Captain, you have your orders, now execute them." As he drove away in his jeep, I began to question the wisdom of the decision to attach me to the division headquarters. However, I had my orders, and I was determined to carry them out. Perhaps the major knew something that was not obvious to me, but I knew I would have a hard time explaining this new mission to my platoon commanders.

On September 7, we left Ap Phuoc Thuan hamlet and marched a mile west along a trail that led to the village of Ap Doi La. There we found Route 14, a one-lane gravel road that led north to join Highway 1 near Da Nang City. We marched northeast along Route 14 until we came to the pass between Hills 244 and 364. There we found the ruins of a Buddhist shrine and a trail leading up a steep ridgeline to the summit of Hill 244. Because the ridgeline was so narrow and steep, we could only move in single file and at a slow pace. I had hoped to find some level ground that was wide enough for the company to establish a perimeter, but this was impossible.

At the top of Hill 244 was an artillery observation post manned by a Marine corporal and three other Marines. Their job was to maintain continuous observation of the area around the hill for any enemy rocket or mortar attacks and to report the enemy's firing location so counterbattery fires could be brought in on the enemy. When we had struggled up the trail halfway to the summit, the Marine corporal met us and told us that there was no place on the trail where we could set up a normal defensive perimeter. Indeed, he said there was no place large enough for even a squad to occupy. With this information, I decided we would dig in on each side of the trail and form a perimeter 200 meters long and only 10 meters wide, with two squad-size security outposts north and south of our perimeter and a few listening posts 100 meters on the western and eastern slopes of the ridgeline. I did not like our defensive posture, but I knew it would be next to impossible for any enemy force to attack us on this steep ridgeline. Despite its limitations, I reconciled myself to the fact that this was the best we could do for now.

Since it was getting dark and the company needed to take some time to dig in, I decided to postpone our investigation of the suspected rocket-launching site the G-3 major had pointed out on his map. Instead, I decided to wait until the next morning, when I knew it would be easier to negotiate the steep terrain. As dusk settled in, I took a moment to look out in every direction. To the north was the summit of Hill 244, dark and forbidding, but to the south, east and north I had an unobstructed view of all the terrain within miles. Below us the lights in the villages, hamlets, and farms twinkled, and to the east we could see the bright lights of Da Nang City and the ships in the bay. We also had a very good view of the air base and the aircraft taking off and landing. There was no doubt that we occupied a commanding piece of terrain guarding one of the main approaches to Da Nang City.

At first light on September 8, I followed the 2nd platoon down the steep, cliff-like east side of the ridgeline until we came to the grid coordinates that the G-3 major had identified as the location the enemy had used for their rocket attack on the division headquarters. After a rather treacherous and hot descent, we found nothing. I sent out patrols for 400 meters' distance from the suspected rocket-launching site and still we found nothing. As I had anticipated, we found nothing more than a very steep hillside, thick with bamboo, brush, and small trees. It was obvious that the location had never been used by the enemy to fire rockets at the division headquarters or anything else.

After searching the area all day, I radioed to the division G-3 and asked to speak to the major who had sent us to this location. I was told that he was at the officers' club eating dinner, but he would get back to me later in the evening. I decided to climb back up to the top of the ridgeline, since it was obvious there were no enemy on the side of the hill. An hour later, when I got back to the top of the ridgeline, my radio operator told me the major was on the radio and wanted to speak to me. He asked me where I was located, and I told him I was on the ridgeline with my company. He then started to berate me for not following his instructions, which were to have my company occupy the grid coordinates he had pointed to on his map and to not deviate from those instructions. When I told him we had found nothing indicating any enemy activity in the area, he angrily told me to take my company back to the location he had pointed out and remain there until further notice. When I explained to him that the area he wanted my company to "occupy" was the steep side of a cliff, he simply reiterated his demand and gave me a lecture about obeying orders. I realized I was not dealing with a rational human being, so I said I would carry out his orders immediately, but I intended to leave a security element on the ridgeline protecting my company below it. He agreed. I knew his demand was ludicrous, so I decided I would obey his instructions but modify them to suit the situation. Instead of taking my entire company down the slope, I took my radio operator and a fire team with me and descended the hill, arriving at the location the major insisted we "occupy" well after last light. The six of us simply huddled together that night, sitting with our backs against the steep slope, trying to find a comfortable position so we could sleep when not on watch. Each hour, I sent in a position report, saying we were "all secure." The Marines with me thought I was crazy, but I was not going to explain to them why we were doing such a foolish thing.

The next morning, the major from the G-3 radioed me to ask if I was where he wanted me to be, and I told him, honestly, that my CP group and I were located exactly where he wanted us to be. I did not tell him that I had kept the rest of my company on the ridgeline where they were safer, more comfortable, and better employed. The next day, the 9th, I left Hill 244 and caught a ride at the base of the hill from a passing Marine jeep that was heading in the direction of the division CP. When the driver dropped me off at the division headquarters, I demanded to see the G-3 of the division. When I told him about what I had done the previous night, sitting on the side of a cliff, he listened for a moment and then asked me to show him on the G-3 map where I had spent the night. After I showed him the location, he remained silent for a moment and then he turned to me and told me to keep my company on the ridgeline where they were now and to send out patrols along the north side of Route 14. He then asked if my company needed any hot chow, and I said it would be greatly appreciated since it had been a long time since we had had any hot food. That evening, waiting for us at the bottom of the ridgeline near the destroyed Buddhist shrine, was a Marine jeep with a trailer loaded with vat cans of hot food and several water cans filled with cold water. Rather than lug the heavy vat cans up the ridgeline, I had the company come down a platoon at a time to eat. That evening I sent a message to the G-3 colonel thanking him for arranging the hot meal and cold water—and in my heart thanking him for changing our mission to reflect the realities of our situation.

During the next few days, we sent out patrols, but we did not see any enemy activity. I spent a lot of my time on the ridgeline using my binoculars to scan vast stretches of terrain to my west and south. From my position I could see for miles, almost all the way to An Hoa. In some ways, sitting on the ridgeline using my binoculars to search for enemy activity reminded me of my days as a reconnaissance team leader. However, there was one big difference—I did not see a single enemy soldier, only the daily routine of a province that looked very peaceful and secure. Had it not been for the occasional sound of distant artillery fire, it was difficult to believe there was a war being fought. From my OP, I was reminded again of the intense beauty of South Vietnam. From the green-blue waters of the East China Sea to my east, to the black-grey mountains to my west, to the multihued green of the rice paddies and tree lines to the south, everywhere I looked, I saw a country as scenic and as beautiful as any on earth. I could not help but think that if ever a country deserved peace and a chance for democracy, South Vietnam certainly did.

Around the middle of the month, I received a guard mail envelope from my company headquarters at An Hoa Combat Base. It contained orders for a five-day R&R to Hong Kong. I was both surprised and a bit unhappy over these orders because I did not want to leave my company for five days, especially when we were under operational control of the division. I radioed the company first sergeant at An Hoa and asked him if there was some mistake since I did not remember asking for R&R. He informed me that a quota had come in for several R&Rs, and the orders were assigned based upon the time a person had been in-country. Since I had been in-country ten months, he thought I was overdue for R&R, and he did not want an R&R quota to go to waste. I told him I understood, but he should have consulted me before submitting my name to regiment. Now, I had only a few days before I was to report to the Da Nang Air Base, which left me little time to prepare the company for my absence. I told the first sergeant to send the executive officer out to our position so he could take over for me.

Since I was under the operational control of the 1st Marine Division and not my battalion, I decided it would be prudent to ask the G-3 colonel if I should take the R&R, or would he prefer I remain with the company. He told me that I should take advantage of the R&R since things were quiet and it was a bit late to have my orders changed.

A second set of orders arrived one day after the first set arrived. These orders were issued by III MAF, and they stated that my request for a six-month extension of my tour of duty had been approved and that I was to report to the III MAF G-1 for further assignment to MACV Headquarters in Saigon. There was no mention of the PRU or any other unit in my orders, so I wondered if my request for assignment to the PRU had been approved or not. I decided to find out and again hitched a ride from the bottom of the ridgeline to the division headquarters to seek out the G-1 personnel officer and obtain some clarity as to what my next assignment would be. When I found the personnel officer, an officious and rather dour major, I immediately had an uneasy feeling. My feeling proved correct because I had no sooner approached the major's desk than he informed me that he had an opening on the division staff that needed to be filled and he was going to cancel my orders to MACV and assign me to this divisional staff position. He began to tell me that the need for "a Naval Academy graduate with a lot of in-country experience was a perfect fit for the job"; but I cut him off in midsentence and told him I wanted to request mast with the division commander immediately. Naturally, the major was not used to having his personnel decisions questioned by a junior officer, and he became quite angry. I insisted that I wanted to be assigned to MACV in Saigon because I had explicitly extended my tour of duty so I could serve with the PRU, and nothing else would do. He told me I was being "obstinate and selfish," but I held my ground and began to get up to seek out the commanding general's office, when he told me to sit down and began mumbling something about seeing his boss about my orders. He left the room for a minute and then returned to tell me he was endorsing my orders to MACV, but he thought I was making a big mistake by turning down his offer to work on the division staff. He told me I would be detached on October 1 and that I should expect to hear from MACV concerning my transportation to Saigon. I thanked him and left his office.

When I got back to my perch on the ridgeline, I told my officers and SNCOs that I would be leaving them on September 30, shortly after I returned from my R&R in Hong Kong. I then radioed the battalion on Hill 65 and informed Lt. Col. Bowen about the need to have a replacement for me by the end of the month. He told me he had received a copy of my orders and was aware of the departure date. He asked me if I had any recommendation for my replacement, and I told him either Lt. Dennis Storm or Lt. Robert Conti would be good choices, since both had served in the company and both were highly respected by everyone for their tactical ability and leadership skills. Since I was due to go on R&R in a few days, he said he would send me my replacement before I left on R&R so the officer would have some time to "snap in" with me and make a smooth transition at the end of the month. An hour later, he told me Lt. T.R. Woolens would be my replacement and would be at my position the next day. I had no knowledge of Lt. Woolens, but when he arrived I was delighted with Lt. Col. Bowen's selection, since it was obvious from the moment I met him that he was a superior officer in all respects. He and I spent the next few days going over everything he needed to know to take command of Company G. When I left for R&R on September 20, I had every confidence that Lt. Woolens would be able to successfully lead my company.

As I was waiting in the outdoor marshalling area of the Da Nang Air Base to board the charter aircraft that would fly me and 200 others to Hong Kong, I heard a Marine standing next to me say, "Captain, take a look at those two planes over there." I looked up just in time to see a South Vietnamese commercial airliner have its left wing clipped off by a U.S. Air Force F-4 Phantom jet. The jet continued over the runway with the pilot and naval flight officer (NFO) ejecting at low altitude just before the jet crashed into the village at the south end of the runway. The commercial airliner seemed to dip its right wing slowly to the right and begin a slow-motion roll that took it into the ground in a ball of flame off the northwest end of the runway. I was later to find out that all but one of the passengers in the Air Vietnam plane had been killed instantly. Only a small child managed to survive. Needless to say, seeing such a horrific crash did not make any of us waiting to board a plane feel very comfortable.

My flight to Hong Kong was uneventful, but as we came in for a landing at Hong Kong's Kai Tak airport, I felt a bit apprehensive upon seeing how close the buildings were to our plane. It took a skillful pilot to land at this airport due to its short runway and the close proximity of many high buildings. We taxied to the exit ramp, where we were met by customs personnel and a Navy officer who gave us a short lecture on Hong Kong and handed us some instructions on what to do if we had any problems during our stay. Inside the terminal we were assigned hotels for our five-day visit, and I was given a room at the Hong Kong Hotel, a new hotel located in Kowloon. A bus took me to the hotel, where I was told by the front desk that my room might be a bit noisy since the upper floors of the hotel were still being finished. That was an understatement—during my entire stay, the noise made by the nearly 24-hour construction project was terrific, making it almost impossible to sleep, even late at night. Still, clean sheets and hot water went a long way in assuaging any sense of discomfort, so I did not complain and remained in my noisy abode for the entire five days.

Each day, I signed up with the hotel's concierge to take a tour bus to various sites in and around Hong Kong, and each evening I went to one of Hong Kong's best restaurants to eat the kind of meals I could never get in South Vietnam. I went to the famous Jimmy's Kitchen twice and ordered their biggest New York-cut steak. I also went to several Chinese restaurants in Kowloon and on Hong Kong Island, often taking the ferry and cabs to get to these culinary destinations. Unfortunately, on my second day in Hong Kong, I developed a case of gastroenteritis and an accompanying fever, which tended to limit my mobility and enjoyment, but the hotel sent a doctor to my room, and he gave me some antibiotics that helped me get over my illness in 24 hours. Since I only weighed 155 pounds, down from my normal weight of 180, I did not take advantage of the many excellent tailors in Hong Kong, but I did have a pair of shoes custom made for me and delivered to my hotel room the day after I was fitted in the shoe shop. Those shoes were the product of true craftsmen and lasted for 30 years. As I looked around Hong Kong, I thought of South Vietnam and how different that country could be if it had the same chances that Hong Kong had. Hong Kong was a beautiful city with a vibrant, entrepreneurial population—in my mind, the perfect model for Asian capitalism and the benefits that accrue to a people and city committed to a market economy. The British ran the colony efficiently and benignly, a difficult task given the problems China was having with their Great Proletarian Cultural Revolution just across the border. While I was riding in a taxicab, I noticed the driver had a copy of Mao Tse-tung's *Little Red Book* prominently displayed on his cab's dashboard where I could easily see it. I wondered if he was a communist or not, or perhaps this display was meant to show the visiting American his disdain for my country. I suppressed my desire to do violence to the driver and opted instead to forego the normal tip.

When I left Hong Kong on September 25, I did not realize that four years later on a future trip to Hong Kong I would meet the girl I would fall in love with and eventually marry, Sarah Zaman. Because I found Sarah in Hong Kong, it has always been my favorite city in Asia and a place I have a strong emotional tie to.

Upon my return to Da Nang, I found out that I was to fly to Saigon on September 1 aboard an Air America flight and check into the Duc Hotel in Saigon, where I would await further instructions. There was an air of mystery when the personnel officer at division told me this information. I knew that Air America was the CIA's private airline, and few U.S. military personnel ever flew on one of their planes, a fact that intrigued me since I had expected the Marine Corps or the Air Force to fly me to my new job. I again asked the personnel officer if he knew if I was being assigned to the PRU program, and he said he did not know and he did not have any interest in "talking to the spooks."

On September 30, I gathered up my meager possessions, said goodbye to my company, turned over command to Lt. Woolens, and walked down the ridgeline for the last time to Route 14. I was met by a jeep from division headquarters, which took me to the division billeting office on Hill 327. There I checked in, grabbed a cot, took a shower, had my orders endorsed by the G-1, and spent a leisurely evening in the officers' club watching a movie, having a few drinks, and chatting with Mai Ly and Dien. They asked me if I was going home, and I told them I was going to Saigon. They joked and said I must have a girlfriend there, but I confidently replied, "Not yet," which provoked several comments from them about how difficult it would be for me to find any girls willing to have me. After a few minutes mocking and teasing me, my friends asked me what my new job would be, and I told them, in all honesty, that I did not know yet. They giggled and looked at me like I was crazy, but both knew me well enough not to pry. The next day, I went to the Da Nang Air Base and found the small terminal used by Air America, where an attractive young Vietnamese woman in an Air America uniform took my orders and gave me a boarding pass for the next flight to Saigon. Within an hour I was flying south toward the capital of South Vietnam and a new chapter in my life, one that would involve mystery, danger, and challenges I never expected.

But before I relate that story, allow me to tell you about the former Viet Cong guerrilla who became my friend and taught me many valuable lessons about how and why a young peasant joined the ranks of "revolutionary fighters."

CHAPTER 10

Qua's Story: The Life of a Viet Cong Guerrilla

"To wish for victory and yet neglect political mobilization is like wishing to go north by driving a chariot south, and the result would inevitably be to forfeit victory."
—Mao Tse-tung

One of the first people I met when I took command of Company G was a 23-year-old Kit Carson Scout named Tran Van Qua. He was part of my command group and served as a combination scout, intelligence gatherer, and interpreter for my company. I had other Kit Carson Scouts assigned to my company during this time, but Qua was the only one who was with me the entire five months I commanded my rifle company, and he was the only one I talked to in any great depth. What he told me about his life as a Viet Cong guerrilla coincided with the fragments of other conversations I had with my other Kit Carson Scouts, so his story is, in my opinion, rather representative of the kind of life a Kit Carson Scout had before rallying to the GVN side and renouncing his affiliation and loyalty to the communist cause.

The facts I present below were obtained from numerous conversations with Qua, primarily when he and I worked together at Liberty Bridge, and later when I asked him to sit down with me in front of a ruined Buddhist shrine a mile west of Hill 65 in August 1969. I was so intrigued by his story, I copied its major elements into my operations notebook. While our conversations covered many topics, the bulk of our discussions involved the genesis of his life as a VC guerrilla and how the communist system worked in his home village. His story formed my understanding of the organizational techniques used by the Lao Dong Party to mobilize and control the rural population of South Vietnam. In my next assignment with the CIA in South Vietnam, this knowledge helped me considerably.

Qua was born in 1946 in a village in the Que Son Valley of Quang Nam Province. His father was a rice farmer who owned a small plot of land barely more than a few hectares in size. On this farm the family produced enough rice and vegetables to feed the family and to have a small portion left over to sell at market and to pay taxes. The family also had a few chickens and ducks but never had enough money to buy and raise pigs. He described his family in the terms used by the communists when they wanted to classify the economic and social status of peasant families in rural South Vietnam; he said his family was "Middle Peasant." When I asked him what this meant, he told me the party classified families in the village into five categories. Those categories were: Absentee Landlords, Rich Peasants, Middle Peasants, Poor Peasants, and Landless Peasants. Much to my surprise, Qua said there were no

Kit Carson Scout Tran Van Qua.

Absentee Landlords or Landless Peasants identified in his village, a fact that made much of the communist propaganda about land reform of little importance to the people living there.

His mother was a typical peasant wife and mother who worked hard in the rice paddies each day and tended to her family with great love and care when her backbreaking labor in the paddy fields was over for the day. Qua's father, who had been a guerrilla fighter with the Viet Minh during the First Indochina War, died when Qua was about 10 years old, leaving Qua's mother with seven children to feed and no husband to help her. Fortunately for the family, Qua's eldest brother, who was seven years older than Qua, was both industrious and strong, so this older sibling was able to take over the management of the farm and serve as the head of the family. Qua loved his brother and idealized him because he was so caring and helpful to everyone in the family.

Qua's village was in an area that had been controlled by the Viet Minh during the First Indochina War against the French, and later by the Viet Cong. It was never under either French or GVN control while he was growing up. Qua said he enjoyed his early village life, even though there was a war going on somewhere in the province most of the time and his family was poor. He remembered seeing French soldiers, probably Senegalese, since he described them as "African soldiers," manning a small fort near his village, but he said there was no actual fighting in his village during the First Indochina War. He noticed a profound difference after the French defeat at Dien Bien Phu in 1954 when Vietnam was divided into North and South by the Geneva Accords. In the years following the French departure, there was a struggle between the people of his village and people who lived near the district headquarters who had sided with the French but were now on the central government's side. The people of Qua's village were sympathetic to the Viet Minh, and they resented being told what to do by these GVN bureaucrats living in a fortified compound at the district headquarters. In the late 1950s, Qua witnessed several violent episodes as the villagers resisted the imposition of a new village chief and village council. Qua would describe these resistance activities as part of the "dau tranh," or struggle movement, organized by the local communist cadres. I would hear him repeat this "dau tranh" phrase many times, as if it had some magical influence on events just by mentioning it. It was, according to Qua, part of the communist mantra and a fundamental part of his indoctrination by the VC political cadres in his village.

I asked Qua why there never was any central government, either French or GVN, in his village before the late 1950s, and he told me an old adage that I had read about in my studies of China, which says, "The emperor's edict ends at the village gate." This saying reflects the relationship between central authority and the village in a Confucian society like South Vietnam. In practical terms, it meant the central government's control extended only down to the district level while village government was left up to the villagers.

Before the VC took over administration of his village, there was a village chief and a village council made up of village elders, a system of local government that went back for over a thousand years. Qua was not certain about the evolution of his village's government, but he thought the village government came under Viet Minh control shortly after the end of World War II. When Qua was a young boy, the local village government had little impact on daily life in the village, and most of its work involved resolving family conflicts, collecting taxes, and arbitrating land disputes. However, this all changed around 1960 when Qua was 14 years old. One day, the old Viet Minh village chief was replaced by a new chief, a much

The author in the ruined Buddhist shrine at My An (2) hamlet.

younger man who was a communist party member. Qua was uncertain how this all took place; all he knew was his older brother came home one day and informed the family that a new village chief had been installed and the new chief wanted to hold a mass meeting of all the adults in the village. Qua, because of his age, was not invited to attend the meeting, but his mother, an older sister, and his older brother did attend.

When they returned, they sat down in their small hut and discussed with Qua what they had heard at the mass meeting. Qua listened intently to what his elders said, their voices rising with excitement as they each tried to remember what the new communist village chief had told them. Qua's elder brother told him that the new village chief had taken over the village administration because the old chief and the old village council were unable or unwilling to resist the imposition of President Diem's policy of organizing the rural population of Quang Nam Province into GVN-controlled, fortified hamlets, called "strategic hamlets." Qua's brother knew and respected the new village chief, so he believed him when he told the villagers that President Diem was "a puppet of the French and Americans," and Diem was determined to turn South Vietnam into an "American colony." The new village chief outlined a bold new plan for the village, based upon the Lao Dong Party's economic policy, a policy that he promised would bring a new primary school, a new health clinic, and a rural cooperative that would share farming implements among the villagers. He also said the Lao Dong Party would resist what he called "rice tax extortion" by the Diem government. The village already had a small security force and a farmers' association, both of which had been formed under the Viet Minh earlier, but the new village chief said the situation in Quang Nam Province was so critical it was now necessary to mobilize the entire population of the village, even the children, to "dau tranh" against the "evil schemes of the puppet Diem and his American masters." This new effort would be "difficult but necessary," requiring a degree of dedication and commitment never before called upon from the villagers.

The new chief said the village security force would be expanded from just a few men to a full platoon of about forty men, and the Farmers Association would now be called the Farmers Liberation Association (FLA) and expanded to include almost every farmer in the village. In addition, the women would be mobilized into a Women's Liberation Association (WLA), and the children of the village would be required to join the Youth Liberation Association (YLA). Originally membership in these organizations was restricted to only 20 percent of the people, but after a few years, just about everyone in the village would belong to one or more of these associations; no one would be allowed to opt out if recommended for membership. The new chief stressed the need for total participation by the people in the village because strength in numbers was needed to counter what he called the "schemes being hatched by the Diem regime in Saigon to subjugate the people" of South Vietnam.

According to Qua, this village chief was a very charismatic leader—tall, strong, intelligent, and highly articulate—a man everyone looked up to and readily followed. He had been a Viet Minh soldier and a member of the famous 1st VC Regiment during the First Indochina War, two things that made him a "hero" in the eyes of most of the villagers and gave him a great deal of credibility when he talked about events outside the village. Qua also thought this man had left the village and gone to North Vietnam when the French were defeated in 1954 and Vietnam partitioned, but had returned a year or two before he was installed as the new village chief.

Shortly after the mass meeting, Qua was invited to join the village YLA, along with most of the other teenage children in the village. His older brother was invited to join the FLA and also to serve as a member of the expanded village security platoon. Qua remembered how proud and envious he was of his older brother because his brother had been given an old Japanese rifle and ten rounds of ammunition by the new village security chief, a young man only a few years older than his brother. Because Qua's mother was a widow, the new village chief directed that she did not have to pay any taxes, a gesture that won the gratitude of Qua's family for the Lao Dong Party and made life easier for them. Qua's mother joined the WLA, and soon became an active member of this mass civic organization, often volunteering to help organize "dau tranh" struggle demonstrations against the GVN district chief.

Although everyone in Qua's family belonged to a communist-led mass organization, no one in his family was a member of the Lao Dong (communist) Party until 1963, when his older brother became the first person in his family to achieve full membership in the party. In fact, according to Qua, there were only a dozen or so full party members in the village, a village with a population of just under 2,000 people. The only party members Qua knew of were the village chief (who was also the village party chairman), the security chief, the party secretary, the finance-economy chief, and the heads of the mass organizations. Qua also thought there were probably a few "secret" party members in the village whose identities were known only to the party chairman and the security chief. A number of other villagers were what Qua called "probationary members" of the party—people who aspired to be full party members but had either not achieved the requisite level of political sophistication or had a class background that required a longer period of evaluation before they could join the ranks of the Lao Dong Party. Qua identified a poor class background as one that included family members working for the Diem government, rich landowners, and the bourgeoisie or merchant classes. A poor class background did not preclude party membership, according to Qua, but it made it far more difficult and time-consuming to achieve. Qua said he achieved probationary membership in the party after two party members recommended him for membership, but he remained in probationary status for nearly a year before achieving full party membership in 1965.

I asked Qua what motivated him to become a member of the Lao Dong Party, and he told me he aspired to party membership because he wanted to gain the respect and prestige party membership conferred. He saw how his brother was respected by the people in the village, and he wanted to be treated in a similar manner. In order to enhance his chances for party membership, Qua volunteered to join the village security platoon because he thought this would make it easier for the party to accept him for membership. He was only 17 years old when he became a local village guerrilla, or as he put it, "a revolutionary fighter."

I was a bit incredulous about Qua's contention that there were only twenty to thirty party members in his village, since I had previously thought that every guerrilla with the VC was a party member and that any member of the mass organizations had to be a party member also. Qua corrected my thinking on this, telling me, "The party is the head of the revolution and the people are the body, but not everyone has the traits and abilities to be a party member. Only those who have the proper class background and the proper political thinking can be a party member. These people are rare." I asked him what percentage of people in his village were actual party members, and he told me no more than 5 percent, at the most. He also said that the party was not always able to fill every party position in the village, a situation that often resulted in party members' occupying more than one position. Qua said the party was very security-conscious, and for this reason the party was highly selective when it came to party membership. He was told that in the late 1950s the party was not as careful in vetting applicants for party membership, and this led to the Diem regime infiltrating of many of the party chapters, seriously damaging the party organization. He also said that every party member was given a party pseudonym that was always used in written communication so "government spies and police" would not know the true identities of the party members if party documents fell into the hands of the Saigon government. By keeping the party leadership small and difficult to identify, the VCI in Qua's village made it difficult for their enemies to infiltrate their organization and neutralize them.

I asked Qua about the education level of the VCI cadres in his village, and he told me that few had more than three years of formal education; however, they made up for their lack of formal education by personal study and training classes provided by the party. He added that the most educated member of the party in his village was the party secretary, who had completed primary school and two years of secondary school. Qua explained that the party secretary was not a very powerful individual in his village, despite his important-sounding title. In the case of his village's party secretary, the individual chosen for this position was simply someone in the village with the proper class background who could read and write well. Someone was needed to read and interpret party literature and directives, and to draft the many reports required by the VC district and province party organization, so it was necessary to have a person with a fair degree of education filling the role of the village party secretary. Although Qua was very intelligent and had mastered English in less than a year of exposure to it with the U.S. Marines, he had only a few years of formal schooling, and that ended when he was 12 years old. He did not view his lack of education as a stumbling block to advancement in the party infrastructure, however. Like many rural peasants I encountered in South Vietnam, he seemed to hold city-dwelling, well-educated people in contempt, often referring to them as "lazy, arrogant turtles," or using Marine jargon, "shit birds."

I was curious about the level of knowledge Qua had obtained about communist doctrine and whether or not he had ever studied the writings of Marx, Lenin, or Mao Tse-tung. Qua's answer to this question surprised me, but in the following months his answer would be echoed by many enemy POWs and Hoi Chanhs I would speak to. He said that he had never read a single Marxist book, but he had read some lectures given by Ho Chi Minh and other leaders of the Lao Dong Party, as well as some NLF training materials that contained portions of the communist doctrine.

Since I had read many of the works of these communist luminaries, I asked Qua a few questions about the main points these writers had made to see if he acquired some knowledge through other forms of education, such as study meetings or lectures. For instance, I asked him what the communist definition of the term "profit" was, and he not only was unable to define the word in Marxist language, he was unable to define it at all. He used communist terminology, but he had no real understanding of the meaning of many of the terms he used. At times, he seemed to be simply repeating phrases he had heard but had never understood. It was evident from many of his comments that he had been exposed to some of the arguments made in Lenin's work on imperialism and Mao Tse-tung's writings about land reform and taxation, but his knowledge was extremely shallow and unsophisticated.

Since he seemed to lack any motivation based upon a theoretical understanding of

Marxism, I asked him why he joined the VC. After a long pause and a bit of deep reflection, he told me:

> I joined the VC because I was young and I wanted to belong to the revolution like my brother and friends. I also hated strangers coming to my village and telling us what to do, especially the people working at the district headquarters. I guess I believed the propaganda I heard from the party cadres about President Diem and how he was suppressing the Buddhists in Da Nang; but to be honest, the biggest reason I joined the VC was because I wanted to be respected the way the party members in my village were respected.

I would hear an answer like this from many of the enemy I interviewed in the coming year. What many Americans failed to understand during the war was the Lao Dong Party provided a vehicle for upward mobility and esteem for many rural people who normally would have no chance whatsoever to achieve high status in their communities. The Lao Dong Party exploited this desire on the part of the disadvantaged and provided a system based on merit for advancement, but only if the person subjected himself to party discipline and dedicated himself to a life of danger as a revolutionary.

I knew that two nationalist political parties were active in Quang Nam Province, and that these two parties, the Dai Viet and the VNQDD, were often in conflict with each other over who would rule the province. When I asked Qua about them, he looked at me quizzically and said, "I have never heard of these parties. The only political parties I know of are the Viet Minh and the Lao Dong. Those other parties must be in Saigon." His answer told me that no other political party had ever reached down into the rural area where Qua grew up. In his village and many other villages in the province, the communist Lao Dong Party had a free hand. There was simply no alternative to the VC in his village. I was beginning to see that the communists were not being challenged in the villages for political control of the population and the enemy was winning by default, at least in large parts of rural Quang Nam Province. The fact that the Lao Dong Party was the only mass-based political party in South Vietnam was a huge advantage for them and an equally huge disadvantage for the GVN. Even the two largest, non-communist parties in South Vietnam, the Dai Viet and the VNQDD, were quite small, with no more than a few thousand members in the entire country.

Since I was intrigued by the evident control of the Lao Dong Party over the rural peasants in Quang Nam Province, I asked Qua to explain what techniques were employed by the party to mobilize the population of his village and why they were so effective. What he told me gave me a deep and abiding respect for the organizational abilities of the VCI. Qua explained that the VCI in his village used the mass organizations, such as the FLA, WLA, and YLA, to achieve every goal set by the party. When I asked him to give me a concrete example of how this worked, he told me the following:

> One day in 1963, when I first joined the security platoon, my chief came to me and told me to get two other guerrillas and come with him to the house of a farmer who had refused to leave his fields with his two sons to dig bunkers for a battalion of the 1st VC Regiment. He explained to me that the battalion would be staying in the village for a few days and hiding in the bunkers being constructed by the villagers. It was a lot of work and the village party chairman wanted a working party of over 200 people to do this work and to do it at night when government spies and aircraft could not observe it being done. This same farmer was always complaining about having to give up his rice tax to the finance-economy chief, so I was not surprised when I heard the farmer was complaining about leaving his fields to dig bunkers. We considered him selfish and stubborn.

When we arrived at the man's house, we saw the village finance-economy chief standing in a crowd of villagers assembled in front of the house. Sitting on the porch was the party chairman, the stubborn farmer, and his two teenage sons. The party chairman was talking in a friendly way with the man, trying to convince him to do his "revolutionary duty" and to not think in a selfish way. He told the man that if he refused to work on the bunkers, someone else would have to send more people from their family, which would create "a hardship" for that family. He stressed that he had known the man for all his life and knew he was a good man, so he could not understand why he would not help his neighbors when they were in such need. He tried to make the man feel guilty. He pointed to the large, and growing, crowd of villagers standing in his front yard, many of whom were yelling phrases like "support your neighbors" and "do your duty." The effect was overwhelming, and soon the resistance of the man began to crumble. His wife came out and begged him to reconsider and work on the village project of building bunkers. Faced with an overwhelming number of his neighbors exhorting him to comply with the party chairman's request to provide labor for the project, the man succumbed and agreed to spend the next few nights digging bunkers for the mobile VC battalion. He knew this work would tire him and force him to neglect his fields, but faced with so much organized opposition from his neighbors, he felt helpless to do anything else but comply.

I asked Qua what would have happened if the man still did not comply. Qua said people rarely stood up to such mass action; but if they did, then there were other things that could be done to force compliance—and all the villagers knew this. When I asked for specific actions that could be taken, Qua said that violence was used but only rarely. Instead, the party leadership would organize continuous "dau tranh" against the man and his family using other family members and the mass organizations to convince the man to change his mind. If that did not work, groups of neighbors from the mass associations would take turns going to the man's house and demanding he change his mind. If that failed, the man and his family would be forced to attend a group meeting, usually led by the head of one of the mass associations, and then forced to confess to "incorrect thinking," or "right deviationism," or some other social crime against the community. Qua said that it was extremely rare for violence to be used unless there was a "collective decision" made at a large struggle meeting that such a drastic measure was necessary. Even then, violent punishment normally had to be approved by the district Lao Dong Party chapter before it could be carried out. Qua explained that the reluctance to impose physical punishment or death upon villagers was based upon a practical understanding of the village. Since most people in the village had familial connections and the use of violence could drive a wedge between these families and foster grudges, the party felt violence would only thwart the objective of the party to mobilize every individual in the village under the party's leadership. In practical political terms, it did not make sense to resort to violence unless absolutely necessary.

While violence was viewed by the party as a last resort against people living in the village, it was used more often when the party itself was threatened by outsiders. For instance, if a GVN spy was uncovered in the village or a GVN militia unit was inserted into the village, violence was the normal course of action in dealing with this threat to the primacy of the party. Any representative of the GVN was viewed as a severe threat to the VCI, and for this reason violence was a far more common reaction to these external threats to party control. Any GVN presence in the village was considered "a poisonous weed" that needed to be rooted out immediately, even if it meant extreme forms of public violence.

Qua admitted to me that once he was forced to take part in the killing of a GVN pediatric nurse from the district health clinic. She had made the mistake of visiting his village to tend to some pregnant women without an armed escort. According to Qua, this murder was carried out "legally," since the woman was brought before a mass meeting and forced to confess she was a government spy. I asked Qua if he thought she was really a spy, and he said it made no difference since she was "an agent of the Diem clique and the Americans," or so the village's party chairman claimed. She was shot in the head by the security platoon chief in front of a crowd of over 500 villagers and then buried in a garbage pit. While Qua said the execution was carried out by his chief, I had a strong feeling that he had carried out this murder himself, and he carried some guilt about his participation in it.

Since Qua had mentioned President Diem often, I asked him about how the assassination of President Diem in November 1963 was viewed by him and his fellow villagers. He said that when news of the murder of President Diem reached his village, it was a source of great rejoicing at first, but it soon became apparent that it was also a problem for the VC. All of the propaganda used by the party had stressed how evil President Diem was and how he was a puppet of the Americans. With Diem gone, the party lost a major motivation for mobilizing the rural peasants. People began to question the party's contention that Diem was a puppet of the Americans. Several people actually questioned the party position on Diem by saying it made no sense for the Americans to kill President Diem if he was their puppet. Qua referred to Diem as a "true nationalist," and he was not convinced by the VC propaganda that Diem was a bad leader. Qua admitted that "many people" in Quang Nam Province thought well of Diem, even if he was not popular in his village.

Qua believed what the party told him would happen once Diem was deposed—the revolution would immediately succeed and the country would be unified under the party's leadership. He was disappointed and surprised when the country did not immediately rise up and embrace the revolution. His platoon commander held several study meetings with the security platoon to go over why the death of Diem did not lead to a general uprising of the population as the party had been telling everyone. Qua was not convinced by the answers given to him, but, like everyone else in his village, he and his neighbors agreed for the need to redouble their efforts to bring about the eventual success of the revolution. He could tell from the party's study materials that they were worried about a lack of support for the VC once Diem was removed. In fact, Qua admitted that a lot of the enthusiasm for the revolution began to wane in the months after Diem's death, and some people actually abandoned the party in 1964 and went over to the GVN.

Until 1965 the GVN had been unable or unwilling to really challenge the control of Qua's village. On several occasions ARVN units made sweeps that took them through his village, but they never attempted to insert a stable GVN presence after these sweeps. When the ARVN troops returned to their bases around Da Nang City, the local party cadres would return from their hiding places in the Que Son Mountains and re-establish control. Qua told me the party feared the strategic hamlet program of President Diem since it greatly complicated the ability of party members to function inside these hamlets, forcing them to live outside and away from their families. His hamlet was never included in the program, but all of his party member colleagues feared that this might happen. With the death of Diem, the strategic hamlet program withered, much to the relief of Qua's VC leaders.

I wanted to know what a local VC guerrilla's primary mission was, since I often found it perplexing that they never seemed to stand and fight like an NVA unit would when confronted by a Marine unit. Qua told me I thought like most Marines and did not understand that a local VC guerrilla's purpose in life was far different from the NVA soldier's job. He said:

> Our village guerrilla platoon had one primary mission and that was to protect the party cadres. When an ARVN or Marine unit came near our village, our mission was to delay them until our cadres could escape. We would fire a few shots and run off in one direction while the cadres ran off in another. We did not really consider it our mission to defend the village since we knew that was impossible given our small numbers and inadequate supply of ammunition. We could only delay an ARVN or Marine unit. We also could plant mines and booby traps along likely avenues of escape so any people following us or our cadres would be killed or wounded by these devices. Once in a while we might try a night ambush, but this was very rare since we often took heavy casualties when we did so. Real fighting was done by mobile VC or NVA units because they had the numbers and firepower needed to fight ARVN and U.S. Marine units.

Like most Marines, I was interested in developing better ways to defeat the VC, so I asked Qua what he thought the major weakness of the VC was. He replied very quickly, as if he had often thought about this same question many times in the past:

> Our biggest weakness is supply. The revolutionary forces, including the NVA units, never have enough equipment, ammunition, and medical supplies, and this weakens our fighting ability. We could always rely on the finance-economy cadres in the villages to provide us with rice and other food items, but we never had enough of the other stuff we needed. In 1966, I was transferred from my village security platoon to a mobile VC battalion because they needed replacements badly. I thought this mobile unit would have more supplies since it was called upon to fight regular ARVN and Marine units, but it was the same thing—we never had enough supplies, especially ammunition and crew-served weapons like machine guns, recoilless rifles, and mortars. Everything like that had to come down from North Vietnam, and the NVA units had the highest priority for these supplies. We always had to do with less, and it cost us dearly. You may find this hard to believe, but there were many times when only half of the men in our battalion had weapons. Even if we had weapons, we seldom had enough ammunition for our operations unless we were to take part in a major attack, and it often took months for us to store up enough ammunition for a major fight. That was a serious problem since even if we had some success, we ran out of ammunition before we could exploit the success. We were always told to make every shot count since most of us went into battle with only thirty to forty rounds of ammunition for our rifles. You can't fight for very long when you only have thirty to forty rounds of ammunition. Once you run out of ammunition, all you can do is run away.

One hot evening in late August, as a dark, red sun slowly drifted behind the mountains to the west of my company CP, Qua came over to where I was sitting. I could tell he was in the mood for conversation. We had been conducting patrols west of Hill 65, protecting the farmers harvesting rice so it would not fall into the hands of the VC tax collectors. We also provided security for the refugee camp nearby. I had established my CP a hundred meters north of the refugee camp near an old Buddhist shrine that was pockmarked with numerous bullet holes. While my company occupied this defensive position, it had become somewhat of a ritual for Qua, Gunny Coffer, my radiomen, and my lead corpsman to sit around and talk until the sun went down.

As Qua approached me, I noticed he had his Cheshire Cat smile on his face, the smile that he often displayed when he had conned a Marine out of some cigarettes. It was getting dark and my radio operator was calling in my night activities to battalion, a nightly task that kept the battalion informed about the locations of my listening posts, ambush sites, and night patrol routes. I had just finished eating a can of C-ration beans and franks when Qua showed up. He eyed the can of C-ration fruit cocktail I had been saving for dessert, so I motioned him over and offered it to him. He readily accepted it since it was his favorite C-ration food. His smile broadened as he eagerly wolfed down the sweet fruit and syrup concoction. When he finished the fruit cocktail, I decided to ask Qua why he decided to rally to the GVN and abandon his life as a VC guerrilla. I knew this was a delicate subject for Qua, so I waited a few minutes while he took out one of the cigarettes he had just cajoled from a nearby Marine and lit it using the C-ration matches he always kept in his boot top. We were both sitting on a pair of 5-gallon water cans in front of the abandoned Buddhist shrine, staring in silence at the mountains as a blood red sun sank behind them. I heated a canteen cup of C-ration coffee while Qua took the first of many long drags on his cigarette.

When I thought the time was right, I posed my question to Qua. He did not answer immediately, but instead held his cigarette in his calloused fingers and stared at it as if the answer to my question could be read in the cigarette's smoke. I was not sure he would answer me since I knew this matter was one Qua felt uncomfortable talking about. I had seen his reaction previously when a Marine asked the same question, and invariably it was one of discomfort and annoyance. Qua was a very proud young man, and he did not like to be questioned on his motives for anything, but he was most sensitive when anyone asked him about his reason for leaving the ranks of the VC. His answer so impressed me, I wrote down what he said in my notebook:

> I was tired of running, of being chased like an animal. At least when I was a local guerrilla in my home village I could get some rest and some good food. As a VC soldier in a mobile battalion, I never seemed to have any rest at all. We were always on the run and always hungry. No matter where we went, the artillery and the bombs followed us, even in the mountains and during the monsoon season. We had to move all the time, never staying in one place for long. We would dig bunkers one day and then move a day later. We did this over and over again. No matter where we went, the Marines or the South Vietnamese soldiers followed us and made us move again. We were never safe. It was awful. I was going crazy.

He went on to explain that two events in 1967 finally pushed him to the point where he could no longer deal with his life as a VC guerrilla. The first event was the death of his older brother. His brother was an established party member by then and had become the chairman of the village finance-economy committee, a very important position and one with a lot of stress. His brother had been very happy when he was accepted as a full member of the party; it was something he had strived for ever since the VC took over control of his village. Qua's mother was proud of the elder brother also. But things began to go bad for him in early 1967 when he was told to collect a large amount of rice and dried fish to put in a cache for an upcoming operation by the 2nd NVA Division in the Que Son Valley. The rice harvest that year was not good, and many of the villagers did not want to contribute their share to the cache. Qua's brother was criticized by the district party committee for failing to fulfill his responsibilities on time, and he had to endure a self-criticism meeting before the assembled people of his village. This hurt him deeply since he felt the criticism was unfair.

While this was going on, Qua was away with his VC battalion in Quang Tin Province and completely unaware that his brother was in trouble with the party. Although his brother was not physically punished, he was made to go to extra lengths to obtain his village's quota of rice and fish, and then to transport it to an NVA base camp near Antenna Valley. He left with a transport party of twenty young men and teenagers from the village and headed off toward the NVA base camp. On the way back from the base camp, the transport party was ambushed, and his brother was killed, along with half of the men with him. Their bodies were left on the trail where they died.

When news of his brother's death reached his village, Qua's heartbroken mother managed to get a message to Qua in the mountains informing him of the sad news. When Qua received the news, he was overcome with grief and severely depressed. All he could think about was how much he had loved his brother and how sad everyone in his family felt over his loss. Now his beloved brother was gone forever. He began to blame the party for his brother's death since the party insisted that his brother take the risk of transporting the rice in broad daylight into an area where the enemy was known to be strong. Qua asked permission to take leave to see his mother, but the political officer in his battalion denied his request and scolded him for requesting leave from the battalion on the eve of an operation in the Que Son Valley.[1]

A second event finally convinced Qua that he should abandon his life as a VC guerrilla and rally to the GVN. This event occurred in late 1967, and it involved Qua's anger with the way the NVA treated his local VC unit. Prior to joining the mobile VC battalion, Qua only had a very cursory exposure to the NVA, since most of his battalion's activities were in an area where the NVA seldom operated. However, during the battles that took place in the summer of 1967 in the Que Son Valley, his battalion was assigned to support the 1st VC Regiment, a subordinate unit of the NVA 2nd Division, and one that had originally been manned with southerners but now was almost entirely made up of North Vietnamese soldiers due to severe attrition. His exposure to these soldiers from North Vietnam angered him. He felt they treated his southern comrades like children and had no respect for them at all. Qua, using the vernacular he learned from his Marine friends, said, "They gave us the shit jobs and always accused us of being lazy."

Qua's VC battalion had suffered very severe casualties during operations in Quang Tin Province in 1965 and 1966, so he and his southern colleagues were in no mood to take this criticism from the soldiers from North Vietnam. Qua's battalion should have had a strength of over 500 men, but due to heavy fighting it was reduced to fewer than 100 men by the summer of 1967. The NVA kept complaining that the VC units, like Qua's, were unable to find enough recruits from the southern population; this was a drain on the NVA, who had to assign men from the NVA units to make up for the lack of southern recruits. He summed up his feeling toward the NVA quite succinctly: "We just did not like the arrogance and the criticism of the NVA."

It all came to a boil in November 1967 when the 2nd NVA Division was forced to retreat from the Que Son Valley back to their bases in the mountains to the west. Due to the heavy casualties suffered by the 2nd NVA Division that summer, Qua was told his VC battalion would be disbanded and its soldiers would be used as replacements for the 2nd NVA Division. Qua did not know it at the time, but the 2nd NVA Division was so beat up from Operations Union I and II that the communist leadership was worried that the division would not have enough men for the 1968 Tet Offensive. Since plans for the Tet Offensive called for the 2nd NVA to play a major role in the attack on Da Nang City and several district headquarters in Quang Nam Province, a decision had been made to take all the southerners they could find to fill their depleted NVA battalions. This decision had the effect of eliminating most of the mobile units in the province made up of southerners.

10. Qua's Story

Unlike the South Vietnamese provinces in the southern three military regions, Quang Nam Province fell directly under the control of the North Vietnamese government's Front 4, so all the VC units in Quang Nam took their orders directly from the North Vietnamese government and not through some entity like the Central Office for South Vietnam (COSVN). Qua resented this since it always seemed to him that the northerners treated him and his southern colleagues with disdain. Whether this was true or not, Qua said he and his southern compatriots felt the North Vietnamese did not appreciate their contributions. Qua insisted his fellow VC felt the same way he did. The decision to disband his VC battalion and absorb the soldiers from his unit into the 2nd NVA Division did not sit well with Qua or the other men in his battalion. According to Qua, several of his friends decided they were not going to obey this order, and they began to actively explore the possibility of deserting. They were tired, hungry, and sick after over a year of constantly moving many miles each day to escape the ravages of ARVN and U.S. ambushes and supporting arms. They did not look forward to another monsoon in the mountains, especially if it would be under NVA command.

On their way from the Que Son Mountains to a new location in the mountains of western Quang Nam Province, they were told they would join elements of the 31st NVA Regiment. As they approached the mountains, Qua saw some Chieu Hoi leaflets lying along the trail. These leaflets, which he had seen before but had been forbidden to read by his unit's leaders, were actually safe-conduct passes that allowed a VC to surrender safely and to be reintegrated into South Vietnamese society after a short period of re-education. Qua was suspicious of the validity of the promises made in the leaflet, but he and several of his friends were desperate, so they decided to hide the leaflets on their persons until an opportune time came to use them. This was an extremely dangerous thing for Qua and his colleagues to do since the communist cell system and the unit's political officer made it very difficult to hide such leaflets or to conspire to defect. Qua knew that once they decided to keep the leaflets, they would have to act quickly.

A few days later, their chance came. Shortly after they had arrived at a temporary base camp near the Nong Son coal mine southwest of An Hoa, Qua was shown a PF fort near the coal mine and told that an American Marine unit was located nearby. That night, he and two others from his cell decided to escape and rally to the PF unit at the coal mine. They volunteered to stand guard together and use this opportunity to abandon their posts and make their escape down a mountain trail that led to the coal mine. The three of them reached the coal mine in only a few hours, taking care to hide near the PF fort until daylight, when they thought it would be safe to surrender. When day broke, they left their rifles in some bushes and simply walked up to the PF fort, a small rectangular fort consisting of little more than an earthen berm with barbed wire strung around it, and called out to one of the PF soldiers standing guard at the entrance. Several children ran up to them at this time and surrounded them, giving Qua an odd feeling of safety since he did not think the PFs would suspect a trap if there were children with them. One of the children actually took Qua's Chieu Hoi leaflet and shook it above his head shouting, "Hoi Chuan, Hoi Chuan!" The PF guard called out to his comrades in the fort, and soon Qua and his two friends were taken into custody by the PF platoon, given food and cigarettes, and told to wait until they could be questioned by an ARVN officer from the coal mine. After a short interrogation by the ARVN officer, the three VC ralliers were taken by helicopter to An Hoa and then to a Chieu

Hoi camp somewhere else in Quang Nam Province. Qua's life as a VC ended that day, and several months later he began a new life as a Kit Carson Scout for the U.S. Marines. Ironically, Qua was in a Chieu Hoi training program when the 1968 Tet Offensive was launched, and he expressed the opinion that had he not decided to rally to the GVN, he would have surely died.

I liked Qua and valued the talents and experience he brought to his job as our scout. He knew how to talk to the local people using the Quang Nam rural vernacular. I also valued his ability to interrogate VC prisoners in such a way as to readily get them to cooperate and provide valuable information. He was taller than most Vietnamese and quite strong, with an athlete's build and reflexes, and he did not back down, even if he got into a confrontation with a much bigger U.S. Marine. He possessed a warrior's ethos, and that endeared him to the Marines he served within our company.

He was also extremely intelligent, although lacking in formal education. I am sure that in terms of IQ he was close to a genius since he was able to read and write both Vietnamese and English and to carry on an intelligent conversation with my officers and SNCOs about topics he read about in the newspapers and magazines our Marines gave him. He never lied to me or sugar-coated the truth, often emphasizing a point with profane language that he had learned from the Marines around him. Probably the two most valuable contributions he made to me were the knowledge he possessed about what motivated the majority of local farmers and his knowledge of how the VC operated in the villages of the province. Much of what he told us could not be found in any intelligence report or course of instruction; it was all firsthand knowledge that only a local boy and a VC soldier could provide. I often found him conducting informal classes for the Marines in my company about enemy booby traps, VC tactics, and the strengths and weaknesses of the communist insurgency. My Marines listened to him, and his words often had a great influence on their thinking. For instance, many Marines had been told that every South Vietnamese villager was a potential enemy and not to trust anyone other than a fellow Marine. Qua did a lot to make the Marines understand that most villagers were not their enemy, but simply people who were living under incredible stress and danger, which often made them wary of the Marines. The average villager was not ideological but practical, as Qua would explain it. Most were not committed to the communist insurgency, but they feared and respected the communists since in many cases the communists were the only functioning government they had ever known. Qua attempted to make the Marines more tolerant and understanding of the plight of the average villager in the province, and this was, in retrospect, his most valuable contribution, since it made it easier for our Marines to live and work in their environment and to treat the villagers they encountered with respect and courtesy.

I felt privileged to have known Qua, and I still think of him with affection and respect. Sadly, I do not think he fared well when the communists finally came to power in 1975. I pray that he survived and found peace in his life, wherever he is.

Chapter 11

The House on Doan Cong Bu Street

When my Air America flight from Da Nang arrived at Tan Son Nhut Air Base in Saigon, I stepped out of the plane into the blinding light and blazing heat, with absolutely no idea what to expect or even how to get to the Duc Hotel from the airport. As I was puzzling over my lack of information, a middle-aged American dressed in a khaki safari suit came over to me and asked if my name was Capt. Finlayson. I told him I was, and without introducing himself, he told me to get into his white van because he was going to drive me and another American to the Duc Hotel. As it turned out, the other American in the van was also a Marine officer, another captain from the 1st Marine Division, and we were both on our way to join the PRU—at least, that is what we thought.

After a short drive through the bustling and foul-smelling traffic of Saigon, we arrived at the Duc Hotel, a rather nondescript whitewashed building several stories high located near the Presidential Palace in the heart of the city. Unlike most hotels, however, the security around this hotel was quite impressive, with several sandbagged bunkers, a lot of barbed wire, and some very tough-looking guards checking the credentials of anyone trying to enter the building. The driver of our van escorted us into the hotel, told the desk clerk to issue us temporary passes, and then told us we would be contacted later that day with instructions for the next day's activities. Although I had already guessed it, the driver told us that the Duc Hotel was where most of the CIA personnel assigned to Saigon lived, and no other "guests" ever stayed there. It was all friendly and informative, but our short conversation in the lobby did nothing to clear up the many questions I had about what I would be doing with the PRU. However, like most Marines, the other captain and I took full advantage of the situation and found the hotel's bar, restaurant, and rooftop swimming pool, and immediately made ourselves at home. Life was too short not to take advantage of every comfort available in a war zone. After dinner that evening, I was given a note by the front desk informing me that I was to be in the lobby at 0830 sharp the next morning to meet my "transportation to the office." That night, as I drifted asleep in my clean, comfortable, and air-conditioned hotel room, I wondered if my future surroundings would be as comfortable and relaxing as the ones I had found at the Duc Hotel.

The next morning I had breakfast in the hotel's dining room and then waited in the lobby for "someone" to meet me and finally tell me what was going on. I was joined by the other Marine captain, who had received the same instructions I had the previous night, and we both spent a few minutes pondering who would meet us at 0830. At exactly 0830, we noticed a rather grim-looking Vietnamese in a tiger-striped uniform and black beret walk

The Duc Hotel, Saigon.

into the lobby and approach the front desk. After speaking to the man at the reception desk, he turned around and looked at us for a moment before slowly walking over to us. He was not tall or stocky, but he looked very tough and he did not smile. His eyes were hidden behind dark sunglasses. In fluent English, he asked to see our military ID cards, which we produced immediately. He examined them for a moment and then handed them back to us, again without smiling.

"Come with me, please," he said. I asked him where we were going, and he simply replied, again without smiling, "You will see soon." Outside, he motioned us to get into a civilian jeep that had U.S. Embassy license plates on it, and soon we were driving at breakneck speed through the streets of Saigon, which were filled with noisy, smoke-belching cyclos and motorbikes also moving at speeds that seemed to invite disaster. After a short, 10-minute ride, we stopped in front of a French colonial-style villa not far from the Presidential Palace. The address of the villa was 1 Doan Cong Bu Street. The villa looked much the same as the other villas on the street, but guarding the entrance of this villa were two heavily armed guards wearing uniforms identical to the one worn by our silent driver. Entering the front door of the villa, we found ourselves in a large, airy foyer that had several desks in the middle and some smaller rooms to the rear and to our left. On the right was a set of stairs leading to the second floor. Behind the desks in front of us were several Vietnamese in civilian clothes busily doing paperwork. We were told to wait by one of the men behind the desks while he fetched "The Tu Da" (The Major).

Soon we were being greeted warmly by a short, rather solidly built Vietnamese gentleman who had an air of complete authority about him. He introduced himself as Major

Nguyen Van Lang, the director of the PRU. He smiled broadly and shook our hands, telling us he was extremely happy that we were "visiting" Saigon and that he hoped our "long journey from Da Nang had not been too arduous." After exchanging pleasantries, Maj. Lang told us he wanted to introduce us to "some men on the second floor" who were eager to see us. We followed him up the stairs to the second floor, where he stopped before a closed door. He surprised me by knocking on the door before entering, something I did not think the commander of the PRU would be expected to do in his headquarters. The door was answered by an American in civilian clothes who ushered us into his office and told us to sit down while he fetched "The General." After we had waited nearly 30 minutes in our seats, the door to another office opened and two Americans entered: one about my age and another in his 40s. Both men were lean, about average in height, and dressed in identical civilian clothes, in this case dark slacks and white, short-sleeved shirts. They introduced themselves to us as Bob and Terry, respectively. Terry, whom Maj. Lang referred to as "The General," asked us a few questions about our background, and then he excused himself and left us with Bob and the man who had opened the door for us. I was later to find out that "Gen. Terry" was, in fact, Col. Terry Allen, USMC, and he used the rank of general as a means of dealing with American and Vietnamese bureaucrats and others who placed obstacles in his path, but respected rank, even if it was not factually accurate.

While our orders were endorsed, Bob told us he wanted to interview us separately, so one of us would have to wait in the office for an hour. I volunteered to wait while the other Marine captain went with Bob into a room across the hall. I spent an hour reading the *Stars and Stripes* newspaper and chatting with the man who had opened the door for us. Since he was in civilian clothes, I assumed he was a civilian working for the U.S. government, perhaps even a CIA agent, so I referred to him as "Sir" while speaking with him. He told me it was not necessary to call him "Sir" since he was not an officer but a U.S. Army sergeant.

When it was my turn to be interviewed, Bob brought me into a small conference room that was bare, save for a table and a few chairs. He poured two glasses of ice water, offering me one, and then he began the interview by saying, "Captain, I do not know what they told you in Da Nang, but your orders do not mean a thing to us. We, and only we, will determine if you are the right kind of military officer we want to work with the PRU. This is in no way a reflection on your abilities as a U.S. military officer, but we know from experience that not everyone is suited for the kind of work we do. As such, I need to tell you that if you do not pass this interview, you will be sent back to III MAF in Da Nang and reassigned." This news bothered me, but I managed not to say anything other than, "I understand."

For the next hour or so he engaged me in a rather strange conversation that seemed to focus more on how I felt toward the Vietnamese, both Northern and Southern, than any other topic. He would ask about my background, including such things as my religion and what part of the United States I grew up in, as well as my combat experience, but he always kept going back to the topic of the Vietnamese, often questioning me about aspects of their history and culture. Fortunately, I knew quite a bit about the history of Vietnam, having read several books on the subject. Oddly, he did not seem impressed with my experience as a reconnaissance team leader or infantry company commander.

Near the end of my interview he asked me if I had any Vietnamese friends. I told him I had several, and I took a minute or two to tell him about each one. This seemed to impress him a great deal, and he pressed me about it. I told him about Mai Ly, Dien, Mr. Smart, and

Tran Van Qua, the four Vietnamese I knew best and considered my friends. He said I was unusual in this regard, since few American military men he knew had a single Vietnamese friend, unless they had been advisors.

As the interview was coming to a close, he asked me if I was familiar with revolutionary warfare. I told him I had been fighting the VC and NVA for over twenty-three months in South Vietnam, and I had learned a great deal about the way the enemy fought from that experience. He was not impressed with this answer and said, "No, I mean do you understand how the VC control the population using their political cadres?" Thinking back to the many hours I spent reading the collected works of Mao Tse-tung and my long discussions with my former Kit Carson Scout, Tran Van Qua, I began to tell him about my understanding of how the communists in China and the VC cadres in Quang Nam Province organized the entire rural population using mass-based social organizations and skillful propaganda to achieve their objectives. I could tell Bob was very interested in what I was talking about, and often he would nod his head in approval after I made a certain point. He complimented me on my attitude toward the Vietnamese people and my knowledge of communist revolutionary warfare, but he ended our interview by handing me a book by Douglas Pike called *Viet Cong*, instructing me to take the book with me back to my hotel and to read it before reporting back to him the next morning. As if to spur me to forego the pleasures of Saigon and concentrate on reading the book, he told me he would quiz me on its contents the next day, and I should be thoroughly conversant with its contents. As I left the interview and got back into the jeep for my ride back to the Duc Hotel, I realized I had not asked him if I had "passed" my interview.

Upon returning to the hotel, I immediately began reading *Viet Cong* and taking notes on the key points made by Pike. I concentrated on comparing my readings of Mao Tse-tung's works and the information I had gained from my conversations with Tran Van Qua with what Pike's book revealed about the organization and methods employed by the Viet Cong in South Vietnam. While there were a few differences, most of what I read in Pike's book matched what I had previously learned from these other two sources. At 0300 I finished the book and managed a few hours of sleep before I received a wakeup call from the front desk at 0630. I dressed and went to breakfast, where I met the other Marine captain, who appeared a bit under the weather from his exploits in the fleshpots of Tu Do Street. Seeing his bloodshot eyes, I was glad I had spent my time reading *Viet Cong* and not accompanying him on his travels the previous evening. As I joined him at his table, I asked him if he had read *Viet Cong*, and he informed me that he had no idea what I was talking about. Obviously, Bob did not seem to feel it necessary for my new-found friend to spend his evening reading the book. Then, to my surprise, he informed me that he was going back to Da Nang that afternoon. I asked him why and he told me he had not been accepted for duty with the PRU Program, explaining that he must have said something during his interview that did not sit well with Bob. I asked him what that might be, and he did not offer an explanation. I expressed regret, which I sincerely felt for him, and said I thought they must have made a mistake. This officer was a very good infantry officer with a strong record, so I was truly confused as to why such a good man would not be acceptable for the PRU Program. I wondered if the same fate awaited me that morning, so I went back up to my room, grabbed the copy of *Viet Cong* and spent a few valuable minutes in the lobby reviewing my notes and key passages I had underlined in the book. I was very apprehensive by the time the same grim-faced, taciturn Vietnamese officer arrived at the hotel with his jeep. And his behavior did nothing to lift my spirits. I feared that I was on my way to a meeting where I would be told I was not good enough for the PRU Program.

At PRU headquarters, I was again ushered to the second floor, where the same three men I had met the previous day greeted me. "General" Allen took me into his office, asked me take a seat, and then sat behind his desk with a very serious look on his face. I was prepared for the worst, but my fears dissipated instantly when he said, "Welcome aboard, Captain." My relief must have been apparent to him because he told me to relax and listen carefully to what he had to say:

> Captain Finlayson, I know you wanted to be assigned to a province up north in I Corps, and under normal circumstances that is where I would assign you, but we have a serious problem in III Corps, and I need an officer up there immediately. I have had to relieve the PRU advisor in Tay Ninh Province and kick him out of the program. I may court-martial him. This officer, a U.S. Army major, has been guilty of both moral and financial transgressions, which have undermined his credibility with the province chief and the Cao Dai religious leadership and caused great embarrassment to the U.S. government. Tay Ninh Province is one of the most important provinces for our pacification effort for a host of reasons. It is the seat of the Cao Dai religion; it is the former location for the enemy's main political headquarters in the south, COSVN; and it has one of the most effective PRU Programs in the entire country. We can't afford to have one man's indiscretions ruin our program there, and we can't afford to leave it without a PRU advisor for another day. I want you to go up there tomorrow and take over the Tay Ninh PRU.

I sat in front of Col. Allen dumbfounded and more than a little worried about what I had gotten myself into. I knew nothing about Tay Ninh Province, the Cao Dai religion, or even what the PRU were or how they operated, and now I found myself on the receiving end of orders from a Marine colonel to leave for this place and this new job in less than 24 hours. I timidly broached the subject of not possessing any knowledge about anything related to my new assignment and even more timidly suggested that some training might be a good idea before I traveled to Tay Ninh Province.

"Nonsense!" Col. Allen roared, "You are a Marine officer, and we don't have time to send you to Vung Tau for training. I need you in Tay Ninh now, not a week or two from now. I have confidence in you and know you will not let me or the Marine Corps down. Bob and Maj. Lang will brief you on all you need to know," he added, as if a few hours with these two men would rectify my total lack of knowledge about my job or my destination for tomorrow. Before I could even say a word, he fired off his last instructions to me and added a terse and pointed warning:

> Captain, your predecessor in Tay Ninh got into trouble there because he had a weak character. I don't think you have a weak character, but before I send you up there, I want you to promise me that you will not do anything immoral or illegal. You and I are both Roman Catholics, so when I say don't do anything immoral, you know I am not just talking about Marine Corps regulations or the Uniform Code of Military Justice. I don't want you to have a Vietnamese girlfriend up there. Keep your God-damned dick in your trousers. Remember, you will be dealing with the Cao Dai religious community, and they expect you to be a paragon of propriety. Got that? If I find out that you are involved with some girl up there, I will relieve you immediately. Also, you will find that the CIA handles their funding a lot differently than the U.S. military, so I expect you to never—repeat never—take advantage of the special trust and confidence they place in you regarding funds. Keep good and honest financial records. And finally, I don't care about any of the shit you have heard about the Phoenix Program and the PRU; but regardless, I don't want you to ever kill or mistreat

anyone unless they are resisting arrest. Your job is not to kill the VCI; it is to neutralize them. The best way to do that is to capture them so we can get more information on their friends and what their plans are. When you take a VCI prisoner, treat him properly, and turn him over to the Provincial Interrogation Center for interrogation—don't you or your PRU soldiers do the interrogating. All you will do is screw things up. Got it? And oh yes, if I find that you did anything unethical, immoral or corrupt, I will personally come up to Tay Ninh and kick your ass in front of everybody before I take you back here and court-martial your sorry ass. Got it?

He then quietly said he had a lot of work to do, and I needed to get with Bob and Maj. Lang immediately, so our "little chat must end." He shook my hand and turned me over to Bob, who took me into another office for the first of my six hours of indoctrination and "training" that day.

I spent three hours with Bob before a very good Vietnamese lunch was sent in to our room for us. After lunch I spent another two hours. Bob's briefings covered a great deal in those five hours with him. He gave me an overview of the history of the Phoenix Program and the role the PRU Program played in it, and then he launched into a series of briefings that included a short course on the origins of the Viet Cong in Tay Ninh Province, the NVA/VC order of battle in III Corps, the VC logistics system, the Tay Ninh PRU's organization, the history of the Cao Dai religion, and, finally, a detailed briefing on how the Phoenix Program was organized in Tay Ninh Province, from the provincial level down to the district level, to include some of the key personalities I would be working with there. It was a lot of absorb, but I thought the briefings were very helpful. I would later find that the information they provided was also very accurate. When we finished, Bob handed me several documents related to the VCI organization in Tay Ninh Province and told me to familiarize myself with the information contained in the documents before I boarded the Air America plane that would take me to Tay Ninh City the next day. As I said goodbye to Bob, I remembered he had not asked me a single question about Douglas Pike's book, but I decided not to pursue the matter and just accept the fact that Bob did not think it necessary to quiz me on its contents.

After I left Bob's office, I went downstairs to see Maj. Lang. He was standing in front of his administrative officer's desk, which was piled high with a surprisingly large number of manila file folders that contained the personal histories of the ninety-two PRU soldiers I would work with in Tay Ninh Province. Maj. Lang, a very affable and intelligent man who spoke perfect English, led the briefing, telling me everything he thought might be helpful to know about the Cao Dai religion, the GVN political leadership in Tay Ninh Province, and the status of the war against the VCI in that important province only 62 miles northwest of Saigon. He told me that Tay Ninh's War Zone C, a large jungle tract north of Tay Ninh City, had been the headquarters of the NLF and COSVN from 1960 until 1967, when the U.S. Army forced them to move across the border into Cambodia to an area near Mimot. He pointed out the various places in the province and in Cambodia where the VCI were active, telling me that ever since Tet 1968 the VC military units in Tay Ninh had been effectively destroyed. Despite this, the NVA had three divisions across the border from Tay Ninh in base areas close enough to the border to be able to move into the province in less than 24 hours on foot. He stressed the important role the VCI played in providing rice and other foodstuffs to these NVA divisions whenever they moved into the province to conduct operations against the American or South Vietnamese army units. He also stressed the importance

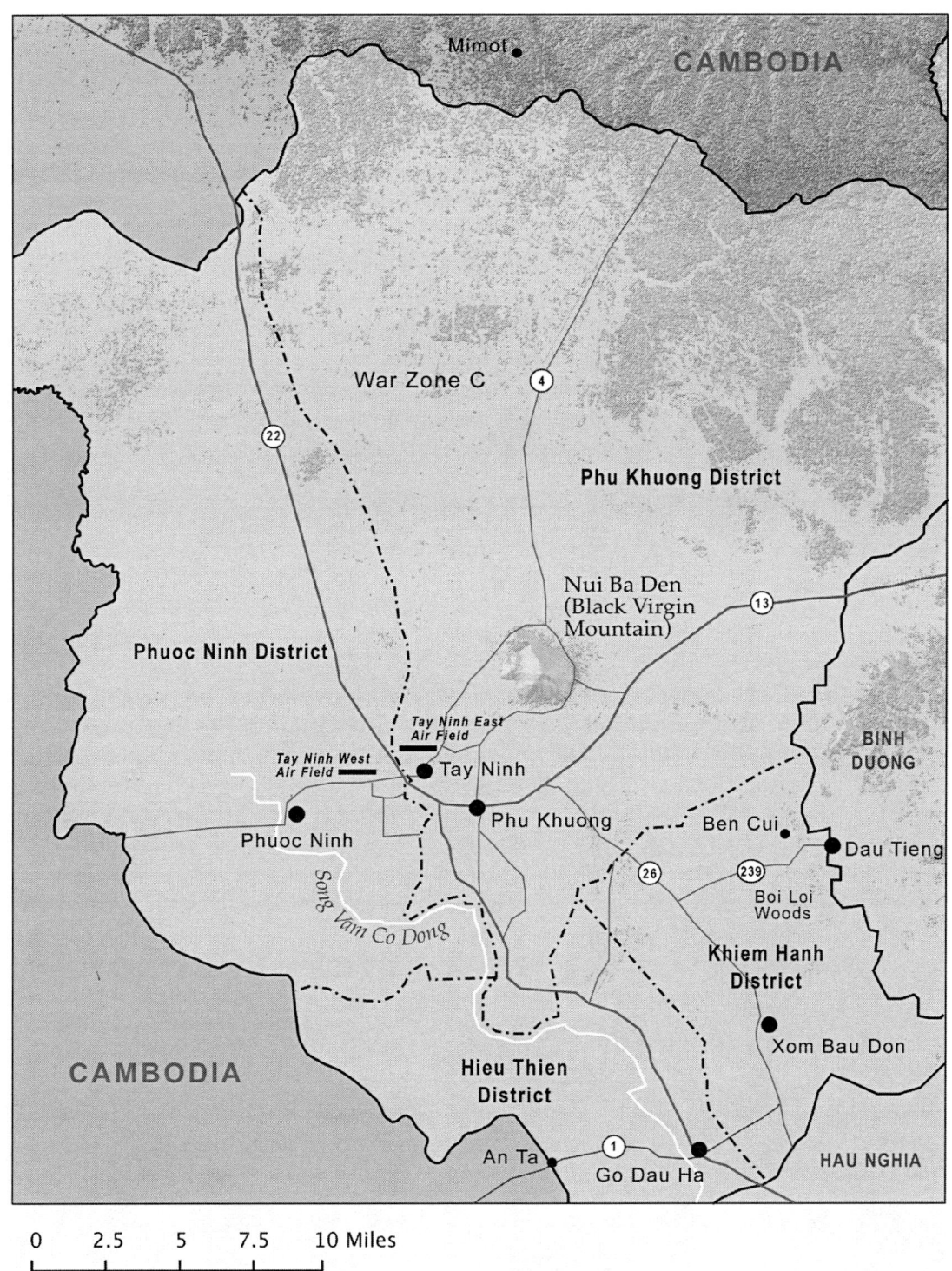

Map 5

Tay Ninh City street scene.

A crowded street in Tay Ninh City.

of maintaining a positive relationship with the religious and political leaders in the Cao Dai religion in Tay Ninh, especially since that relationship had been subject to many strains in the past and was still not on a solid footing. Pointing to a wall map of Cambodia, he mentioned that the Cao Dai Giao Tung, or "Pope," Le Van Trung, was living in exile in Cambodia, which made matters worse. Maj. Lang offered that the Cao Dai Pope was in contact with the communists and could not be trusted.

While I was impressed with the detail and breadth of Maj. Lang's knowledge of the situation in Tay Ninh, the more I listened to him, the more concerned I became about the complexity and difficulty of my mission there. When he finished his briefing, he turned the meeting over to his administrative officer, who began to tell me about the men occupying the leadership positions in the Tay Ninh PRU. Their names and positions were a blur to me, since it was difficult for me to remember the names and the positions associated with them, but one thing did impress me from this personnel briefing—these men possessed a high level of experience and were committed anti-communists. The PRU leaders were men in their 30s and 40s who had been fighting all of their adult lives. Some had been members of the French airborne battalions fighting the Viet Minh, while others had been members of Trinh Minh The's Cao Dai militia that had fought against the French and then joined President Diem to defeat the Binh Xuyen pirates in vicious street battles in Saigon in 1956. Still others had fought as members of the Civilian Irregular Defense Group (CIDG) or as special intelligence agents working for the American Special Forces. As for the rank-and-file members of the Tay Ninh PRU, they also possessed similar military or intelligence experience and had a reputation for being extremely tough and determined fighters. Almost all of them were members of the Cao Dai religion, although there were one or two Roman Catholics and Buddhists in the unit as well. All but two were ethnic Vietnamese, and those two were Cambodians.

The administrative officer ended his presentation by giving his assessment of the quality of the unit in terms of its strengths and weaknesses. He said the Tay Ninh PRU soldiers were "outstanding fighters with a very good operational record," and they had "a very good commander, Mr. Chinh, who was honest and brave"; but they were "weak in administration, often reporting late or holding back information the headquarters needed." He also said they had training weaknesses, which I should seek to rectify once I had assessed these weaknesses for myself. I found the briefer's comments a bit cryptic, so I asked him what, specifically, he felt were the major weaknesses I needed to work on. He looked at Maj. Lang, as if to see if he should respond, and then he simply said, "Intelligence management and proper reporting." With this very general description, I made a mental note to look into these alleged "weaknesses" when I got to Tay Ninh Province.

The last thing I did at the PRU villa was to sign for my South Vietnamese National Police ID card and a packet of documents that gave me a false identification. The packet contained a set of business cards with my cover name on them, identifying my job as a U.S. Department of the Army civilian engineer assigned to the 69th Heavy Construction Group in Saigon. There was also a U.S. government driver's license made out to my cover name. I used my National Police ID card frequently, but I never had to use any of my false ID documents.

I spent my last night in Saigon at the Duc Hotel memorizing my cover story and preparing for my early-morning flight to my new assignment. I felt woefully unprepared for my new job, but determined to do the best I could under the circumstances.

CHAPTER 12

The CIA Embassy House

On October 3, I boarded an Air America Pilatus Porter plane at Tan Son Nhut Air Base and made a short flight to Bien Hoa, where I checked in with the CIA's senior officer in Region III, Daren Flitcroft. Mr. Flitcroft looked like the kind of man a casting director in Hollywood would choose for a film about American spies. He was tall, ruggedly handsome, and supremely confident and assured. When he introduced himself he mentioned that he had grown up in New Jersey and had served as a Marine officer before joining the CIA in the early 1950s. I only spent a few minutes in his office, but those few minutes were very instructive. He told me that I had been specifically chosen for the job of PRU advisor in Tay Ninh Province because the province was of the utmost importance to the CIA, and Col. Allen thought I had what it takes to do a good job there. When I asked him why Tay Ninh was so important, he gave me a rather cryptic answer. He said, "Andy, when you get to Tay Ninh, Chuck Stainback, your boss there, will tell you everything you need to know." A few minutes later I was boarding the Pilatus Porter plane again and on my way to Tay Ninh Province.

From the air, Tay Ninh City did not look like a city at all. Instead, it looked like a sprawling collection of individual houses tightly packed between the Song Vam Dong River to the south and Nui Ba Den Mountain to the north. I could not make out any structures from the air that appeared to be larger than two stories.

The Air America plane, which was specifically designed to operate in rough terrain and make short landings and takeoffs, made a steep and rapid descent into a small airstrip on the western side of the city, called Tay Ninh East Airfield. The airstrip was only 1,000 feet long, but the single-engine Pilatus Porter landed in less than half of the runway, using the reverse pitch of its engines to bring the aircraft to a rapid halt. I jumped out of the aircraft, pulled my footlocker and B-4 bag behind me, and dragged them

Daren J. Flitcroft, the CIA's Region III Officer in Charge.

over to the edge of the runway while the plane quickly turned around and took off in what appeared to be less than 100 feet. I marveled at this plane's ability to take off and land in such short distances, and for a moment I stood on the side of the runway, oblivious to the swirling dust the plane produced as it took off down the runway and quickly ascended into the sky. I soon realized I was alone. I stood in the sweltering heat for a few minutes, glancing up and down the short runway, half expecting to see someone there to meet me. But I saw no one, save for some CIDG soldiers manning a bunker at the B-32 Special Forces Camp that occupied the eastern side of the airfield. They silently stared at me, probably wondering what this American in civilian clothes was doing standing in the sweltering heat and looking like he was lost. For some reason, Noel Coward's song "Mad Dogs and Englishmen" came to my mind as I stood there.

As I was about to go into the Special Forces camp to ask for directions to the Embassy House, I noticed a green Toyota jeep with U.S. Embassy license tags approaching me at great speed from the other end of the runway. The jeep came to a screeching halt beside me. Inside I saw the smiling face of Bernie, who introduced himself as the logistics officer for the Embassy House in Tay Ninh City. Bernie, I was to find out later, was a Filipino citizen who worked for a company contracted to the CIA for logistics services. He was about 30 years old and had an easy smile and friendly manner that immediately set me at ease. He also possessed the easy grace and articulate manner of speaking that marked a man of considerable education. A few weeks later, I learned he possessed a university degree in civil engineering.

As I climbed into the jeep, he informed me that the pilot of the Air American plane had waited until the plane was on the ground before he radioed the Embassy House, and that was the reason why he was late in picking me up. I took an immediate liking to Bernie and hoped everyone else at the Embassy House was as friendly and gracious as he was.

The ride to the Embassy House took only five minutes. We stopped in front of a pleasant-looking, one-story, French-style colonial villa and waited for a moment while Chinese Nung security guards dressed in camouflage uniforms and brandishing M-16 rifles opened the front gate. We drove into the side yard and Bernie parked the jeep under an open carport nestled against the whitewashed wall of the adjoining MACV compound. As we walked toward the villa, Bernie pointed out two very well-constructed concrete bunkers on one side of the villa's yard, along with several tropical fruit trees he seemed to think merited my attention. Across the street from the Embassy House was a Catholic church, and further down the street a high school for girls and a National Police compound.

I entered the front door of the villa with Bernie leading the way. He showed me my room, which was the second one on the right after entering, and told me he would tell "Mr. Chuck" that I had arrived. I quickly surveyed my new quarters and found them to be far better than any previous quarters I had occupied during my many months in South Vietnam. My room was spacious and clean, with a high ceiling and walls painted in two shades of light green. It contained a bed, a night stand, a large metal desk, a chair, a chest of drawers, a bookcase, and a filing cabinet that had a large padlock and security bar on it. My room had only one window, which was boarded on the bottom and had an air conditioner on the top, so no natural light was allowed into my room. As I began to relish the cool relief of my room's air conditioner, Bernie returned and announced that "Mr. Chuck" was waiting to see me in his room down the hall.

"Mr. Chuck," it turned out, was Mr. Charles O. Stainback, a career CIA officer who was the Agency's Provincial Officer in Charge (POIC) in Tay Ninh Province, meaning he was the senior CIA officer in the province and the boss of our very small contingent of CIA operatives. Chuck greeted me warmly with the courtly manners and charm that seems to come naturally to Southern men of good breeding. He was Virginia born and bred, a true Southern gentleman in every sense of the word, and I took an instant liking to him as he began to speak to me about my duties as his PRU commander.

He started by telling me a little about himself and what had brought him to South Vietnam. He told me he had grown up in the Tidewater area of Virginia, and from a young age he had been fascinated by flying. During World War II, he became a U.S. Navy pilot and, after the war, he used the G.I. Bill to finish college at the University of Virginia with a degree in geology, a degree he hoped to use to land a job with a large oil company. His plans changed, however, when a friend suggested he apply for a job with the CIA. The CIA sent him all over Asia and the Middle East on covert missions. He told me that he had worked in CIA postings that took him to Taiwan, Turkey, Afghanistan, and Pakistan. I wondered why a CIA officer with so much experience in the Middle East was posted to South Vietnam, but I thought I would raise that question with Chuck at some future date. He anticipated my question by telling me there was a critical shortage of career CIA officers, and the war required far more case officers than the CIA could provide. This meant that even career case officers with little or no experience in Southeast Asia were needed to fill jobs in South Vietnam.

Chuck gave me a brief overview of Tay Ninh Province and why it was so important to the U.S. government. He explained that the province had once been the headquarters of COSVN, but U.S. operations in 1967 drove COSVN out of South Vietnam and into base

Charles "Chuck" Stainback, the CIA's Provincial Officer in Charge for Tay Ninh Province.

areas in eastern Cambodia. Despite this setback, the enemy still maintained an extensive and well-organized political network in the province, although many of the VCI had been killed, captured, or driven into exile across the border into Cambodia.

I sat there enthralled as he related the story of the CIA's long history in Tay Ninh Province, beginning with Colonel Edward Lansdale's meeting with the famous Cao Dai militia commander, Trinh Minh The, in 1956. These meetings were a successful effort by Lansdale to convince this Vietnamese nationalist to bring his 12,000-man guerrilla force to Saigon to help President Diem defeat the Binh Xuyen pirates, who were threatening to oust Diem and replace him with a government that was more amenable to retaining a strong French presence in South Vietnam. As he told me this fascinating story, Chuck walked over to his safe, opened it, and handed me a thick file that had been written by Col. Lansdale after he had returned to Saigon from his meetings in Trinh Minh The's jungle headquarters on Nui Ba Den Mountain.

As I opened the file, I noticed several black-and-white photos taken in 1956 showing Col. Lansdale and Gen. The sitting around a bamboo table in what looked like a treehouse. Later on, I would read this file in its entirety and come away with two strong impressions: first, that Col. Lansdale was a gifted writer, since his memoranda were filled with sound analysis, crisp prose, and highly detailed analyses of the strategic situation in South Vietnam; and second, that Gen. The was a very brave, intelligent, patriotic, and totally ruthless nationalist who viewed President Diem as the least of several evils. It has been rumored that Col. Lansdale bribed Gen. The to support President Diem, but there was nothing in this classified file that would indicate that. In fact, the file's memoranda and reports seemed to indicate Gen. The did not need to be bribed to support Diem. Lansdale's reports and other reports from the Saigon station indicated that the primary motivation for Gen. The's support of Diem was a hatred of both the French and the communists. Gen. The told Lansdale that his animosity toward both the French and the communists was reciprocated, and he had been threatened with assassination by both, leaving him with no other alternative than to side with President Diem, whom he referred to several times in Lansdale's reports as "the strongest non-communist patriot in the country."

Chuck asked me about what training I had in intelligence, and I told him I had no training whatsoever. He said he was surprised by this since most PRU commanders coming from the U.S. military had at least attended several weeks of training at the PRU training facility at Vung Tau before taking over as PRU commanders, and many of them had received up to half a year of training by the CIA in the United States before their assignment to the CIA's program in South Vietnam. I informed him that my experience so far had been in U.S. Marine reconnaissance and infantry units only. I could tell that Chuck was not at all pleased with this news, but, like the gentleman he was, he simply said he felt confident that I would adapt and learn quickly. He also said he would guide and instruct me in the craft of intelligence and cautioned me about going off on my own without first clearing my actions with him. This promise of Chuck's expert advice and training lessened my anxiety about my obvious deficiencies. I promised him I would do everything possible to justify his confidence in me.

During my initial conversation with Chuck, it became apparent that he was unaware of the exact justification for the relief of his former PRU commander, a U.S. Army military intelligence major. When I told him that Col. Allen had relieved this officer "for cause," he seemed to think it was because of some conflict with how the Army major administered the PRU program. I told Chuck that Col. Allen gave me the impression the reason for the relief of my predecessor had been moral and financial lapses of judgment. Chuck said only that he had been in the province a few months and was unaware of any serious problems with his PRU commander, aside from some missing weapons and some financial irregularities in the PRU account. He went on to tell me that the financial accounting procedures he found when he took over were in total disarray and highly unprofessional, requiring him to devote too much of his time rectifying this problem. Rather than belabor the rationale for my predecessor's departure, I told him I intended to maintain a thoroughly professional approach to my job and to keep careful and accurate records of everything logistical and financial. This comment had a visible and favorable effect on Chuck. I told him that I had received explicit instructions from Col. Allen about how I was to conduct myself in Tay Ninh Province and the consequences if I did not adhere to his orders.

Chuck told me that two CIA men, one of whom was the PRU commander for the province, had been lured to their deaths by a female VC agent a year or two earlier, so he understood why Col. Allen had instructed me to avoid socializing with Vietnamese women in Tay Ninh Province. He informed me that no women were allowed inside the Embassy House compound unless they had a security clearance, and no women were allowed in the compound at all after dark. He indicated that this policy had been instituted shortly after he took over his post. Judging from the tales I had heard from other PRU advisors, this policy of not fraternizing with Vietnamese women was highly unusual. As if to put an exclamation point on this policy, Chuck said, "Andy, I know how hard it can be leading a celibate life when so many pretty Vietnamese women live nearby, but I recommend that if you want to have your ashes hauled, you take a day or two off and go to Saigon, where you will find plenty of opportunity to find satisfaction." Chuck, always the Southern gentleman, had a way with words that was both courtly and soothing, even when he was conveying unpleasant or difficult requirements.

I spent nearly an hour talking to Chuck, and then he suggested we have lunch and meet the rest of the Embassy House team. Having lived a rather austere life as a Marine infantry officer, with very few comforts and luxuries, I was pleasantly surprised by the lunch that was prepared for us and served in the villa's dining room. Everyone sat at one table with Chuck at the head. The meal was served by the Embassy House cook, a middle-aged woman named Ba Thu, whom Chuck and others in the house had taught to cook western meals, in addition to her excellent Vietnamese dishes. That first lunch consisted of a delicious vegetable soup with a rich beef stock, spaghetti with meat sauce, French bread, and a side dish of mixed fresh vegetables prepared Vietnamese style. Iced tea and Cokes were the beverages. Having had an early breakfast at the Duc Hotel that day, I was ravenous and thoroughly enjoyed this new and delicious cuisine.

Chuck introduced me to the four men sitting around the table with us. John was the Special Branch advisor, and his job was to provide advice and assistance to the GVN National Police Special Branch. John explained that the Special Branch was similar to the FBI's counterintelligence division and the British MI-5 organization. As he put it, "We are in the business of catching spies." During our introduction John mentioned that he was a retired U.S. Army colonel. I would later find out that John was a retired U.S. Army major with a counterintelligence background, and, unlike Chuck, he was not a career CIA employee but a contract employee.

Ba Thu, the housekeeper and cook at the Embassy House.

Sitting directly across from me was Mickey, the Provincial Interrogation Center (PIC) advisor. His job was to advise the Vietnamese National Police personnel at the province's interrogation center and to carry out interrogations of selected prisoners and Hoi Chanhs, all of whom were processed through the PIC. Mickey said he was a retired U.S. Army Special Forces lieutenant colonel, but later on, I found out that he had been a Special Forces sergeant and never an officer. I wondered why both John and Mickey would choose to lie about their previous ranks in the Army, something I felt was distasteful and unnecessary, unless they intended to pull rank on me in some way. Even Chuck was not sure of their previous ranks in the Army. I only found out about their duplicity a month after arriving, when a Special Forces officer from B-32 told me the truth about their Army ranks and offered an explanation. He said both John and Mickey needed to impress their Vietnamese counterparts with a false rank so they would be accorded the added respect and access these ranks would provide. I found this explanation a weak one, but since it did not affect my work, I decided to overlook it.

The other two men at the table were Bernie, our Filipino logistics officer, and SFC Robert Smith, U.S. Army, a Special Forces NCO assigned as the Assistant PRU Commander. Unlike John and Mickey, he did not inflate his rank, and he was more willing to talk about himself and his job. SFC Smith and I did not get off to a good start. He was entirely too casual with me and seemed to resent my presence. I suspected he felt he should have been given sole responsibility for the PRU mission, and he did not need an officer to tell him what to do. I listened to him as he called me by my first name and expounded on his many accomplishments and contacts in the Special Forces community, but I decided lunchtime was not the time to talk to him, so I remained silent. After lunch was finished, I asked him to see me in my room.

In my room and out of earshot of the other men in the house, I began to question SFC Smith about how he expected our relationship to be. He immediately knew what I was talking about because he began to tell me that he had been with the U.S. Army's Special Forces for most of his career and that the relationships between officers and enlisted men in that organization were less formal than in regular Army units, with both officers and enlisted soldiers on a first-name basis. He added that most officers assigned to the Special Forces were only assigned for a few years, and then they left for other jobs while the NCOs were there for many years continuously, so they really ran the Special Forces. He ended by saying his assignment to the CIA was no different, and he intended to treat me like any other officer he had ever served with.

I then told him that I was going to immediately ask for his transfer from Tay Ninh back to the Special Forces, where he would be more comfortable, since I had no intention of having someone with his attitude working for me. I could tell he was surprised by my answer, but he was not going to give up quickly. He said, "Let's talk to Chuck about this." I replied that I would be glad to talk to Chuck, but I doubted that Chuck would be able to do anything, since assignments were made by MACV and Col. Allen. Besides, I was confident Chuck would support me if I asked him to transfer my assistant. Furthermore, I told him that I expected an NCO in the U.S. Army to refer to me either by my rank or "Sir," and the use of my first name was disrespectful. I could tell from his body language that he did not like what I was saying, and he was pondering what he should do or say. He sat in silence for a moment and then simply said, "I guess there is no more for us to talk about," and he rose to leave my room. I told him to sit down; I was not finished talking to him. He sat down, and I began to grill him about the Tay Ninh PRU and about the U.S. Army officer I was replacing. I noticed that he began to say "Sir" when talking to me, which I took as a good sign. In the next few months, I would find that SFC Smith was a highly experienced and knowledgeable NCO, whom the PRU soldiers respected and admired. I also would find that he was an exceptionally good man in the field, the result of his extensive combat experience. I think we grew to respect each other, but I never really felt comfortable with him as my assistant, and I was glad when he was transferred to another province.

SFC Smith told me the PRU in Tay Ninh Province was, in his estimation, one of the best in the entire country. He attributed their success to several factors. First, he said Mr. Chinh, the PRU chief, and his four district team leaders were thoroughly professional in all respects, and they were outstanding natural leaders. Second, they were all local men who grew up in Tay Ninh Province, and they knew the people and terrain with an intimacy that gave them an advantage over anyone else in ferreting out the VCI. He also told me that most of the PRU soldiers had extensive military experience, some of them having fought against the Japanese during World War II. I could tell he genuinely respected the PRU leaders and men. I would find his assessment of them to be entirely accurate.

I told SFC Smith that PRU headquarters in Saigon had originally intended to assign me to a province in I Corps, but at the last minute had decided to send me to Tay Ninh because the American PRU commander had been relieved "for cause." SFC Smith then told me that my predecessor had been engaged in a number of illegal and unethical activities, which resulted in his relief. When I told him that Col. Allen might court-martial this man, SFC Smith told me that would never happen because this individual would go to the press and tell them everything he knew about the CIA's operations in Tay Ninh Province. I found this to be a rather weak threat, since revealing classified information would probably result in additional, more serious, court-martial charges against this officer.

The next comment from SFC Smith was my first indication that there was something unique and very important being done in Tay Ninh—something so important, the revelation of it could absolve an individual of any legal action against him. He said, "Sir, the major knows something that the United States cannot afford to get into the press. I don't know what it is, but I know when he threatened to go public with it, the CIA told Col. Allen to back off and forget about any legal action." I wondered what exactly was so important that Colonel Allen would not press charges against someone who was in clear violation of the Uniform Code of Military Justice (UCMJ) and had damaged the U.S. PRU program in Tay Ninh Province. Since this was history and I thought I had enough of a challenge ahead of me trying to get the PRU program back on track, I put SFC Smith's cryptic comment out of my mind and concentrated on picking his brain for everything he knew about the PRU. In the coming months, however, this "something" that was so important to the CIA would crop up again several times until I finally found out what it was.

My first evening in the Embassy House was spent getting to know the other five men living there. After a very good dinner served by our Vietnamese cook, Ba Thu, the five of us retired to the living room and had a few after-dinner drinks. Each man had a bottle or two of his favorite whiskey behind a small bar on one side of the living room. Since I did not have my own bottle, Chuck graciously offered me a drink of Scotch from his bottle, and I settled down in one of the comfortable chairs in front of the house's TV set and watched the AFTV evening news program from Saigon. I had never watched TV before during my previous time in South Vietnam, so this was a real treat for me and something I looked forward to each evening. After the news, I spent a few minutes talking to each man, trying to be as friendly as possible since I realized I would be living and working in close proximity to these men over the next few months. While all of them were friendly, I noticed that none of them really shared much information with me about their work. They seemed reticent to talk about what they did, unless it was couched in the most general of terms, and they often changed the subject if I delved too closely into their work. As Chuck would often tell me, "We are compartmented and for good reason. You and the others need to know your own jobs. I am the only one who needs to know what everyone is doing."

While I understood the need for secrecy and agreed with Chuck's dictum, I could not help but feel that there was something special about what my compatriots knew but did not want to share with me. This was especially true whenever the subject of "sources" and "assets" came up. Chuck had told me the first day in Tay Ninh City that the CIA's new Chief of Station (COS) in South Vietnam, Ted Shackley, wanted the CIA in-country to focus their efforts more on developing strategic intelligence and less on pacification. This meant that the main effort for the CIA was to recruit spies from the ranks of the enemy, and my work, which was destroying the VCI, would have a relatively lower priority. I assumed that Chuck, John and Mickey were focused on this new requirement to recruit spies, and since I was not involved in that work, I had no need to know what they were doing. I took Chuck's guidance to heart and did not probe any of these men for information on their work. The importance of this was driven home to me by the answer SFC Smith gave me to a question I posed to him one day shortly after my arrival. I asked him if anyone besides the two of us went to the field on operations. He said, "Sir, the CIA would never risk the capture of anyone else but us. Chuck and the others know too much. You will find out that they seldom go outside the city, let alone on operations in the field. They very seldom leave the embassy house at night, either. They travel to the CIA's Region III Headquarters in Bien Hoa or the Embassy in Saigon, but seldom by road. They use the Air America's daily service for that travel. Their work is so secret, they don't even allow anyone without a top secret clearance inside the Embassy House unless that person is escorted at all times and leaves as soon as their business is completed. Unlike other Embassy Houses, we are not allowed to have women in the house at night." Although it was unspoken, I sensed that this last restriction was the most onerous in the mind of SFC Smith.

SFC Smith went on to tell me that while the other men in the Embassy House did not go on operations in the field, he and I were not restricted in any way from accompanying our PRU soldiers on their operations. He also said that there were times when it was not possible for us to accompany the PRU soldiers to the field, especially during daylight hours. Even if we were dressed in black pajamas, our size and mannerisms would give us away if we were seen traveling to a target in daylight. Some PRU operations demanded we accompany our men, primarily those in which the PRU was operating with U.S. military forces, or for which we were needed to radio requests for U.S. supporting arms or helicopter medevacs. SFC Smith indicated that we could normally expect to go to the field three or four times each month.

On my second day in Tay Ninh Province, I was scheduled to meet the Province Chief, Lt. Col. Thien, and my PRU leaders. SFC Smith and I drove over to the provincial com-

Tay Ninh Provincial HQ, Tay Ninh City.

pound, a large walled facility that contained the buildings used by the French-colonial government prior to 1954. Most of the buildings were large, airy, whitewashed, two-story buildings in the French-colonial style with porches on both stories and large ceiling-to-floor shuttered windows. The newer buildings in the compound were far less grand and imposing than those of the French-colonial period.

As we entered the provincial headquarters, we were escorted to Lt. Col. Thien's office on the second floor and told to wait until he was ready to see us. A minute passed, and then the door to his office opened and a rather small, pleasant-looking South Vietnamese Army officer walked out, smiled broadly, and said, "Mr. Robert, how nice to see you this morning. What brings you to see me?" SFC Smith introduced me, and then we entered Lt. Col. Thien's office and sat down in large wicker chairs facing his desk, which was filled with papers and reports. Behind his desk he had pictures and plaques from various events in his military career. On the wall to his right was a large South Vietnamese flag, and next to the flag was a picture showing President Thieu and Lt. Col. Thien standing together in front of the president's office in Saigon.

Our meeting was not a long one. Unlike many South Vietnamese officials, the province chief did not waste anyone's time with small talk before getting to the essence of a meeting. However, he did maintain the universal courtesy of giving us tea, brought to us by one of his clerks. He told me I was replacing a "PRU advisor" who had made some "serious mistakes," and he hoped I would not make these same mistakes during my time in his province. He did not go into the details of these "mistakes," but instead told me that it was important for me

Mr. Nguyen Ngoc Chinh and the author at PRU HQ, Tay Ninh City.

to understand what my position was in the scheme of things, especially as it pertained to my relationship with him. He said the PRU worked for him and no one else. I noticed that Lt. Col. Thien looked directly at SFC Smith when he said this, and I thought of what I had been told by Col. Allen in Saigon—that I worked for the POIC in Tay Ninh and not the province chief. He went on to say that under the U.S. government's policy of Vietnamization, the PRU would soon be subsumed into the South Vietnamese National Police, and they would no longer operate independently under CIA supervision. Since this was the agreed-upon policy of both the South Vietnamese government and the American government, he expected me to take my orders from him. He said there was no need to physically check with him on every operational matter—my PRU Chief, Mr. Chinh, could do that—but it was essential that every mission be cleared by him before it was executed. He said he was responsible to President Thieu directly for everything that was done in the province, and he did not want to be surprised by some action taken by the PRU without his consent or knowledge. He strongly suggested that I obtain an arrest order prior to seeking out a suspected VCI cadre, since this would protect both the PRU and me from accusations that the PRU was an extralegal force. He promised me that he would sign, or have a magistrate sign, any arrest order brought to him that was backed up by solid evidence that the person named in the arrest warrant was a communist cadre.

I would meet with Lt. Col. Thien several more times during my time as a PRU commander, and each time I would come away more impressed with him. He spoke English well, was always professional, and seemed to know everything that was going on in his province. It was also apparent that he was genuinely committed to improving the lives of the people in his province and protecting them from the VC. He was always cordial and friendly with me, treating me with both respect and consideration. In short, I considered him an ideal province chief and a pleasure to work with.

After our meeting with Lt. Col. Thien was concluded, SFC Smith and I met my interpreter, Mr. Nguyen Hoang Lam, and together we went to meet Mr. Chinh and the PRU team leaders. Since the PRU headquarters building was located in the same compound as the province chief's headquarters, it took us less than two minutes to arrive in front of the PRU headquarters building, a far more austere building than the one that housed the province chief. It consisted of a few sparse rooms inside an aging one-story building with a wooden annex that served as the barracks for the PRU City Team. It was very Spartan, but clean and neat in appearance. Greeting me at the door was the PRU Chief, Mr. Nguyen Ngoc Chinh, a distinguished and wiry-looking man in his mid–50s who had the appearance and demeanor of a professional military man—a man who stood erect and proud, a man who demanded and deserved respect. From the minute I met Mr. Chinh, I was impressed with everything about him.

Mr. Chinh, who spoke little English, asked us to come into the PRU Operations Room, where I would receive a briefing on the Tay Ninh PRU and meet the district team leaders and a few of the headquarters staff. Mr. Lam, who was actually a PRU soldier, but worked at the Embassy House as my interpreter, translated the briefing given by Mr. Chinh and the Operations Officer, Mr. Tran Quoc Tho. Tea was brought in, and I was introduced to the five team leaders and the PRU's administrative officer, Mr. Chuong. For a few minutes Mr. Chinh asked about my family and my military background. Mr. Chinh seemed very pleased that I was a qualified parachutist, and he volunteered that he had been a parachute infantry officer in the French Army during the war with the Viet Minh and had made several combat jumps.

Using large cardboard briefing charts, Mr. Chinh went over the mission, organization and equipment of the Tay Ninh PRU. I listened as Mr. Chinh explained that there were four districts in the province, and each district had an eighteen-man team assigned to it. An additional eighteen-man team was assigned to Tay Ninh City and was used to carry out missions inside the city limits or to reinforce the district teams, if needed. The City Team was commanded by the Tay Ninh PRU's deputy chief, Mr. Nghiem. There was a total of ninety-two PRU personnel for the entire province, a province that had a population of nearly 400,000 people. When I asked Mr. Chinh if he thought his unit was rather small considering the number of people living in the province, he quickly replied, "We are small, but highly effective." I would later find that he spoke the truth.

When the briefing addressed equipment, I was told the PRU soldiers were well-equipped by the CIA with the latest versions of M-16 rifles, M-60 machine guns, and M-79 grenade launchers. They also had enough PRC-25 radios for each team to have at least one. Where they were deficient, in the view of Mr. Chinh, was the paucity of transportation assets available to them. They had only two Toyota pickup trucks and a few Japanese motorcycles to cover a province that was 30 miles long and 25 miles wide. This forced them to use American helicopters from the U.S. Army's 25th Infantry Division at the Tay Ninh West base

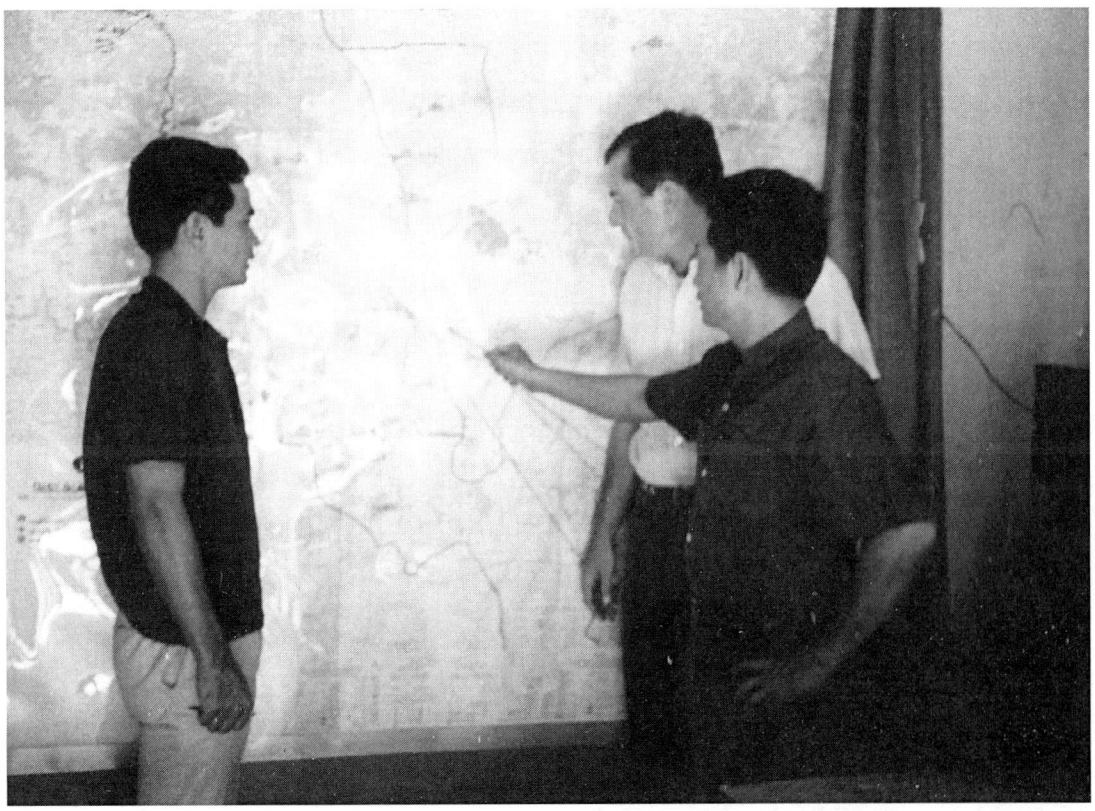

Mr. Tho, the author, and Mr. Nghiem planning a PRU mission.

camp for many of their operations, or to use local commercial transportation, such as dump trucks, three-wheeled cyclos and taxis. Even bicycles were used from time to time to transport PRU soldiers on missions. As for uniforms, I was told that the PRU soldiers dressed in a wide variety of clothing depending on the mission. The standard uniform was the tiger-striped camouflage uniform with a black beret, but they also wore the peasants' ubiquitous garb of black pajamas, as well as VC and NVA uniforms and civilian street clothes.

After the organizational briefing ended, Mr. Chinh turned the meeting over to Mr. Tho, who presented a briefing on the current operational situation in Tay Ninh Province. Mr. Tho was a handsome man in his early 30s who had once been a South Vietnamese movie actor, a fact that was not lost on many young women in the province, who often recognized him and sought out his company. He was extremely intelligent, produced well-written and complete intelligence reports, and spoke fluent English, which was rare among the PRU soldiers. Out of patriotism, he said, he decided to put his film career on hold and volunteer for duty with a U.S. Special Forces CIDG unit. After several years fighting the VC as a CIDG officer, he joined the PRU and rose to his current position of operations officer for the unit. I would spend more time with Mr. Tho during my stay in Tay Ninh Province than with any other Vietnamese, aside from Mr. Lam. We became fast friends and saw each other on an almost daily basis.

Mr. Tho stood in front of a large map of the province mounted on the plaster wall of the Operations Room and began to speak. Normally, this map was hidden from view by a large U.S. government-issue green blanket, which was only drawn aside when some item needed to be updated on the map. A guard was posted at the door of the Operations Room each night to ensure that no prying eyes saw what was written on this map, a wise precaution because the map was the primary means for planning future operations and posting recently obtained intelligence on the VCI. Mr. Tho began by giving a short history of the VCI presence in the province, including where the communist political headquarters, COSVN, had been located prior to 1967, a large jungle tract in the northern portion of the province called War Zone C. Mr. Tho mentioned several high-value targets who had been neutralized during the past few years, stressing the point that due to the attrition suffered by the VCI after the 1968 Tet Offensive, few of these targets remained. He reviewed the Phoenix Program's categories of VCI targets for my benefit, informing me that Category A consisted of COSVN and provincial-level VCI; Category B consisted of district- and village-level VCI; and Category C VCI were low-level village and hamlet guerrillas, couriers, civic organization leaders, and tax collectors. He produced figures that showed a large spike in the number of VCI captured by the Tay Ninh PRU in 1968, including several of whom were in the first two categories. Since that time, the number of killed and captured VCI had dropped off, with most of the VCI eliminated occupying the lowest category of VCI, Category C. Mr. Tho attributed this decline in high-value VCI eliminations to two primary factors: the inability of senior VCI to move freely around the province since their security, primarily the regular NVA 5th, 7th, and 9th divisions, had been driven out of the province and into Cambodia; and the improved intelligence on the identities of high-value VCI who surfaced during the 1968 Tet Offensive. He concluded by saying most of the provincial-level VCI were either dead, in prison, or living in exile in Cambodia, but some district-level VCI had taken over the duties of the provincial-level cadre and were still operating in the province, albeit at much lower numbers.

I asked Mr. Tho where the Tay Ninh PRU obtained most of their intelligence on VCI targets and his response surprised me. He said that the PRU had their own intelligence system, and that it produced most of the operational leads on VCI in the province. I had been told at the PRU headquarters in Saigon that the PRU functioned as the "action arm" of the CIA's contribution to the Phoenix Program, and as such the Provincial Intelligence Operations Coordination Center (PIOCC) and District Intelligence Operations Coordination Centers (DIOCC) were tasked with the responsibility of collecting targeting intelligence from multiple sources and then assigning missions to the PRU and other security units, such as the National Police or the military, to affect the capture of the target. Since that was my understanding of how the process was supposed to work, I asked Mr. Tho why it was necessary for the PRU to have their own intelligence system. He replied that the PIOCC in Tay Ninh City and the DIOCCs in the districts were supposed to coordinate all the intelligence on the VCI and task the PRU to mount operations to neutralize the VCI, but in practice this did not always work. I then asked him why it did not work, and he said, "Not everyone wants to share their information with us." I could tell that Mr. Chinh and Mr. Tho were both uncomfortable talking about this subject, so I made a note to myself to talk to Chuck about it when I returned to the Embassy House that afternoon.

At the end of the briefing, which lasted nearly two hours, I had an opportunity to talk for a few minutes with the four district team leaders. All of them were larger than most Vietnamese, with two of them, Mr. No and Mr. Siem, nearly 6 feet tall and possessing strong, athletic builds. All appeared to be very tough.

I asked one of them, Mr. Nguyen Van Siem, why he had decided to work as a PRU soldier, and his answer was both shocking and representative of many of his colleagues in the unit. He told me that he had been a Cao Dai militia leader and local farmer until 1966, when a VC assassination squad came to his village and killed his entire family. They had waited until he had left to sell his rice crop in Tay Ninh City, and then they entered his village at night looking for his house. They took his wife, father, mother, and five children out of the house and murdered all of them, leaving placards on their bodies warning everyone else in the village that this would be the fate of anyone who sided with the government of South Vietnam. That same night they also murdered the village school teacher, a young unmarried man they accused of being a government spy. This event had been Mr. Siem's epiphany. From that moment on, he was an implacable enemy of the communists. He had a reputation for being fearless, but Mr. Lam told me that his bravery stemmed from the fact that he had nothing else to live for after the communists had murdered his family. Oddly, Mr. Siem, who was born in 1935, had been a member of the Viet Minh as a teenager and had fought with one of their local units until 1954. His story was not unique; most of the PRU soldiers I spoke to told me similar tales of atrocities committed against their families by the VC. Not surprisingly, when the communists finally conquered South Vietnam in 1975, Mr. Siem did not surrender to them, but chose instead to take most of his men and disappear into the jungle, where he waged guerrilla warfare against the communists for several years as a member of the Yellow Dragons, a Cao Dai resistance group.[1]

As we were leaving the meeting, Mr. Tho suggested I visit the PIOCC to see how that important component of the Phoenix Program worked. It was located only a short distance from the PRU headquarters building and occupied a building similar in size to the one occupied by the PRU. Inside the PIOCC, I found the Provincial Security Officer, Mr. Anh, who

Mr. Anh, the Tay Ninh Security Chief; his wife Ba Quyen, our radio operator; and their three children at their home.

informed me that he supervised the various watch officers in the PIOCC. He explained that each organization involved in the fight against the VCI was represented in the room by a watch officer, and these watch officers manned the PIOCC 24 hours a day, seven days a week. Sitting at desks around the room were representatives from the National Police, the National Police Special Branch, the Provincial Sector S-2, the U.S. 25th Infantry Division, the U.S. 1st Cavalry Division, the ARVN Airborne Division S-2, the Chieu Hoi Program, the Revolutionary Development Program, and the Provincial Military Security Service (MSS). Mr. Anh explained that the PIOCC received reports from each of these agencies and organizations, maintained dossiers on all the known VCI in the province, and submitted recommendations to the provincial Phoenix Committee on actions needed to neutralize the VCI. In essence, the PIOCC served as a central clearinghouse for all the information gathered in the province on the VCI and for any actions needed to be taken to defeat them. He pointed out that prior to 1967 when the Phoenix Program was started, there was little coordination between these agencies and organizations, and there was also a lot of duplication of effort. The end result was a rather haphazard and inefficient attack against the VCI. "Now," he said, "the VCI are being systematically destroyed because we are now coordinating fully and working efficiently as a team."

In order to draw out the information from Mr. Anh that I had just received in the PRU briefing concerning the lack of operational leads coming from the PIOCC, I asked Mr. Anh if the PRU had a representative on the PIOCC. He replied that they were not physically represented on the PIOCC, but they were part of the PIOCC's operations section, and in this capacity they received arrest orders and missions from the PIOCC. Mr. Anh was quick to add that the PRU generated many very accurate intelligence reports, which they submitted to the PIOCC and the DIOCCs, and he said the PRU was the most effective action arm of the PIOCC since they were able to go anywhere in the province, usually in secret, to find VCI targets. He also went out of his way to praise Mr. Chinh and Mr. Tho, even referring to them as "patriots" and "the bravest men in the province."

I decided to bide my time concerning what I had heard about the lack of operational leads given to the PRU and shifted the conversation to how well the four DIOCCs were functioning in the province. Mr. Anh said the DIOCCs mirrored to a large degree the composition of the PIOCC, having most of the same representative agencies and organizations that the PIOCC had, but involving lower-level representatives who concentrated on the VCI in their respective districts. He pointed out that the American district advisors, usually U.S. Army captains and majors, were doing an excellent job of using the information developed on the VCI by the DIOCCs to mount effective combined U.S. and GVN counter–VCI operations and to ensure the information coming into their DIOCCs was being sent to the PIOCC for analysis and action.

Mr. Anh was a rather tall, thin, bespectacled man in his late 30s who looked more like an energetic bank clerk than the senior intelligence officer in the province. However, in the coming months, I would grow to appreciate how intelligent, industrious, humorous, and engaging he was and to value his judgments concerning the war against the VCI. I would also find out that he was married to the Embassy House's radio operator, the very beautiful and charming Phung Thi Quyen, or Chi Tam, as her friends called her. She worked during daylight hours in the Embassy House Annex behind the main villa, receiving and sending unclassified radio traffic between our province and other CIA stations in Region III. The

Embassy House Annex consisted of two small rooms: one for Chi Tam and her radio equipment, and our two interpreters, Mr. Lam and Mr. Phong; and the other for the financial officer and his two finance clerks. There was also a small closet in the annex that contained drawers filled with Census Grievance maps and reports on the province—maps and reports that would play an important role in my work in the near future.

After dinner that day, I spoke with Chuck about what I had heard during my visit with the province chief, the PRU staff, and Mr. Anh. He seemed genuinely concerned that there appeared to be a difference of opinion about whether or not the PRU were receiving operational leads from the PIOCC, and he promised to look into the matter with the view of making sure the PIOCC functioned in accordance with the Phoenix Program's policies. When I told him Lt. Col. Thien had said he was the sole authority on the employment of the PRU, he explained that "technically" Lt. Col. Thien was correct, since the combined U.S.-GVN agreement on the Phoenix Program identified the province chief as the chairman of each province's Phoenix Committee. However, Chuck quickly pointed out that the PRU was fully organized, trained, equipped, and paid for by the CIA and, as such, they were under the direct operational, as well as administrative, control of the CIA. As if to stress the point, he added, "This means they work for me, and as my PRU commander, they are under your command, not the province chief's." I began to see that my relationship with Lt. Col. Thien was going to be far more delicate than I had anticipated, but I resolved to work around this problem so as not to jeopardize the war against the VCI. I decided to work out a system that would smooth out any rough edges, and perhaps allow both Lt. Col. Thien and Chuck to control the PRU with a minimum of conflict.

One topic I did not bring up with Chuck was the revelation that the PRU had their own intelligence-gathering system. I assumed Chuck knew about this PRU intelligence system since he periodically met with Mr. Chinh and was thoroughly familiar with most aspects concerning the PRU. I never did discuss the PRU intelligence system with Chuck, and this proved to be a mistake that I would later regret.

Chuck suggested I visit each district headquarters and speak with the district chiefs and their American advisors about their PRU teams. He said it was possible to drive to each district headquarters in the province in less than an hour or two, depending on the quality of the roads used, but he thought it best to spend an entire day at each district so I would be able know the district chiefs and their American advisors well enough to gauge their appreciation for their PRU teams and to ascertain for myself whether or not the PRU teams were being employed properly and effectively. I heartily agreed with this suggestion, and during the next four days Mr. Lam and I drove to each district headquarters. By 1969, the security situation in Tay Ninh Province was quite good, making it possible to travel safely on most of the roads. Chuck told me it was safe to drive anywhere in the province now, but two years prior, it was hardly safe. I would spend many hours driving around the province during the next eight months, sometimes alone in my jeep, but more frequently accompanied by Mr. Lam, and never once did we encounter any problems. We carried M-16 rifles with us and our side arms, but nothing more, and we never had to resort to using these weapons or traveling with a security escort. I felt safe driving along the roads of Tay Ninh Province, but I never let this feeling reduce the normal security precautions needed in a war zone.

After visiting the districts of Phu Khuong, Khiem Hanh, Hieu Thien, and Phuoc Ninh, I felt fairly confident that the relationships between the PRU teams in each district and the district chiefs were on a sound footing, and, in some cases, were highly developed with a degree of mutual respect that I did not really expect to find. I also was impressed with the young American military advisors in the districts, who seemed to have a firm understanding of the security situation in their districts and the level of VCI activity. Each district had a functioning DIOCC, which was manned continuously, and several of the DIOCCs actually had a PRU liaison officer working in them most of each day. I was particularly pleased with the many favorable comments I heard from the Americans about how effective the PRU teams were in going after the VCI. One district advisor told me, "The PRU are, without doubt, the best Vietnamese force in the district and the only force I can count on to aggressively go after the VC cadres."

Although the district advisors gave high marks to the PRU teams in their districts, they mentioned two significant logistical shortcomings—they did not have enough radios or ground transport, which forced them to often rely on American units for communications and transportation support. They suggested that each district PRU team be given at least one pickup truck and four motorcycles, as well as three PRC-25 radios. I took note of their recommendations and brought it to the attention of the PRU headquarters in Saigon.

After my visits to the districts, I settled into a daily routine that was only altered when I went to the field with the PRU forces on operations. This routine involved a daily meeting at 0900 with Mr. Tho on the porch of the Embassy House. Mr. Tho would arrive on his motorcycle, stop at the gate, and wait for the Nung guard on duty to open the metal gate and close it after him. The two of us would sit at a small table on the porch and talk for an hour or so about the previous day's activities, the latest intelligence reports written by the PRU, and what plans were being developed for future operations. Often our housekeeper and cook, Mrs. Thu, would bring us cups of strong coffee as we talked.

The only distraction we ever had was a pleasant one. Occasionally, we would look up from our discussions and take a moment to admire the graceful beauty of dozens of ao dai–clad high school girls walking or riding by on bicycles to the school up the street. I often thought of these girls as graceful swans moving along the road to their school, their movements so languid and flowing. The cool morning scene was largely silent as they passed, with only the sound of a few occasional giggles or the ring of their bicycle bells to break the silence of the scene passing in front of us. Mr. Tho and I both acknowledged that one of the added benefits of our early-morning meetings was this flow of youthful beauty passing before our eyes each day.

After the meeting with Mr. Tho, which often included Mr. Lam when some translation work was necessary, I would go into my room and read the various GVN intelligence reports that Mr. Lam had translated into English for me. I would also take his translations of the PRU intelligence reports and edit them before typing them in English on my IBM electric typewriter so they could be distributed to the American intelligence community in the province and also sent to the CIA regional headquarters in Bien Hoa. A copy of each Tay Ninh PRU intelligence report was sent each month as an attachment to my monthly report to PRU headquarters in Saigon. This administrative work would often take me until lunchtime, when my colleagues and I would gather for one of Mrs. Thu's delicious meals. If I finished my morning work early, I would drive to the Tay Ninh East Airfield and run around the small airstrip for three miles, or go to the private Chinese school in Tay Ninh City and play basketball there for an hour. After lunch, I would usually spend an hour or two at the PRU headquarters in the provincial compound or drive to Tay Ninh West Airfield to coordinate a future operation with the G-3 of the 25th Infantry Division brigade located there. I would also visit the B-32 Special Forces camp at the Tay Ninh East Airfield to talk to them about any intelligence they had on VCI activities their agent net had developed. I seldom visited the MACV compound next to the Embassy House because Chuck told me to avoid going there unless absolutely necessary. There had been some tension between Chuck and the senior American advisor in the province, a State Department foreign service officer, so Chuck wanted to make sure he was the only one in our house who dealt with this individual. I never found out what led to this tension, but the result was I had little contact with Americans working in the MACV compound. I left everything that had to do with MACV up to Chuck. During my eight months in Tay Ninh City, I never saw anyone from the MACV compound inside our villa, but Chuck often would visit their compound via a small door he had built into the wall we shared with them. Like many things done by Chuck and the other CIA officers in the Embassy House, I was not privy to what transpired when Chuck visited the MACV compound.

On very rare occasions, late in the afternoon, Chuck would send me to attend the daily Phoenix Committee coordination meetings held at the provincial compound. Normally Chuck attended these meetings, but John, Mickey, and I were sent when Chuck could not make them. Chuck always told me to keep quiet and not discuss anything at the meeting that had not been cleared with him beforehand. On one occasion, I overstepped my bounds in this regard, and Chuck let me know he was not amused. I had mentioned that he was pursuing the development of a possible penetration of the VCI in a village south of the city. Chuck had told me about his desire to recruit spies inside the enemy's political apparatus and mentioned that one possible source was living in a village a few miles south of the city. He was extremely angry when I told him I had mentioned this in the Phoenix Committee, and from then on I was not asked to attend the committee's meetings. I had naively assumed that since everyone at the meeting had a top secret clearance and was involved in the effort to eliminate the VCI, it was acceptable to share this bit of intelligence with the members of the committee. I was wrong—dead wrong—and Chuck had every right to be angry with me. I was not an intelligence professional like he was, and I had no understanding of the sensitivity of the work Chuck was doing to recruit spies from the ranks of the VCI. Chuck told me a few days later, after this faux pas, that he blamed himself for my mistake. In a fatherly way, he explained that I had a specific job to do as the PRU commander, and it did not include intelligence management, except at the tactical level. He reminded me that I lacked the training and experience needed for work involving intelligence management, a fact I understood all too well. Strategic or high-level political intelligence was clearly and exclusively under the purview of the POIC, and he had been wrong to even discuss a small portion of this work with me. He ordered me to never, under any circumstances, discuss his work outside of the Embassy House with anyone, including the Americans at PRU headquarters in Saigon. Chastised, and feeling guilty at having let Chuck down, I told him I would obey his order completely. I made up my mind that evening to restrict my activities solely to my job and not involve myself in anyone else's work. I resolved to keep what I was doing to myself, unless it required the authorization of Chuck. While this prevented me from making any more mistakes revealing sensitive information, it would lead me to make an even bigger mistake later on, one that I will address in a following chapter.

Chapter 13

First Impressions

The first two weeks into my stay in Tay Ninh were spent getting to know my PRU leaders and men, visiting each district to determine if the PRU teams in these districts were performing properly, coordinating with the various U.S. and GVN organizations that provided intelligence to the PIOCC and the DIOCCs, studying the PRU files in the Embassy House to see what my predecessors had done, assessing the training and logistics needs of the PRU, and spending at least an hour each day talking to Mr. Tho and making plans with him for future PRU operations. I also took several aerial reconnaissance flights of the province with SFC Smith aboard U.S. Army scout helicopters from the U.S. Army's 25th Infantry Division. I was quite busy and found I had little time to talk to Chuck or the other members of our household about my activities. They also seemed to be very busy with their jobs, often staying in their rooms until late at night, typing up field reports that they would put in the "pouch," to be flown to Region III headquarters in Bien Hoa. It seemed the only time we socialized was at meals, when our conversations were guarded due to the presence of Mrs. Thu and her 15-year old-daughter, Missy, who often helped her mother after school preparing and serving our evening meal. I began to adapt to this professional isolation. It seemed to be a routine part of the "compartmenting" of the CIA officer's life. Conversation in the Embassy House always seemed to revolve around small talk and seldom involved topics of a classified nature. If intelligence matters were discussed, it was always done in one's room with the door closed. In many respects, the work done by Chuck, John and Mickey was a complete mystery to me since no one shared more than a very cursory aspect of their work with me. In my initial meeting with Chuck, he explained the need for this secrecy. He told me that the work SFC Smith and I did with the PRU, especially our field work, made it possible that we could be captured by the enemy, and the less we knew of the CIA operations in the province, the better. I took his explanation at face value and did not pry into the affairs of any of my colleagues.

At the end of my first month, I prepared my initial monthly report for submission. This report, which was the only administrative requirement levied upon me and the other PRU commanders, was far different from the long, tedious, and often inane reports required of me in the Marine Corps. I could literally prepare this report in an hour and have it in the pouch to Region III the very day I wrote it. To make the report as simple as possible, the CIA devoted most of it to filling in numbers representing such categories as "VCI killed," "VCI captured," "VCI rallied," "weapons captured," "intelligence reports submitted," and a few other items of interest for those collating information on the war against the VCI. There

Nui Ba Den Mountain.

were also categories for such things as the number of PRU soldiers on the muster rolls, PRU casualties, and money expended on operational requirements. All of this numerical information was typed on the first page of the report. There was only one section at the end of the report devoted to a narrative of the month's activities, and this narrative portion could lengthen the report to two or more pages. The following narrative for my first month in Tay Ninh Province is illustrative of the kind of information this section contained:

> PRU operational results for the month of October (1969) were greater than the month of September with the number of VCI captured in October exceeding the average for the previous five months. In light of the reduced level of enemy activity in the province, this is most encouraging.
> Again, the bulk of the PRU activity and productivity could be found in the efforts of Team 1 in Khiem Hanh district and Team 2 in Hieu Thien district. I believe that this trend is not just a function of a disproportionate amount of VCI activity in these districts, but rather a direct result of the superior leadership of the team leaders, Mr. Le Minh Khoi and Mr. Le Van No and their excellent intelligence nets, especially the Hieu Thien net. Even a cursory evaluation by this reporting officer of all of the PRU intelligence efforts has indicated that the PRU informant nets in Hieu Thien and Khiem Hanh districts have a far greater proficiency and have a far more closely monitored, controlled, and exploited organization than those in Phu Khuong and Phuoc Ninh districts. The PRU leaders in these latter two districts have been apprised of this deficiency and have assured me that they will take the necessary actions to bring their [intelligence] operations up to the level of the other two districts.
> During the month of October, a penetration [of the VCI] was achieved by the Hieu Thien district PRU of a village finance-economy organization. The agent, a member of the village's finance-economy committee, placed himself at the service of Team 2 after the VC shot and killed his brother. His authenticity is presently being established, and his actions closely monitored with the intention of further exploitation of this penetration. Team 2 hopes to cultivate this agent until such time as a large target is acquired or a higher level penetration can be achieved.

The author with PRU soldiers near Nui Ba Den Mountain.

13. First Impressions   195

During the period of October 21–23, an operation [Cliff Dweller II] was conducted by forty PRU assets, and [the U.S. Army's] C/3/22 involving the movement of these units from the top of Nui Ba Den [Black Virgin Mountain], down the steep east slope to close with a blocking force at the base of the mountain. As a result of this movement, the blocking force engaged a company-size NVA force on the night of October 21 and killed twenty NVA soldiers by body count and captured three individual weapons and five crew-served weapons. At 1400 on October 23, elements of C/3/22 and the PRU force, commanded by Mr. Chinh and accompanied by SFC Smith and me, engaged two VC hiding in a cave vic. XT296592, resulting in two VC KIA with no friendly casualties. No indication of any VC district organization, the intended target for the operation, was found in the area. Four American Bronze Star medals were awarded to PRU assets Chinh, Nghiem, Sen, and Lam for this action and were presented at the 1st Brigade, 25 Infantry Division headquarters at Tay Ninh West Airfield (USA) in ceremonies on October 26.

The Phoenix Committee for this province is a problem. Unfortunately, almost all targets assigned to the PRU have been the result of their own intelligence-gathering system and not from the Phoenix Committee's Acquisition System. The PRU Chief, Mr. Chinh, and the Phoenix Chief, Mr. Anh, enjoy a close personal relationship, but unfortunately, the Phoenix Committee does not seem to possess the administrative ability or the intelligence insight required to effectively acquire and assign VCI targets with reliability or rapidity. I have attempted to remedy this situation by establishing a close relationship with the Phoenix advisor, but it appears that the real source of the problem lies on the Vietnamese side of the fence, and progress has been slow. Every effort will be made, however, to work within the Phoenix framework and to improve its functioning as far as PRU activities are concerned.

The relationships between the PRU teams and their respective district chiefs are good overall with mutual respect the prevalent mood. In the cases of Team 3 of Phuoc Ninh district and Team 4 of Phu Khuong district, a strong and genuine bond of friendship appears to exist between the PRU team leaders and their district chiefs. There is, however, a problem existing between PRU Team 2 of Hieu Thien district, commanded by Le Van No, and the chief of that district. Team 2 is the most efficient and productive team in the province and possesses a reliable and extensive net of sympathizers and informants. The fact that they are successful and relatively honest has gained them the disfavor of the district chief, who is, according to the PRU and several other sources, heavily involved in graft ... and, in short, a detriment rather than an asset to the counter–VCI effort in the province. A recent example of his poor judgment and questionable motives was his covert release of two VCI POWs the day after they were captured and turned over to him by the PRU. A formal complaint was lodged by Mr. Chinh to the province chief, but as yet, no satisfactory explanation for the district chief's actions has been provided. I am seeking an emollient to this situation through American channels ... a more thorough investigation and separate report will be made.

Of continuing concern are the problems involving reimbursement of PRU asset Tran Van Pha and the pressing need for action on the request for construction of a new PRU building within the Hieu Thien district headquarters compound. Both items have been addressed in previous communications with ROIC III.

Of further interest is a piece of information gathered by two separate PRU sources indicating that a meeting has been held recently within Cambodia between representatives of the Free Cambodia (Khmer Serey) movement and the KKK organization, and this meeting has resulted in an agreement between these two groups on some sort of united armed action to take place inside Cambodia within the next two months. If further details are obtained, they will be furnished immediately.[1]

I have included this first monthly report's narrative in its entirety because it highlights several key issues confronting the PRU Program in general, not just those that apply to Tay Ninh Province in late 1969. For instance, the importance of personal relationships between the PRU and the province chiefs and district chiefs they served were often the difference

American award ceremony for PRU soldiers. *Left to right*: author, Mr. Ngo, Mr. Dung, Mr. Chinh, Charles Stainback, SFC Smith.

Mr. Tho in foreground and SFC Smith on the right, Nui Ba Den Mountain, Operation Cliff Dweller II.

between success and failure in the fight against the VCI. This was because the provincial and district Phoenix Committees were chaired by the provincial chiefs and district chiefs, and they could effectively block coordination and intelligence sharing between the committees they chaired and the PRU. Where the PIOCCs and DIOCCs worked as they were intended to work, the VCI were systematically destroyed. When personal feuds and bureaucratic conflicts existed, the Phoenix system did not function at peak performance and the war against the VCI suffered. What has always amazed me is how effective the Phoenix Program was, even though many obstacles were placed in its path by both the American and South Vietnamese governments and by poorly trained or poorly motivated Americans and South Vietnamese assigned to it.

The first of my monthly reports also contained a few clues about a mysterious source of high-level strategic intelligence who was so valuable to the Americans that they sacrificed many opportunities to roll up the VCI in Tay Ninh Province in order to protect him. This often resulted in restricting intelligence to the PRU that might result in even the slightest chance that PRU operations might threaten the identity or the life of this mysterious "Tay Ninh Source." For instance, the target for the operation conducted on Nui Ba Den Mountain was the VCI district committee that contained this mysterious "source," but in order to warn the "source" of the impending operation, it was delayed 24 hours. When the operation was finally launched, no VCI were caught in the net, even though we had received good intelligence that elements of the VCI district committee were located near the southern slope of Nui Ba Den. At the time, I chalked up the failure of the operation to faulty intelligence, but Mr. Chinh told me afterward that he thought the operation had been compromised somehow. He was right, but at that time we did not know why or by whom.

Our first real indication that someone was tipping off the enemy about our PRU operations occurred in late October, shortly after the conclusion of the Nui Ba Den operation with the U.S. 25th Infantry Division. Our city PRU team received reliable information concerning the location of the VCI district headquarters for their Duong Minh Chau district, which was roughly aligned with the GVN district of Phu Khuong. An informant who had reported reliably in the past told the PRU that the VC District Chief, Sau Bau (party code name), and his staff were located in a wooded area called the Boi Loi Woods in the southeastern part of the province, not far from the border with Binh Dong Province, and they were guarded by only a depleted squad of seven VC guerrillas. The informant warned that while the location of the VCI district headquarters was accessible by several trails leading to it from both Routes 26 and 29, any attempt to use these roads would be discovered by the enemy, thus giving the enemy time to escape. For this reason, Mr. Chinh, Mr. Tho, and I decided I would request an assault helicopter package from the U.S. 25th Infantry Division consisting of five UH-1H transport helicopters, two helicopter gunships, and a command and control helicopter.[2]

When I visited the Tay Ninh West base camp to coordinate my request with the S-3A for air operations, I also arranged for an aerial reconnaissance flight for Mr. Tho and me the next day, and I showed them the operation plan that the PRU had prepared for the capture of the VC Duong Minh Chau district headquarters. The S-3A and his assistants were eager to assist us, and we easily ironed out the details of our combined operation. The next day Mr. Tho and I boarded a U.S. Army light observation helicopter and flew over the target area, observing it from a distance so as not to reveal our intention of conducting an operation there. I could see why the informant had warned us about using any roads or trails near the site, since most of the area was open, making observation of any approach easy. The area was not populated and consisted primarily of abandoned fields with knee-high grass and individual stands of trees a few hundred square meters in size. I could readily see that there was no approach to the target area that would allow us to remain unobserved, even at night. Mr. Tho and I both agreed that the best course of action would be an assault directly on top of the enemy location, using surprise to gain the advantage over the enemy.

I briefed Chuck about the operation, and he immediately approved it. It was then coordinated with the PIOCC so no friendly units would get in our way. We scheduled the assault for the day after our visual reconnaissance (VR) flight of the area and placed the PRU assault team, consisting of the entire City Team and eight PRU soldiers from the Hieu Thien district PRU, in isolation at the City Team's barracks. Mr. Chinh, Mr. Tho, SFC Smith, Mr. Lam, and I were also added to the PRU assault team, giving us a total force of thirty-one, more than enough, we thought, to quickly overcome a depleted squad of VC. Just hours before we were to launch the operation, we were told there would be a delay of 24 hours. No reason was given for the delay, so I went to Tay Ninh West base camp to find out why. When I asked the U.S. Army officer who was our liaison for the operation about the delay he said he did not know why there was a delay, but the division commander had been told by MACV that the operation could not be launched until 24 hours had lapsed. I was completely perplexed by the answer I was given, but I respected the professionalism of the Army officer we had been dealing with, and if he said he did not know why there was a delay, I believed him. While I knew intelligence on the location of the VCI was a very perishable commodity and time was extremely important, I reconciled myself to the delay. Still, in the back of my mind, I had the nagging feeling that something was amiss here since no one seemed to know the reason behind the delay.

On the day of the helicopter assault, our PRU force was picked up at the Tay Ninh East Airfield and transported quickly to the objective area. I told the pilots not to make any dry passes but to put us down as quickly as possible. I also requested that no prep fires be used since I knew this would only alert the enemy and allow them to flee. The pilots did not like my instructions, so we compromised. The gunships would fly directly in front of the transport helicopters and strafe the LZ as we came in for our landing. Everything worked well—too well. We landed in a large open area 100 meters south of our objective and immediately began to move toward it, using fire and maneuver. We received no fire on landing and no fire as we assaulted the objective. It was obvious no one was there. After setting up security, we searched the area and found what initially looked like a covert base camp consisting of several covered foxholes, the remnants of a cooking fire, and some trash scattered about, including some pages from a notebook with a speech by Ho Chi Minh written in it. At first we simply felt the enemy had seen the helicopters and fled, but Mr. Chinh looked closely at the ashes of the campfire and the trash left at the site, and soon he was telling me he thought the entire camp had been "staged" to make it look like the enemy had fled only a few minutes before our arrival. He pointed out that the ashes in the campfire were cold and the trash left behind did not make any sense since most of it consisted of commercial food wrappers and empty cans of fish that appeared to be several days old. He also pointed out that there was no latrine in the vicinity, and he could not smell any human urine nearby. We were all disappointed with the outcome and decided we would analyze the events leading up to this "dry hole" when we returned to Tay Ninh City.

Left to right: Mr. Nghiem, SFC Smith, Mr. Chinh, and the author, Tay Ninh East Airfield.

Tay Ninh PRU soldiers at the conclusion of an operation near the Boi Loi Woods.

After two "blown" operations in one month, both of which were targeted against the communist Duong Minh Chau district VCI cadre, Mr. Chinh and I convened a "murder board" to review why both operations seemed to have been compromised. The meeting was held at the PRU headquarters in Tay Ninh City in late October and was attended by me, Mr. Lam, Mr. Chinh, Mr. Tho, and the Deputy PRU Chief, Mr. Nguyen Van Siem, whose agent provided the initial report about the location of the communist meeting place in the Boi Loi Woods. We spent several hours discussing the timelines for the initial receipt of the intelligence used to justify both the Nui Ba Den and Boi Loi Woods operations, and we came to the conclusion that there was a high degree of probability that both missions had been compromised. Since the PRU team members who participated in both operations were isolated in their barracks prior to receiving their orders and were not briefed until 24 hours in advance of the operations, we precluded them from our list of people who could have contacted the enemy and revealed our plans. We made a list of everyone who had knowledge of both of these operations and found that the list was larger than we had anticipated. It included everyone in the PIOCC, including the province chief and the five PRU members who actually worked on the operation plans. We finally agreed that the most likely source of the compromise was a communist spy either in the PRU or the PIOCC. We determined that twenty-nine Vietnamese had knowledge of both operations and had enough time to warn the enemy. When Mr. Chinh went over the list of names, he said he could not believe anyone on the list was a likely VC spy.

During this meeting, I asked Mr. Chinh if there were any other historical examples of PRU missions being compromised like these recent ones, and he said the only times he could remember that something like this had happened before were a few instances during the past two years when operations directed against district-level targets north of the city had been unsuccessful, causing him to think there might be a spy inside the PRU. Mr. Chinh said he would take up our concerns with the province chief and see if some investigation could be initiated to find the spy. We agreed that I would also discuss the matter with John, the National Police Special Branch Advisor, when I returned to the Embassy House. After I said this, Mr. Chinh took me aside and told me to be careful about what I said to "Mr. John" and "Mr. Chuck" because he did not want anyone in the Special Branch to be assigned to investigate a possible enemy spy within the ranks of the PRU. Mr. Lam told me after the meeting that Mr. Chinh and the National Police were not on good terms, and the police were always looking for some way to bring Mr. Chinh and the PRU under their control.

When I returned to the Embassy House that day, I remembered Mr. Chinh's request not to discuss the potential of an enemy spy with Chuck or John, but I approached Mickey, the PIC advisor, and asked him if he had ever heard of any spies in the PRU. I was surprised when he told me that he thought the PRU administrative officer, Mr. Pham Van Chuong, was a VC spy. I became angry with Mickey that he had not shared his suspicions with me before, but he simply retorted, "You never asked before."

I demanded to know why he suspected Mr. Chuong of being a VC spy, and he only cryptically replied, "I have heard this from several sources, but you had best talk to John about it since he knows more about it than I do."

I immediately went into John's room and found him, as usual, banging away at his typewriter on one of his many field reports. I asked him if he thought Mr. Chuong was a spy, and instead of answering, he stood up shielding his typewriter so I could not see what he was typing. He took me to the other side of his room and had me sit in a chair while he sat on his bed. He told me that Mr. Chuong was under suspicion because some PRU personnel information had been found in the possession of the VC, and the most likely source of this type of information was Mr. Chuong. I asked him how he knew that this PRU personnel information had been given to the enemy, and he said, "Andy, I can't tell you that because you don't have a need to know."

Now I was angry with John, and I yelled at him, "God damn it, John, don't you think it would be a good idea to tell me and SFC Smith that there might be a spy in the PRU since we work with these people every day and go to the field with them on operations?" John then said that he thought the PRU headquarters in Saigon had investigated the matter and cleared Mr. Chuong, so there was no reason now to worry about it. I was still not satisfied with this answer and decided to follow it up by taking a trip to Saigon to talk to Col. Allen in person about this matter. In the back of my mind, I had a strong suspicion that both Mickey and John were not telling me the truth, and I wondered why they would lie to me about such an important issue.

That evening I asked Chuck if I could take Lam with me to Saigon and visit the PRU headquarters. Since I had been in Tay Ninh for a month and my pay was handled in Saigon at the U.S. Navy MACV liaison office, he agreed that it would be a good idea to go to Saigon for a day and attend to my administrative and pay matters. I mentioned I wanted to stop by the PRU headquarters in Saigon and give Col. Allen a personal assessment of PRU operations in Tay Ninh Province, and Chuck readily agreed. He also gave me a few other items to discuss with Col. Allen, among them the imminent transfer of SFC Smith to a new assignment and some missing 38 cal. revolvers that had been on the PRU supply books—weapons Mr. Chinh had denied ever receiving.

Early the next day Lam and I drove our Toyota jeep to Saigon, taking Route 22 to Go Dau Ha, and then on to Saigon using Route 1. The drive took a little over two hours since both of these roads were hard surfaced. The closer we got to Saigon, the more traffic we encountered, especially as we neared Tan Son Nhut Air Base. Whenever I entered Saigon, I was struck by how different it was from the rest of South Vietnam. There was a decaying charm about the city with its old French-colonial buildings and villas and bustling river port. There was also a seedy aspect to it with its many bars, brothels, and black-market stalls selling stolen PX items at inflated prices. I never warmed to Saigon, and I never felt at ease there.

After getting paid by a woman U.S. Marine major at the MACV Navy Annex, which was situated very close to a large Vietnamese brothel posing as a massage parlor, Lam and I drove over to the PRU villa. There I spoke to Col. Allen about my first month in Tay Ninh Province, and he complimented me on my first monthly report, which he had just received from the ROIC for Region III. He said I should continue to provide the kind of detail my report contained since it gave him a much better idea about what the PRU teams were doing. He made a few derogatory remarks about "the numbers game," referring to the numbers in the categories in the monthly reports against which the success of the pacification program was measured. "Shackley [the CIA station chief] is a total numbers guy, just like that bastard McNamara was," he grumbled. "You don't win wars with numbers, but I guess I don't have to tell you that." I must have caught him on a bad day, because he spent the first 10 minutes of our conversation railing against "the insatiable demands for data from the U.S. Embassy," the American press corps in Saigon, the U.S. State Department, and a South Vietnamese province chief in I Corps. After venting his anger, he settled down and asked me what was on my mind.

"Sir, can you tell me if any member of the Tay Ninh PRU has been the subject of an investigation about spying for the enemy?" I asked.

"Not that I can remember, but let me ask Maj. Lang, since he would be the one who conducted such an investigation. Let's bring him in and ask him."

A moment later, Maj. Lang entered Col. Allen's office, and we put the question of a possible enemy spy in the Tay Ninh PRU directly to him. He thought for a moment and then said he wanted to check some files he had on past investigations—investigations that predated his assignment to the PRU. He left the office and returned 30 minutes later and announced, "No, we have never conducted an investigation of the Tay Ninh PRU. In fact, we consider them one of the most difficult units for the enemy to penetrate or proselytize because just about all of them are Cao Dai." After giving a clean bill of health to the Tay Ninh PRU, he told us several stories about enemy attempts to penetrate the PRU, primarily by VC who falsely rallied to the GVN with the intent of penetrating the PRU or some other GVN organization. While he said there had been attempts, most, if not all, had failed. Col. Allen added that the PRU had a very thorough vetting process and also a counterintelligence capability, which he described as effective. I thanked both men and left. As I did so, Maj. Lang told me that if he had the slightest inkling there was an enemy agent inside the PRU in my province, he would let me know immediately. When I returned to the Duc Hotel to meet Lam, I wondered why John and Mickey had tried to tag Mr. Chuong as a VC spy, but

I decided not to discuss the matter with Lam or anyone else until I could speak to Mr. Chinh back in Tay Ninh City.

Since it was rather late in the day, and I wanted to see a bit of Saigon, I radioed Chuck and asked him for permission to return the next day. After gaining his permission, I asked Col. Allen and his deputy, Maj. Hyslop, to join me for dinner at the Hotel Continental and a bit of bar hopping on Tu Do Street afterward. The Hotel Continental was a place that made me think of a Graham Greene novel and the movie *Casablanca*. It had an airy, French-colonial-style veranda where tables were arranged within a few feet of the pedestrians walking by, and waiters wearing clean white coats and black bow ties served excellent French cuisine and wines. Sitting around us were people who could have been right out of central casting for a James Bond spy movie. Western men sat with willowy and beautiful Vietnamese women. Vietnamese men smoking cigarettes and drinking cognac with soda talked in hushed tones despite the cacophony of taxi horns and noisy cyclo engines going by. A rich, dense, foul-smelling blue haze of smoke clung to the street and competed with the aroma of our food. Col. Allen seemed to know a great deal about Saigon, and over dinner he gave me a short history of the city, the current political situation, and the names of several good restaurants in the city, such as Le Paris and L'Amiral, which he strongly suggested I visit on any future trips to Saigon. He even pointed out several "famous" people sitting at tables near us as we ate.

At one table sat a group of American and Vietnamese journalists and a couple of very attractive Vietnamese girls. Col. Allen told me the journalists were from either *Time* or *Newsweek*. I asked him how he knew who these men were, and he said that his cover for his PRU assignment was that of a MACV public affairs officer, so he had frequent contact with

The Continental Palace Hotel, Saigon.

the Western press in order to maintain his cover. As Col. Allen talked about the men occupying the nearby table, I could see he did not have a high opinion of them. He explained that he thought most of the American press corps and their Western colleagues were entirely too dependent upon their South Vietnamese sources, and much of what they wrote amounted to little more than "Saigon café gossip." When I told him I seldom saw any American journalists during my previous two years in South Vietnam, he told me he was not surprised, since his contact with the Western press gave him an insight into how most of them operated when they covered the war. He said almost all of the dangerous journalistic work was done by third-country nationals, normally South Vietnamese or Taiwanese; they fed reports and film from the field to the Western reporters in Saigon, who would then voice-over the film or write their reports as if they had actually observed the action on the ground. He went on to say that during his two years in Saigon, he had met only one American journalist who could speak Vietnamese, identifying this journalist as Zalin Grant of *Time* magazine. He mentioned several other Western journalists he respected, but none of them were names I recognized. No one knew it at the time, but there was a North Vietnamese spy working in the *Time* office in Saigon, and this enemy spy used his position to obtain highly classified information from American civilian and military officials who had provided this information as background to *Time* magazine's American journalists. This spy's name was Pham Xuan An, and he did more damage to the U.S. and Vietnamese military forces than any other enemy spy during the war.[3]

After dinner, the three of us went to a nightclub, where we sat at a small table, ordered some drinks, and watched the floor show. One of the acts was a young singer named Khanh Ly, whom I had met two years earlier when she was singing at the Stone Elephant Officers Club in Da Nang City. She was very attractive and had a sweet, melodious voice. Most of her songs were popular Vietnamese ballads written by the famous contemporary songwriter Trinh Cong Son, but a few were in French. As we sat there, I noticed an older Western gentleman leave his seat and walk toward the small stage where Khanh Ly was singing. When she finished one of her songs, he whispered something to her and then he returned to his seat. The song that this man had requested was the famous and much-loved French ballad "Non, Je Ne Regrette Rien" ("I Have No Regrets,") which was made famous by Edith Piaf. The room fell silent as she began singing, and I noticed the man who had requested the song was standing at his table with tears running down his cheeks. He remained standing until the song was finished, and then he bowed to Khanh Ly and sat down. I asked a South Vietnamese man sitting at an adjacent table why the man was crying and he said he did not know, but he would ask someone and tell me later.

At the end of the evening, as we left the nightclub to return to the Duc Hotel, I was followed by the man I had asked about the reason for the old man's tears when Khanh Ly sang. He explained to me that the man was an old legionnaire from the 13th Demi-Brigade of the French Foreign Legion. That unit had been at Dien Bien Phu during that famous battle and was nearly wiped out. Edith Piaf had dedicated the song to the fallen at Dien Bien Phu, and it had been an unofficial anthem for the French Foreign Legion ever since. Now I understood the old legionnaire's tears. To this day, the image of this old man standing at attention in a smoke-filled Saigon nightclub, his face streaked with tears, haunts me, probably because his image seems to symbolize all the trauma and sadness that soldiers have had to suffer fighting for lost causes.

CHAPTER 14

Bad American Policy—A New Focus

In early November, our luck changed, and we conducted a classic operation exploiting excellent intelligence provided by a PRU informant reporting to the Khiem Hanh District PRU Chief, Mr. No. The informant told us that VC Rear Service Group 83, an enemy unit that provided logistical support to enemy mobile units, was located in a marshy area two miles west of the Ben Cui Rubber Plantation in the far eastern part of the province. This time, Mr. Chinh and I decided to keep the planning for this operation to only a select few PRU leaders and to keep the location and identity of the enemy unit a secret until six hours before we launched the raid. We suspected that the two operations in late October against important VCI targets had been compromised, so we tried to minimize the number of people with knowledge of the operation and to maintain a list of those who had knowledge of the operations order prior to its implementation. If there was a compromise, we wanted to be able to ascertain who was responsible.

Since the target area for this operation was far from any PRU team's compound and was in an uninhabited area of the province, we decided that we would need to obtain a U.S. Army helicopter package to transport our PRU force to the objective area. Mr. Chinh and Mr. Tho also suggested that we incorporate the Phuoc Ninh district Combined Reconnaissance and Intelligence Platoon (CRIP) for added firepower. The CRIP were platoons of light infantry made up of American soldiers and Vietnamese militia, similar to the Combined Action Platoons (CAP) made up of U.S. Marines and Vietnamese PF soldiers. Like the CAP, the CRIP were highly effective and produced a good blend of American expertise and firepower with Vietnamese local knowledge and intelligence. Mr. Chinh also thought having the CRIP along with us meant more Americans would be going on the operation, making our request for American helicopters more likely to be approved. As usual, he was right. When I went to the operations officer for AirOps for the 1st Cavalry Division, he eagerly approved a helicopter package consisting of two Cobra gunships and nine HU-1H transport helicopters for the mission. After arranging for the helicopter package, I drove to the Phuoc Ninh district headquarters and coordinated with the Phoenix advisor and the American commander of the CRIP. Once this was done, I returned to PRU headquarters in Tay Ninh for a planning meeting with Mr. Chinh and Mr. Tho. Together we worked on our operation plan the rest of the day. At the same time, Mr. Chinh placed a PRU force of forty-seven men in isolation in the barracks and issued them their ammunition, rations, and radio batteries.

The next morning, November 5, I told Chuck we were going to launch an operation near the Ben Cui Rubber Plantation and the operation would commence at noon that day.

He approved the operation and agreed that speed was important if we wanted to capitalize on the intelligence we had received the day before. At 1030, fifteen men from the CRIP joined the forty-seven PRU soldiers at the Tay Ninh East Airfield and Mr. Tho and I briefed the assembled assault force and the helicopter pilots on the mission. Mr. Tho told me he had informed the PIOCC of the operation late last night, thus making it virtually impossible for any VC spy on the committee to warn the enemy before we conducted the raid. At 1200 sharp, the first HU-1H helicopter lifted into the air and headed east toward the Ben Cui Rubber Plantation and a rendezvous with the VC Rear Service Group 83. This lead helicopter carried me, Mr. Tho, Mr. Lam, and five PRU soldiers from the City Team.

As our assault flight of eleven helicopters flew east toward the border with Binh Duong Province, Mr. Tho and I followed our flight on our maps. At first we flew over the sprawling city of Tay Ninh, and then picked up Route 26, a long dirt road that took a sharp turn to the southeast just a mile or two outside of the city's limits. I could see large tracks of abandoned fields, clumps of thick vegetation and stunted trees, bomb craters filled with water, and numerous footpaths crisscrossing the largely uninhabited terrain. After a few minutes of flight following Route 26, we came to where this old French road intersected with Route 239, another dirt road that took us east in the direction of the Ben Cui Rubber Plantation. I told the pilots to make a false insertion a few miles west of our objective in the hope of fooling the enemy into thinking we were landing five miles to the west of them. We swept in low for a landing on the western side of Route 26, just south of the intersection with Route 239, remaining in an abandoned rice paddy for a few seconds before lifting off again, so it would appear that we were returning to Tay Ninh City. I hoped this ruse would work, and we could catch the enemy unawares.

A minute later we broke to the east and rapidly flew to our objective area, a wooded area a few hundred meters northeast of the tiny hamlet of Bau Anh. We landed in an open area in the forest, quickly formed into a skirmish line, and advanced toward the location our informant had told us about. We had gone only 100 meters when we came under fire from a sniper. We returned fire, and I was able to detect one VC running away to the north. I fired at him with my rifle and sent a PRU team of six men after him, warning them to be careful since this VC sniper was probably trying to divert us either into an ambush or away from our primary target. The rest of our force then assaulted into the wooded area, where our informant told us we would find the VC Rear Service Group 83. We quickly saw that the informant was correct because we found a camouflaged base camp under the trees consisting of three large earthen bunkers with logs for overhead cover and 20 fighting holes, also with overhead cover. It was evident that the camp had been hastily abandoned. There was a cooking fire still burning and several pots containing water near the fire. Inside the bunkers we found ten fish traps, eight large fish nets, 100 pounds of dried fish, 100 pounds of salt, a case of canned fish, two Chinese hand grenades, and many documents. As we cleared the area, set up security, and sent out patrols to the east, the six-man PRU team that had been chasing the sniper returned with him in tow. He had sustained a gunshot wound to his shoulder. Mr. Lam was carrying our radio, so I went over to him and radioed to the helicopter pilots to come back and medevac our prisoner. While the prisoner was waiting for the medevac, we heard the two Cobra gunships firing to our east. They had spotted five VC running away from us and were taking them under fire. They killed two of them, and one of our PRU security patrols found the bodies and retrieved a Chinese SKS rifle from one of the dead

VC. Mr. Tho was able to interrogate the VC prisoner before he was placed on the medevac helicopter. He told us his name was Phan Van Xa, and he was a member of the VC Rear Service Group 83. Further interrogation revealed that this enemy logistics unit was seriously depleted due to casualties and desertions. He told us there were only eight men left in his unit, which at one time had over 50. He also gave us the names of five VC guerrillas from a nearby village who provided security for the unit, but were absent on this occasion.

This operation was a complete success since we killed two VC and captured one without a single friendly casualty. In addition, we gained some valuable intelligence from the documents we captured and from the prisoner we interrogated. The VC Rear Service Group 83 was seriously damaged and their base camp destroyed. Unfortunately, this operation, which was successful in large part because of good intelligence and the close cooperation between the PRU and American Army units, would be the last such successful combined operation for the month of November due to a new and extremely bad policy change made by MACV.

Mr. Tho and author planning an operation at PRU HQ.

I did not know it at the time, but this operation would be the last time I would personally engage in a firefight with the enemy, a direct result of the new MACV policy prohibiting U.S. military advisors from accompanying the PRU on field operations. My monthly report for November 1969 put this dilemma in stark perspective:

> PRU operational results for the month of November were below the results obtained in the previous month. This was due to the increase in the employment of PRU assets in night ambush operations to counter the mid–November VC "high point" and the reduction of the operating range of PRU operations, the direct result of the Station policy of not allowing U.S. advisors to accompany PRU teams on combined operations. As a result, the monthly total of VCI captured dropped from 22 to 8.

I knew I was whipping a dead horse by harping about this change in policy, but I wanted to make sure the written record contained the negative results this policy had on the war against the VCI. I would obey orders, but I would not allow anyone to think I was complying with them because I thought they were a good idea. I summed up my frustration in the same November report in a later paragraph:

> After the implementation of the Station policy (preventing U.S. advisors from accompanying the PRU teams on operations), one major operation was aborted and two curtailed as the result of the non-availability of PRU advisors for combined operations. It is interesting to note that after November 7 not one PRU operation in Tay Ninh Province took place more than 3,000 meters from a PRU district headquarters and then never more than 1,000 meters from a main road due to the PRU's fear of not being able to medevac their wounded. Of course, this is not unreasonable since the only allied force in Tay Ninh Province that does not now enjoy the capability of helicopter medevac is the PRU.

When I was assigned to the PRU, I had no idea that Gen. Abrams had already decided to place some very severe restrictions on the military personnel assigned to the program. Due to adverse publicity surrounding the Phoenix Program in general, and the PRU in particular, much of it false or based upon fraudulent claims made by military personnel with only a tangential relationship to the Phoenix Program, Gen. Abrams issued instructions that U.S. military officers assigned to the PRU must no longer command these units, but only serve as advisors; and they must not accompany the PRU teams when they conducted operations. These instructions were issued in October 1969 but were not fully implemented until late November 1969. The restrictions were done to protect the U.S. military from any blame for the misemployment of the PRU by the GVN, and thus insulate MACV from any criticism that the U.S. was involved in illegal or extralegal activities. Unfortunately, this policy did great damage to the pacification program and actually facilitated any potential misuse of the PRU since it removed an American presence when the PRU went on an operation, thus eliminating any chance to report abuses or to prevent them. In essence, it blinded MACV to what the PRU was doing.

In addition, the policy also had a deleterious effect on the morale and operational range of the PRUs, two problems that I had to confront early in my assignment. Because the PRU teams lacked adequate transport assets and limited communications, they relied heavily on American support for operations conducted far from their bases. American aviation units were very reluctant to provide this support without an American with the PRU, and even more reluctant to land a medevac helicopter for a PRU team with casualties unless there was an American with them controlling the medevac. This had the practical effect of restricting PRU operations to those close to their bases and rarely far from a road. It also diminished the regard the Vietnamese had for their American advisors, since it appeared the Americans did not trust their lives with their Vietnamese colleagues when it came time to sharing the dangers of field operations. I was informed of the new restrictions on November 8 when Maj. Hyslop, the U.S. Marine executive officer for Col. Allen, came to visit me in Tay Ninh City.

I was so outraged by these new orders, I immediately went to see Chuck to determine if they were indeed accurate, since all I had was Maj. Hyslop's verbal order. Chuck said he was unaware of any change in my status, but he would check with Daren Flitcroft, the ROIC at Region III, to ascertain the validity of the change in policy. He told me to continue to go to the field until further notice and not to tell the Tay Ninh PRU anything in the meantime. Like me, he thought the new restrictions would hurt operations and might even kill the

14. Bad American Policy—A New Focus

entire program. He then told me that he thought the genesis of the new restrictions was the report in the press that the U.S. Army Special Forces had killed an alleged double agent on June 20, 1969, by throwing him out of a helicopter and then blaming this criminal act on instructions from the CIA. This incident sparked outrage in both South Vietnam and the U.S., and caused MACV to overreact by placing restrictions on the U.S. military personnel assigned to work with the CIA. In MACV's effort to insulate the U.S. military from any blame by the U.S. press and politicians back in the U.S. for sanctioning the murder, they seriously damaged the pacification effort.

Chuck told me that the CIA never authorized the murder of an agent and that the Special Forces officers involved in this incident were merely trying to deflect their guilt onto the CIA, aided and abetted by senior U.S. military officers who were feeding false information to the American and foreign press in Saigon about the alleged CIA involvement. He went on to explain that the term "terminate with extreme predjudice," which the Special Forces used to explain why they took the murderous action they did, was clearly understood by all U.S. intelligence organizations to mean that any agent employed by the U.S. intelligence services who was found to be untrustworthy or seriously flawed was to be fired and every other pertinent U.S. intelligence organization was to be warned not to recruit or employ this agent. He said the best that could be said for the people responsible for the murder is they did not understand a basic term used in U.S. intelligence operations, but he seriously doubted this was the case.

This placed me in a predicament, since I had conflicting orders from Maj. Hyslop and Chuck. I decided to obey Chuck's orders until he could clarify the accuracy of those from Maj. Hyslop. I was prepared to face the consequences for failing to obey the new orders, but I felt confident that such foolish orders were either misunderstood or would be rescinded shortly when the lunacy behind them was examined by more rational people higher up the chain of command. Events would prove me wrong about the validity and permanence of these orders.

When Chuck came to me a few days later with a guidance letter in the courier pouch from Bien Hoa, we both found out that the instructions from Maj. Hyslop were correct. Henceforth, no U.S. military personnel, including those assigned to the CIA as PRU commanders, would be allowed to accompany the PRU on any mission. In addition, the status of the U.S. military assigned to the PRU would be changed from "commander" to "advisor," which meant we would no longer have operational control of our PRU. I was infuriated by this news, and hotheaded as I was, I drafted a scathing letter to PRU headquarters in Saigon outlining why I thought both the operational restrictions and my new advisor status were serious mistakes. Chuck endorsed my letter and recommended it receive "favorable attention" by MACV.[1] No reply to my letter was ever received, although on the next visit by Maj. Hyslop to Tay Ninh City he told me they had received the letter and forwarded it to MACV. To my surprise he told me that he and Col. Allen both concurred with my position, but "politics in Washington" precluded any possibility of changing the new instructions.

What was so immoral about this policy was the cynicism behind it. Instead of using the leadership and oversight of the U.S. PRU advisors to prevent any alleged misuse of the PRU, the American leaders simply sought to absolve themselves of any responsibility for the actions of the PRU by saying the American advisors were not present to witness the transgressions. This callous and cynical policy did nothing to prevent those who opposed the war from dreaming up alleged "crimes" by PRU "assassins"—it just made it easier to ignore any real misuse and to limit the PRU's effectiveness. Like many policies surrounding the PRU and the Phoenix Program, this was just another obstacle placed in the path of a successful pacification program by an American government that tended to believe what the U.S. press wrote about the Phoenix Program and not the reporting from their own employees working in South Vietnam. It is no wonder that most American PRU advisors, including Col. Allen, felt our own government did more damage to the PRU than anything the enemy did.

During Maj. Hyslop's visit, he offered me a friendly warning, one that had been offered to me before and would be repeated to me several times over the course of my career as a Marine officer. He explained that he would never be promoted again and was lucky to have been promoted to major, all because he had challenged his commanding officer over some minor issue and received a single bad fitness report for it. "You are far too outspoken," he said, "and this trait of yours will get you into serious trouble sometime. You need to think before you speak or write, or you will pay a high price for failing to do so. There are times when you need to go to the mat over something, but those times are very rare. Choose your battles carefully." I thanked him for the advice and resigned myself to my new role as advisor to the Tay Ninh PRU. I also began to plot how I could make this new bad situation as good as possible through innovation, adaptation, and a little bit of cunning.

One thing I could still do under the new restrictions was train the PRU. I had seen enough during my first month in Tay Ninh to know that there were certain areas that needed improvement. I asked Mr. Chinh what training deficiencies he thought his unit had and what I could do to help him remedy them. I did not try to impose my views on him or criticize the capabilities of his unit since I knew that would serve no useful purpose and might even cause an unintended rift between us. Instead, I simply listened to his comments to see if he saw things the same way I did. For the most part, his analysis of the training deficiencies coincided with mine, so I quickly agreed with him and we set about finding ways to correct the problems. Since we both recognized the PRU needed more marksmanship training, I arranged with an ARVN unit to use their rifle range for three days so the PRU could practice their marksmanship skills. During a routine inspection I found out that most of the PRU's M-16s had not been "zeroed," meaning they had not used a 1,000-inch range to determine their battle sights (used to achieve a point of aim—point of impact hit on a target at 300 meters). Mr. Chinh and I took twenty-eight PRU soldiers to the ARVN range, and the first day we "zeroed" each PRU soldier's rifle and began firing at targets at 100 meters. On the second and third day, I had each PRU soldier fire twenty rounds from a standing position at 100 meters, twenty rounds from a sitting position at 200 meters, and twenty rounds from a prone position at 300 meters. Mr. Chinh, Mr. Tho, and I carefully coached each shooter and recorded hits and misses in an improvised shooter's card we had mimeographed at the PRU headquarters. Since many of the PRU had received formal marksmanship training before with the ARVN and the U.S. Special Forces, they quickly recovered their dormant skills.

During the last day of our training on the rifle range, I won the admiration of the PRU soldiers when I challenged their best marksmen to a contest. I told them I would give any man who beat me firing five shots at a target 300 meters downrange a cash prize of 20,000 piasters, or around $10. All of the PRU soldiers wanted to compete, but Mr. Chinh chose only six men to respond to my challenge. We placed seven targets on a berm 300 meters downrange; then the seven of us got into the prone position and fired our five rounds at the targets. Only one PRU soldier was able to put all five rounds on his target, and his shots were not in a tight group. I placed all of my five shots into a tight group of less than six inches in circumference. Mr. Chinh declared me the winner of the contest, and from that moment on, I enjoyed a reputation with the PRU as a man who knew how to shoot a rifle. In this case, and in many other instances, my Marine Corps marksmanship training paid off for me.

In mid–November, I received a classified message from the PRU headquarters informing me that I was to attend a meeting of all PRU chiefs and U.S. PRU advisors in III Corps, to be held at the PRU training facility in Vung Tau, a small city on the coast of South Vietnam and a favorite seaside resort. The purpose of the meeting was to go over the new instructions from Gen. Abrams concerning the command relationship between the American PRU advisors and the Vietnamese PRU chiefs, and to review the details of President Nixon's Vietnamization policy as it pertained to the Phoenix Program and the PRU. Another topic for discussion was an analysis of the results of the first full year of the Phoenix Program in III Corps.

Mr. Chinh and I flew aboard an Air American Pilatus Porter aircraft from Tay Ninh East Airfield to the airport at Vung Tau, a flight that made two stops in neighboring provinces to pick up some other PRU chiefs and American advisors. When we arrived, we joined the other III Corps attendees at the training facility and began our meeting with a delicious Vietnamese meal. Approximately twenty American advisors and their Vietnamese PRU counterparts were in attendance, along with a half-dozen American and Vietnamese from the U.S. Embassy and the PRU headquarters. After lunch, Maj. Lang addressed us in a large conference hall and reminded everyone that he would be discussing highly classified matters, and for this reason, he did not want anyone to take notes during his briefing.

The first topic he addressed was President Nixon's policy of Vietnamization and what that meant to the PRU program. Essentially, he said the PRU would rapidly transition from a combined CIA/MACV and GVN program to a totally Vietnamese program, and this transition would begin immediately and be completed by the end of 1971. He warned his Vietnamese PRU chiefs that they would have to adapt to having far less American support as the American military began to withdraw from the country. He also predicted they would have to rely solely on the GVN to provide everything from weapons and equipment to pay and housing in the near future. He acknowledged that this transition would be difficult, but there was no alternative. When he finished speaking, he took several questions from the audience, questions that reflected serious concerns with how the new policy would affect the PRU. The most contentious questions involved the news from Maj. Lang that the PRU would be subsumed into the Vietnamese National Police, an organization that obviously did not enjoy a good reputation with many of the PRU chiefs attending the meeting. There were also some practical questions about how they would go about requesting support from the National Police and if the new policy would change the PRU chiefs' command relationship with their respective province chiefs. It was fairly apparent that the audience did not think much of the Nixon doctrine of Vietnamization, a fact not lost on Maj. Lang as he struggled to allay the fears and apprehension his comments generated.

When Maj. Lang finished his briefing, an American whom I did not recognize and never saw again gave a briefing on the Phoenix Program, starting with its history and ending with a province-by-province breakdown of the status of the pacification program in III Corps. Since we were not allowed to take notes, the specifics of this briefing are beyond my ability to recall, aside from the most salient points made. The American briefing officer told us the Phoenix Program had its origins in the northern part of South Vietnam, where the CIA saw the need to find some mechanism for coordinating all of the disparate programs involved with pacification. This was needed because the pacification effort was not functioning efficiently, what with so many different organizations, both American and Vietnamese, operating independently without much coordination between them and a great deal of duplication. The model for the Phoenix Program countrywide was only adopted in late 1967, just prior to the Tet Offensive of 1968. It was instituted just in time to take advantage of the Tet Offensive, which caused many VCI to surface during the "General Uprising" and thus reveal themselves.

The briefing officer mentioned several VC and NVA POWs and Hoi Chanhs who confirmed that the enemy's political cadres were facing serious attrition problems in every province. He also pointed to several classified VC documents that indicated this erosion of the VCI was seriously undermining the ability of mobile VC and NVA forces to operate inside South Vietnam. These same documents expressed deep concerns at COSVN that this attrition of experienced VCI cadre had caused COSVN to resort to using Lao Dong party members from North Vietnam instead of southerners as replacements. While success was uneven and there were still some problem areas, the briefer produced facts and figures that clearly demonstrated the enemy was losing the war in the villages as more and more of the VCI were neutralized and the GVN took control.

The last topic addressed was the contentious issue of the role of the new American advisors to the PRU and why Gen. Abrams had imposed restrictions that made it illegal for any American military personnel to accompany the PRU teams on operations. The American briefing officer made no attempt to hide his disdain for this new policy, but he said it was now in place and nothing could be done about it. He also repeated the order I had received from Col. Allen when I first joined the PRU program and had heard the first day I was in Tay Ninh Province from Chuck Stainback—that none of us were to ever do anything in violation of the UCMJ, and we were required to report any violation we witnessed to PRU headquarters via our POIC. Many of the American military advisors present expressed their anger at the implication that they had done something in the past that was illegal or immoral, and they felt offended by this new restriction placed upon them. One U.S. Army Special Forces NCO assigned as a PRU advisor said what we were all feeling:

> Gen. Abrams is trying to cover his ass with this policy. Everyone knows there have been examples of the PRU and other units fighting the VC going too far at times, but those instances are few and far between. Just because one person or one unit does something bad does not mean everyone and every unit does these things. For God's sake, we are at war. I don't need some candy-ass general in Saigon telling me how to behave. I know what an illegal order is. I don't obey illegal orders, and I don't condone illegal actions, so why are we being treated like this?

His sentiments were applauded by every American advisor in the room, but the American briefer simply listened to us bitch, and then he said, "Gentlemen, that is the way it is."

A week later, I received a letter from MACV headquarters that required me to sign an affidavit that I would not take any action that was in violation of the UCMJ and report any violation I witnessed. Chuck and Mr. Chinh were also required to sign the affidavit. We all viewed this unnecessary and insulting letter as yet another example of the American political and military leadership responding to scandalous and fraudulent claims made against the PRU by those who did not support the war. I can state categorically that I never participated in any illegal action by the Tay Ninh PRU or witnessed any PRU soldier committing an illegal act. I cannot vouch for all the PRUs in every province, but I can for mine.

When I returned to Tay Ninh City with Mr. Chinh, we stopped off at the Embassy House to tell Chuck the results of the meeting at Vung Tau. When my explanation of the Station policy concerning my new status as an advisor to the PRU and the proscription against accompanying them on operations came up, it soon revealed my hotheadedness and my lack of support for the policy. Chuck calmly changed the subject since he did not want to discuss the American policy in the presence of Mr. Chinh. I admired Chuck immensely and saw the wisdom of his restraint, so I took up a new subject and calmed down. When Mr. Chinh had departed, Chuck told me that I must learn to control my anger and not allow the new policy to affect my judgment or my relationship with Mr. Chinh and the PRU. He explained that he had been trying to advance the policy objectives of the United States for all of his adult life and he had often encountered the kind of obstacles that I was facing now, but his experience in such matters told him that our positions did not allow us to question the authority of our government, and that meant we must execute our orders without question, unless those orders were clearly illegal. In a firm but fatherly way, he told me to get on with the war and stop whining about the new policy. I knew he was right, but I did not like it.

In the course of our discussion that day, Mr. Chinh had mentioned that there were Cao Dai followers in other provinces in South Vietnam, not just in Tay Ninh Province. He also said the VC were always trying to proselytize his coreligionists in these provinces, but he did not know how effective the enemy had been. I asked him about my old stomping grounds, Quang Nam Province, and he said he knew there was a sizeable number of Cao Dai in that province. Chuck thought it might help for me to take a flight to Quang Nam Province and investigate the loyalty of the Cao Dai living in that province and then write a field report on my findings. While there was a certain logic in Chuck's idea, I realized that the main purpose of his suggestion was to get me away from the Tay Ninh PRU for a few days and get my mind off the new Station policy. He arranged for me to fly to Da Nang the next day and check in with the CIA Region I headquarters located there.

When I arrived in Da Nang, I was told the Cao Dai leader in Quang Nam Province was Nguyen Hong Khue and I could find him in Hoi An City south of Da Nang. I borrowed a CIA jeep and drove down Highway 1 to Hoi An, where I quickly found Mr. Khue. We sat down for tea in his home and began to discuss the reason for my visit. I could tell Mr. Khue was very nervous and apprehensive. After all, when an American wearing civilian clothes and carrying a snub-nosed Colt .38 cal. pistol arrives at one's home in a civilian jeep with U.S. Embassy license plates, it is not a routine occurrence for a South Vietnamese cleric. Since I had studied the doctrine of the Cao Dai and was familiar with its history, I tried to put Mr. Khue at ease by asking him some generic questions related to his religion.

After a few minutes discussing these innocent topics, I began to ask him about what he thought of the Ban The Dao, the new Cao Dai political organization created in 1968 by the Hiep Thien Dai, or "legislative body," for the religion. He clearly felt uncomfortable

Highway 1 south of Da Nang.

talking to me about the political activities of the Cao Dai, so I decided to change the subject to how he felt about the war and whether or not the VC threatened his congregation. He suggested that I might obtain more accurate information on this subject from an ARVN sergeant, named Hoa, who was the leader of the Cao Dai Youth Program in the province. When Sgt. Hoa joined us, Mr. Khue seemed more at ease, and both men began to speak freely about the VC and the war. We spoke for nearly three hours, and I took copious notes that I later turned into a field report when I returned to Tay Ninh City.

The most significant information these two Cao Dao leaders provided concerned what they described as "many acts of terrorism" against the Cao Dai refugee camp in the province and the continuous VC attempts to infiltrate the Cao Dai Youth Program and recruit Cao Dai youth to join the communist cause. Both men stressed that the Cao Dai religion was antithetical to communism, and therefore the VC attempts to proselytize the Cao Dai youth had not been successful.

When I asked about an alleged attempt by former Cao Dai military leaders, such as Gen. Thanh, to form a Cao Dai political party, Mr. Khue said he knew nothing about this and he was still adhering to the explicit instructions he had received from Cardinal Sang in the Tay Ninh Holy See that forbade any political activity whatsoever. As far as he was concerned, every Cao Dai member was to follow the politically neutral "co-existence line" set down by the Cao Dai leadership. When I asked for the rationale behind this proscription on political activities by the Cao Dai, both men spoke about the very perilous situation that the Cao Dai found themselves in Quang Nam Province, a situation that made political activity by their religion fraught with danger. As they put it, they were caught up in the dual struggles between the GVN and the VC, and the two powerful nationalist political parties

14. Bad American Policy—A New Focus

vying for control of the province, the Dai Viet and the VNQDD. They stated emphatically that it was necessary for the Cao Dai to strictly stay out of all political activities since nothing good could come from it.

After meeting with Mr. Khue and Sgt. Hoa, I drove back to Da Nang and spent the remainder of the day visiting some of my Vietnamese friends before going out to dinner with two CIA officers at the U.S. Navy Officers' Club, the Stone Elephant. Much to my surprise and pleasure, the beautiful singer, Khanh Ly, was performing at the club that night, and I had an opportunity to talk to her between sets about the night I saw her bring tears to the eyes of the old French Foreign Legionnaire a few weeks earlier in Saigon. She was lovely and charming to talk to, so I was not eager to leave the club. However, my CIA colleagues reminded me that I had an early Air America flight back to Tay Ninh to catch in the morning, so I would have to wait a few more months to again talk to the toothsome Khanh Ly and listen to her beautiful voice.

On the approach to Tan Son Nhut Air Base, I came very close to death. After receiving clearance from the tower to land his Pilatus Porter aircraft, our Air America pilot banked his plane sharply and descended. When we were only a few hundred feet above the runway, a lone ARVN helicopter rose off the runway below us. The ARVN helicopter was hidden from the view of the pilot, and it was obvious the ARVN pilot did not see the Air America plane above him. It looked like we were going to collide, so I yelled at the pilot that there was a helicopter below us. The pilot quickly banked hard to his left and increased his power, allowing us to escape a certain crash by only a few feet. The pilot swore loudly at the ARVN pilot, made another pass, and landed safely. He was still angry when we landed, and he let the tower know it. According to the tower, the ARVN helicopter did not request clearance to take off and was clearly in the wrong. Of course, it would have made little difference whose fault it was when my charred body was pulled from the wreckage of our plane.

After catching the next Air America flight to Tay Ninh City, I sat down at my IBM typewriter in my room and wrote my field report on my findings about the Cao Dai in Quang Nam Province, and Chuck put it in the pouch to send to Region III. Always helpful and concerned about me, Chuck asked if I had calmed down a bit during my trip up north and whether or not I was ready to work around the operational problems the new Station policy created. I told him I was prepared to work around my new restrictions, but an event took place within a few days that ignited my anger again and substantiated the negative impact that this policy had on operations.

On the afternoon of November 17, Mr. Tho came to the Embassy House with information that a VC guerrilla from a mobile VC battalion, called C-40, had just taken advantage of the government's Chieu Hoi Program and rallied to the PRU team in Phuoc Ninh district. I asked if the Hoi Chanh had been turned over to anyone yet, and he informed me that he was still with the PRU at the Phuoc Ninh district headquarters compound. I immediately asked Mr. Lam to come to my office, and the three of us jumped into my jeep and drove to the Phuoc Ninh PRU barracks west of Tay Ninh City. When we arrived, I began to interrogate the VC guerrilla, who told us he had just left his unit four hours previously. He was very cooperative, and we quickly learned the exact location of the C-40 battalion, which was only 5,000 meters north of our location. He revealed that the battalion's strength was only fifty-four men armed with recently acquired new Chinese AK-47 rifles and three Chinese 82 mm mortars from an NVA base area in Cambodia. He told us his unit had the

PRU Phuoc Ninh District compound.

mission of attacking the American base at Tay Ninh West Airfield using the newly acquired mortars.

I immediately sought out the district chief and the platoon commander of the Phuoc Ninh CRIP, and we decided to launch a mission against the C-40 unit that day so as to take advantage of the Hoi Chanh's information before the enemy could react. The rallier told us he was willing to show us where his unit was located and go with the PRU assault force. Since we only had an eighteen-man PRU team at Phuoc Ninh and the enemy unit had fifty-four men and heavy weapons, we decided we needed a more robust force than just me and the PRU team. The district chief and his American advisor, a very capable and aggressive U.S. Army officer, quickly put together a plan to use a combined PRU, CRIP and U.S. Army infantry operation. The district advisor contacted a U.S. Army infantry company operating a few thousand meters north of the C-40 battalion and informed them that a combined PRU and CRIP force would soon be moving north from the Phuoc Ninh district compound trying to push the C-40 battalion toward them. We also coordinated with a U.S. Army artillery battery to provide fire support for the operation. It would be a classic "hammer and anvil" operation with the PRU and the CRIP acting as the "hammer," pushing the enemy against the U.S. Army infantry company's "anvil."

All of the planning and coordination for this operation was accomplished in less than an hour due to the efficiency of the district chief and his American advisor. By 1700 we were about to send the combined PRU-CRIP force of thirty-nine men on the mission when the PRU team chief, Mr. Dung, asked me and Mr. Lam where we would be located in the maneuver force. He was shocked when I told him that I was no longer allowed to go on field operations with the PRU. He then asked me who would be going with them to coordinate with the American units involved, and I told him he would have to rely on the U.S. Army enlisted men with the CRIP. He then requested that the PRU team not participate, since he felt he would not be able to effectively communicate with the CRIP Americans, who would be operating at some distance from the PRU as they swept north. I had a great deal of admiration for Mr. Dung and did not question his courage, so I informed the district chief that the PRU would not be going on the operation because I was prohibited from going with them. He was surprised by this news, and both he and his American advisor accused me of lacking courage. I explained to them that a new MACV policy, one they had not heard about, prevented me from going on any more PRU operations. With this, they both agreed that the entire operation should be aborted until a sufficient force could be assembled using a Regional Force company the next day. The American district advisor was so angry, he told me he was going to report me to his boss and have me brought up on charges. As was my nature, I became very angry and informed the American officer that I was not about to disobey my orders, but I would not allow him or anyone else to question my courage. I told him to call for a U.S. Army helicopter from Tay Ninh West Airfield, and I would personally take the VC rallier with me on a flight north to locate the exact location of the C-40, and I would then call in an artillery mission on that location. This seemed to mollify the American advisor, and he volunteered to accompany me on the flight.

 Within an hour, the rallier, the American district advisor, Mr. Lam, and I were on a HU-1H helicopter heading north. After just a few minutes, we were over the vicinity of where the rallier had told us his battalion was located. As we approached the area, I asked the pilot to contact the artillery battery we had coordinated with earlier and request they be ready to receive a fire mission shortly. Like most enemy soldiers, the rallier had never been in a helicopter before, and he quickly became disoriented having to look for a location on the ground from such an altitude. I had seen this before, so I asked the pilot to fly to a location the rallier could readily identify, and then I would direct the pilot to fly along a path the rallier knew led to his unit. I began to have doubts about our rallier because when we finally came to the area he recognized as the location of his unit, I could not see any indication whatsoever of human activity, let alone a VC battalion. Mr. Lam cupped his mouth to my ear, and over the noise made by the chopper, he told me the rallier was sure this was the location of his unit, and the reason we could not see anything is the unit had dug camouflaged bunkers to hide in, making it nearly impossible to see them from the air. I had the pilots make several low passes over the area in the hopes the enemy might reveal themselves by firing on the helicopter, but nothing happened. I decided to take the rallier at his word, and I asked for one last low pass by our helicopter so I could mark the target with a smoke grenade and thus help with the adjustment of any artillery fires. The pilot of our helicopter called in several "repeat" fire missions, resulting in nearly 100 rounds of 105 mm and 155 mm artillery landing in or near the area marked by my smoke grenade. We observed two secondary explosions but did not see any enemy personnel. We returned to the district headquarters convinced we had, at best, done only a little damage to the C-40 battalion. I was not convinced the rallier had actually shown us the correct location, so I decided he needed to be further interrogated at the PIC in Tay Ninh City. As it turned out, the next day the U.S. Army infantry company swept through the area we had hit with artillery and found five dead VC and a small cache of mortar shells. Unfortunately, the rest of the C-40 battalion had escaped.

On November 20, I sent a scathing memorandum to Daren Flitcroft, the Region III Regional Officer in Charge (ROIC) at Bien Hoa, reporting on the aborted operation against the C-40 battalion and informing him that a mortar attack against Tay Ninh West Airfield had been launched shortly thereafter from an area close to the location where the aborted mission was to be conducted. In my memorandum, I blamed the new Station policy for the failure to destroy the C-40 battalion and to prevent it from attacking Tay Ninh West Airfield.[2] Chuck agreed with me completely and wrote a strong endorsement to my memorandum requesting the Station review the new policy and allow U.S. PRU advisors to at least accompany the PRU when U.S. military coordination was required. As with my previous efforts to reverse the Station policy, this one was denied without comment. Seeing my frustration and anger, Chuck told me he would try to obtain some flexibility with the new policy, but it would be done personally and not with any more memoranda. Chuck had considerable diplomatic skills and was less prone to anger than I was, so I decided I would cease writing memoranda to higher headquarters and continue to work around the restrictions with the help of Chuck.

There was one very good aspect of the new Station policy that I did not initially appreciate, but one that would become both important and valuable in the months ahead. That good aspect was a much greater interest in the PRU intelligence system and how it could be best used to hurt the enemy. This all evolved after Mr. Chinh and I decided to hold a meeting with the PRU district team leaders on how to best implement the new American policy of "Vietnamization." We decided to hold a day-long meeting in the Tay Ninh City PRU headquarters to discuss various actions we needed to take to allow for a much more robust involvement of the PRU in the transition from American to South Vietnamese control of the pacification programs under the Phoenix Program. During the course of this meeting, I asked the PRU leaders what they thought was the greatest threat to Tay Ninh Province, and they uniformly replied that it was the North Vietnamese Army, specifically the three NVA divisions occupying bases inside Cambodia and poised to attack whenever an opportunity presented itself. I then asked them what we, as the PRU, could do to counter this threat of the NVA forces. After nearly an hour of discussion, we concluded that the VCI element that made the movement of the NVA forces inside Tay Ninh Province possible was the finance-economy cadres who supplied these NVA divisions while they were operating in the province. When I heard this, I immediately thought of my Kit Carson Scout Qua's comments about how important the finance-economy cadres were in supplying his mobile unit in I Corps. I remembered how Qua explained the way VC and NVA main-force units were supplied using caches of food and ammunition pre-stored along their direction of attack, using local villagers organized by the party's finance-economy cadres. Qua had said that without the finance-economy cadres, the main-force units could not move or sustain themselves. We decided our best course of action was to focus our efforts on identifying and neutralizing the finance-economy cadres in Tay Ninh Province. This decision would pay off handsomely in the coming months as we systematically disrupted the ability of the NVA to move units into Tay Ninh Province. We understood that without the food caches, the labor parties, and the locally bought medical supplies that the finance-economy cadres provided, the NVA plans for any operations of long duration in the province would be greatly complicated.

As I said previously, until this time I did not pay close attention to the PRU's intelligence system. In fact, I felt too much effort was being devoted to intelligence gathering by the

PRU, especially when I thought the PRU needed to spend more time on training and operations. The Phoenix Program was established so the DIOCCs would provide the PRU with the targeting information they needed to mount counter–VCI operations. We were, in theory, supposed to obtain operational leads from the Special Branch, the Military Security Service, and the other intelligence organizations represented on the district DIOCCs. While the PRU would occasionally obtain operational leads from these sources, I felt the number and value of these leads were minimal. It seemed that many of the GVN and American intelligence organizations were reluctant to share any important intelligence with the PRU. Since the PRU had a good intelligence system in place, I decided to use it to concentrate our effort against the enemy's finance-economy cadres and not rely on the DIOCCs for the information we needed to target the enemy's supply system.

Once we had formulated our plan of attack on the province's finance-economy network, I took it to Chuck for his blessing. I always valued Chuck's opinion on anything related to intelligence since he had years of experience gathering intelligence and he always provided his knowledge and advice in the most helpful manner. In addition, Chuck had a great deal of experience with paramilitary operations during his career as a CIA officer, so he had a keen understanding of such operations and how they should be conducted. Chuck listened to the plan and promised to enlist the aid of John and Mickey in providing useful leads on finance-economy targets. He also asked me to enlist the aid of the PRU in identifying any potential spies among the enemy's finance-economy cadres since they would obviously have knowledge of any upcoming NVA military plans inside the province. I knew that the new CIA Station Chief in Saigon, Ted Shackley, was very interested in developing sources of strategic intelligence, and Chuck considered this his highest priority. I promised him that I would do my best to develop a valuable source, if possible. He cautioned me to be extremely careful with any attempt to recruit a finance-economy cadre and to turn over to him any attempt at recruitment. He reminded me, in his discreet-and-friendly manner, that I was not an "intelligence professional," and I lacked the training for the task of recruiting and controlling a spy, so it was best to leave the mechanics of recruitment to him.

He also instructed me to inform him if the PRU had information on any possible VCI Hoi Chuan before that individual made his attempt to rally to the GVN. Timing was critical in recruiting a spy, and he did not want a potential spy to do anything that might cause suspicion early in the recruitment process. Once an enemy surrendered or rallied, his utility for recruitment as a spy was normally over since the enemy counterintelligence system would never trust that individual again. He instructed me to always keep this in mind and turn over the name of any potential recruit as soon as the PRU believed that an individual was contemplating defection to the GVN side. I agreed and told him I would pass on the names of any potential recruits to him as soon as I knew about them. Listening to Chuck talk about the recruitment of spies and their handling, it was clear to me that he had a great deal of experience with this process and he considered it imperative that the recruitment of spies in the communist camp was vitally important. What Chuck did not share with me during our discussion was the fact that he already had under his control the most valuable spy America had working for us, a spy who was reporting on strategic intelligence of incredible value and accuracy. I will explain in the next chapter how I found out about this valuable spy we had within the enemy ranks.

As part of our plan to concentrate the PRU teams against the finance-economy cadres

Mr. Nguyen Hoang Lam, PRU interpreter.

in the province, Mr. Lam and I began to delve into the archives kept in the Embassy House Annex. Mr. Lam had told me about the Census Grievance maps and reports we had on file there; but, despite his suggestions that I might find them interesting, I had devoted most of my time to training the PRU and planning their operations, tasks that I felt were far more interesting and productive than poring over dusty files in the annex. "Poring" was an apt phrase for this work, since the annex was very hot during the day, and even at night the heat and humidity caused us to perspire profusely as we examined the maps stored there. Droplets of sweat often dripped off our chins onto these maps as we labored into the night searching for information concerning finance-economy cadres living in the province. At first, I found this a distasteful and fruitless task, but Lam assured me the Census Grievance maps held little nuggets of intelligence that might help us narrow our search and make it more efficient. He was right.

The Census Grievance maps were detailed, hand-drawn maps of each village and hamlet in the province. This work had been done a few years earlier by Census Grievance teams that were part of the Revolutionary Development (RD) Program and managed by the CIA before it was turned over to MACV. These Census Grievance teams would visit the homes of every person in the province and interview them to find out how many people lived in each house, their names and ages, and other pertinent census information. They would also ask the head of each family a series of questions that were intended to obliquely ascertain the loyalty of the family members, as well as determine what the grievances those family members might have toward their local government and the government in Saigon. The answers to these questions produced a color-coded map based on loyalty. A house that was colored green was friendly toward the local government and the GVN, a house that was colored red was considered friendly toward the VC, and a house colored yellow was deemed neutral. Although the information on these maps was rather dated, it soon became apparent to me that the color-coding system provided us with a means of concentrating our efforts in hamlets and villages that had a significant percentage of "red houses" in them.

During these late night searches of the Census Grievance maps and on many other occasions, Lam and I would talk about our respective lives. As our professional relationship matured and we spent more and more time working with each other, he and I became close friends. I came to admire Lam for his wit, intelligence, sincerity, and devotion to his country and people. Lam's father died when Lam was quite young, leaving Lam responsible for his family's welfare at a young age. He lived with his mother and younger sister in the Cholon section of Saigon. When he was a young boy, he was enrolled in a school run by an American missionary, despite the fact that Lam was a Buddhist and never fully converted to Christianity. At this school, he learned English and excelled in all of his other studies. Since he had no father, was poor, and lacked the connections needed to advance in South Vietnamese society, he decided to offer his services to the American Special Forces as an interpreter and translator, a job he was eminently qualified for, given his many years of schooling by English-speaking teachers. The Special Forces used him in a number of different jobs, many of which were quite dangerous, such as fighting as a member of a CIDG company, and later as a member of a long-range reconnaissance team.

Despite his training and life as a soldier, Lam's character and demeanor were more akin to those of a scholar. He was a voracious reader and could talk to me for hours about Vietnamese literature and the Chinese classics. At heart, he was a philosopher who enjoyed examining his life—a Vietnamese Socrates, of sorts. Lam introduced me to two Vietnamese classics, *Kim Van Kieu* and *Cung Oan Ngam Khuc,* both sad tales of sacrifice and devotion. He gave me English and Vietnamese translations of these books, often taking hours of his time to explain to me the nuances and hidden meanings within the pages of these books. Lam felt that one could not really understand the culture of Vietnam without understanding the underlying significance of these books.

During the many times we waited for Mr. Tho to show up for our morning meetings on the Embassy House porch, Lam and I would talk about what it meant to be a Vietnamese nationalist. It was evident to me that much of Lam's opposition to the communists was based on his Buddhist beliefs and his devotion to the ideals he had read about and embraced in the works of Jean-Jacques Rousseau, Immanuel Kant, Blaise Pascal, and Voltaire. When I told him I had read several books by the French existentialists, he told me he rejected the socialist philosophies of Albert Camus and Jean-Paul Sartre, calling them "selfish, petty men, with little ideas that absolved the average man of any number of sins." Although he had read some American books, I could never find any indication that they made an impression on Lam, at least not in a political or philosophical sense. Classical Vietnamese works and European philosophical books seemed to have made a far deeper impression on him.

Although he worked closely with the Cao Dai members of the PRU, he did not embrace any aspect of that religion, but he was careful not to disparage it, at least not in my presence. He firmly rejected Marxism, calling it "a socialist heresy" that ran counter to human nature and "would never work in a rural country like Vietnam with a tradition of personal ownership of land and a very small worker class." If I could sum up Lam's philosophy of life, I would describe it as a complex blend of classic Confucianism, Buddhist theology, and some aspects of Protestant Christianity mixed together with French Romanticism and a strong belief in the ancient Greek concept of "arête," or heroic excellence through struggle. I was always amazed by Lam's depth of knowledge and his broad interests. Talking to him was something I always looked forward to and valued. If ever there was a soldier-philosopher, Lam was certainly one.

Sadly, my conversations with Lam revealed he had many tragedies befall his family. He told me his mother was a widow, and his lone sibling, his younger sister, had been severely wounded by a VC rocket that exploded in front of their house in Cholon in 1968, a wound that reduced her to the mental capacity of a young child. Two years prior to her injury, she had won a scholarship to attend college, and she was excelling at her university studies when this tragedy struck. During one of my visits to Saigon, I met his mother and sister, a meeting that filled me with a deep sadness over how life had treated them. I realized that without Lam they would be completely lost and without hope. With a widowed mother and an invalid sister, Lam was a man with many cares, yet he always seemed to be optimistic and cheerful. I marveled at his toughness and his calm acceptance of life's trials.

Two incidents took place in November that gave me my first inkling of how important the work being done by Chuck and John was. The first event was a visit to the Embassy House by a man described as "a technical officer," who spent the better part of a day with Chuck and John hidden away in Chuck's office. Later in the day, before this technical officer was due to be driven to Tay Ninh East Airfield for his return trip to Saigon, Chuck came into my room and asked me if I would like to learn something about "dead drop technology," explaining that I might find this useful with my PRU duties. I was delighted that Chuck

14. Bad American Policy—A New Focus

thought this new technology might be beneficial to the PRU. I always welcomed any opportunity to learn the "trade craft" of the intelligence business, and especially if it was imparted by a true professional like Chuck. I eagerly accepted Chuck's offer and went into the Embassy House living room to meet the technical officer and find out what he had in his technical bag of tricks.

I found the man sitting behind one of the tables in our living room. On the table he had assembled the latest devices used to communicate with a spy. He showed me hollow rocks, pen-like camouflaged cylinders that could hold small messages and could be driven into the ground so only a small extraction ring on the top was visible, and everyday items with small hidden chambers in them that could hide a slip of paper or a piece of microfilm. He also demonstrated some small radios disguised as kitchen tools and other everyday items that might be found in a Vietnamese home. I was amazed at the number and ingenuity of these devices and would have gladly spent hours talking to this interesting man. I asked the CIA technician if I could use some of the items he showed me to help the PRU to communicate with their agent network, and he told me that I would have to ask Chuck to make a request to Station before he could give any to me. He added that he thought it unlikely that such a request would be approved. With my usual lack of tact, I began to question the man as to why my PRU were not important enough to use his dead-drop inventions. He responded that these items were to be used very sparingly and only by "agency assets of great value." Of course, I considered the PRU "assets of great value," so I did not take this comment very well and the technical officer suddenly decided to end his little class for me. Chuck later came by and told me the items I had been shown were experimental, and he felt confident that soon they would be approved for use by the PRU. Chuck knew how to calm me down, and his explanation served its purpose. Still, I had the lingering feeling that this "technical officer" had come to Tay Ninh to help with some very important "asset" that I knew nothing about.

The second incident occurred when two British MI-6 officers from Hong Kong visited the Embassy House. I did not know they were even in our villa until I sat down to lunch, and they were seated across from me at the table. I was introduced to them but not told anything about them. All I knew was some Brits were having lunch with us, which was a highly unusual occurrence. I was not even told they were intelligence officers. At lunch they talked about events going on in China, English Premier League soccer, and American domestic politics—all subjects that one could find in any newspaper. One would never have guessed they were MI-6 intelligence officers from the conversation we had that day at lunch. I spent the afternoon with the PRU at their headquarters, but returned around 4 p.m. to find the two British intelligence officers sitting in our living room and having a drink. I made a drink and joined them. They asked me what my job was, and I told them I was the PRU advisor for the province, which produced a conversation about the PRU and the Phoenix Program.

By now, I had been told that these visiting officers were from Hong Kong, and they were in Tay Ninh to brief Chuck on information they had relating to the North Vietnamese using the Cambodian port of Sihanoukville to supply NVA units in the eastern border area of Cambodia. Whether it was the alcohol or their belief that I was privy to everything going on inside the Embassy House, they began to talk to me about subjects I was totally ignorant of, specifically a "high value agent" they, the British, had inside North Vietnam who regularly reported to them about the supplies being shipped from North Vietnam and the People's

Republic of China to Sihanoukville. They told me they knew about the shipments before the NVA in Cambodia knew about them, and they even had copies of the invoices for the shipments. They explained that the primary means inside Cambodia for the shipment of these vital military supplies to the enemy was a front company called the Hak Lee Shipping Company. This company, they informed me, was financed by the People's Republic of China using a bank in Hong Kong. They also said President Sihanouk and his wife were receiving massive amounts of money to allow these shipments to be transported by the Hak Lee Shipping Company inside of Cambodia.

Since I expressed an interest in the VC supply system, they spent a few minutes explaining to me the workings of the North Vietnamese organization tasked with supplying the NVA in South Vietnam, the shadowy Unit 559. I sat in amazement as these two men explained how Unit 559 moved critical supplies and troops south through Laos and Cambodia. I mentioned the U.S. air campaign and the CIA use of Lao mountain tribes to attack the enemy's supply routes in Laos and their response shocked me. They said the efforts of the Americans in Laos were not preventing Unit 559 from moving either people or supplies south, and they opined that the Americans would have to someday occupy Laos with American and South Vietnamese troops if they ever seriously hoped to choke off the enemy supply lines there. I offered the opinion that the American bombing campaign in Laos was helping to restrict the enemy's ability to supply their troops in South Vietnam, and they cut me off short with a comment along the lines that "figures don't lie and even you Americans know the figures are correct."

They then said something that gave me the first real hint that our Embassy House controlled a very valuable spy inside the VCI. As if to make their point about "the figures" relating to the movement of supplies and men from North Vietnam, they said, "Even your own source knows those NVA units across the border are not lacking for supplies, and he would surely know the true figures." This was the first time I had heard of a mysterious "source" who was reporting to us on such strategic intelligence. I pretended that I was aware of this source and his reporting, but decided it would be better to let this subject drop and take it up with Chuck later.

When it came time for Bernie to drive the British intelligence officers to the airfield for their Air America flight back to Saigon, John came in to say goodbye to them. Unfortunately, they mentioned in this brief conversation that they had had "a good conversation with your special police man, Andy." I could tell by the expression on John's face that this concerned him. A few minutes after the Brits departed with Bernie for the airfield, John came into my room and asked me what I had discussed with the MI-6 officers. When I told him we had talked about the Hak Lee Shipping Company in Cambodia, he angrily told me that I was out of line discussing Special Branch activities with them, or anything else for that matter, outside the realm of PRU operations. Since his reaction was very intense, I decided not to tell him about their comments concerning Unit 559, the Ho Chi Minh Trail, or the "source" in Tay Ninh.

I liked John and always found him to be friendly and cooperative, but I could tell he was not happy about my conversation with the Brits, and he warned me not to delve into matters I was not cleared to know about. When I angrily replied that I thought there was no harm in talking to Brits about the enemy's supply system, he told me that I had no need to know of these activities outside the purview of the PRU. He reminded me that since I went on field operations with the PRU, there was always the chance that I could be captured by the enemy and forced to reveal vital information. He soothingly told me that it was not a matter of trusting me; it was simply a matter of good operational security given my vulnerability to capture. His reasoning made sense to me, and I let the matter rest. I remembered what Chuck had told me when I first reported to Tay Ninh Province about the need to minimize shared methods and sources of intelligence so the enemy would only be able to extract information that pertained to our specific operations and not what other members of our team were doing.

Chuck had reinforced this remark with the story of an event that occurred a few years earlier. The Tay Ninh PRU advisor and the RD advisor had both been ambushed and killed while driving in Tay Ninh City on their way to meet the PRU advisor's girlfriend. They could have just as easily been captured, and anything they knew would have been extracted under torture. With this example in my mind, I decided I would take John's advice and not try to delve into what the other occupants of the Embassy House were doing and concentrate solely on PRU business. Still, the comments of the British MI-6 officers stimulated my interest and made me aware that there was a lot going on in the Embassy House that I did not know about.

The remainder of November and the first two weeks of December, I devoted myself to arranging some much-needed training for the PRU soldiers in the use of supporting arms, taking them to a U.S. Army firing battery, and having them call in and adjust artillery fire missions in both Vietnamese and English. Many of the PRU had a rudimentary understanding of English, so it was not too difficult to find a few of them who had enough mastery of the language and the requisite map-reading skills to draft a fire request and then transmit it over a radio. When we finished this training, we had at least two or three men in each team who could perform this vital skill.

I also began spending a few hours each day at the PRU headquarters, going over the information Lam and I had culled from the Census Grievance maps and correlating it with the dossiers we had on file in the PIOCC of known VCI cadres. Not surprisingly, we found that most of the VCI we were looking for came from villages and hamlets with a very high percentage of red houses marked on the maps. Based on the information we gathered from our map analysis and the dossiers from the PIOCC, Mr. Chinh developed a list of the most likely VCI cadres still alive and working in the province. We then assigned the VCI targets to those district teams where the VCI were last known to live or where their family members were located. Mr. Chinh instructed his team leaders to approach the family members of these VCI and to try to convince them that it was best for their communist family member to rally to the GVN. However, he cautioned them that this approach must be done very carefully so as not to jeopardize the chance to recruit these VCI as spies. He explained that as soon as the PRU effort to proselytize a VCI appeared to be bearing fruit, the name of that VCI should be sent to Mr. Chinh immediately before any overt action was taken. Mr. Chinh would then contact Chuck, and together they would determine how to handle the potential spy. Once our plan was fully developed, we cleared it with the province chief and then began to execute it. As November came to a close, I felt confident we had a plan in place that would seriously damage the enemy's supply system and potentially develop a spy or two inside the enemy's political organization.

CHAPTER 15

London Interlude

Since I had volunteered to extend my tour of duty from thirteen months to nineteen months, I was granted a thirty-day leave to any place in the world with my airfare paid for by the U.S. government, a very generous deal that I looked forward to taking advantage of. I decided I would first fly to the U.S. and spend the Christmas holidays with my family. Then I would board a plane at McGuire Air Force Base, New Jersey, for a flight to England, where I hoped to spend a few weeks seeing the sights and visiting Capt. Robert Asprey, the noted author on guerrilla warfare, who was living in Oxford at that time. I had not been home for a year, so the prospect of seeing my family again during the holidays made me forget my anger and frustration with the new, restrictive Station policy and to concentrate on making sure the PRU were able to function well in my absence. Chuck arranged for a temporary replacement for me since he felt it was essential that the PRU have American coverage and support at all times.

On December 16, I traveled to Saigon by jeep with Lam, obtained my travel orders from the U.S. Marine liaison office at the MACV Annex, and checked into the military liaison office at Tan Son Nhut Airport. As I waited in the terminal, I noticed that the U.S. military personnel traveling with me seemed to take a keen interest in me. I was definitely the odd man out on this flight since I was the only person wearing civilian clothes and I had my .38 cal. Colt Cobra revolver in a holster attached to my belt. I overheard several American soldiers speculating who I was. The words "narc," "CID," and "spook" were the ones I heard whispered within earshot of me. One of them even came up to me and asked me who I was. When I told him I was a Marine Corps captain, he looked at me in disbelief and said something to the effect that I had the haircut, but no Marine he knew wore civilian clothes and carried such an exotic weapon. Since I was on my way home, I couldn't care less what anyone thought about me, so I ignored his comment. A few minutes later, I gave my pistol to Lam to keep for me and boarded the plane. Like everyone else on that plane, I settled into my seat with that pure joy that comes with the knowledge that one has when leaving South Vietnam in one piece and anticipating a warm welcome back in the States.

I arrived at the Philadelphia International Airport to find my parents waiting for me. I was not prepared for the shock of the winter weather, however. As soon as I stepped off the plane, I was chilled to the bone after spending a year in the tropical climes of South Vietnam. I soon forgot the cold air when I saw my parents and basked in the warmth of my family's happiness at seeing me home again. On the ride from the airport to the family home in Merchantville, my mother and father brought me up to date on what my sisters and brothers had been doing over the past year. Both noted I had lost a lot of weight, but I assured them I was in good health.

During the first few days at home, my mother cooked several very delicious dinners for me, including my favorite of roast pork with all the side dishes I loved, and showered me with her warmth and love. I exchanged gifts with my parents and my sisters and brothers at Christmas and attended Midnight Mass with them, just as I had done many times before at Christmastime. I visited my cousins, the Kelleys, and attempted to find a date with some girls I had dated in high school, only to find out that most of them were married and had already started families. As I had encountered on my last trip home from the war, no one called me or visited me to welcome me home. It was as if, once I had left my hometown, no one even remembered me outside of my own family. Only this time it did not hurt as much since I had resigned myself to the fact that no one really cared about the war or those who were fighting in it. I suppose I realized it was something they did not want to think about, and the presence of someone like me only brought up unpleasant and inconvenient thoughts.

One day after Christmas, my father asked me if I still intended to make the Marine Corps a career and offered his assistance to me if I decided to leave the Corps and pursue an advanced degree in law or business. I told him my military obligation was over in June 1970, only six months away, but I did not think I would leave the Marine Corps at that time since I had no real desire to do anything else but serve my country in the Marine Corps. He listened quietly, but I could tell he did not think I should pursue a military career. He knew me well and did not try to persuade me to take up a civilian career, but he mentioned that several Naval Academy graduates from my high school had left the service and pursued graduate studies at Harvard and the University of Pennsylvania, using their GI bill benefits to pay for this elite education. I listened and agreed with him that these men would be successful in life and would enjoy many material comforts and advantages that would be denied to me, but I ended any hope he had that I would follow in their footsteps when I told him I felt I was called to military service the way a priest is called to the church. After that comment, he never raised the idea of a civilian career with me again.

After I had spent a very enjoyable, if lonely, ten days with my family, my father drove me to the nearby McGuire Air Force Base where I took a flight to the U.S. air base at Menderhall, England. From there, I traveled to London and checked in at the American bachelor officer quarters (BOQ), which occupied the former Astor estate at Lancaster Square. During World War II, the Astor family had donated their London estate to the U.S. government, and it had been turned into an upscale officers' quarters. When I arrived, I was greeted by a distinguished-looking gentleman dressed in a morning suit, every inch the proper English gentleman. He was the Lancaster Square BOQ's concierge, and I immediately took a liking to him when he pronounced my name perfectly (*Fin lah sin*) and began to tell me about the Finlayson Clan's history in Scotland. From my first day at this luxurious BOQ in one of the most fashionable neighborhoods in London, this courtly and friendly man took charge of my stay. He showed me the wood-paneled dining room and bar and all the other facilities this military hotel offered, and he gave me a list of things I should see and do in London, with instructions on how to reach them using the Tube, bus, or taxi services. Each day he would greet me when I came down for breakfast and ask me where I was going that day, offering his assistance with any transportation needs I might have. He even arranged for the dining room to prepare a boxed lunch for me several times so I would not have to buy my lunch during a day-long trip. I visited every important tourist attraction in London and a few he recommended to me that were not normally on the list of things to see by tourists. If I wanted to go to the theater to see a play or movie, he arranged for my tickets. I suppose he was helpful and kind to every guest, but he seemed to go the extra mile for me. When I asked him how he came to be the concierge at the BOQ, he told me he had been a soldier once, and he wanted to treat soldiers with the respect and honor that was due them. I have never met a more gentlemanly or considerate hotel employee anywhere in the world, and that covers a lot of hotels in many countries.

Near the end of my stay in London, I called Capt. Robert Asprey, USMC (Ret.), and arranged to meet him at his home in Oxford. I took an early-morning train from Paddington Station, sharing my first-class compartment on the train with a lovely English beauty on her way back to university at Lady Margaret College. I am rather shy by nature, so I remained silent and read a book for the first half hour of the three-hour train ride to Oxford; however, after a few awkward efforts at small talk, we both began to converse freely. She asked me what brought me to England, and I told her I was on leave from South Vietnam. She responded by saying she knew I was in the military by my close-cropped hair, which was not in vogue at that time by any civilian. She began to ask me many questions about South Vietnam and the war, listening intently and without any visible indication as to her views on the war. All of her questions were carefully framed in such a way as not to be controversial or judgmental. As she put it, "I do not possess an informed view on the war since you are actually the only person I have spoken to with firsthand knowledge of it." This was a disarming way of approaching such a delicate subject with a stranger, but it was not a completely honest approach. Clearly, this young, well-educated, and well-bred young woman had formed a view on the war, and something told me it did not conform to my view in any way. She had a decidedly socialist political orientation with a strong pacifist sentiment as well, which she could not hide, even with the most judicious choice of words. She found it difficult to believe that I actually had Vietnamese friends and that I admired Vietnamese culture. I think she expected me to say I hated the Vietnamese, and several times she asked me questions that were clearly framed in such a way as to invoke a response that would reveal some hostility toward the Vietnamese. Since I was sincere in my comments about my respect and admiration for the Vietnamese, she finally conceded that I had surprised her and made her question her preconceived notions about the American military, if not the war itself. I enjoyed the company of this attractive woman, so I treaded lightly with any questions that might result in an argument over the war. Still, I could not help but ask her near the end of our journey whether she had come to a conclusion as to which side of the war had the higher moral purpose. Her answer finally gave her away and made me angry when I heard her words. She said, "I tend to support anti-colonial and progressive movements, so I suppose I think the Vietnamese people would be better served by a government free of foreign influence and an exploitive economy."

When the train pulled into Oxford station, this lovely socialist handed me a piece of note paper with her address and telephone number on it, and she told me we should get together again during my stay in Oxford. I thanked her and took the note she handed to me, but I did not take her up on her offer, despite her attractiveness and friendly manners. As I said goodbye to her at the Station and wished her good luck in her studies, I could not help but hear a voice deep in my subconscious say, "She is the enemy."

15. London Interlude

After checking into a small hotel on the main street of Oxford, I called the home of Robert Asprey to arrange a time and place where we could meet. When he answered his phone, he told me his home was not a suitable place to meet and he suggested we meet in a local pub nearby. I took a cab from my hotel to the pub, finding upon my arrival that he was already there waiting for me. For the next three hours we drank beer and talked about my experiences in the war and the book he was working on, a two-volume history of guerrilla warfare.

For the most part, our conversation was friendly and enjoyable, but it became tense and strained after I told him about my conversation with the young lady I had met on the train to Oxford. He offered that her views were common among the university community in Oxford. Then he surprised me by indicating he shared the young lady's pessimism about the war. I had great respect for Mr. Asprey, a World War II Marine veteran, but I began to see that he was opposed to the Vietnam War, but not for the same reasons that the young lady on the train had. I was tired from my long train journey and still a bit angry at the young woman from Lady Margaret's College, so I was not as patient as I should have been when Mr. Asprey began lecturing me on how badly the war was going because "the Americans were fighting the wrong kind of war." In the argument over "conventional versus counterinsurgency strategies," he came down clearly in favor of counterinsurgency, stating emphatically that until the South Vietnamese government became something akin to a Jeffersonian democracy and the Americans devoted all of their resources to civic action and pacification, the outcome was a foregone conclusion, a communist victory. It was obvious that he was an ardent proponent of the strategy endorsed by the British counterinsurgency expert, Sir Robert Thompson, and he seemed oblivious to the conventional threat that the North Vietnamese Army posed. When I told him my experience in the war told me that the pacification side of the conflict could work perfectly and we would still lose unless we found some way to keep the North Vietnamese Army out of South Vietnam, he bristled and told me that the NVA would not be able to operate in South Vietnam if the "people genuinely supported the GVN." He seemed surprised when I told him I thought the VC were merely "annoying" and incapable of having any real strategic significance and the real threat to South Vietnam was from the heavily armed, more conventional forces of the NVA.

We had exchanged letters several times during my two tours of duty in South Vietnam, but these letters had been rather short and dealt primarily with specific tactics and weapons used in the war, not with the overall strategy. Now I could see that my views did not conform to his at all and seemed to provoke him. He began to refer to the writings of several American reporters who had been stationed in Saigon in the early years of the war, such as Neil Sheehan and David Halberstam, and I told him it was a mistake to rely on the reporting of these men and others in the press corps in Saigon since I had been told by Col. Allen and several CIA officers that the Saigon press corps was riddled with enemy agents and was also the target for every disenchanted U.S. military staff officer and South Vietnamese café politician in Saigon. I pointed out to him several key mistakes the American press corps had made, such as believing the NLF was a purely southern political movement that included representatives of non-communist parties, that the North Vietnamese were not using Laos to move troops and supplies into South Vietnam, and that the communist Tet Offensive in 1968 was a success when it was clearly a military failure. Since he relied heavily on the U.S. press for many of the quotes and footnotes in his book on guerrilla warfare, he did not enjoy hearing my words concerning the lack of accuracy contained in the press reports coming from South Vietnam or my belief that many of these articles were filled with information provided by dubious sources. We parted as friends, but I could tell a gap had opened up between us. That gap would lead to a complete severance of our relationship in 1973 when I brought several factual errors in his book to his attention and he refused to correct them.

I had planned to fly back to South Vietnam from London, but when I went to the U.S. Embassy with my orders to arrange for a commercial airline ticket, the naval attaché, a U.S. Navy captain, told me I had to fly back to McGuire Air Force Base and catch a military charter plane from there back to the war. Despite my orders, which clearly stated I was to be provided with a commercial plane ticket, the attaché was adamant. I decided not to argue with a captain in the U.S. Navy, and instead returned to the U.S. air base at Mendenhall to catch a military flight back to New Jersey. I spent a day or two with my parents at home and then left on my long journey back to Tay Ninh Province and the war.

CHAPTER 16

America's Most Valuable Spy

When I returned to Tay Ninh Province in early January, I found that Chuck had gone home on leave and a replacement CIA officer was standing in for him. Unlike Chuck, this other officer, who called himself "Don," did not pay much attention to me and spent almost all of his time working with John and Mickey. He was pleasant and cordial whenever we spoke, but he seemed uninterested in anything the PRU was doing, an attitude that I found mildly annoying. When I went to him to gain his advice or approval concerning a PRU operation, he would act as if it was not necessary to bring up such topics with him. He gave me the impression that he had bigger fish to fry and PRU operations were very low on his scale of interests. Given his attitude, I began to clear PRU actions with the province chief only and merely convey the results in my monthly report to the CIA office at Region III in Bien Hoa.

During Chuck's absence an incident took place that would haunt me for nearly 40 years. It involved a spy controlled by the CIA who was so valuable to the United States, his actual name was known to only a handful of people because the CIA went to great lengths to keep his identity a secret. To this day his CIA file remains completely classified, even though he has been dead since 1975. This spy, who was controlled by John, was the highest penetration of the VCI during the Vietnam War. He provided strategic intelligence on the enemy's plans for over a decade. The spy's existence was first tentatively revealed to me during Chuck's leave and only confirmed many years later when I read a paper written by Mr. Merle Pribbenow, a retired CIA case officer and author.[1]

I probably never would have known about the "Tay Ninh Source" had it not been for a combination of circumstances that began with a simple incident that spurred my anger over what I felt was a cavalier attitude toward my personal safety. Ever since SFC Robert Smith had been transferred from Tay Ninh Province, I was the sole PRU advisor in the province. A rather important PRU operation was planned by our PRU City Team that required my presence since it involved coordination with, and support from, the U.S. 25th Infantry Division. The area of the operation was northeast of Nui Ba Den Mountain, around the southern fringes of War Zone C. Since the area for the operation was far from friendly lines, an English-speaking radio operator was required to be with the PRU contingent so U.S. helicopter medevacs could be called in and supporting arms employed in the event the operation went bad. I knew I was not allowed to go on strictly PRU operations, but since this operation involved U.S. units with the PRU in a supporting role, I decided to consider it a combined U.S.-GVN operation and one that justified my presence. The only way for the PRU to communicate effectively with the American units was to have me go along on the operation. Although the rationale I was using was a bit of a stretch, I took solace in an old Marine Corps adage—it is better to beg forgiveness than to ask permission when tactical necessity is involved.

Two days before the operation was to kick off, I went to arrange for Mr. Nguyen Van Phong, our Special Branch interpreter/translator, to go on the operation with me as my interpreter, since Mr. Lam was on vacation in Saigon. I fully expected that Phong would participate because I had been told by Chuck that Phong was the backup interpreter for Mr. Lam. When I approached Phong in his office in the Embassy House Annex to inform him that he would need to prepare to go on the operation with me, he politely but firmly declined. I argued with him a bit, but he did not back down. I asked him why, if he was Mr. Lam's backup, he could not go on a PRU operation with me. He simply smiled and told me I should talk to "Mr. Mickey" about it. I went into Mickey's room and told him about Phong's refusal to go on a PRU mission with me, and I solicited his assistance in obtaining Phong's participation. Mickey surprised me by telling me that Phong would not be going to the field with me on this operation or any other operation. I blew up at Mickey and told him it was unrealistic to send me with the PRU without an interpreter, especially since I would be the only American with them on the mission. Mickey was adamant, but he refused to tell me why Phong was not available. I never got along very well with Mickey, so I decided to see if I could talk some sense into Chuck's replacement as POIC.

I found Don typing a report in his room. Since Don was only an interim replacement for Chuck, I didn't think he knew how much or how little I knew about the intelligence operations conducted in Tay Ninh, but I think he assumed I knew more than I did. In any event, when I confronted him with my dilemma, he was sympathetic, but he insisted that Phong was "too important to risk on a PRU mission." I exploded again and asked him why Phong was so valuable and why I, an American, was not. He said he could not tell me that, but I should simply accept this and get on with my job or cancel the mission.

By this time, I was very angry and emotional about the situation. I threatened Don by telling him that I was going to Bien Hoa to talk directly with his boss, Daren Flitcroft, to complain about how I was being treated. As I started to get the keys to one of our jeeps, he stopped me and ordered me back into his office. He told me that Phong was "more than an interpreter," and his work made it too risky for him to go to the field with the PRU. In essence, he said that Phong's life was more important than mine. He then went on to tell me Phong was really a Vietnamese Police Special Branch case officer, and "he controlled a very valuable asset." He insisted that any complaint to the ROIC by me could jeopardize "ongoing operations critical to the war." I was somewhat mollified by Don's explanation, but I was not entirely convinced of Phong's importance relative to mine. I had never seen Phong in any other light than as an interpreter, so it was difficult for me to associate this rather timid, docile, and scholarly person in the role of a Special Branch case officer. Regardless, I let the matter rest and canceled the operation since I could not go with the PRU.

Following this heated discussion with Don, he went out of his way to be nice to me during the remainder of his month-long stay in Tay Ninh, even suggesting that I should become "a unilateral officer" since he felt there was a pressing need for one in the province. He suggested I start by developing contacts with several Cambodian Khmer Serey leaders in Tay Ninh, saying recent events across the border in Cambodia were heating up and we needed to tap into the Khmer Serey's informant net for any information their agents could provide.

I accepted his offer to become an ad-hoc "unilateral officer," despite my absolute lack of knowledge as to what a "unilateral officer" did or how to do it. This did not seem to deter Don in the slightest because he pulled out a file from his safe and wrote down the names of three Cambodians living in Tay Ninh Province who were affiliated with the Khmer Serey movement, instructing me to develop a relationship with them so I could find out what information they had on the events unfolding in Cambodia. One of these men was Mr. Tran Thu, the senior Khmer Serey representative in Tay Ninh, who was assigned to the U.S. Special Forces CIDG unit at the B-32 Special Forces camp at the Tay Ninh East Airfield. I met Tran Thu several times, but nothing really panned out, aside from some vague predictions about a future coup to overthrow Prince Sihanouk. In retrospect, I realized this was a ruse by Don to distract me from questioning the rationale behind Phong's importance. Don wanted me to concentrate on events unfolding in Cambodia and not the "very valuable asset" Phong was controlling.

About a week after my problem with Phong, John, who was having one of his very difficult times, came into my room one evening very drunk and crying. I was shocked to see him in this condition. I liked John and always found him to be very friendly, if overly coy about the work he was doing. He apparently felt he could talk to me since I was "an outsider" and had an "unbiased attitude," as he put it. He was so upset, he was barely coherent, but after a few minutes, it became clear why he was so emotional. He felt that he had been "betrayed" by Chuck because Chuck had signed a field report that John had written just prior to John's departure on home leave. In John's mind, the report he had written had been "stolen" by Chuck. I tried to assuage his anger, which I felt was totally unjustified, by telling him I thought what Chuck had done was clearly acceptable when someone was absent from Vietnam. I added, "Besides, it's only one field report, and we send lots of them out each month." John then told me that the field report he was so upset about was not just *any* field report, but one that involved the most important enemy spy we had under our control. He told me the source was so close to him that the spy had requested he go to Hong Kong with him on some sort of vacation. I did not know if I should believe John or not, given his emotional state, but I soon came to realize he was telling the truth about this valuable spy.

John began his tale by informing me that he was the only person who could control this valuable asset, and over the past year he had developed such a strong relationship with this spy that no one could take his place when dealing with him. For more than an hour John talked about the spy and how he had taken over control of this valuable source of strategic information on the enemy, turning a poorly handled and little exploited asset into the most valuable spy the United States had in South Vietnam. John kept telling me that before he showed up in Tay Ninh Province, the spy was not professionally managed, but he now had everything in place to manage him properly.

I was a bit dubious about the true value of this spy, and I suppose my reaction to this news only angered John more, because he left the room, telling me as he left, "I will prove to you that I am not overreacting about this!" A few minutes later he returned and handed me a report he had prepared a few months previously. The report was a verbatim text from his spy concerning a briefing the spy had received while attending a COSVN meeting inside Cambodia. The subject of the report was COSVN Resolution 9, the Lao Dong Party's analysis of the 1968 Tet Offensive and the party's plans for 1969. As I recall, the report did not contain a copy of COSVN Resolution 9, but only the key points of the document that the spy had memorized and then transcribed once he had returned to his home in Tay Ninh Province.

As I began to read the agent's report, I was immediately struck by the level of detail and the accuracy he described. For instance, he outlined the enemy's plans for several attacks inside Tay Ninh Province months before they actually took place in 1969. His report also contained a great deal of analysis the North Vietnamese leadership made concerning the 1968 Tet Offensive and the remedial actions the Lao Dong Party needed to take to recover from this disaster.

I only had a few minutes to read the report, which was several typewritten pages long, but even a quick reading of the document convinced me that John had, indeed, a very valuable spy under American control and this spy was providing detailed intelligence on the enemy's strategy and plans well in advance of their execution. As I read this report, I felt elated that we had such valuable information in our possession, and I began to see why this spy had to be protected at all costs from exposure.

Probably the most interesting information this spy conveyed to John was not contained in the report John showed to me, but in comments John made to me when I asked him if the spy had ever told him about the reason for the enemy's decision to launch the Tet Offensive in 1968. By 1969, it was generally considered that the enemy had made a disastrous decision to launch their General Offensive-General Uprising during the Tet holidays of 1968, and judging from the contents of COSVN Resolution 9, the enemy had come to the same conclusion. While the countrywide attacks had panicked the American press in Saigon, undermined the morale of the public in America, and convinced President Johnson and his advisors that the war was lost, the truth was the Tet Offensive failed miserably and did not achieve any of the goals set for it by the communists. The enemy realized it was a disaster, and the report indicated they were intent upon not repeating the mistakes they made in 1968. Given the disastrous military results of the Tet Offensive, I was intrigued as to why the enemy decided to launch their offensive when they did. John explained that he had asked this question of the "source" and was given an explanation that differed from any I had heard previously or since, but one that made a lot of sense.

The enemy spy told John that the decision to launch the 1968 Tet Offensive was based on the Lao Dong Party's "reasoned and objective analysis" of several factors in the spring of 1967. According to the "source," there were three main reasons why the party decided to risk everything with an attempt at provoking a general uprising against the Thieu regime. First, they had come to the conclusion that the military balance in South Vietnam was shifting in favor of the Americans and the South Vietnamese government. They were particularly worried about their base areas that were overrun inside South Vietnam, forcing their main-force units to move into areas far removed from South Vietnam's populated areas. As their bases in South Vietnam were attacked and destroyed by American and ARVN units in 1966 and 1967, they found it necessary to spend more and more time in their sanctuaries in Laos and Cambodia and the mountains of western South Vietnam. Their military commanders in the south told the leadership in Hanoi that they were finding it increasingly difficult to both mass and move inside South Vietnam, especially in the areas of III and IV Corps. They were also having morale problems, which the source attributed to the effects of devastating U.S. air power, especially the B-52 raids on their base areas.

Second, their revolutionary doctrine called for the party's political infrastructure in South Vietnam, the VCI, to support any large-scale military operation by using their mass-based organizations to provide manpower, logistical, and intelligence support for large-scale, mobile military operations, but this was becoming more difficult as more and more territory was falling under the control of the Saigon government. Compounding this, the party had recently learned that the U.S. government was about to institute a new pacification policy that the party feared would seriously erode the capability of the southern party members to mobilize the masses of South Vietnam to support the revolution. According to our spy, COSVN had obtained the complete American and GVN pacification plans in early 1967. After carefully studying these pacification plans and realizing the full implementation of the plans was less than a year away, the party came to the conclusion that the new pacification program posed a very serious threat to the VCI and had to be disrupted before its full implementation.[2]

Finally, and most important, the "source" told John that COSVN had received information from Hanoi's spy service that the United States planned to invade Laos and Cambodia in the summer or fall of 1968 to cut the Ho Chi Minh Trail and destroy the extensive communist base camp system used to support the movement of NVA troops and supplies south. They had obtained a general outline of this secret plan, along with information that Gen. Westmoreland intended to gain approval for the invasion of Laos from President Johnson when the two men met in the fall of 1967. Hanoi's leaders thought President Johnson would be briefed on the invasion plan before the end of 1967 because they thought Gen. Westmoreland needed at least six months to move the additional U.S. troops to South Vietnam from the United States. This knowledge led the Lao Dong Party to decide to thwart the American invasion plans by launching a major attack against the populated centers of South Vietnam and to secure the eastern approaches to the Laos panhandle.

The "source" told John there were three goals for this countrywide offensive: First, damage the ARVN to the point where they would be ineffective or rally to the VC side; second, seize the political centers of the GVN; and, third, create a general uprising of the population with the objective of either seizing power completely or enough territory to force the United States to accede to the formation of a coalition government under communist control. Once the coalition government was in place, it would demand the withdrawal of all American forces from South Vietnam.

When Hanoi's leaders were told about the American plan to invade Laos, they feared that a successful attempt to cut the Ho Chi Minh Trail, especially one that would permanently extend the defensive barrier along the DMZ between North and South Vietnam to the Mekong River on the Laos-Thailand border, would spell disaster for them. Hanoi's leaders knew the bulk of the manpower and almost all of the weapons and ammunition needed by the communist forces in South Vietnam came through the panhandle of southern Laos. Any American barrier anchored on the Mekong River in Laos would effectively isolate their forces south of the DMZ. The Tay Ninh Source told John that cutting the Ho Chi Minh Trail was an existential threat to the communist plans to unite North and South Vietnam. According to the Tay Ninh Source, the communist leadership in Hanoi knew that the Americans planned to use the U.S. Marine combat base at Khe Sanh as the main logistical base for the planned invasion of Laos and that is why they attempted to overrun it prior to the Tet Offensive and devoted so much combat power to that effort.

I have no idea what, if anything, John did with the information his valuable spy gave him concerning Hanoi's reasoning for launching their General Offensive–General Uprising in 1968 or whether this information ever reached anyone beyond our Embassy House. Perhaps, when the CIA declassifies the field reports from Tay Ninh Province, we might have the answer. One thing is certain: the Tet Offensive put an end to any planning by the Americans to extend their barrier along the northern border of South Vietnam into the panhandle of Laos. The perception among the American people was the war was stalemated and the VC had achieved a great victory with their offensive. This made it impossible for Gen. Westmoreland to execute his plan for an invasion and occupation of Laos in 1968, or any time after that. While the communists and the American military both considered the Tet Offensive a massive military failure for the VC, the press corps in Saigon and the U.S. public did not see it that way. The negative and often inaccurate reporting of the Tet Offensive sealed the fate of President Johnson and undermined the faith of the American people in the possibility of victory.[3]

While John had almost total confidence in the reliability of the spy, he told me many CIA analysts had doubts about the "source's" reasons for the communist Tet Offensive. He said they based their doubts on the belief that the "source" did not occupy a sufficiently high position in the VC political hierarchy to have access to such highly classified information on decision-making in Hanoi. They also did not believe the "source" would know how such highly classified American plans, such as the pacification plan or the operational plan for the invasion of Laos, were obtained. They thought the "source" might be either repeating rumors he had heard on his visits to COSVN, or he was just trying to enhance his value to the CIA by making these claims.

When John spoke of the CIA analysts' doubts, I had no way of assessing the validity of their doubts. I was unaware of the position held by the Tay Ninh Source inside the communist hierarchy, so I was not in a position to judge whether or not he would have access to such strategic intelligence. Still, I respected the professional abilities of John, and I knew the information contained in the report John showed me was clearly accurate, so I tended to believe John's assessment of the value of the Tay Ninh Source.

After venting for an hour, John left my room and staggered back to his room, pale and nauseous. Later I heard him vomiting in the bathroom down the hall, and I went down to check on him. He looked terrible, so I helped him back to his room and put him in his bed. The next day I did not see or hear John all day, but I had our cook, Mrs. Thu, send in his dinner before she left for the day. Unfortunately, John would have relapses like the one I observed that night, brought on, I believe, by a combination of separation from his family, whom he missed terribly, and the strain of controlling the Tay Ninh Source.

I was so taken with what I had heard from John, I wrote down the main points later that night so I would not forget them. While John never told me the name of the Tay Ninh Source, he did provide some interesting personal information on this individual and how John managed him. John told me the "source" lived in Tay Ninh Province near Nui Ba Den Mountain and he had originally been controlled by the South Vietnamese military intelligence people, the Military Security Service (MSS), but was later controlled by the South Vietnamese National Police Special Branch. He was first recruited in 1965, but poorly handled, so his strategic intelligence value was not exploited until 1969 when John started to manage him. According to John, the "source" passed several polygraph tests and the intelligence he provided was considered to be "gold standard" and accurate, at least by John. His motivation for coming over to our side was his anger over the party's decision to deny him a promotion he felt he deserved, something John felt was quite plausible since the "source" was very egocentric and self-assured. According to John, the "source" traveled regularly to Cambodia to attend COSVN and VC provincial-level meetings, despite the danger and difficulty such trips entailed. Because COSVN was located in the border region north of Tay Ninh Province, the "source" was able to make the journey in one day with little difficulty. John never told me how this cross-border journey to COSVN was made.

According to John, no American ever met the source unless the meeting was held in a safe house in Saigon. All contact with the source in Tay Ninh City was done with dead drops—and that was why "technical people from Saigon" had visited Tay Ninh to demonstrate several of these dead-drop techniques. Probably the most interesting thing John told me about the Tay Ninh Source was the man had a photographic memory and was able to recall, almost verbatim, what he had heard during the COSVN meetings he attended in Cambodia. According to John, the COSVN meetings were so secretive, the attendees were forbidden to take any notes of the proceedings, so the photographic memory of our spy was of inestimable value.

During this late-night visit by John, I did not mention Phong and his refusal to go on the PRU operation with me, but I suspected that Phong was involved with this valuable spy in some way. My suspicions about Phong would prove correct, but I would not know this until 2007. John never told me the name or the position held by this valuable communist cadre, but at the time I assumed, *incorrectly,* that he must have been a provincial level or higher cadre. After a few days of reflection, I began to see there might have been some connection between the failed operation against the Tay Ninh City District Committee meeting and what John was talking about. Perhaps this mission was aborted because it threatened the safety or identity of the Tay Ninh Source. I began to see why no one in the Embassy House had told me of his existence: had I been captured on a PRU operation, I might have been forced to reveal what I knew about this spy, thus placing his life in jeopardy and removing America's most valuable source of strategic intelligence.

Aside from this one conversation with John, I never discussed the Tay Ninh Source with anyone, even Chuck. On a few occasions, I was able to engage Chuck in discussions related to operational matters, but he never once mentioned the Tay Ninh Source or any other spy he knew about. He always provided me with sound professional advice and wise counsel on PRU operational matters, but he never mentioned anything specific about his work and certainly never anything involving a CIA asset. John and I never discussed the Tay Ninh Source again while I was in South Vietnam, but several years later, I met John for lunch near his home in Northern Virginia, and he reiterated most of what he told me that night in the Embassy House, adding only his belief that the spy had a relative or close friend who was a senior COSVN Lao Dong Party member who provided much of the intelligence the "source" obtained. Whether or not this relative or close friend provided this information knowing it would reach the American CIA was something John did not tell me. John also told me that the source provided the CIA with every strategic plan developed by COSVN from 1967 until the end of the war.

In 2007, I attended a conference at Texas Tech University where a former CIA officer, Merle Pribbenow, presented a paper that provided additional information about the Tay

Ninh Source, including his name and tragic fate. His name was Vo Van Ba, and he was arrested on April 30, 1975, and died while in custody under suspicious circumstances on June 8, 1975. At the time of his capture, he was the Lao Dong Party Secretary of Phu Khuong District and had been a controlled agent for over ten years. His primary duty for the Lao Dong Party was the recruitment of Cao Dai religious leaders. His identity was revealed to the North Vietnamese security service shortly before the end of the war by Mr. Phong. Mr. Phong was captured in Bon Me Thuot in the Central Highlands by the NVA, and he allegedly traded his safety for the identity of this valuable CIA spy.

To this day, the case of the Tay Ninh Source is taught to Vietnamese counterintelligence students as a classic example of how the CIA can penetrate even the highest level of a police state's security system and keep such a spy hidden for many years.[4] The communist Vietnamese government is careful not to reveal in any public document exactly what Ba revealed, but from my understanding, he revealed every important plan that COSVN made from 1968 until the end of the war. Despite having almost perfect knowledge of the communist plans provided by Mr. Ba, the American intelligence community failed to take full advantage of his knowledge. Why this important source of strategic intelligence was not exploited fully is a story that only the CIA can explain. Since everything related to Mr. Ba is still classified by the U.S. government, we may never know the answer to that question. Until the reports he provided are declassified, the reason why his information was not properly exploited will remain a mystery.[5]

Another significant incident took place in early 1970, one that resulted from a PRU effort to recruit a VCI as one of their informants. I made a serious mistake in my handling of this incident, a mistake that was a combination of my lack of intelligence training, my failure to follow up on the recruitment of a potentially valuable source, and my personal sense of honor. It was a hard lesson to learn and one I regret to this day.

It all began with a visit to the Tay Ninh Embassy House by the CIA's Inspector General (IG) in South Vietnam, retired U.S. Army MajGen. Charles J. Timmes. During the course of his IG visit, Gen. Timmes asked me if I had received any good leads from the Special Branch or the PIC lately. I informed him that I had received very few operational leads from either of these organizations. Naturally, Gen. Timmes was both surprised and concerned about this revelation, and he went to see Chuck about it. After meeting with Gen. Timmes, Chuck came to me and expressed his disappointment that neither John nor Mickey had given me the support he had demanded of them. He also said he intended to speak with John and Mickey to confirm this lack of cooperation, and if true, to correct it. Despite Chuck's intervention, nothing significant materialized as a result of his talks with these two men. How much of this reluctance was due to the need to protect Mr. Ba, the Tay Ninh Source, or their unwillingness to share in the glory of a VCI capture, I never found out. I decided not to force the issue, leaving the matter in Chuck's hands, since he was far more effective in dealing with John and Mickey than I was.

While I left Chuck to work with my colleagues in the Embassy House on developing operational leads, I spent most of the month of January working on improving cooperation between the DIOCCs and the PRU by visiting each district headquarters and enlisting the aid of the American district Phoenix advisors. I knew we could not rely on the PRU's own intelligence system entirely to gain the targeting information we needed. This was especially true when it came to developing actionable intelligence on the province's VC finance-economy network. While the legitimate and appropriate sources of intelligence that were represented on the DIOCCs, such as the Special Branch, MSS, SubSector S-2, PIC, Chieu Hoi Center, and Rural Development, provided some good leads on the low-level VCI, we seldom succeeded in getting much information on district- or province-level cadres. To make up for this deficiency, I had several meetings with Mr. Chinh and Mr. Tho to see if we could develop better operational leads using our own net of informants.

These discussions led, for the first time, to a thorough examination of the PRU intelligence system.[6] Up until then, I had only a very cursory and shallow understanding of how the system worked. The PRU seldom said anything to me about it; they just showed me the results. Since they had been using their own system for many years, I assumed it was fully functional and capable of developing accurate intelligence on the VCI. When I got into the details of the PRU intelligence system, I found that it was based upon the use of PRU family members and other Cao Dai coreligionists. Many of the PRU informants were old women who often visited family members and friends in areas where the VC operated. They could provide very plausible reasons for their travels and were highly skilled at asking questions in a manner that did not appear suspicious. I was surprised to learn that the PRU agents were not paid for their services. Mr. Chinh explained that paying agents was a mistake. He said an agent who wanted money for information was just as likely to sell information to the enemy as to us, so he insisted all PRU agents must be unpaid and motivated by factors other than money. According to Mr. Chinh, the best agents were those motivated by anger over some atrocity committed by the VC against their families, or because their religious convictions led them to see the communists as a threat to the Cao Dai religion.

Mr. Tho explained that the PRU net of agents was rather small, perhaps only a dozen informants to cover the entire province, so he stressed the need to ask ourselves how to best employ these limited assets to damage the VCI. We concluded that the most important VCI, in terms of support for the three NVA divisions in Cambodia, were the finance-economy cadres, since they arranged for supplies of food and medicines to be strategically staged in caches for NVA troops coming into the province. They also collected taxes that could be used to pay for food to feed the NVA troops in Cambodia. Without these local tax collectors, the NVA would not have food to eat, bunkers to hide in, or guides to direct them around U.S./ARVN ambushes when they moved through the province. In sum, these finance-economy cadres were the essential element of the North Vietnamese Army's logistics system inside South Vietnam. Without them, the NVA were forced to remain in their sanctuaries in Cambodia, incapable of sustained operations inside South Vietnam.

We also considered another element of the VCI as having an important role to play in supporting the NVA in Cambodia, the commo-liaison cadres who carried communications back and forth between COSVN and South Vietnam. Mr. Chinh contended that the NVA "were blind" without the intelligence these commo-liaison cadres carried between local VCI and the NVA units in Cambodia. We decided to make the VC commo-liaison cadres our next priority target after the finance-economy cadres.

Mr. Chinh and Mr. Tho recommended we add a third set of VCI targets to our list of communist cadres—the VCI security and reconnaissance units in the province that collected tactical intelligence on American and ARVN forces. Mr. Chinh informed me that he and Mr. Tho knew of a small, squad-size reconnaissance unit that was targeted against the American Tay Ninh West Air Base. They said this unit reported directly to COSVN and did not go through any village-, district- or province-level communist organization. This information about a special reconnaissance unit collecting intelligence on U.S. forces was completely new to me, but I was so interested in thinking of ways this valuable source might be used to identify and arrest VCI in the province, I made the serious mistake of not asking Mr. Chinh if he had reported this information previously to anyone besides me. I naively believed he had, although at the time I remembered thinking that I had not read about this enemy unit in any PRU intelligence report that had crossed my desk previously.

At the end of the meeting, I told them I would try to enlist the support of the American Phoenix advisors in the DIOCCs to develop operational leads for the PRU for targets that were finance-economy, commo-liaison, and security/reconnaissance cadres. Our goal was to eliminate as many of these cadres as possible and, thus, cripple the ability of the NVA main-force units to transit Tay Ninh Province or, at least, curtail their stay in the province due to the lack of logistical support and tactical intelligence.

As we developed our plan, I found myself asking more questions of Mr. Chinh about our own PRU intelligence system, but found he only wanted to discuss it in very general terms, often telling me that Mr. Tho or someone else had more detailed knowledge of the system. After a few minutes of my questions, he excused himself and never came back to the meeting, leaving me with many of my questions unanswered.

The next morning, when Mr. Tho came to the Embassy House for our daily coordination meeting on the front porch, he gave me a written invitation from Mr. Ngo Van Dung, one of the PRU district team leaders, to accompany him on a guided tour of the Cao Dai Holy See, the Vatican of the Cao Dai religion. Mr. Dung was not fluent in English, and I only knew some very basic Vietnamese, so I suggested I bring Mr. Lam along to assist in translation. Mr. Tho said Mr. Chinh insisted that I was to go alone to the meeting with Mr. Dung. Mr. Tho quickly added that I should not worry about Mr. Dung's English.

The next day I drove alone to the gate of the Cao Dai Holy See and met Mr. Dung there. He bought me a coconut juice drink at one of the shops outside the gate, and we sat down at a table and struggled to communicate with each other. It was hot, and I was beginning to feel like my afternoon with Mr. Dung was going to be a long and difficult one. Just as I was about to end our tortured conversation, we were joined by a tall Vietnamese man wearing a white shirt and dark trousers. He was young, about 30 years old, slender, quite tall for a Vietnamese (about 5 feet, 10 inches tall), and athletic-looking. He spoke English well and, after introducing himself as Mr. Tran, he suggested we should enter the basilica of the Holy See for his guided tour of this impressive Cao Dai church.

After entering the gate to the Holy See, Mr. Tran explained how the Cao Dai religion came into being in the 1920s and how the Holy See was built without any formal plans or engineering expertise. We spent a few minutes inside the basilica looking at the ornate interior as Mr. Tran pointed out various statuary and architectural aspects of the building. Both Mr. Dung and Mr. Tran were obviously very eager to explain their religion to me and to express their pride in the basilica's architecture.

After an hour, we started to leave the Holy See grounds, but Mr. Dung suggested we sit in the shade and talk for a few moments before leaving. I was eager to get back to the Embassy House, and I told Mr. Dung I could not stay much longer. He and Mr. Tran said we would only take a few minutes more, and they motioned me to a wooden bench under a tree where we sat in silence for a moment before Mr. Tran started to tell me about the

The Cao Dai Holy See.

The Cao Dai Holy See.

meeting I had had with Mr. Chinh. I did not know Mr. Tran and was hesitant to talk to him about Mr. Chinh or the PRU, but I did not want to be impolite or offend him since he and Mr. Dung seemed to be very good friends. I began to think that Mr. Tran might be one of Mr. Dung's informants. I decided to simply listen to what he had to say and maintain a polite silence.

He told me that the Tay Ninh PRU had a very good system for finding out about the VCI, but the details of this system had to be kept secret since there were "many VC spies everywhere." He went on to say that this system was based on family connections and long-established friendships, and therefore was "very reliable." At this point, I became a bit suspicious of Mr. Tran. Since I had never met him before and knew he was not on the PRU payroll, I told him I really could not talk about this matter any further. When I said this, Mr. Dung interrupted Mr. Tran and began to talk to him in a very forceful manner. I did not understand exactly what they were saying, but it was obvious that Mr. Dung wanted Mr. Tran to talk to me about a subject of great importance to him.

Mr. Tran began by saying, "Mr. Dung wants you to know that you must never share any information the PRU gives you unless it is in the form of the written reports they file with the PIOCC." I told him that I never had any other information to share—that the only information I ever passed on was contained in the written reports Mr. Tho gave to me. Mr. Dung and Mr. Tran then spent a few minutes talking to each other before Mr. Dung turned to me and said (in fractured English), "Dai Uy (Captain) Andy, do you promise to keep certain secrets and not share them with anyone, even your American bosses?" I told him I could not do that and that I trusted every American who worked with me. Then Mr. Tran said Americans can be trusted, but they talk to their counterparts all the time and the PRU have sources of information that cannot be revealed to anyone since the provision of the information would reveal the sources. I said I understood the need to protect their informants from VC retribution, but I also knew that information on the VCI needed to be shared if we were going to succeed in neutralizing them.

It was then that Mr. Tran told me that he was not talking about the PRU's Cao Dai informants (the old women he talked about earlier), but a very important source of information—"someone at the very heart of the enemy." When he said this, I immediately thought of the Tay Ninh Source and wondered how this man knew about him. However, I was *wrong*. Mr. Tran was talking about someone entirely different, but I did not know that then. I trusted Mr. Dung, but I was suspicious of Mr. Tran's motivation for raising this topic with me, and I began to think he might be planting false information with me in an attempt to get me to finance a PRU operation that was based on some fictional source. I had been warned that the South Vietnamese had used this ruse on occasion to obtain funding from the Americans. I again repeated that I was honor-bound to report all the information on the VCI that came to my attention.

My instincts told me that I should end this conversation and discuss what Mr. Tran had told me with John or Chuck since they were far more knowledgeable about such matters. I told Mr. Dung and Mr. Tran I needed to leave and get back to the Embassy House for an important meeting. Mr. Tran said he was sorry I could not work with them, but he understood why. At the time, I simply did not believe the PRU had access to any high-level VCI, and I was angry that Mr. Dung and Mr. Chinh thought I was gullible enough to fall for such a story. I suspected the worst—an effort to extract money from the CIA to finance this operation using me as the conduit. Given the paucity of high-level information developed by the PRU during my tour with them, I simply found Mr. Tran's claim about a high-level VCI source lacked credibility.

Later that afternoon at the Embassy House, I questioned John about whether or not he thought the PRU had any intelligence sources of significant value. He said he did not think so. He said the PRU had been cooperative with intelligence sharing, but they had never provided any information to the Special Branch that was very exploitable, at least during his time with the Special Branch. He qualified his comment by telling me the information the PRU provided, while low level and tactical, was usually accurate, something that was not the case with many other sources. John's assessment of the PRU intelligence system was that it was not sophisticated, but it was effective in developing VCI targets in the B and C categories, meaning most VCI cadres below district level.

Taken together, I decided to forget about this alleged "high level" VCI source that Mr. Dung said existed. After all, I was not a trained intelligence officer, just a Marine infantry officer with a lot of practical combat and long-range reconnaissance patrolling experience. I was satisfied at the time with what the PRU were doing to develop targets, and I was not particularly interested in the mechanics of their intelligence-gathering system—only the results. My rationale for this thinking was the fact that I was not expected to be an intelligence officer; that was the job of Chuck and the others in the Embassy House. I thought my job was to exploit the intelligence they and their counterparts developed and to use my military skills to train and support the PRU. *This was a major failing on my part.*

Just before I left Tay Ninh in June 1970, I went on a final visit to each district PRU headquarters to inspect them, to ascertain if there were any last-minute logistics requirements that needed my attention, to bid them farewell, and to make one final coordination visit with each district's American Phoenix advisor. On this trip I had a chance to speak privately with Mr. Dung. Mr. Lam, as usual, accompanied me during this trip. Mr. Dung said he was sorry I was leaving, but he thought his team would function well in my absence, even if a new American PRU advisor was not assigned.

Almost in passing, I asked him if he had any new information concerning his "high level" source in the VCI. It was then that Mr. Dung shocked me with the revelation that this source had recently provided an accurate list of the enemy personnel in a COSVN security unit called "Section 7 of the D46 Ground Reconnaissance Battalion." According to Mr. Dung, this unit was responsible for gathering tactical and *political* intelligence for COSVN in Tay Ninh Province. He explained that Section 7 did this by employing three squad-size teams in the western half of the province.

I asked him if this information had been conveyed to the DIOCC in his district, since I had never heard anything about this unit before. Mr. Dung was embarrassed and started to change the subject. I could tell he did not want to discuss the subject further, but I pressed him on it because I was angry that such valuable information, if true, had not been reported previously. I was still dubious about his high-level VCI source, but I had never known the PRU to deliberately withhold information before. Mr. Dung then said he had not reported it because he wanted to protect the source. He was keeping this information to himself because he wanted to exploit it in good time by arresting the members of Section 7 under circumstances that would not indicate they had been betrayed by a provincial-level VC security cadre. I told him it was a mistake to keep this information a secret since such a high-level cadre was too important to waste on tactical intelligence. I still doubted him, but I could see no reason for him to lie to me. He never asked for funds, and he was always honest and forthright with me in every instance previously. As our meeting ended, I took him aside and told him he must have Mr. Chinh talk to Mr. Stainback about this source. Mr. Dung said he would do it "soon," but only if I promised not to tell anyone about it until he had discussed it with Mr. Chinh. I gave him my word and left Vietnam three days later. I regret not telling anyone in the Embassy House about this conversation, but I believed then that Mr. Chinh would follow up and discuss this source with Chuck. As it turned out, Mr. Dung never told Mr. Chinh to contact Chuck, or Mr. Chinh decided not to tell Chuck about Mr. Dung's source.

In March 1986, I helped Mr. Tho resettle in the United States after he escaped from South Vietnam. He had been captured by the communists shortly after the fall of Saigon and had spent several years in re-education camps and prisons before he walked across Cambodia and found sanctuary in a refugee camp in Thailand. When he arrived in the United States, I rented a small house for him and his family near Camp Lejeune, North Carolina, the Marine base where I was stationed at the time. He lived there for six months that year before leaving with his family for California. While he was in North Carolina, he and I talked a great deal about Tay Ninh and what happened to the PRU after the fall of Saigon.

In one of our discussions, Mr. Tho indicated that Mr. Dung had, indeed, developed a very valuable source of information on the VCI. Mr. Tho seemed to think, based upon Mr. Dung's unguarded comments, that this VCI informant was a relative of a PRU soldier in

Phuoc Ninh district, where Mr. Dung was the PRU team leader. He also thought this informant lived in Cambodia most of the time and even had a second wife there. According to Mr. Tho, the PRU spy seemed to have detailed information on both the internal and external security units assigned to COSVN, as well as the names of several Tay Ninh provincial-level cadres living in Cambodia. Mr. Tho thought this spy first started to provide Mr. Dung with information in the summer of 1969, but he stopped doing so in either 1971 or 1972 for reasons unknown. We both thought that either this informant was caught by the North Vietnamese security service, or, more likely, the informant viewed the departure of American forces as the prelude to the eventual abandonment of the South Vietnamese government by the Americans and broke off his contact with Mr. Dung. In retrospect, I think a case could be made that this PRU spy was legitimate, and given his position in the VCI, a strong effort should have been made for the Police Special Branch and the CIA to recruit him. I sincerely regret not informing Chuck before I left South Vietnam about this potential spy; however, I had my doubts about his existence, and I had also promised Mr. Dung I would not discuss my conversations on this subject with anyone. My sense of honor got in the way, I am afraid.

In a later telephone conversation with Mr. Tho in California, some additional information about Mr. Dung's high-level source came to light. Mr. Tho remembered that Mr. Dung told him the special COSVN security unit, Section 7, had been formed as a result of COSVN's dissatisfaction with the normal intelligence-gathering efforts of the VC in Tay Ninh Province and elsewhere in III Corps. The informant told Mr. Dung that COSVN did not trust the intelligence provided by the VCI in Tay Ninh Province after Tet 1968. In addition to this lack of confidence in the VCI reporting, many of the normal VC intelligence-gathering teams had been destroyed by the Phoenix Program in the months following the Tet Offensive. As a result of these developments, COSVN decided to form a special reconnaissance unit that would be under direct COSVN control, thus eliminating their reliance on reporting from the district and provincial VCI organizations in Tay Ninh Province.

Surprisingly, the informant also revealed that the majority of political intelligence collected by COSVN (post–Tet 1968) came from open sources, primarily daily Saigon newspapers and *not from spies*. They considered these open sources so valuable that they arranged for multiple deliveries of Saigon's daily newspapers via commo-liaison cadres who used a variety of transportation modes to get the newspapers to the Cambodian border, and ultimately to COSVN. In so doing, these newspapers were in the hands of COSVN analysts within 24 hours of their publication. I still find it difficult to believe that COSVN would place such importance on open-source newspapers, especially when they had so many high-level spies working for them, such as Pham Xuan An, who had good access to both American and GVN government officials and military leaders. Still, Mr. Tho told me the PRU captured several of the commo-liaison cadres transporting these newspapers between Saigon and the Cambodian border, so there must be some truth to the source's claim that they were important to COSVN. As I recall, Mr. Tho mentioned that COSVN considered the Saigon daily *Chinh Luan* the best source of political intelligence available to them. According to a State Department analyst who was working in Saigon around this same time, this newspaper was so full of useful political intelligence, it was read avidly by American analysts in Saigon to stay abreast of the latest South Vietnamese political developments.

CHAPTER 17

The PRU Winter Offensive of 1969

Shortly after Chuck returned from his home leave, I briefed him on the PRU plan to concentrate their efforts against the finance-economy, commo-liaison, and security/reconnaissance cadres in the province. He seemed pleased with it. He also said he would encourage John and Mickey to have both the Special Branch and the PIC provide any information they could on these cadres and provide whatever assistance we needed to make the plan a success.

We began to see results shortly after we implemented our plan. We captured two village-level finance-economy cadres in early January, and then on January 25, we captured a district-level finance-economy cadre after receiving a tip from a Special Branch informant. The enemy cadre, Nguyen Tan Hiep, had been on our list of priority VCI targets for over a year, so his capture by our City Team was a high point for our entire program that month.

Wearing civilian clothes and traveling in two groups of three men each, six PRU soldiers from the city team left the city on foot and walked two miles to the home of a family member of Mr. Hiep, where the informant said Mr. Hiep could be found hiding. As they approached the house, two armed men opened fire on them. The PRU soldiers returned the fire, killing both men. They then tackled Mr. Hiep as he attempted to run out of the back of the house. Along with the capture of Mr. Hiep, the PRU soldiers recovered a pistol and a rifle from the dead guerrillas.

Later that day when I was debriefing the PRU team on their successful mission, one of the PRU soldiers told me that the marksmanship training I had arranged for him a month earlier had paid off for him in this firefight. He was not able to speak English well, but he knew enough to explain to me why the training had paid off when he said, "I shoot one shot, use sight picture, kill one VC." It felt good to know the training I had arranged for him had paid off in a successful operation.

Some very incriminating documents were found on Mr. Hiep's person and hidden in the roof of the house he was hiding in, documents that clearly proved that Mr. Hiep had been skimming VC tax money and using it to purchase farmland for himself and his family. When I told John, the Special Branch advisor, about this example of VCI corruption, he told me this was far from unusual. Mr. Chinh also told me of several examples where VC were involved in corrupt practices, most of which involved skimming taxes or demanding protection money from farmers, woodcutters, and local tradesmen. When I read the translation of the documents captured with Mr. Hiep, I saw that he had amassed a small fortune by skimming taxes and hiding this crime from his communist colleagues. His older brother and a cousin were accomplices in this scheme to steal tax money from the party so they could buy high-grade farmland east of the city. At Mr. Hiep's trial in Tay Ninh City, which I attended, he was convicted of being a VC and sentenced to two years in prison—a very light sentence, in my opinion. Mr. Chinh made sure the corruption practices of Mr. Hiep were read into the trial's record because he believed the communists would punish Mr. Hiep far more severely when he was released if they knew he had been stealing from the party for several years.[1]

February was not a particularly productive month for the Tay Ninh PRU, but Mr. Chinh attributed this more to the Tet holidays than to any lack of action by the PRU. Still, we had a few very successful operations against the enemy's finance-economy network.

Mr. Tho launched an operation involving fifty PRU soldiers and six PRU informants in Hieu Thien district, in an area between the Song Vam Co Dong River and the Cambodian border southwest of Tay Ninh City. We had received numerous agent reports that identified this area, which stretched for 10 miles along the Cambodian border, as the location for several major enemy supply and commo-liaison routes. Dressed in civilian clothes, with hidden weapons, and acting as farmers, woodcutters, and ox-cart drivers, these PRU soldiers tried to entice the VCI finance-economy cadres to tax them. At first, I was a bit dubious about the ability of the PRU to blend into the local area, but my fears were quickly allayed when a village finance-economy cadre, named Nguyen Van Danh, was captured trying to tax a PRU soldier posing as an ox-cart driver. The PRU soldier pulled out his hidden .45 cal. automatic pistol when Mr. Danh asked him to turn over 2,000 piasters. He then transported Mr. Danh in the back of his ox cart to the Hieu Thien district headquarters, bound hand and foot like a pig on the way to market. Using this same technique of disguised PRU soldiers, another lower-level VCI finance-economy supplier was captured on February 26. Both prisoners were cooperative, spoke freely about their activities, and were turned over to the PIC for further questioning.[2]

On February 27, we again had a successful operation against the VCI supply system when we arrested the supervisor of agriculture at the Cau-Khoi Rubber Plantation, Mr. Mai Than Pho. We had received a tip from Mickey after he had interviewed a Hoi Chanh who had recently turned himself in to a PF platoon near the Cau-Khoi Rubber Plantation. This plantation was located a few miles east of Tay Ninh City on the border of Phu Khoung and Khiem Hanh districts. The Hoi Chanh told Mickey that Mr. Pho had been providing a sanctuary on the plantation for small units of NVA soldiers conducting reconnaissance missions in the province, as well as purchasing hard-to-obtain items of supply, like typewriters, mimeograph machines, printer's ink, and medicines for NVA units in Cambodia. He was also accused of providing huge sums of money to the VC Duong Minh Chau district finance-economy section.

I questioned Mr. Pho after his capture in an attempt to discover how he was able to move his supplies from the rubber plantation to Cambodia, a distance of eight miles. He was very cooperative and explained in great detail how these valuable supply items were hidden in the false bottom of one of the plantation's stake-bed trucks and driven to a spot near the An Ta Border Station on the South Vietnamese-Cambodian border. Here the items were picked up and carried by porters across the border near the destroyed village of Xom Ba Ao. He also revealed that supplies for the enemy were being transported from the Michelin Rubber Plantation in neighboring Binh Duong Province, using this same route. He thought many high-value supply items were knowingly provided to the VC by the Corsican manager of that French-owned plantation. The information provided by Mr. Pho turned out to be accurate, and we later successfully ambushed an enemy supply column near the An Ta Border Station. We also passed the information about the manager of the Michelin Rubber Plantation to the Binh Duong Province PRU, who arrested him.[3]

On one of the last days of February, I was offered a chance to make a low-level reconnaissance flight in a U.S. Army OH-6A helicopter. This small and very fast helicopter was new to me and was not part of the Marine Corps inventory of aircraft, so I welcomed this chance to take a flight in it. It had a two-man crew, was small, very fast, highly agile, and able to fly at treetop level with ease, making it an ideal aircraft for conducting aerial observation missions. The PRU had received two agent reports about a finance-economy cell operating in War Zone C, and I wanted to check out the area the agents identified to see if there were any trails or huts in this largely uninhabited part of the province that would indicate the presence of such a VC cell.

My pilots for this flight were both young U.S. Army warrant officers who seemed to possess an abundance of flying skill and an almost total lack of fear. We flew north from Tay Ninh West Airfield toward Nui Ba Den Mountain, passing it on the right as we hurled through the sky at over 100 miles an hour at an altitude of around 50 feet. I had never experienced such a ride before or after—it was breathtaking, to say the least. Trees, brush, water-filled bomb craters, and abandoned paddy fields raced past us as we skimmed over the terrain toward our destination. When we arrived over the coordinates given by our informants, the pilots made several low-level passes so I could get a good look at what lay below. I searched the area for several minutes, but all I saw was flooded marshland with a few clumps of trees interspersed at intervals ranging from 50 to 100 meters. The terrain did not look like a very good place for a VC finance-economy cell to operate in, so I told the pilots to return to base.

On our way south, I noticed a set of intersecting trails and what looked like a man walking beside a bicycle on one of them. Since the surrounding area was devoid of any habitation and was remote, I thought it odd that someone would be out there with a bicycle. We circled the man, who stopped and stared up at us. I could see the fear in his face as we circled above him. I suspected he might be a VC, so I asked the pilot to land the helicopter so I could capture him. The pilot did not think it was a wise course of action, but he agreed nonetheless, quickly setting down in an open area just off one of the trails 100 meters from the man on the bicycle. I jumped out of the helicopter, drew my only weapon, a Colt Cobra .38 cal. snub-nosed revolver, and began running along the trail toward the suspected VC. As I approached the man, the thought struck me that perhaps I had been a bit rash in taking the action I did. I pondered what I would do if he was armed, a thought that had escaped me when I asked the pilot to land his helicopter.

Fortunately for me, God smiles on fools. The man raised his hands as I approached, dropping his bicycle, and trembling in fear from the sight of this odd-looking American dressed in civilian clothes with a pistol in his hand. I asked him for his ID card, which he quickly produced. I tried to ask him a few questions but the noise from the helicopter's rotor blades made communication almost impossible. His ID looked in order, but I still could not figure out what a man would be doing in War Zone C, so far from any village or town. I decided to take him back to Tay Ninh West Airfield so he could be questioned. Throughout the 20-minute flight, I kept my pistol trained on the young man while he stared outside the helicopter in stark terror. I was not sure what he was more afraid of, the man holding the pistol aimed at him or the hair-raising flight at treetop level. In any event, when we finally interrogated our terrified passenger at Tay Ninh West Airfield, we found out that he was just an innocent teenager out looking for turtles and frogs to take home to his family for dinner. I apologized to him for the inconvenience and told him I would reimburse him for the bicycle he left out on the trail. The National Police provided him with a ride home that evening, where I am sure he had a hard time explaining to his family where he had been since he left home that morning.

During February, I saw a graphic example of the superiority of the CIA's supply system. I had asked for the construction of a new headquarters building for the Hieu Thien district PRU, since their current building, not much more than a few cramped huts built close to each other that also served as quarters for their family members, was neither adequate nor safe. Since I was only familiar with the U.S. Marine Corps system of supply, I expected my request to take at least a month to be approved and then even longer for the building to be constructed. To my surprise and pleasure, my request was approved a day after it was submitted, and just five days later, on February 23, two flatbed trucks showed up at the Embassy House and their drivers asked me where I wanted the building erected. I hurriedly called for Mr. Lam, and he and I led the two trucks south along Route 22 to the town of Go Dau Ha, where the PRU team had their headquarters. The drivers unloaded the prefabricated metal building, called a Butler building, and immediately set to work digging a foundation and then laying a concrete slab for the floor. Mr. Lam and I looked on in amazement as the two Filipino drivers and their two South Vietnamese assistants rapidly went about their tasks. They told me they would erect the frame, walls, and roof of the building the next day after the concrete was settled. The next day, true to their word, they had completed their work. In just two days, they had erected a shiny new metal building measuring 50 feet by 30 feet. The eighteen-man PRU team from Hieu Thien now had enough room to sleep comfortably in the new cots I had obtained for them from a friendly U.S. Army officer at the Tay Ninh West base camp. The construction crew even built an outdoor shower for the team behind the building and ran a pipe from it to the main water supply of the Hieu Thien district compound. When I saw the finished product, I thought to myself that even the U.S. Navy's Seabees would have had a difficult time doing this work faster.

The PRUs and the Phoenix Program have often been accused of extralegal arrests and the wholesale assassination of both VC and innocent civilians, but my experience with the Tay Ninh PRU and the information I gleaned from other U.S. PRU advisors led me to believe these claims are false.

A good example of this occurred in January and February of 1970, when the PRU began to investigate allegations that two individuals living in the Cao Dai Holy See were members of the VC Duong Minh Chau district party committee. A Special Branch informant identified Mr. Le Van Mang as a VC lieutenant colonel in charge of the VC district's "Assassination Section," and a Mr. Le Hoang Dan as Mr. Mang's bodyguard. The Cao Dai Holy See was off-limits to both the American and South Vietnamese governments because an agreement had been negotiated between the Cao Dai religious leaders and the GVN that the Cao Dai would police the Holy See and prevent it from being used by the communists. For this reason, no one who was armed was allowed on the grounds of the Holy See and no uniformed American or GVN personnel were allowed to visit it. Under a special agreement with the

Cao Dai religious leaders, the members of the Tay Ninh City PRU team were given permission to operate inside the Holy See, but they could not make an arrest there. This meant that investigations had to be carried out in a very discreet manner, and any arrest had to be made outside the Holy See.

Mr. Chinh and I discussed the agent report about Mang and Dan and decided to use Chuck to approach his contacts in the Cao Dai to gain their permission to insert a three-man PRU surveillance team to work undercover inside the Holy See for a month so evidence on the two VC suspects could be developed. Chuck obtained the permission, but after a solid month of observation, no evidence was obtained that could be used to make an arrest. We also tried to locate Hoi Chanhs from the VC Duong Minh Chau district party committee who could identify Mang and Dan as members of that communist organization, but this also produced negative results.[4] Still, Mr. Chinh was convinced Mang and Dan were VC, but he knew the province chief, Lt. Col. Thien, would not approve an arrest order unless there was solid evidence that these two men were what the informant claimed they were. If the PRU had been an "assassination" unit, as some have claimed, then why did they not just kill these two suspected VC instead of spending a month trying to obtain evidence, if there was no need to do it?

During the eight months I was the PRU advisor in Tay Ninh Province, I never once received an order to assassinate anyone and neither did the PRU. In fact, we considered any VCI killed in an operation as a loss since we much preferred to capture VCI so we could either interrogate them for information on their colleagues or attempt to "turn" them and have them spy for us. Most of the VC the PRU killed were local guerrilla fighters who were providing protection for the VCI cadres, or were armed VCI cadres who resisted arrest. Although many VCI were apprehended without violence, the majority chose instead to engage the PRU in a firefight rather than surrender, especially if they had a security detail protecting them.

One thing that became apparent as we interviewed captured VC was the fact that the ranks of the VCI were severely depleted in our province by early 1970, with many villages having no VCI cadres at all. This paucity of VCI was due to several factors, but the work of the PRU and the other elements of the Phoenix Program was the primary reason, according to statements made by VC POWs and Hoi Chanhs. We also found that many of the VCI targets we developed from our analysis of the Census-Grievance maps and those contained in the "Current List of VCI Executive and Significant Cadres," a report prepared by the PIOCC, simply did not exist any longer. We found that nearly 80 percent of the VCI we identified on these lists had been neutralized through death, capture, or rally to the GVN. It was becoming impossible for the VCI to function in Tay Ninh Province because as soon as they tried to govern in their villages and districts, our spies would identify them, and the PRU, National Police, or PFs would kill them, arrest them, or drive them out of the province. In fact, most of the VCI we identified as still alive were living in exile in Cambodia and could not return to their villages for fear of arrest.

This fact caused us to investigate the possibility of conducting cross-border operations inside Cambodia, even though that country was off-limits to American forces. We never received permission from Station to send PRU teams into Cambodia, but Station did not say anything about PRU informants. This lack of a proscription for the use of informants inside Cambodia was not lost on Mr. Tho and Mr. Chinh, both of whom admitted that they had been sending informants into Cambodia in search of VCI for several years. This cross-border activity was not done on a small scale. In fact, they had mounted thirty-seven such intelligence-gathering missions into Cambodia during the months of February and March. During these missions inside Cambodia, our informants located several high-ranking VCI living in Cambodian towns close to the border with South Vietnam. Some of the PRU informants had ethnic Vietnamese family members living in the eastern provinces of Cambodia, and these family members regularly reported the presence of VCI living among them. In order to make sure we received the informant reports quickly, Mr. Tho established three border listening posts at the An Ta Free Market, the Cay Me Free Market, and the Phuoc Tan area.[5]

In addition to sending us information on the VCI via the border listening posts, these PRU informants began to send us reports in late 1969 of unrest in Cambodia and increased tensions between the NVA troops living close to the border and the local Cambodian citizens and soldiers of the Cambodian Army. These reports increased in frequency shortly after Christmas 1969. In February 1970, I provided this information to Chuck, who wrote several field reports to Station informing our Embassy of these developments.

The heightened tensions in Cambodia led us to believe that these events might cause those VCI living in exile in Cambodia to attempt to return to South Vietnam. With this in mind, we launched an operation to contact the family members of known VCI in the hope we might be able to convince these returning VCI to surrender to us. We knew that many of the families of the exiled VCI were in dire financial straits due to the absence of their men who were living in Cambodia, so we tried to influence their families living in Tay Ninh Province with financial aid and medical assistance. While the families of these VCI seemed grateful for the assistance we provided to them, we were not successful in our efforts to get these families to convince their missing husbands, sons, and fathers to rally to the South Vietnamese government.

During February, we began to receive reporting on Cambodian demonstrations and acts of violence directed against the NVA in the border regions of Cambodia, along with reports that the NVA divisions in Cambodia were planning for a major summer offensive. Our informants told us that the NVA 5th, 7th and 9th Divisions were receiving very large amounts of new weapons and ammunition to support this impending invasion of South Vietnam. This was coupled with intelligence from our informants inside South Vietnam that VCI finance-economy cadres had been directed to begin storing rice in caches for this offensive. As a result, we redoubled our efforts to neutralize these finance-economy cadres.[6]

In March, the volume of reporting on the turmoil inside Cambodia spiked dramatically. The CIDG unit located at the Tay Ninh East Airfield, which was an ethnic Cambodian unit, had several of its soldiers request leave to travel to Cambodia to help the Khmer Serey (Free Cambodia) forces fight the NVA, a clear indication that the situation in Cambodia was rapidly reaching the crisis point. I spoke with several of the American Special Forces soldiers assigned to the CIDG unit, and they informed me they had been told to expect a coup against Prince Norodom Sihanouk soon. The Cambodian CIDG troops told them the Cambodian people were angry over the prince's reluctance to take action against the large number of North Vietnamese communist forces controlling much of the eastern part of the country. This loss of sovereignty and several attacks upon the Cambodian Army by the NVA had produced a loss of faith in Prince Sihanouk. There was also growing tension between ethnic Vietnamese living in Cambodia and the local Cambodian citizens. The Cambodian inhabitants of the border region resented the presence of both the ethnic Vietnamese minority and the NVA. According to these American Special Forces officers and NCOs, their Cambodian CIDG unit was on the verge of mutiny since their Camdodian soldiers all wanted to cross the border into Cambodia to assist the Cambodian Army in what they expected would be a violent confrontation with the NVA.

While we monitored events in Cambodia and continued to pursue the VCI in Tay Ninh Province, the PRU experienced one of those incidents that plagued the program from time to time—the misuse of the PRU by South Vietnamese officials who did not fully understand the mission of the PRU or the chain of command for this CIA-controlled anti–VCI organization.

I was sitting on the porch of the Embassy House with Mr. Lam and Mr. Tho, sipping coffee and conducting our daily meeting, when one of the City Team PRU soldiers drove up to the front gate on his motorbike with a message for me that the province chief wanted to see me and Mr. Chinh in his office immediately. This was highly unusual and I suspected the province chief had some important mission he wanted to discuss with us, or else there had been an incident involving the PRU that needed our immediate attention. In this case, the latter applied.

When we went in to see Lt. Col. Thien, he seemed calm and relaxed, but after a few casual remarks about how much good work the PRU had been doing, his demeanor changed as he stated the real purpose for our hastily called meeting. He informed us that there had been a serious confrontation between Mr. Ngo Van Dung, the PRU team leader for Phuoc Ninh District, and his district chief. The district chief had ordered Mr. Dung and his entire team to establish an ambush position near the district headquarters on three successive nights and at the same location. Mr. Dung had refused to send his team out on the third night because the ambush was not related to any counter–VCI objective. Mr. Dung also did not want his entire team awake all night, making them too tired to conduct surveillance and intelligence operations the next day. I was also concerned when I heard that the district chief insisted that the PRU ambush be located in the same site for three successive nights, something I felt was exceedingly dangerous and foolhardy.

I could not argue with the logic used by Mr. Dung for refusing to obey the district chief, but I could see the dilemma his refusal caused the province chief. I also knew that Mr. Dung could be very quick to anger, and at times quite violent. A few months previously he had caught an ARVN airborne sergeant making inappropriate remarks to his wife in a small soft drink shop she owned, and this confrontation led to Mr. Dung's beating the South Vietnamese paratrooper to death in the street in front of the shop. Unlike many South Vietnamese, Mr. Dung was solidly built and extremely strong, despite his short stature. He was a devout Cao Dai, a committed anti-communist, and one of the best field leaders I have ever encountered. In short, he was a very valuable PRU asset, and I did want to see him leave his post in Phuoc Ninh District.

After discussing the matter for a few minutes, I could see that the province chief was forced to support his district chief, although he candidly told us he thought the district chief was primarily to blame for this incident. Mr. Chinh and I agreed that Mr. Dung needed to be replaced, and the best place to employ a man of his ability and talents was in the Tay Ninh PRU City Team. The province chief, who understood the mission of the PRU and had been a strong advocate for the correct employment of his premier anti–VCI unit, apologized to me for the need to replace Mr. Dung, and he suggested it might be a good idea for me to go to Phuoc Ninh to talk to the U.S. district advisor there to explain why Mr. Dung was leaving and to enlist his aid in convincing the district chief he should employ the PRU in that district in a manner more in conformance with the PRU mission.

The next day, Mr. Lam and I drove to the Phuoc Ninh district headquarters where we met Mr. Dung and got his side of the story before we met with the U.S. district advisor. The young American Army officer who was the district advisor did not know that he and I had the same rank or that I was a U.S. Marine officer, so he always referred to me as Mr. Finlayson, thinking I was a CIA officer and giving me far more respect and cooperation than he normally would have had he known my true rank and service affiliation. Since this misunderstanding only benefitted me when I spoke with the province's district advisors, I did nothing to correct their thinking.

As was the normal course of events during my visit to this district, the U.S. Army district advisor and I got along well and discussed the problem with Mr. Dung in a friendly and collegial manner. We had discussed the need for the district PRU team to be used exclusively on counter–VCI operations on a previous occasion, and the American officer had agreed then that he would try to convince the district chief that this was the proper way to employ them. He explained that the district chief was worried about an impending NVA attack on his district headquarters and wanted to use every available asset to counter this threat, thus employing the PRU team in a strictly military role as district headquarters security during the day and ambushes at night. The district advisor praised the district's PRU team and Mr. Dung, telling me the PRU was the best fighting unit in the district. It appeared that it was these very qualities that motivated the district chief to use the PRU in a security role when he felt his headquarters was threatened.

I listened to the U.S. advisor carefully explain the rationale for the district chief's employment of the PRU team, but I could tell that he did not fully support his district chief's reasoning. I did not seek a confrontation, only a solution, so I suggested in the future more consideration should be given to using the RF Company or local PF forces for such missions, since these forces were better suited for purely military missions. He agreed, but cautioned that he had to maintain a good working relationship with the district chief and he could not force his views on him. We both agreed that it was important for the district chief not to "lose face" by confronting him on this issue, but to work in private with him to see if he would change his policies. We also agreed that the district chief should be reminded in private that the province chief had recently spoken with him about how to properly employ PRU forces in his district. I was impressed with the American officer and sympathized with his situation, so I decided to do nothing or say anything that might hurt his relationship with his district chief. I could have played hardball with the district chief and pulled the entire team out of his district until he promised to use them correctly, but that would have only made matters worse. I could also have reminded him that the PRU were under my command and not his, but this would only undercut the evolving Vietnamization process, whereby the PRU would ultimately come under the control of the Province Chief and the National Police, so I refrained from making this comment when we met later that morning. Instead, when the U.S. district advisor and I had our meeting with him, I simply apologized for the problem caused by Mr. Dung's refusal to obey orders and that I was transferring Mr.

Dung to a new position in the province immediately, pointing out that this decision had the approval of the province chief. To my surprise, the young ARVN officer asked me to reconsider the decision to transfer Mr. Dung, explaining that Mr. Dung was a highly effective leader and fighter who simply had made a mistake in judgment. For a moment I was tempted to leave Mr. Dung in place, but based on what I had heard from the U.S. advisor and Mr. Chinh, I informed the district chief that it was necessary to relieve Mr. Dung of his duties in Phuoc Ninh district because he had openly challenged the authority of the district chief and this failure could not be glossed over. After a few comments by me about the need to concentrate on arresting VCI finance-economy cadres in the district and suggesting we better coordinate our operational use of the PRU in Phuoc Ninh District, I left the headquarters and went over to the PRU compound to take Mr. Dung back to Tay Ninh City and his new duties. On the way back to the city, Mr. Dung informed me that it was a good thing he was being transferred because he intended to call the district chief out to a fistfight. As we approached the city, I thanked God for not changing my mind about his transfer.[7]

Shortly after we transferred Mr. Dung to the City Team, we conducted an almost textbook PRU operation resulting in the capture of a female commo-liaison cadre along the road leading to the An Ta Free Market on the Cambodian-South Vietnamese border. This operation worked the way every Phoenix operation should have worked if everyone involved in the effort played their roles properly and in conformance with the Phoenix Program's procedures.

In this case, a PRU informant provided information to the Hieu Thien District PRU team that a female commo-liaison cadre would be transporting communist documents from Cu Chi to the An Ta Free Market for follow-on movement to COSVN headquarters inside Cambodia. This information was provided to the PRU by the informant on the afternoon of March 10 and forwarded by PRU courier to PRU headquarters that evening. I was informed by Mr. Tho early the next day, and together we took an arrest order to be signed by the province chief. At the same time, Mr. Chinh placed six PRU soldiers in isolation at the PRU headquarters barracks and began planning for an operation the next day to capture this communist cadre on her way to the Free Market. After receiving permission to arrest the commo-liaison cadre from the province chief, Mr. Tho and I met with Mr. Chinh to finalize our planning for the next day's operation. We waited until nearly midnight to inform the PIOCC of the impending operation in order to prevent any potential leaks to the enemy. The next day, Mr. Lam and I traveled to the Hieu Thien District Headquarters to establish a command post there and to inform the district chief and the DIOCC that an operation was planned in their district. The U.S. district advisor arranged for a reaction force to respond if the operation encountered difficulties, and he also alerted a nearby U.S. artillery battery. While Mr. Lam and I set up our radio to communicate with the capture team, three of the six PRU men, along with the informant, traveled in a borrowed taxicab to a small bridge on Highway 1 leading to the Free Market. They knew the commo-liaison cadre would have to cross the bridge on her way to the border station. The capture team, dressed in civilian clothes and posing as traders, sat down in a small drink shop near the bridge while the informant waited inside the taxicab, where he could clearly see the faces of anyone crossing the small bridge.

The informant had met the commo-liaison cadre on a previous occasion, and therefore he was confident he could identify her. If he spotted her, he would signal the capture team by dropping a towel he had around his neck. Another three-man team was positioned in a truck at the intersection of Route 22 and Highway 1 in case the operation went badly and help was needed quickly. The capture team had been in position for only a few hours when they saw the informant signal their intended target was crossing the bridge. Within seconds, the woman was captured, placed in the back of the taxicab, and transported to the Hieu Thien district headquarters, where we interrogated her before turning her over to the National Police for further questioning. She was uncooperative and denied she was a VC, but when we found coded messages written on small scraps of paper inside several oranges she was allegedly transporting for sale at the Free Market, her story begin to unravel. Shortly thereafter she was convicted in court of being a VC courier and sentenced to two years in jail.[8]

The above PRU operation was flawless and demonstrated what was possible when every organization in the fight against the VCI cooperated and coordinated as the Phoenix Program intended them to do. The intelligence on the target was exploited rapidly; in this case less than 48 hours passed between the time the information on the target was provided and the time of arrest. The PIOCC and Hieu Thien DIOCC functioned in accordance with procedures established for them. Permission for the arrest was obtained quickly, and the PRU team that carried out the arrest acted quickly, successfully, and safely. The prisoner was interrogated at the Provincial Interrogation Center, where the coded messages were forwarded to Saigon for decoding and she was remanded to trial by the National Police. The intelligence obtained from the prisoner and the coded messages was processed quickly, and the PIOCC sent this information to the pertinent security and military organizations for exploitation. The Phoenix apparatus did not always work as smoothly as it did on this operation, but when it did, the results were usually just as successful and productive.

On March 18, the situation in Cambodia reached a climax with a coup against Prince Sihanouk, led by Gen. Lon Nol and the Cambodian Army. On that day, one of our Cambodian PRU soldiers who often doubled as an interpreter and translator, Mr. Thone, came to the Embassy House to see me. I had known Mr. Thone only in his capacity as a translator of captured Cambodian and Vietnamese documents, so I assumed he wanted to speak to me about some recent translations. We sat on the front porch, and Mrs. Thu brought us some coffee and locally made French baguettes to eat, since it was getting late in the afternoon and dinner was still several hours away. I asked Thone for any papers he had for me, and he answered that he did not have any papers, only a request. I asked him what the request was, and he informed me that he wanted seventy-five PRC-25 radios and several hundred batteries for the radios. I was shocked by this request, and at first thought he was making some sort of joke, but his serious look told me his request was sincere. He said he was a secret member of the Khmer Serey and he had received a request from the Khmer Serey government in exile to obtain as many radios as possible from the Americans so the Khmer Serey forces fighting the NVA would be able to coordinate operations with Lon Nol's army. I told him I did not have such a large number of radios, and even if I did, I would not be authorized to give them to him based upon what he had told me. Instead, I referred his request to Chuck, who invited Thone to come back the next day to see him. That was the last I heard of the matter, but I assumed Chuck did not arrange for the transfer of any radios to the Khmer Serey forces fighting in Cambodia. This was just one of many incidents that told me the Tay Ninh PRU had many secrets hidden within its ranks, and I was unaware of most of them.

After the coup in Cambodia, I began to hear the distinctive sound of B-52 "Arc Light" carpet bombing across the border from Tay Ninh Province. Like most Americans in South Vietnam, I rejoiced at the news that President Nixon had finally made the decision to unleash the B-52s against the NVA sanctuaries inside Cambodia. The distant rumbling sound of these bombing raids had a dramatic and uplifting effect on the morale of the South Vietnamese, with many of them going out of their way to express their gratitude to me for the courageous and long-overdue decision to attack the enemy sanctuaries. Unfortunately, the antiwar movements in the United States and Western Europe were not so enthusiastic about this development, and they took up the propaganda line from Hanoi that the bombing was an "expansion" of the war. For me, the bombing signaled a major and positive change in U.S. policy—the final realization that the sanctuaries inside Laos and Cambodia needed to be destroyed if there was ever going to be a chance to prevent the North Vietnamese from moving their troops and supplies down the Ho Chi Minh Trail. For the first time I felt that the United States might be finally doing something about this all-too-obvious strategic necessity, and we might win the war after all.

As March ended, I noticed several of the intelligence reports we were receiving from our informants in Cambodia indicated the NVA were planning something out of the ordinary. These reports told of NVA units commandeering hundreds of ox carts from local civilians and using them to transport NVA wounded and supplies to new locations—locations that we had never heard of before and could not locate on any map. We also received a report that a large meeting had been held on March 27 between two VC security units and the families of ethnic Vietnamese living in Cambodia, informing these people they would be protected by the VC from the new Cambodian government, but it might be necessary for them to move to new, more secure locations in Cambodia soon. These reports and others like them seemed to indicate the NVA and VC in Cambodia were not preparing for a new offensive inside South Vietnam, but were instead intent upon fighting the new Lon Nol army inside Cambodia. One thing was certain from reading these reports—the enemy was planning to move away from their base areas along the border regions with South Vietnam and deeper into Cambodia, at least temporarily.[9]

CHAPTER 18

The Cambodia Invasion

During the month of April, the Tay Ninh PRU conducted 123 intelligence operations as part of their effort to arrest returning VCI cadres displaced from the fighting going on in eastern Cambodia between the NVA and the new government in Phnom Penh. Unfortunately, very few of these operations bore fruit since the VCI living in Cambodia were not returning to their homes in South Vietnam as we had anticipated, but instead were choosing to move deeper into Cambodia, away from the allied invasion force. On April 22, Mr. Chinh and I decided to cancel these surveillance operations since it was obvious they were not productive; we felt we could use our PRU soldiers better by going after any remaining VCI finance-economy cadres in the province. We captured eight VCI in April, among them a person of high value, Mr. Do Van Ky, a 62-year-old village finance-economy chief from Phu Khuong District. In our interrogation of Mr. Ky, we found he had recently received instructions to cancel any further preparations for the movement of NVA forces through his village. He said he did not know the reason behind this cancellation of plans, but he suspected it had to do with developments inside of Cambodia. He also gave us information on a large NVA supply depot located in the enemy's Base Area 354, just a few kilometers across the border inside Cambodia. He had visited Base Area 354 two months previously, and there he saw massive amounts of weapons, ammunition, and supplies buried in underground bunkers. He went on to say the bunkers were very well camouflaged, several of them having been built under existing rice paddies. From what he had personally observed, it appeared most of the weapons and supplies in these bunkers were from the People's Republic of China. We asked him to point out on a map where Base Area 354 was located, and he identified an area 10 miles northwest of Tay Ninh City.[1]

As part of our operations to obtain intelligence on events inside Cambodia, Mr. Chinh had established three listening posts on the border with that country. These listening posts sent PRU agents into Cambodia and then interviewed them when they returned from their missions or collected written agent reports from dead drops located within a few kilometers of the listening posts. One such listening post was located at the Phuoc Tan Border Post. Two PRU soldiers manned this listening post, collecting intelligence there for nearly a month until the post came under a mortar and ground attack by the VC on the night of April 13 and 14. During the ensuing firefight, one PRU soldier was killed and the other seriously wounded. These were the only serious casualties my PRU suffered during the eight months I served with them. The body of the dead PRU soldier, Mr. Tran Quoc Thanh, was brought back to Tay Ninh City, where Mr. Chinh, Mr. Lam, and I took possession of his body and made arrangements for his burial. We found his body lying in a room inside the provincial compound wrapped in a blood-matted mosquito net. We were angry that such a brave soldier's body was treated this way, so we immediately had his body removed and sent to a funeral home, where it was cleaned and prepared for burial. I had seen many dead bodies, but Mr. Thanh's was particularly gruesome. The entire top of his head was missing, leaving the lower skull cavity empty of any brain matter; one of his eyes hung from strands of tendons on his cheek; and he had numerous shrapnel holes in his torso with his intestines protruding through a large hole in his stomach.

After we paid the funeral home owner to have Mr. Thanh's body cleaned and prepared for burial, we went to the home of his young wife to pay our respects and to give her Mr. Thanh's back pay and the standard three-month death gratuity, along with some money we had collected from his fellow PRU soldiers and me. She expressed concern that because she was young, female, and without a family, her situation might result in people trying to take advantage of her. She requested that she be allowed to continue to live in her house and the PRU provide protection for her. Mr. Chinh and I both agreed that the PRU would provide her with protection, but we suggested she move to a new house closer to the provincial compound so it would be easier to keep her under protective surveillance. I obtained employment for her in the base laundry on the U.S. Tay Ninh West base camp, a fairly good-paying job for a South Vietnamese worker. A month later, Mr. Lam and I visited her again, and she told us she was coping with the loss of her husband and liked her work on the U.S. base. Despite her brave face, she started to cry when we began to leave her modest quarters. She looked forlorn and pathetic, sobbing with her hands clenched on her lap, her chest heaving, a child-like figure sitting in a room full of shadows—a picture of overwhelming grief and helplessness. The death of her husband had left her alone in the world and without any family to help her. We both felt deeply saddened by her plight. As we left, Lam whispered to me, "We must pray for her, Mr. Andy."

The most successful PRU mission for the month of April occurred on April 21, when the Hieu Thien District PRU team received information from one of their informants that a hidden VC supply tunnel was located near the Ba Manh Canal in the southern part of the district. Mr. Le Van No, the PRU team leader, took eleven PRU soldiers to the location of the tunnel and found its camouflaged entrance in the middle of an area of lush vegetation, exactly where the informant said it would be. They searched the tunnel but found it was empty; however, while they searched the surrounding area, they found a second tunnel entrance. As they approached this second tunnel entrance, they were fired upon by three VC hiding inside. Mr. No and his team assaulted the tunnel and killed all three of the VC without sustaining any casualties. They captured an SKS rifle, a B-40 rocket grenade launcher, fifteen B-40 rounds and ten Chinese hand grenades. Documents found on the bodies did not identify any VC unit, but the team was confident that they had killed members of a local VC finance-economy cell.[2]

In early May our beautiful radio operator at the Embassy House, Ba Quyen, invited me to join her and her husband, Mr. Anh, the provincial security chief, for a weekend vacation at the beach town of Vung Tau on the South China Sea. Chuck approved my absence but suggested I take Mr. Lam along for security and use one of the Embassy House vehicles so I could radio back to him while we were on the road. One of our finance clerks, whose nickname was "Map Map," joined the party, and the five of us loaded into my Toyota jeep for our road trip to Vung Tau.

Mrs. Phung Thi Quyen, the radio operator at the Embassy House.

Our trip south along Highway 1 through Cu Chi and Bien Hoa to the coast went without incident, and we all enjoyed the warm, sunny weather, the clear blues skies, and the rural countryside along the way. However, one sight we saw reminded us of the horrors of war in a hideous and graphic way. As we drove near Bien Hoa, we passed a small town with a fortified area that appeared to be a district headquarters. We had to slow down to avoid some potholes and chickens in the road, and as we did, we noticed what looked like two large scarecrows lying up against a barbed-wire fence with their arms outstretched, looking very much like a crucifixion scene. Mr. Lam, who was driving the jeep, slowed down and stopped near the barbed-wire fence where the "scarecrows" hung. It was a decision we would all regret. There before us were the decomposing bodies of two VC, one of whom was missing the entire bottom half of his body from his navel down. A group of dogs were beside the bodies, feasting on the human flesh. A line of bluish-gray human entrails lay in the mud beneath the dead VC's body. The sightless eyes of both dead men were thick with bloated black flies, and several black bullet holes in their torsos were also thick with flies.

For some odd reason, the sight of the dead man's entrails lying in the mud made me think of the ancient Etruscan soothsayer, the "haruspex," who was able to tell the future by examining the entrails of the dead. I began to tell Lam about the haruspex, but before I could get very far in my explanation, I heard the sound of Ba Quyen desperately begging him to drive on. Crying, she told us she was ill and she would vomit if we stayed a moment longer. It was a truly horrible sight and one I will never forget. Still, as we drove away, I wondered what an Etruscan haruspex would have divined from the gruesome sight we were passing.

Once we arrived near Vung Tau, the smell of the ocean air and the cool breezes helped us to forget the evil sight of the decaying VC bodies we had just encountered a few hours earlier on the road. Mr. Anh had arranged for us to stay at a small hotel in Vung Tau a few blocks from the sea, but he failed to tell me beforehand that all five of us would be sharing just one room and a communal bathroom. It was awkward at first, but since Ba Quyen did not seem to mind having to share a room with her husband and three other men, we all settled down and found ways to preserve her modesty while we changed into swimming suits.

We spent two wonderful and relaxing days on a relatively deserted beach outside of town, swimming in the surf, taking pictures, and eating a picnic meal that Ba Quyen had prepared for us each day. In the evenings, we went to the Grand Hotel on the strand, where we ate some of the best seafood dishes I have ever tasted, washed down with some of the most expensive French wines I have ever bought. Sitting on the hotel's veranda overlooking the strand and the beach, we would continue to drink wine until late in the evening before returning to our humble hotel for the night. As I sat talking to my friends, looking on the tranquil scene before me, I felt as if I was in some seacoast town in southern France, not a town in war-torn South Vietnam.

On this excursion to Vung Tau, I realized how fortunate I was to have such good Vietnamese friends, the kind of friends who seemed to genuinely enjoy my company and wanted to share their enjoyment with me. I got to know them far better than I had during the previous seven months I had worked with them. Perhaps it was the relaxed setting by the South China Sea that enabled us to freely talk about anything that came to our minds or to share experiences that were meaningful to us, but whatever prompted the warm feelings of friendship, it had a profound impact on me. Aside from many long conversations with Mr. Lam at work, I seldom found the opportunity to talk to the others about anything other than our work. During this trip we talked of our childhoods, our families, and some of the humorous incidents in our lives that we would never think of discussing back at the Embassy House. In the case of my Vietnamese companions, I think the good French wines we consumed helped to break down their natural reserve.

The short vacation had been therapeutic for all of us, especially for Mr. Lam, who had been under a great deal of strain lately due to the situation with his family in Saigon and the responsibilities he owed to his widowed mother and invalid sister living there. It was good to see them all laugh heartily as we frolicked like children on the beach and in the waves. For a brief and happy moment, we could forget about the war, as if it really did not exist; as if it were all some bad dream, and the sun, sand, and friendship we found on the beach at Vung Tau was the real world we were meant to live in.

When we returned to Tay Ninh Province, we saw large numbers of trucks, tank transporters, and troops lining the roads and staged in and around the city. It was obvious to everyone that a major military operation was about to be launched, and we all knew the target would be the NVA divisions across the border in Cambodia. On May 1, that attack started as units of the U.S. 25th Infantry Division and the U.S. 1st Cavalry Division began to move across the border. The night before, President Nixon had announced to the American people that American and ARVN forces would be attacking NVA sanctuaries inside Cambodia, an announcement that set off a wave of antiwar demonstrations in the United States. For those of us fighting the war, both American and South Vietnamese, the announcement was greeted with joy. We had suffered for years from the silly restrictions imposed on us concerning Laos and Cambodia, restrictions that enabled the enemy to use these supposedly "neutral" countries as sanctuaries from which to attack us. We felt that finally some sanity and logic had been applied by President Nixon and his national security advisor, Henry Kissinger. As the attack progressed, jubilant crowds of South Vietnamese people gathered along the road leading to the border, cheering for the troops and presenting gifts of flowers and food to them.

Operation Rock Crusher, as the Cambodian incursion was called, was enthusiastically supported by the Americans and South Vietnamese, but that enthusiasm was soon tempered by the announcement that the American units participating in the incursion would only penetrate 15 kilometers into Cambodia and would be withdrawn after just sixty days. This news made no sense to us at all, since we knew the enemy had received advance warning of the incursion and had moved its forces and COSVN headquarters away from the border well in advance of the American and ARVN attack. When I spoke to officers of the 25th Infantry Division shortly after the invasion began, they spoke derisively of President Nixon's restrictions and said they had come as a complete surprise to them. In their view—and mine—the restrictions made no military sense at all. Of course, none of us were fully aware of the political pressure on President Nixon from the anti-war movement and their allies in Congress and the press, so we did not understand his reasoning for the restrictions.

The South Vietnamese we talked to were equally dismayed by the restrictions and felt betrayed once again by the actions of the American political leaders. I felt very uncomfortable when the PRU team leaders asked me why these "stupid" restrictions on the depth and duration of the attack into Cambodia had been imposed by the American president. Mr. Chinh actually accused President Nixon of making a secret deal with Hanoi to allow the NVA to escape, and he asked me what Mr. Nixon had gained for America in exchange for this "deal." I could offer no reasonable answer to his question since the restrictions made absolutely no military sense to me. The decision may have made sense to the politicians at home, but it had a devastating effect on South Vietnamese morale and caused many American soldiers to question the seriousness of our country's resolve to defeat the North Vietnamese communists.

Almost immediately after the first U.S. and ARVN military units entered Cambodia, several American military commanders and district advisors requested that our PRU teams accompany the forces invading Cambodia. Since we had several PRU agents already operating in Cambodia and we had compiled a list of VCI living in Cambodia, these requests made a lot of sense to me. The American commanders rightly thought that it would be beneficial to have PRU teams with them to help identify any VCI among the many POWs they were rounding up as they attacked west into Cambodia. As a result, Chuck wrote a memo on May 5 to the Saigon CIA Station requesting permission to use PRU assets inside Cambodia.[3] Despite a very compelling argument for the use of the PRU teams operating with American and ARVN units in Cambodia, the request was denied without explanation by CIA Station Chief Ted Shackley.

Although my PRU teams were not allowed to accompany the U.S. and ARVN forces entering Cambodia, that did not lessen their activity inside South Vietnam. Unfortunately, the Cambodian invasion had an unintended negative impact on our primary mission of neutralizing the VCI. We found that the Cambodian incursion increased the need for security measures around the American and ARVN bases in Tay Ninh Province, which meant many of the PRU teams were diverted from their normal counter–VCI operations to perform strictly military operations. They were called upon by the province chief to conduct numerous night ambushes and take up static defensive positions near local government buildings and installations, tasks that were better suited to military forces and not the specialized police of the PRU. Although I had advocated strongly in the past to reduce such military-type missions, I did not complain to the province chief this time. When I met with him shortly after the imposition of these military duties, he promised me that the need for the PRU to conduct such missions was temporary and, as soon as the security situation in the province became more stable, he would release the PRU to perform their normal duties. Still, these new requirements had a negative effect on our plans to aggressively go after the VC finance-economy cadres still operating in the province. Both in terms of VCI neutralizations and intelligence-gathering operations, the month of May was a far less productive month for the PRU than we would normally have anticipated.

As the invasion of Cambodia continued during the month of May, we began to see the tangible results the invasion was producing. Huge caches of weapons and supplies were being uncovered by our forces. The size of these stocks of captured items was truly staggering. I got my first inkling of how massive these captured enemy supplies were when Mr. Tho came to the Embassy House one day and told me to come to the Provincial Headquarters to view some of the weapons captured by the U.S. 1st Cavalry Division in Cambodia. The source of these weapons was a huge, one-square-mile supply dump called "The City" by the American recon team that found it. The cache of supplies was so large, most of it had to be destroyed, but the display of weapons I saw inside the provincial compound was still amazing.

Mr. Tho and author at the Tay Ninh Provincial HQ examining enemy weapons captured in Cambodia.

There, lined up by weapon type throughout the grounds of the compound, were hundreds of new, crew-served weapons, such as mortars, rocket launchers, antiaircraft machine guns, recoilless rifles and RPD machine guns. There were also thousands of individual weapons on display, such as new AK-47 rifles and SKS rifles. One of the American U.S. Army officers serving as a provincial advisor told me the American and ARVN forces were finding NVA supply caches inside Cambodia with quantities of weapons and ammunition that surprised everyone. He told me they had even captured new Chinese and Russian trucks left behind by the enemy.

The Cambodian invasion produced some unusual benefits, one of which was the capture of several senior NVA officers. As a result, a unique opportunity was presented to me in early May when Chuck informed me that several NVA prisoners who had been recently captured by American forces in northeastern Cambodia were being held in Tay Ninh Province and were now available for us to interrogate. Several of these prisoners had been captured in an NVA hospital, and they included some very high-value personnel, such as a code clerk and a political officer with the rank of senior colonel (equivalent to a U.S. brigadier general). The prisoners were being temporarily held in Tay Ninh Province until they could be transferred to Saigon, and Chuck had been offered the opportunity to interrogate them prior to their movement to the capital. Since these were considered military, not VCI, prisoners, I would not normally have been afforded the opportunity to interview them, but Chuck believed they might possess information on VCI in Cambodia, so I was given the chance to spend a few hours with several of them.

One prisoner I spoke with was a wounded NVA captain who provided very little useful information about the VCI in Cambodia, but did tell me several things that I found most informative. He was cooperative and eager to talk to me, probably because he was sincerely grateful for the medical treatment he had received since his capture. He told me that his unit was often warned about impending B-52 strikes, receiving these warnings via radio transmissions from Hanoi. In some cases, these radio warnings from Hanoi came more than 24 hours in advance of the B-52 strikes. Most of the time the warnings came early enough to allow the NVA units to move to a safe location before the bombs could inflict any casualties. He did not know how Hanoi knew about the B-52 raids in advance, only that the information conveyed from Hanoi was normally very accurate. I asked him if he could remember any of the dates of the raids he had been warned about, and he provided several dates in late April when he was sure he had received prior warnings for the raids. I took down the dates and locations of these raids and reported them to a U.S. Army military intelligence (MI) officer when I left the interrogation room.

My second interview was a far more interesting one since it was with a high-ranking NVA political officer. He had been questioned extensively by American MI officers prior to my interview with him, so I did not see any useful reason for questioning him about military information. I decided, instead, to ask him about his knowledge of intelligence matters, especially anything he knew concerning the VCI in Tay Ninh Province and any support these VCI provided to the NVA in Cambodia.

Rather than immediately questioning him on this subject, I asked him about his life as an NVA soldier, hoping that such a banal subject might make it easier to transition into a discussion on more important matters. He told me that he had come south several years ago traveling on foot down the Ho Chi Minh Trail and had been in South Vietnam or Cambodia ever since. He was captured by the Americans while he was staying in a jungle hospital inside Cambodia where he had been recovering from a serious bout with malaria. I told him I had also had malaria, and I could understand how he suffered. He mentioned that he had contracted malaria several times previously, including one serious case that nearly killed him during his initial trip south along the Ho Chi Minh Trail in eastern Laos. According to him, the malaria in Laos was far more virulent than the malaria NVA troops contracted in South Vietnam, often causing death within a few days.

I moved the discussion into a more profitable area by asking him about his experiences during the 1968 Tet Offensive, since I knew many southern VC considered the performance of the NVA during this campaign to be incompetent at best and duplicitous as worst. I wanted to get his side of the story. He did not want to talk about what he did during the Tet Offensive, but he did mention that after the Tet Offensive of 1968, the communists analyzed their failure, and one of their findings was the local VC failed to provide adequate support, both logistical and political, for the NVA and main-force VC units moving against Saigon. To remedy this problem, COSVN reorganized the areas around Saigon into six "subzones," which looked like slices of a pie radiating out from the center of Saigon for many miles. A senior VC or NVA political officer was placed in charge of each sub-zone, with the job of making sure the VCI in each sub-zone provided adequate support to any NVA units moving toward Saigon. I asked him what this support entailed, and he said it involved staging supplies of food, building bunkers, and other field fortifications for transiting units; providing labor parties to help with the movement of supplies and wounded fighters; assigning guides and runners; and establishing way stations along routes of advance toward the city. When I asked him why he did not include a mission of provoking a general uprising of the South Vietnamese people, he simply replied that "it is not possible now."

After he had explained how these new sub-zones would function during any future attack on Saigon, I asked him if he felt this system was fully established and was working well. His answer surprised me somewhat because he began to complain about the attitude of the southern VC, especially those in Saigon. He told me the southern communists were not up to the task and were very unreliable. He even accused them of lying to COSVN about their state of readiness and the numbers of cadres they had on their rolls. Since I was interested in the support provided by the enemy's VC finance-economy cadres, I asked him how he felt about their contribution to the revolution. His answer seemed to justify the efforts of the Tay Ninh PRU because he told me the Finance-Economy cadres in most of III Corps had been severely degraded due to the Phoenix Program, which he referred to as "The Puppet Government's Pacification Program."

He went on to make several comments about the lack of faith many party members had in the strategy that led to the failure of the 1968 "General Offensive–General Uprising," and the belief that prevailed now that the southern party infrastructure was no longer able to fulfill a primary role in any future attack on Saigon. According to him, a new strategy was needed to compensate for the weakness of the VCI and their inability to provide adequate logistical support or to create the conditions necessary for an uprising by the southern population.

Since his comments seemed to portray a rather bleak assessment of the situation, I asked him if he thought the party had lost the war, especially now that their sanctuaries in Cambodia had been overrun. On the contrary, he told me he was sure of ultimate victory. When I asked him why he was so sure, he smiled and said I already knew the answer to that question. When I said I did not, he smiled again and said, "You are far from home, and you do not understand the strategic realities in this country. Your strategy is seriously flawed, and your people will grow weary as they see more and more Americans dying without anything to show for that sacrifice. Your president has already said you are leaving. We will wait until you are gone and then we will attack, attack, and attack until the puppet regime falls from its own weight. Victory for us is inevitable."

His confident answer intrigued me since the recent events in Cambodia appeared to me to be a significant setback for the communist cause, and I thought he would be somewhat demoralized by it. Because he seemed so sure of final victory, I decided to ask him what made him so confident that the communists were assured of victory over the Saigon government, especially given the sorry state of the southern VCI and the recent setbacks the communists had suffered on the battlefield. I expected him to give me some propaganda-laden cant about the inevitable triumph of Marxist theology or the undefeatable fervor of the revolutionary masses, but what I got instead was a very succinct and sensible answer devoid of the political clichés I often heard from other prisoners I had interviewed. He said:

> It is all very simple. We will win, even if it takes 100 years, because you have never solved the problem of the western approaches to South Vietnam and because we know of all your plans as soon as you hatch them. We can always counter your plans because they are known to us. And one thing we have always known is you think you can win this war inside the borders of South Vietnam only. Your strategy has failed because you do not view the geographic boundaries of the war the

way we do. We view Vietnam, Laos, and Cambodia as the theater of operations, but you look at these as separate areas. How can you fight a war in just one part of the theater of operations? As long as you see things this way, we will always be able to move freely along the western border of South Vietnam and attack whenever and wherever we want. This places you and the Saigon regime on the defensive forever, and you cannot win a war on the defensive. You will never be able to defeat our forces as long as you only fight in South Vietnam. It is obvious to us, but hidden to you.[4]

I became a bit angry with his arrogant answer, so I decided to play upon it by asking him if he thought there was anything we could have done that would have made it impossible for them to win. I expected him to say we could have done more to win over the loyalty of the South Vietnamese people or employed a better counterinsurgency strategy, but that was not the answer he gave me. He said:

I am not in the business of giving advice to my enemy, but even if I did, it is too late for you now. If you had really wanted to win this war, you would have changed your strategy and disregarded the neutrality of Laos and Cambodia. You were doomed from the moment you signed those accords [the 1962 Geneva Accords on the Nuetrality of Laos and Cambodia]. The Russians knew it, the Chinese knew it, and we knew it, but you foolishly pursued a strategy that anyone with any sense would have seen was hopeless.

The NVA colonel was fatigued and weakened by his malaria, so I ended our interview and left him. As I rose to leave the room, I placed a pack of Marlboro cigarettes on the table for him, but he pushed them away and said he did not like the taste of American cigarettes. Although he was cooperative and answered most of my questions, I could tell his contempt for me was clearly palpable.

At the time of my interview with this NVA colonel I did not have a very clear understanding of the 1962 Geneva Accords, or, for that matter, the overall American strategy for the war, so the significance of his words had little impact on my views. However, with the passage of time and a great deal of study, I came to realize that what he was telling me made a great deal of sense. In the last chapter of this book, I will explore our flawed strategy in more detail.

Chapter 19

My War Ends

In mid–May, Mr. Chinh and his team leaders invited me to have dinner with them at a local restaurant we occasionally dined at after a particularly successful operation. It was to be our last social gathering, and Mr. Chinh insisted that he pay for the meal, which would be the specialty of the house, called "Seven Kinds of Beef." This was a huge meal of seven courses, all involving some form of beef, starting with a delicate beef soup and ending with beef fried rice. Chuck provided several bottles of Martell's cognac for the dinner, but he did not attend since he considered it extremely risky for a CIA case officer to eat at a local restaurant. When Mr. Lam and I arrived at the restaurant, which was a rather humble affair made of chicken wire, weathered planks, and corrugated steel with only four or five tables set on a dirt floor, we found Mr. Chinh, Mr. Tho, and the five district team leaders waiting for us. Outside the restaurant were a dozen heavily armed PRU soldiers, and inside there were no other customers. If the VC wanted to kill us, they would have a fight on their hands since all of us were armed and every approach to the restaurant was covered by the PRU.

Since I had received orders home, Mr. Chinh wanted to send me off with a first-class Vietnamese meal and the companionship of some of the bravest, toughest, and most devoted fighting men I have ever known. Over a truly delicious meal we made several toasts and talked about some of the more humorous situations we had experienced during my stay with them. They even joked about my nickname, "The Superior Monk," and how they marveled at my inability to find a local beauty for a girlfriend. I told them I was often tempted since there were so many beautiful women in Tay Ninh Province, but with so many choices I just could never make up my mind. I told them I hoped to make up for any lost time when I returned to the States. After a final toast to the Tay Ninh PRU and Mr. Chinh, I thanked all of them for their devotion to duty and their friendship, which I promised I would always cherish. It was the last time I would see all of them together. As the dinner ended, it became clear that Mr. Lam and I were suffering from the effects of too much cognac, so we had one of the PRU soldiers drive us the short distance back to the Embassy House. The Nung guards thought we looked hilarious as we stumbled up the steps to the porch and into the front door. The next day my head felt like I had been in a fight with a water buffalo—and lost!

Since I would be leaving Tay Ninh Province and returning to the United States in June, I began to arrange for my departure and take care of some last-minute administrative and logistical problems. On May 13, I signed over two recently refurbished pickup trucks and several motorcycles to the PRU, along with a dozen new M-16 rifles. I knew there would be no replacement for me since Gen. Abrams had made his decision to remove all U.S. military

PRU soldiers on operations disguised as VC.

advisors to the PRU Program by the end of 1970. With this in mind, I wanted to make sure the PRU in Tay Ninh had all the equipment, supplies, and weapons needed for them to continue to operate effectively.

Chuck informed me that the CIA would be taking over the advisory duties for the PRU, but only one CIA case officer would be responsible for advising all of the PRU teams in III Corps, a huge task and one I doubted a single individual could do with any degree of success. Chuck tended to agree with me, but he said as long as the Department of Defense had made the decision to remove the U.S. military advisors, there was little else to be done. He promised he would work closely with the CIA officer who would be taking over the III Corps PRU advisory duties and to look out for the Tay Ninh PRU. Always the professional, he reminded me that I should prepare a briefing for the new III Corps PRU advisor since he would be visiting Tay Ninh before I left, and that officer would need all the advice and information I could provide. I immediately set to work on a "turn over file" for this as-yet unknown individual.

One of the last PRU operations I was involved in occurred on May 19, and it demonstrated both the skill and bravery of the PRU chief for Hieu Thien District, Mr. Le Van No. Mr. No was, along with Mr. Siem and Mr. Dung, one of the three best PRU leaders we had. He was both intelligent and courageous, but he coupled these two attributes with a natural ability to develop and manage a group of incredibly effective secret informants, primarily old women who spread out over his district daily doing routine domestic chores while collecting intelligence on the VCI. One of these female informants told Mr. No that a VCI cell was operating in the Binh Thanh Border region, an area near the border with Cambodia. Mr. No sent one of his men to the PRU headquarters to inform Mr. Chinh of this information and to request the issuance of a general arrest order for this VCI cell. I was at the PRU headquarters when this information was passed to Mr. Chinh, and the two of us immediately went in to the province chief to seek his approval of Mr. No's request to conduct a clandestine operation that night using a four-man PRU team disguised in captured NVA uniforms and carrying AK-47 rifles. Lt. Col. Thien, the province chief, did not like the idea of disguising the PRU soldiers in NVA uniforms, but he finally agreed when Mr. Chinh said it was probably the only way the PRU soldiers would be able to get close enough to the VCI to make an arrest.

Because we would have PRU soldiers on a mission dressed as NVA soldiers, it was essential that any friendly units near the area be made aware of their presence. We did not want to have an intramural firefight. In order to coordinate this operation with the American and ARVN military units in the border region, the U.S. Army Phoenix district advisor and the Hieu Thien district chief established a No Fire Zone around the target area and a secure corridor for the disguised PRU team to take once they left the PRU compound at Hieu Thien. Mr. Chinh and I informed the PIOCC two hours before the PRU team was scheduled to leave on their mission to minimize any potential for the enemy to hear about it in time to react or allow the target to escape. Mr. Chinh and I monitored the operation from Tay Ninh City via secure radio with the Hieu Thien DIOCC.

Around ten in the evening, the four disguised PRU left on their mission and traveled quickly and silently to the Cambodian border, where the informant said the VCI cell was hiding. As they approached the area, they were challenged by a VC sentry. Fortunately, the enemy sentry was fooled by the NVA uniforms and allowed the PRU soldiers to advance to within a few feet of him. When the PRU failed to use a proper password, the sentry raised his rifle and the PRU team leader shot him at point-blank range, killing him instantly. In the darkness, the PRU saw five VCI running away toward the border, and they took the fleeing VCI under fire but stopped pursuing them when they crossed into Cambodia. A search of the body of the sentry produced documents identifying him as Mr. Do Van Ve, a 37-year-old native of My Thanh Dong Village in Long An Province and the VC security section chief for border surveillance of sub-region 2. The PRU recovered an AK-47 rifle and other documents indicating the men who escaped were members of VC sub-region 2 who had moved into South Vietnam from a base camp in eastern Cambodia to escape from the allied forces who had overrun their base camp two weeks earlier. The PRU team returned to Hieu Thien district headquarters without incident at first light and were debriefed by the district chief and the district sub-sector S-2. Later in the day, I drove to Hieu Thien district to congratulate the team on their successful operation and to help retrieve the body of the VC they had killed.[1]

As the end of May approached, I began to feel pangs of guilt about leaving the PRU without an advisor. I knew they would be able to carry on with their missions, but I also knew they depended on me for a great deal of support, especially support involving training, supplies, and coordination with U.S. military forces for helicopter transport and fire support. I doubted that someone advising the PRU from Saigon would be able to do this effectively, and this bothered me. I voiced these concerns with Chuck, but he told me it was time for me to go home, and I should feel grateful I had survived the war. He then told me the man who would be replacing me and managing all the PRU teams in III Corps would be visiting Tay Ninh Province that very day, and I should be ready to give him a full briefing on the local PRU.

Shortly before lunch that day, Bernie drove through the front gate of the Embassy House with a man sitting beside him dressed in civilian clothes and carrying a Swedish K machine pistol on his lap. Chuck went out to greet this stranger while John, Mickey, and I watched from the front porch. Chuck had told me nothing about the man who was taking over the PRU in III Corps, aside from a cryptic remark about the man being "a legend in the agency's paramilitary world." Chuck brought the man on to the porch and introduced us to him. I was the first to shake his hand. He said, "I'm Felix Rodriguez, and I need to talk to you about the Tay Ninh PRU."

Before that introduction to Felix on the front porch of the Embassy House, I had never heard of Felix Rodriguez. All I knew was Felix was going to take over my job, and he needed me to brief him on the PRU in Tay Ninh Province. I was soon to find out why Chuck had referred to him as "a legend in the CIA," but that would come later in the day.

Since it was lunchtime, the Embassy House team and Felix went into our dining room and sat down to one of Ba Thu's great lunches of spring rolls, chicken fried rice, iced tea, and vanilla layer cake. After lunch, Felix and I sat at the dining room table, and the two of us went over what I thought he needed to know to manage the PRU. I gave him several information papers with subjects like: "The Tay Ninh PRU Key Personnel," "The VCI in Tay Ninh Province," "Problem Areas and Unresolved Issues," "The PIOCC and DIOCCs and How They are Functioning in the Province," and "The VCI Situation in Cambodia." As I went over each information paper, Felix asked very few questions, choosing instead to listen intently and to take notes. Chuck came in near the end of our chat and told Felix about his assessment of the PRU, reinforcing much of what I had already gone over with him.

As I was about to wrap up my briefing with Felix, I told him about the PRU plan to neutralize the VCI finance-economy cadres and why I thought he should continue to implement this plan. I pointed out on a map the base areas for the NVA divisions in Cambodia and how the finance-economy cadres in Tay Ninh Province made it possible for these NVA divisions to move through the province on their way to attacking friendly forces and populated centers between the border and Saigon. He seemed to agree with the rationale for the operations against the logistical system the communists used, but he was noncommittal as to whether or not he would advocate the continuation of those operations. Nearing the end of my briefing, I gave him a paper that showed the results achieved by the Tay Ninh PRU from October 1, 1969, to May 31, 1970, the months covering the period I was their advisor. I ticked off the numbers: 274 operations launched against the VCI, 60 VCI captured, 34 VCI suspects apprehended, 28 VCI killed, and 156 intelligence reports written and disseminated through the Phoenix system.[2] He seemed impressed with the figures I cited and even told me that he had heard that the national PRU headquarters considered the Tay Ninh PRU one of the most effective units in the country.

At the end of the briefing, I asked him if he wanted to meet the PRU Chief, Mr. Chinh, or any of the other PRU leaders, and he said he would do that on a subsequent trip; this trip was his initial one to the province, and he wanted to formulate his overall plan for III Corps before he met any of the PRU chiefs. I was very impressed with Felix's confidence that he could handle multiple provinces from Saigon, but I felt compelled to warn him that I thought it was necessary to actually live in a province to understand it well. Managing all the PRU in III Corps from Saigon would be, in my opinion, a very daunting task. I explained that the simple task of paying all the teams in III Corps each month would prove very difficult. He agreed that the job would not be easy, but he dismissed my concerns with a statement to the effect that he had faced bigger challenges in the past and he felt confident he could do what the agency expected him to do. He graciously thanked me for the information papers and the briefing, and then he went into Chuck's room to talk to him.

I spent the rest of the afternoon at the provincial compound, so I did not see Felix again until we all sat down to dinner. At dinner I noticed that John was not eating with us again. Periodically, John would remain in his room and not join the rest of us for meals. I attributed this to a combination of homesickness, since I knew he missed his family terribly, and to the strain he was under managing the Tay Ninh Source. Still, his absence always seemed to increase the tension in the house, and we all knew it was best not to disturb him when he was in one of these moods. Chuck broke out a bottle of French wine in honor of Felix's visit, and Ba Thu cooked spaghetti and meat sauce, which was her attempt to find something in her culinary repertoire that approximated Cuban cuisine. During dinner, Chuck and Felix did most of the talking, often referring to men they had worked with over the years and about the increased emphasis on developing strategic intelligence on the enemy now that Ted Shackley was the station chief for the CIA in Saigon. Since Felix came from the paramilitary side of the CIA, a few of his comments indicated he was not all that enthusiastic about the new emphasis on developing strategic intelligence and what he perceived to be a reduced emphasis on pacification.

After dinner, John left his room and joined the rest of us in the living room, but he remained distant and uncommunicative, a fact that I could tell was not lost on Felix and annoyed Chuck. In order to ease the tension, Chuck suggested that Felix tell us about how he captured Che Guevara, the Cuban revolutionary, in Bolivia in 1967. Like most Americans at that time, I had only fragmentary information about the death of Che Guevara, and I certainly had no idea that a CIA operative named Felix Rodriguez played a central role in the operation against the legendary Marxist guerrilla. I was a bit incredulous at first, but as Felix began to tell his tale, like everyone else in the room, I became completely enthralled with his astounding saga.

Felix told us that he and another Cuban CIA operative had been sent to Bolivia to advise a Bolivian Army Ranger battalion that had been trained by the U.S. Special Forces and had been given the mission of tracking down Che Guevara and the other Cuban guerrillas with him in a jungle base in the mountains of eastern Bolivia. This band of Cuban communists was trying to spark a revolution in that South American country, but having a very difficult time doing it due to a number of factors that could best be summed up as planning failures on the part of Che. Foremost among these planning failures were Che's underestimation of the Bolivian peasant's desire for revolution and the weakness of the Bolivian Communist Party outside of the country's urban areas.

As we sat around him on that hot, humid evening in the Embassy House, with geckos scurrying across the ceiling in search of mosquitoes and each other, Felix began his story with his arrival in Bolivia and ended it with his description of the capture and death of Che. What he told us was, in large part, exactly as he later related it in his autobiography, *Shadow Warrior: The CIA Hero of a Hundred Unknown Battles*, written in 1989 with John Weisman—but there were a few differences, some of which I consider significant.

For instance, in the autobiography, Felix said he gave the order to execute Che Guevara, but when he told the story to us in Tay Ninh, he said the Bolivian government gave that order, and they did so because the CIA told him via radio that they would not agree to take Che out of Bolivia unless Che agreed to cooperate with the CIA, something Che refused to do, despite Felix's best efforts to convince him to do so. This forced the Bolivian government to execute Che because they did not want another show trial like the one they had just endured when they put one of Che's guerrilla comrades, the French Marxist Regis Debray, on trial in April of 1967. This trial created a soapbox for the fiery French Marxist and a huge embarrassment for the Bolivian government as the foreign press repeated every propaganda-laden word Debray uttered, thus turning him into the focus of leftist adoration throughout the world. The Bolivian government had made the decision that they could not afford another trial like the one that Debray inflicted on them, so Che had to die if the CIA was unwilling to take him out of the country.

Another discrepancy involved the disposition of Che's body, which Felix claimed in his book he personally delivered to the Bolivian government after taking it with him on a helicopter to Vallegrande Airport. In Tay Ninh, Felix told us the body was taken away by the Bolivians on a helicopter, and it was either dumped from the helicopter into the jungle below or it was taken to an undisclosed location and buried. Felix said he did not know exactly what happened to Che's body since he stayed behind at the execution site when the Bolivian helicopter with Che's body took off.

Probably the biggest discrepancy between the story Felix told us in Tay Ninh and the one in his autobiography entailed how the CIA found out that Che Guevara was in Bolivia and how Che and his guerrillas were finally located in their jungle hideout. Unlike the version in his book, which told of getting their leads from the interrogation of Regis Debray and another captured guerrilla, Jose Castillo Chavez, Felix revealed to us that Che's lover, an East German woman named Tamara Bunke Bider, who was with Che and the guerrillas, had played a far greater role in revealing Che's location than recounted in the book. It turned out that Ms. Bider was not only Che's lover, but also a KGB agent, sent by Moscow to keep an eye on Che. The Soviets did not approve of his revolutionary ambitions in South America, and they considered him a dangerous radical who could damage Soviet interests in that hemisphere. Che was so smitten with Ms. Bider, he made her his radio operator, an extremely foolish decision given her status as a KGB spy and not a Cuban. Felix also told us about several other sources of information on Che's activities in Bolivia, but in the interest of security, I will not reveal what they were. Suffice it to say, Felix was quite cagey about what he chose to reveal in his book. He did not fabricate anything in his autobiography, but he chose only to tell part of the story. The real story is far more interesting and is a testament to the success of the CIA and other U.S. intelligence organizations during the Cold War. One day, the classified files about Che's capture and death will be revealed, but for now they must remain a secret.[3]

A few days before my departure from Tay Ninh Province, I went on a final tour of my district PRU teams, driving to each location with Mr. Lam in our rugged and well-worn Toyota jeep. At each district, I thanked each member of the team and spoke with the district team leader about what he thought needed to be done in the coming months now that Felix Rodriguez would be advising them from Saigon and not Tay Ninh City. I also paid courtesy visits to each district chief and met with each district's U.S. Phoenix advisor. In most cases I felt the district chiefs and their Phoenix advisors would employ the PRU teams properly and would continue to wage the war against the VCI effectively. I was particularly interested in ensuring that the Phoenix advisors arranged for the coordination of the PRU operations with the American and ARVN units in the province and that medevac services continue to be provided to them. While I still did not think the PIOCC at the provincial level functioned as well as it could, I came away from my visits to the districts with a very high level of confidence in the DIOCCs and their ability to coordinate counter–VCI operations.

At one stop on my last circuit of the district PRU teams, I was treated to a barbeque lunch attended by all eighteen PRU soldiers on the Hieu Thien district team, along with the district chief and several other Vietnamese officials. The lunch consisted of strips of water buffalo meat cooked over a wood fire, rice, and local fruit with substantial amounts of warm Vietnamese beer. I was deeply touched by this honor and thanked Mr. No and his team for their hospitality and friendship. As a parting gift, I gave Mr. No an engraved Dunhill cigarette lighter with his name on it and told him that I hoped I could light his cigarette with it when he came to visit in the United States. I never did get the opportunity to light his cigarette with that lighter or any other lighter, since he was captured by the NVA in April 1975 and died in captivity.

On the day of my departure from Tay Ninh, I spent the morning saying goodbye to Chuck, John, Mickey, Bernie, and our South Vietnamese employees. Mr. Lam requested to drive me to Saigon and to see that my baggage was properly packed for shipping to the United States. When I went into the Embassy House Annex to say goodbye to our staff, they were all lined up except Ba Quyen, who was sitting at her radio crying. I was overcome with emotion seeing her cry at my departure. I told her that I wished her and her husband good luck and that I would never forget their friendship and assistance, but I cut short my farewell because I was afraid I might allow my emotions to get the better of me. As I walked out of the annex, I looked back and saw everyone, including Ba Quyen, standing by the door waving to me. I can still see them standing there in my mind, a permanent fixture in my subconscious of people I had come to know and love during my eight months working with them. I realized for the first time that they meant far more to me than I had ever realized before. A feeling of intense guilt came over me as I turned away to leave. I could not help but feel that I was abandoning these brave and dedicated colleagues and friends. For them, the war would continue for another five years and end in great tragedy for all of them.

Mr. Lam and I climbed into the jeep and were beginning to leave the front gate of the Embassy House when our cook, Ba Thu, ran out of the house and handed me several sandwiches she had made and wrapped in wax paper. She pressed the sandwiches into my hands and said in perfect English, which I am sure she had practiced for many days, "Goodbye Dai Uy Andy; I will never forget you." As we drove out of the front gate, the Nung guard stood at attention and saluted me. My eyes were moist, and I had a huge lump in my throat.

When we reached Saigon, Lam dropped me off at the Duc Hotel and we agreed to meet later that evening for dinner at a Vietnamese restaurant Lam liked in the Cholon section of Saigon. I spent the afternoon checking out at the PRU headquarters, but was unable to see Col. Allen since he was out on a mission. Instead, I said my goodbyes to his executive officer, Maj. Hyslop, and to the PRU Commander, Maj. Lang. I also stopped by the Navy section of MACV to get paid, have my orders endorsed, and arrange for my Air America flight to Da Nang, where I would board a commercial contract aircraft for my flight back to the United States. With all of my administrative duties attended to, I returned to the Duc Hotel, where I decided I would take one last dip in the hotel's rooftop pool before dinner with Lam.

After taking a few laps in the hotel pool, I sat for a few moments in one of the lounge chairs soaking up the bright sunlight and basking in the warmth of its tropical rays. While I was sitting there, I heard a voice next to me say, "Hey, Jarhead, what brings you to this den of iniquity?" The voice belonged to Tucker Gougelmann, the gruff, profane, and thoroughly insensitive former Marine I had met on my first trip to Saigon. Tucker did not suffer fools gladly, and he always told you exactly how he felt, never sugarcoating his opinions. Everyone loved Tucker for his honesty, work ethic, and complete devotion to his country and the CIA—everyone, that is, except petty bureaucrats, "pencil-pushing turkey necks," and "limp-wristed liberals." These are just a few of the printable descriptions he used when talking about people who did not see things his way or stood in his way when he was trying to do what was best for his country.

I respected Tucker, who was about my father's age, and thoroughly enjoyed listening to him describe what it was like working for the CIA in Saigon. He joined the agency shortly after World War II because he had been badly wounded as a U.S. Marine fighting in the Pacific, and his medical condition precluded any further service with his beloved Corps. He still limped badly from the wounds he suffered during the war.

I never heard him talk about anything in his past, but he always had plenty to say about what was wrong as far as fighting the war in South Vietnam was concerned and how difficult it was to work with some of his American and South Vietnamese colleagues. His favorite targets were the U.S. military and their lack of support for the pacification program, the U.S. State Department for the restrictions they placed on CIA operations in Laos and Cambodia, and the Saigon press corps for "undermining every attempt to win the war" and "creating a defeatist attitude among the public," both in South Vietnam and the United States. Using a level of profanity that only a U.S. Marine could fully appreciate, he spoke to me as a fellow Marine and not as the young, inexperienced military officer that I was. He paid me the highest compliment he could convey when shortly before we parted company he told me he and Daren Flitcroft had spoken about my work in Tay Ninh Province and they both thought I should leave the U.S. Marine Corps and join the CIA. Sadly, when Saigon fell in 1975, Tucker, who had retired from the CIA by that time, was captured by the communists. He had returned to Saigon as a private citizen so he could help rescue several friends of his, but in the chaos of the fall of Saigon, he was unable to escape with the last helicopter flights out of the U.S. Embassy. He was forced to go into hiding for several weeks before he was finally captured and imprisoned. He was tortured and died under interrogation just a few months after his capture. His body was returned to the United States a year later, showing clear signs of his savage treatment while undergoing interrogation by the communists.

My last evening in Saigon was spent with Lam, eating a truly memorable meal of Chinese and Vietnamese delicacies at a restaurant near Lam's home in Cholon. Unfortunately, our jeep was stolen while we ate our meal, even though we had paid a security guard to keep watch on it. Back at the Duc Hotel, I called Chuck and informed him of the theft of one of his vehicles, and he told me to write up a report and deliver it to the U.S. Embassy before I left for Da Nang the next day. I was embarrassed by this loss of government property, especially knowing the vehicle had U.S. Embassy license plates and could be used by the enemy if it fell into their hands. When I delivered my report to the U.S. Embassy, I was told by one rather officious employee there that I would likely have to reimburse the government for the cost of the vehicle, and he made a copy of my military ID card and my orders so the U.S. government could find me when the bill came due. Fortunately for me, the matter was quickly forgotten, and I never was required to pay for the stolen jeep.

When my Air America flight arrived in Da Nang on June 14, I went to III MAF headquarters and presented my orders to the personnel officer, who informed me that I was two days late, and therefore guilty of missing movement, a serious offense under the UCMJ. In my usual patient and circumspect way of dealing with staff officers, I told the personnel officer that my orders specifically called for me to report to MACV, Saigon on June 14 for transportation to Da Nang and did not give any further instructions. He reluctantly conceded the point, but said I should have known better because my date of estimated return from overseas (DEROS) expired on June 14 and that was the date I should be leaving South Vietnam. Rather than belabor the point, he went ahead and arranged for me to fly out on the next flight to the United States in two days.

With two days to wait for my flight, I borrowed a CIA jeep from the Embassy House in Da Nang City and took one last trip around the area to see some of my friends. My first stop was to see Mai Ly and her husband in their small house in Dogpatch. I was asked to take a seat at the family dinner table, the only piece of nice furniture in their tiny but immaculate quarters. Mai Ly brought her baby out of the only other room in their house and proudly placed it on the table in front of me, and then she went over to a small stove and began to boil water for tea. I complimented the young parents on their baby, and both of

Mai Ly with her newborn baby, her husband, and sister at their home.

them beamed with pride. Her husband, a South Vietnamese Air Force lieutenant, said I would probably prefer a beer and rushed out to purchase some. I was left with the baby while the parents were occupied with other tasks, which turned out to be a less-than-fortuitous situation for me.

When the baby began to cry, I reached down to lift it up. But before I could cradle it in my arms, it started to urinate all over the table and my hands. Mai Ly laughed so hard, I thought she would pass out. She scooped up the baby, washed it off (the Vietnamese did not use diapers on their babies, preferring instead to keep them naked from the waist down), and continued to laugh as the water came to a boil on her little stove. For my part, I tried to hide my embarrassment by telling Mai Ly I often had strange effects on babies.

As Mai Ly poured a glass of tea for me, her husband returned with two bottles of brand Ba Muoi Ba (Number 33) Vietnamese beer. Although it was barely 10 o'clock in the morning, I drank the beer quickly and started to tell my friends that I was about to leave Vietnam for a second time. I told them I had orders to the Marine Corps' Basic School for officers at Quantico, Virginia. They said they were sorry I was leaving, but happy I would soon be home with my family again. They told me they had purchased some farmland in southern Quang Nam Province and hoped to begin a new life of farming once the war was over. Her husband offered to buy me another beer, but I told him I had to leave since I had more business to attend to. As I left their home, Mai Ly told me she thought I would return soon, which so surprised me, I asked her why she thought that. She replied, "Lieutenant Andy, you love Vietnam, even when there is a war here. You will come back to see us again, I am sure of it." She was both right and wrong: I did love Vietnam and its people, but I would never return to Vietnam again.

Later on I drove to Hill 327 and saw Mr. Smart in his shop. We talked as military trucks rumbled by, sending a mist of dust into the air and covering the screening and wall on his storefront. He told me he was thinking of moving to Hue to live with his daughter and her family. He said he would miss our little talks. When I got up to leave, he asked me to wait while he went into the back of his shop. When he returned, he had a red velvet box in his hands, and he presented it to me as a parting gift. It contained an exquisite, lacquered Vietnamese rice bowl and some ornate chopsticks. I was touched by his gift and told him he must come to the United States one day and stay in my parents' home. He thanked me but said, "I would dearly love to visit your home in America, but I do not think I will ever be so fortunate." Like Mai Ly, he told me he thought I would return to Vietnam soon, and he said he hoped that when I did, I would be sure to look him up if he moved to Hue. He then gave me the address of a friend of his in Da Nang who would know how to contact him. In 1985, I wrote to this friend asking about how I could contact Mr. Smart, but after a long delay, I received a letter from the man informing me that Mr. Smart had "disappeared" in 1979 and no one knew where he was. I sent another letter a few months later, but it was never answered.

I wanted to say goodbye to Dien and her husband, but when I went to their small house near the Da Nang Air Base, I found they were no longer living there. A neighbor told me they had moved to Saigon, where Dien's husband was assigned to a South Vietnamese Air Force unit at Tan Son Nhut Air Base. The neighbor did not have a new address for them, so I lost contact with her and never saw her again.

My final stop was at the Catholic Orphanage, where I said goodbye to Ngo Hue and Ngo Dung, my two orphans. They proudly spoke to me in English and produced their report cards for me, which showed they both were in the top 20 percent of their classes. I gave each boy a Cross pen and pencil set I had bought in Saigon for them, but Sister Marie told me she would take charge of these gifts until the boys were older, since these items were expensive and easily stolen or lost at the orphanage. I told the boys they could write to me any time they wanted to and that I would continue to help them with a check to Sister Marie each month to cover their school fees and meals. Since the boys needed to return to class, Sister Marie had them pose with me while an older boy took a picture of all of us standing together in front of the orphanage.

Before leaving the orphanage I had a short conversation with Sister Marie alone about my future support of the boys, and true to form, she suggested I send additional funds to help with other orphans in need of American charity. Sister Marie was a born saleswoman. Since I knew it was impossible to argue with such a strong-willed woman who I had every confidence could charm the skin off a snake, I decided to change the subject. Fully aware of her powers of persuasion, I knew any continued talk about financial matters might well result in having my entire paycheck turned over to her. I asked her about the war. That was a mistake.

Sister Marie had no military experience and certainly had never read any books about military strategy, but she was highly intelligent and knew South Vietnam and the VC well, the result of spending many years dealing with the tragic results of the conflict. She and I sat down at a small table in her office in the orphanage, and she prepared some tea, boiling the water on a small propane stove she had "borrowed from a Marine friend."

Over several cups of strong tea, she told me she was very disappointed in the Americans. Her displeasure with America made me feel uneasy, especially since I did not expect her to say anything like this to me. In the past, she had restricted her conversations with me to such banal topics as my health and the health of my family, and practical comments about how I should go about helping my two orphans. I also half expected her to tell me she would miss me and wish me a safe journey home; instead, she started to berate me in the way only a Catholic nun can do—and get away with!

"I suppose you feel your work here is finished, don't you?" she began. Before I could reply to her question, she said, "Captain Andy, tell me if what I read in our newspapers is true, that the Americans are selling out the Vietnamese and making a deal with the communists? Because if you are, I can only say I am very disappointed in you and your country. Don't you know that the communists will oppress the Church when they come to power? Religious people like me will be arrested, maybe even killed. Don't tell me you don't know this. I know these people and they are completely ruthless and Godless."

I had not expected Sister Marie to berate me this way on my last day in South Vietnam. Instead, I had expected her to tell me about her plans for the education of Ngo Hue and Ngo Dung, or how I should go about sending her money for the support of these two orphans. I was not prepared to respond to her questions, so I simply muttered something like, "I don't know of any American plans to sell out the South Vietnamese, and I sincerely doubt there are any."

"I pray that you are correct," she said. "However, I am afraid no one here really believes that the United States is not abandoning us to the communists."

I asked her what made the people she talked to believe the United States was abandoning them, and she said, "Captain Andy, you have lived in South Vietnam only a short time, but

I have lived here many years. I have seen how the communists work and know why they fear the Catholic Church and the other organized religions so much. Did you know that Ho Chi Minh learned how to organize the people from the Catholic Church? It's true. He lived in France, and he saw how we organized the people into social groups so everyone had some affiliation with the Church. He knew that these social organizations were the glue that held the Church together. The communists will never tolerate the Catholic Church, or the Hoa Hao, or the Cao Dai because we all have organizations that parallel theirs. You can't be loyal to a church organization and to a communist organization at the same time. If the communists seize power, they will do exactly the same things they did in Russia, China, and North Vietnam; they will arrest the clergy and the lay leaders of the Church and destroy the seminaries. You will see."

"I don't think it will come to that," I countered. "The South Vietnamese government and the army are quite strong now, and we have just about destroyed the VC in the villages. If the Americans continue to provide financial aid, military equipment, air support and advisors, the South Vietnamese people will not need American ground forces."

Sister Marie looked at me with a rather annoyed expression and even rolled her eyes at what she considered the naiveté of my remark. I could see she was actually becoming very angry, but she managed to get a grip on her emotions before she spoke again, saying, "I cannot believe you do not know what needs to be done to stop the war. You allow the communists to come down from North Vietnam and attack us. You don't stop them or you can't stop them; either way, it means we will have to go on fighting forever. The cancer is in North Vietnam, yet you Americans don't deal with it. You know what to do. I hate to tell you this on your last day in this country, and I don't mean to seem ungrateful, but your country is run by fools. Do not fight the North Vietnamese communists in South Vietnam where all you do is hurt our people with all your guns and bombs. The way you fight the war only helps the VC. Why can't you fight the North Vietnamese in North Vietnam and stop them from coming down here?"

I wanted to tell Sister Marie that was impossible given the domestic politics in the United States, but decided that would only discourage her more, so I engaged in a little wishful thinking, saying, "I am sure the American government has a good plan for defeating the North Vietnamese. Surely, they don't expect you to go on fighting forever."

With a look of exasperation, this diminutive, kindly nun saw that her words had no effect, so she ended our conversation by standing up, extending her hand, and saying, "Goodbye, Captain, I will remember you in my prayers. Please remember us in your prayers also."

I left the orphanage, never to see Sister Marie or the two orphans again. In 1977, I received a letter from Sister Marie. She had been arrested and imprisoned by the communists after the fall of South Vietnam in 1975, a fate that she had predicted on our last meeting. After her release from prison, she had been deported to her native Philippines and had lost contact with all of her orphans, including Ngo Hue and Ngo Dung. I never answered her letter. I was too ashamed to do so.

Early the next day, on June 16, I boarded a contract commercial airliner at the Da Nang Air Base for my flight back to the United States. Like every other Marine on the flight, I was jubilant that I was leaving for the country I loved and the lifestyle I had not enjoyed for 19 months. I looked around me in the plane and saw row upon row of happy faces. As the plane began to taxi out to the runway, I caught a glimpse of Dogpatch and Hill 327 and wondered if I would ever see these two places again. I knew the United States did not intend to keep combat forces in South Vietnam after 1972, so I thought it unlikely that I would return with a U.S. unit, but I thought it possible that I would be able to return sometime in the future as an advisor. In my mind, I did not think the communists would prevail. It seemed inconceivable to me that the United States would allow the North Vietnamese to triumph after spending so much blood and treasure defending South Vietnam. I also felt the South Vietnamese were capable of defending themselves as long as the United States continued to support them. However, the words of Sister Marie echoed in my mind: "Your country is run by fools.... You allow the communists to come down from North Vietnam and attack us.... Why can't you fight the North Vietnamese in North Vietnam and stop them from coming down here?" I wanted to think about what I would do on leave in the United States, the new duty station I was going to, and how good it would be to see my parents and brothers and sisters again; but instead, I thought about what Sister Marie had said, and I could not get her words out of my mind.

As the commercial airliner took off down the runway and climbed steeply over the Da Nang Bay, I looked out my window and saw the same sight I had seen on my first flight to South Vietnam in February 1967—the dark, cloud-shrouded Annamite Mountains. Those mountains were the last things I saw as the plane gained altitude and flew east. A flood of memories of patrolling in those mountains came back to me, and for a fleeting moment, I saw the faces of my Vietnamese friends: Mai Ly, Mr. Smart, Dien, Qua, Lam, Mr. Tho, Mr. Chinh, and Ba Quyen. As the plane reached its cruising altitude, I remembered Eric Barnes and Tom Dowd, my two friends who had died fighting for their country and for the salvation of South Vietnam. I should have felt relieved that I had survived another tour of duty in what seemed like a war without end, but instead I felt a strong sense of guilt at leaving with the job unfinished. That sense of guilt would remain with me right up to the moment that I write these words.

Epilogue

One day in the spring of 1985, fifteen years after I had left South Vietnam for the last time, I was having lunch with my faculty advisor at the Naval War College, Professor Robert Megagee, when another faculty member joined us and asked what we were talking about. Professor Megagee, who had taught me diplomatic history at the U.S. Naval Academy as an undergraduate, told this distinguished academic that we were discussing the Vietnam War. Professor Megagee's colleague immediately blurted out, "There is no practical use in such a discussion because there was nothing we could have done to win that war." This comment caused me to challenge our tablemate. I told him that wars are not deterministic or ordained by some immutable truth—they are won or lost based on many factors that can be modified and adjusted to affect an outcome. The historian, who was on leave from Harvard University to the Naval War College, looked me straight in the eye and said, "I challenge you to prove that. Tell me how the United States could have won the Vietnam War, given the constraints imposed on it and the superior will and strategy of the North Vietnamese."

This challenge led me to begin a lifelong study of the war and why the United States lost it. An intermediate analysis three years later resulted in the publication of an article for the *Marine Corps Gazette* in which I laid out the basic reason for our failure to win the war.[1] Additional study and the publication of new materials, especially those from North Vietnamese sources, have served to reinforce my original conclusion.

For any person who has participated in a war, the experience is unique and they see the war through the eyes of their own experience. This often makes it exceedingly difficult to be objective about the general conduct and outcome of any war. Each veteran of a war tends to analyze the overall reasons for success or failure in that war through a very narrow range of vision, one that is often clouded by emotion and trauma. I realize I am not immune to this constraint on objectivity and any analysis I might offer should be viewed with skepticism since there can be little doubt that the Vietnam War had a deep and lasting effect on me. Because I was so affected by the war, I spent many years studying it, primarily with the hope that I might find a cogent answer to the central question that plagued me: Why did the United States lose the war? I have examined every reason put forth by a host of writers, carefully examining their arguments, discussing them with other military analysts and veterans, and revising my findings in the light of my own experience in South Vietnam. From North Vietnamese generals, former VC politicians, and international journalists to military historians and U.S. and ARVN veterans of the war, I have attempted to find the root cause for the defeat of my country.

One may question the utility of even attempting to ascertain why the United States lost the Vietnam War; after all, it is over and done with and the strategic balance of power in the world has been little affected by its outcome. Although historians continue to this day to argue about why the United States lost this war, few other people give it any thought. I would count myself among the latter, if the war had not had such a profound effect on me and I thought the United States would never again make the same mistakes it made in South Vietnam. However, after over four decades of study, I am concerned about the "lessons learned" that many historians and other analysts have drawn from the Vietnam War. I see many of these "lessons learned" as false and dangerous, especially when applied to many of the challenges facing my country today. I have seen some of these "lessons learned" applied with disastrous results by well-meaning and intelligent men and women serving my country today. For this reason, I offer my personal assessment of the primary reason why we lost the war in South Vietnam in the hope that future political and military leaders will not pursue a path that leads to defeat.

To be as succinct as possible, the United States lost the war because its national leadership pursued a fatally flawed strategy based upon wishful thinking, hubris, and incorrect assumptions. They did so not because they were fools or lacked the necessary information needed to formulate a winning strategy. No, the requisite information for the proper strategic analysis was available as early as the end of the First Indochina War in 1954, but a combination of factors caused our strategic planners to overlook or dismiss the analysis. Unfortunately, the North Vietnamese had a far greater appreciation for these factors than our own leaders, which resulted in the communists' forging a far more effective strategy for the achievement of their goals—and to do so despite some extremely burdensome and potentially lethal constraints.

I will not address the reasons for our intervention in South Vietnam or why we remained there long after it became apparent we would be unable to successfully affect its outcome. I think the historians have drawn the correct conclusions for the rationale our leaders used in both cases. Whether those reasons were correct or necessary, I leave to the historians to settle. What I will do is identify the objectives of the major protagonists, their respective strategies, and the root cause for failure of the American strategy, a strategy that was, in my opinion, doomed from the beginning without a major change in policy.

For the North Vietnamese, or more accurately for the Lao Dong Party, the goal they set for themselves and one they never abandoned or modified was the complete unification of Vietnam and the domination of the Indochina peninsula, to include Laos and Cambodia. This goal, which was clearly and openly pronounced by the Lao Dong Party during the First Indochina War, became feasible when the Chinese Nationalists were defeated by the Chinese Peoples' Liberation Army (PLA) in 1949, giving the Lao Dong Party's Viet Minh a secure border with China, bases and sanctuaries on that border, and massive amounts of captured Kuomintang weapons and ammunition, to include the artillery used with such effectiveness at the decisive Battle of Dien Bien Phu in 1954. Using doctrine developed by the Chinese communists, secure bases in southern China, and firepower that could match the French, the Lao Dong Party led the Viet Minh forces to victory, expelling the French from the Red River Delta and all of the northern part of Vietnam.

However, their goal of unifying all of Vietnam under their control was thwarted by the 1954 Geneva Accords, which the Soviet Union and the PRC imposed upon them. These accords, which the U.S. was not a signatory to, called for elections in 1956 to determine the political future of a united Vietnam. The Lao Dong Party was confident that it could win a nationwide election in 1956, and most observers agree with that assumption. However, the United States decided that any election held in 1956 would result in a unified country dominated by the communists, a situation that threatened to destabilize their allies in Southeast Asia and lead to communist regimes in most, if not all, of the countries in the region. Given that there were active communist insurgencies in several Southeast Asian countries in the late 1950s and early 1960s, it was correct to assume many of these countries might succumb to these insurgencies if the United States allowed South Vietnam to fall to the communists.

At this time, the United States' grand strategy was one articulated by George Kennan in his famous "long telegram," which called for the containment of the Soviet Union and later the PRC. This grand strategy called for the United States to resist any further expansion of communism, a strategy that led to the Marshall Plan for Europe, the Korean War, numerous other conflicts on the periphery of the Eurasian land mass, and the Vietnam War. While Mr. Kennan would later dispute that his grand strategy for the containment of the Soviet Union should have been applied to the U.S. decision to intervene in South Vietnam, U.S. policy makers in the early 1960s were definitely thinking in terms of containment when the policy discussions concerning South Vietnam were being conducted. Therefore, the U.S. objective was to prevent South Vietnam from falling under the control of a communist government allied with the Soviet Union and the PRC. For domestic and international political reasons, the United States articulated several other goals, most of which were irrelevant or impractical, such as fostering liberal democracy and protecting religious freedom in South Vietnam.

For the South Vietnamese government, their goal was to avoid defeat by both the internal and external threat posed by the Lao Dong Party and to remain in power. From time to time, the GVN would also echo the goals of the United States, but the GVN endorsement of these goals was always tepid at best and done more to mollify the Americans than to be taken seriously. For the GVN their paramount interest was survival in the face of aggression from North Vietnam. Unlike the Americans, the GVN had a more realistic appreciation of the threat and often rejected the advice given by the Americans, which they knew was either irrelevant or infeasible given the cultural, political, and strategic realities in their country. While the GVN had many weaknesses, their military leadership understood the strategic dynamics better than their American allies, who clung to the mistaken belief that tactical brilliance and technological superiority could compensate for strategic incompetence.[2]

The strategy employed by the North Vietnamese to achieve their goal of unification of all of Vietnam and control of Laos and Cambodia was no mystery to the United States. Lao Dong Party documents obtained by the French in the early 1950s clearly laid out the communist strategy. The North Vietnamese knew by 1956 that any hope of achieving their goal through elections in South Vietnam and subversion in Laos and Cambodia was impossible, given the decision of President Diem and the Americans not to hold elections in South Vietnam. They recognized they must resort to violent means to achieve their goal, and they quite logically adopted a strategy that was based upon their successful experience in the First Indochina War. Initially, this strategy called for the Lao Dong Party to build a modern military force capable of defending North Vietnam using equipment and munitions provided by the Soviet Union and the PRC, while at the same time using southern Lao Dong cadres to organize the rural population of South Vietnam and lay the groundwork for future military actions.[3] The Lao Dong Party understood that they could not rely alone on a southern insurgency to achieve their goal, although they hoped the insurgency would so weaken the GVN that a coalition government that included the communist front organization, the National Liberation Front (NLF), would come to power and set the stage for eventual control of the entire south. The Lao Dong Party did not strictly adhere to the Chinese communist model of revolutionary war that placed complete reliance on a guerrilla army; instead, the party planned to use a guerrilla army in South Vietnam to weaken and distract the GVN while it built up a modern, mobile army in North Vietnam that could intervene at the decisive moment when the situation in South Vietnam made it possible to use this modern army to achieve a decisive result. While the North Vietnamese model included the three types of military forces—local, regional, and main-force units—that the Chinese communists used in their successful campaigns against the Japanese and the Kuomintang in China, they placed a greater emphasis on conventional forces for striking a decisive blow. This model was not endorsed by the PRC and often led to theoretical conflicts with the Chinese during the Second Indochina War.

The North Vietnamese were always concerned about military intervention by the United States, so they developed a strategy that would take into account that intervention. They realized that the United States possessed a huge material advantage over their forces, especially in terms of naval and air power, but they had fought a modern army during the First Indochina War, and they knew that they could defeat such an army if they employed a strategy similar to the one they used against the French. Although there were some variations to their strategy to take into account changing events in South Vietnam, the North Vietnamese strategy was remarkably similar to the one they used to drive the French out of North Vietnam during their campaigns from 1950 to 1954. Fortunately for the North Vietnamese, few Americans understood how the Viet Minh strategy worked or why it was successful, and those who did were either ignored or dismissed as pessimists.

During the First Indochina War, the Viet Minh had few successes until the Chinese communists came to power in late 1949, giving them the sanctuaries and the equipment they needed to achieve success. The Viet Minh had been using the Chinese communist model of revolutionary war, with its three stages, as their theoretical model ever since Ho Chi Minh returned from China to lead the communist revolution in Vietnam. These three stages of revolutionary war are: Stage One, which entails "organization, consolidation, and preservation"; Stage Two, which calls for "progressive expansion"; and Stage Three, the "decisive engagement and destruction of the enemy."[4] Since this three-stage model for revolutionary warfare had worked so well for the Chinese communists, it was logical that it be adopted by the Viet Minh.

From 1945 to 1950, the Viet Minh were unable to progress from Stage One to Stage Two, and in fact had suffered several severe losses when they attempted to expand their military operations in the Red River Delta of North Vietnam. This all changed when southern China fell to the communist forces of Mao Tse-tung in late 1949. This development spelled disaster for the French because it created all of southern China as a sanctuary and base for training and logistical support for the Viet Minh. It also meant that the French now had a hostile border with China that was 1,306 kilometers long. It was now physically impossible for the French forces to defend such a long border, forcing them to give up much of the territory north and west of the Red River Delta. The French knew they could not attack the PRC, so the Viet Minh bases in southern China were beyond their reach. The Viet Minh were quick to take advantage of this strategic windfall and began developing a system of supply routes that led from southern China into North Vietnam. The strategic initiative passed from the French to the Viet Minh once the PRC provided the Viet Minh with a safe haven for their forces to attack the French, along with the military equipment and supplies the Viet Minh forces needed to conduct sustained operations inside North Vietnam. Compounding the French dilemma, the Korean War reached a negotiated stalemate in 1953, freeing up vast quantities of military weapons and equipment from the PRC, which the Viet Minh put to good use immediately.

Some prescient American strategists, like Generals Eisenhower and Marshall, understood the situation clearly and cautioned against involving U.S. forces in the war between the French and the Viet Minh. They understood that the French were doomed in Indochina as long as the Viet Minh had sanctuaries in China and an unlimited supply of weapons and ammunition from their Chinese comrades to carry on their war against the French. Despite local victories by the French, it was inevitable that the balance of forces would always favor the Viet Minh as long as they had access to secure bases in China and the material support of the PRC. It is for this reason President Eisenhower rejected the French request for U.S. air support at Dien Bien Phu, the decisive battle in the First Indochina War. He knew that even if U.S. air power saved the French at Dien Bien Phu, the French would never overcome the problem of the Viet Minh sanctuaries in China and the almost inexhaustible supply of manpower the Viet Minh could devote to the war. As a result, the United States attempted to limit the Viet Minh gains to North Vietnam by using diplomacy while it built up an anticommunist regime in the southern part of Vietnam.

With the defeat of the French at Dien Bien Phu, the diplomats took over from the generals. A conference was convened in Geneva to end the hostilities, and the Vietnamese communists expected they would achieve their goals of removing all foreign troops from Indochina and establishing themselves as the masters of a united Vietnam. Unfortunately for them, the diplomats did not give them the victory they thought they had won on the battlefield. Instead, the Chinese and the Soviet delegates forced them to accept an agreement that left the southern half of Vietnam outside of their political control, with the understanding that free elections would be held in 1956 throughout Vietnam to determine what kind of government a united Vietnam would have. The United States and the South Vietnamese did not sign the Geneva Accords, and therefore did not feel obligated to hold elections in 1956. The United States realized that any election held in 1956 would most likely result in a unified and communist-dominated government in Vietnam and would eventually lead to communist-dominated governments in Laos and Cambodia. This expansion of communism ran counter to the U.S. national strategy of containment and threatened several other countries in the region that were dealing with communist insurgencies, such as Thailand, Malaysia, the Philippines, and Indonesia. The United States had just finished fighting a costly war on the Korean peninsula against the communist regimes of China and North Korea, so it was not about to let three more countries fall under communist domination and possibly fuel a series of additional "wars of national liberation" in other countries in the region, some of which were strong allies of the United States.

So the stage was set for a confrontation between North Vietnam and the United States, which could only be resolved by force. The North Vietnamese communists wanted to expand their control over South Vietnam and their influence, if not outright control, over Laos and Cambodia, while the United States was committed to a policy that called for resisting any further communist expansion anywhere in the world. Neither side was willing to compromise. These two conflicting goals would collide with catastrophic results for both countries.

When elections were not held in 1956, the North Vietnamese, under the leadership of the Lao Dong Party, decided to use military force to achieve their goal of unification of the country. Like most strategies, their plan was simple to conceive but difficult to execute, and based upon many assumptions, some of which proved to be false. It called for the organization of a mass-based party infrastructure in South Vietnam, the purpose of which was to provide three things: intelligence, manpower, and logistical support for mobile military forces. In effect, it called for the Lao Dong Party to establish itself in every village and hamlet of South Vietnam so the rural peasantry could be mobilized and controlled in support of the revolutionary military forces. The Lao Dong Party knew from its experience during the First Indochina War that guerrilla forces alone were incapable of achieving a decisive result against a well-armed and technologically advanced military force like the one the Americans had. To achieve victory over a foe as strong as the United States, they knew they would have to avoid decisive engagement, while at the same time inflicting heavy casualties on the Americans and their GVN allies in order to erode the national will of both governments and their respective populations. In essence, they embarked on a protracted war of attrition, but one that allowed them to modulate the level of violence so as not to risk defeat. To achieve this, they first needed to make sure they maintained the support of the three elements identified by Carl von Clausewitz in his classic book of military strategy, *On War*, which are essential if a country decides to wage war. Those three essential elements of support are: the people, the government, and the military. The North Vietnamese clearly understood this dictum for the foundation of a successful strategy, but unfortunately, the Americans either did not or they chose to ignore it.

Since the Lao Dong Party ruled unopposed in North Vietnam, had complete control over the sources of information their population received, had a system of government that made internal security tight and comprehensive, had a military that was under the complete control of the party, and had a recent tradition of victory over a superior foreign military force, this first and most important requirement for a successful strategy was achieved. Their next step in the formulation of their strategy was to take into account every possible action their opposition might take and to develop a strategy that could successfully counter these actions. During the initial stages of the development of their strategy, they hoped that the United States would not intervene militarily in South Vietnam, but they planned for that eventuality from the beginning. As early as 1959 they decided that it was likely that the United States would use military force to thwart their plans, so they developed a strategy that was highly flexible and could be changed rapidly to adjust to any level of U.S. military intervention.

This Lao Dong strategy was based on their experience in their war against the French, but adapted to the reality that the Americans possessed far more economic and military power than the French had. The specifics of their strategy of attrition involved a combination of political and military actions that would erode the will of their adversaries and cause their opponents' governments, militaries, and populations to accede to the goals of the Lao Dong Party. It was a strategy that was not dependent upon timetables or assumptions about the motivations of their opponents; instead, it was a carefully crafted strategy that capitalized upon their opponents' weaknesses and minimized their own vulnerabilities with an open-ended commitment to persevere no matter how long it took.

What then was the strategy the Lao Dong Party employed against the GVN and the Americans? In its broadest terms, their strategy consisted of several actions that had the aggregated effect of neutralizing their adversaries' advantages and preventing them from taking the steps needed to defeat them. These were:

First, the primary concern of the Lao Dong Party was to secure North Vietnam from invasion. This was done by aligning themselves with the Soviet Union and the PRC, making any attack on the territory of North Vietnam by GVN or American ground forces a potential cause for war between the United States and these two countries. It also ensured that these two communist allies would provide the military equipment and economic aid needed to withstand any attack on its soil and to sustain its attack against South Vietnam. In addition, the Lao Dong Party embarked on a sustained program to build a modern military defense force capable of withstanding a conventional attack on their homeland. This effort included the acquisition of modern aircraft, sophisticated armored vehicles, mobile artillery, and technologically advanced air defense and communications systems, almost all provided at no cost by their communist allies.

Second, they appealed through the extensive worldwide propaganda system of communist, socialist, and other leftist organizations to influence public opinion against the GVN and the United States. The formation of the National Liberation Front (NLF) and other front groups to hide the actual identity of the leadership of the insurgency in South Vietnam and provide a patina of non-communist participation in the leadership of the insurgency was an example of how the Lao Dong Party attempted to influence external observers. This was part of their "dau tranh" campaign on a worldwide scale to promote the Lao Dong Party's position and gain support for their cause outside of Vietnam. They found a ready audience for their propaganda among leftist groups throughout Western Europe and the United States.

Third, they built a modern military capable of regional power projection, using extensive support from the Soviet Union and the PRC. Certain units were designated for special training in mobile warfare and supplied with equipment that would enable these units to operate far from North Vietnam in Laos, Cambodia, and South Vietnam. This military buildup was begun shortly after the end of the First Indochina War and was largely completed by 1964.

Fourth, the Lao Dong Party began to build an extensive political infrastructure in South Vietnam with its primary focus on organizing the rural areas of that country. Using cadres from the First Indochina War, the Lao Dong Party created the Viet Cong Infrastructure (VCI) in these rural areas using the same organizational techniques they had employed against the French. This model had a long history, beginning with the system perfected by Chinese communist cadres, who spent several decades building their powerful rural political base in their war with the Kuomintang. The Lao Dong Party adapted the Chinese communist model of political organization to Vietnam but strengthened this system by integrating the lessons they had learned from their experience during the First Indochina War. The purpose of the VCI was to mobilize the peasants of South Vietnam to create a mass-based political organization that paralleled the government of the GVN but extended down into the village and hamlet level. The primary objective for this mass-based political organization was the provision of three basic requirements for mobile military warfare: intelligence, recruits, and logistical support. The strategy of the Lao Dong Party was highly dependent on the VCI in South Vietnam for these three requirements, especially the logistical support needed by North Vietnamese military units. The Lao Dong Party realized that without the logistical support of the VCI in South Vietnam, their ability to conduct large-scale, sustained, mobile military operations was severely curtailed, if not eliminated. While not the only reason for their concern about any successful GVN pacification program, it was the Lao Dong Party's primary reason for concern, since any degradation of the VCI threatened the ability of the North Vietnamese military to operate in South Vietnam.

Fifth, the Lao Dong Party needed a secure logistical system to support mobile warfare in South Vietnam. Phase III of their doctrine of revolutionary war called for the defeat of the conventional forces of their enemy using modern, conventionally armed, mobile mainforce units. To do this, they needed a means of supplying such units. This entailed maintaining the VCI in every strategically important part of South Vietnam and establishing a system of resupply and reinforcement external to South Vietnam. This logistical system was managed by Unit 559, which received its designation from the date of its inception, May 1959. Unit 559 was given the mission of establishing an extensive and sophisticated system of transportation routes, supply depots, training areas, and medical facilities running for over 3,500 miles in length from North Vietnam through Laos and Cambodia to Saigon. This system was known to the Americans as the Ho Chi Minh Trail and to the North Vietnamese as the Truong Son Strategic Supply Route. The system was truly massive; in Laos alone it covered 1,700 square miles. All along the Ho Chi Minh Trail system were multiple roads and trails, some of them all-weather and hard-surfaced, and along these trails and roads were numerous staging areas, truck parks, petroleum pipelines, bivouac sites, hospitals, farms, supply depots, and command and control hubs, all carefully camouflaged to prevent detection by U.S. aircraft and CIA and U.S. Special Forces reconnaissance teams. Providing maintenance and protection for this huge and long logistical system were over 100,000 North Vietnamese troops in Laos and Cambodia and an additional 15,000 Chinese in Laos.

This supply system was in complete violation of the 1962 Geneva Accords, which called for the neutrality of Laos and Cambodia, but the North Vietnamese were left with no viable choice for an alternative means of supplying their military forces fighting in South Vietnam. Their early attempts to infiltrate men and supplies through the DMZ were unsuccessful and costly. Besides, the North Vietnamese military strategy called for cutting South Vietnam in two in the Central Highlands of Military Region II, and this plan necessitated a secure infiltration route to base areas in eastern Cambodia. They also realized that any final push against the capital of South Vietnam, Saigon, necessitated secure supply bases in southeastern Cambodia. Given their military strategy, it was only logical for the North Vietnamese to use the eastern regions of both Laos and Cambodia to build the Ho Chi Minh Trail. Since the trail was essential to their strategy, they viewed any attempt to successfully cut it as an existential threat to their overall strategy for the conquest of South Vietnam. Many Western historians have tended to ignore or play down the vital importance of the Ho Chi Minh Trail, but the North Vietnamese communists do not share these views. In fact, some among the victors of the war have openly admitted that the failure of the Americans to cut the Ho Chi Minh Trail in southern Laos was the biggest mistake the Americans made during the war, and had the Americans cut the Ho Chi Minh Trail, the outcome of the war would have been far different.[5] For the North Vietnamese, the Ho Chi Minh Trail was both their biggest advantage and their most significant vulnerability—and they knew it.

Finally, once the Lao Dong Party had accomplished the steps mentioned above, they were ready to embark on the final phase of their strategy to defeat the Americans and overthrow the GVN. I will not go into the specifics of their strategy inside South Vietnam, but only broadly explain that it entailed the conduct of an attrition-intensive campaign designed to protect their bases inside South Vietnam, Laos, and Cambodia, and to conduct military and terrorist campaigns designed to erode the will of both the American and South Vietnamese governments to continue the war. As long as the North Vietnamese had secure sanctuaries, a secure supply route from North Vietnam to South Vietnam, and a secure rural political infrastructure capable of providing intelligence, recruits, and logistical support, their success was assured. Even with over 500,000 American troops, it was impossible for the United States to secure the 1,400-mile border that ran from the East China Sea west along the DMZ and then south through Laos and Cambodia. The Americans surrendered the initiative to the North Vietnamese when they steadfastly refused to invade Laos to cut the Ho Chi Minh Trail. All the North Vietnamese had to do was maintain pressure on the Americans and the GVN by waging a war of attrition and avoiding a decisive engagement. They knew they could bleed the Americans indefinitely and simply withdraw to their sanctuaries to avoid decisive engagement or intolerable casualties. They felt confident that the United States would weary of the endless list of casualties and withdrawal, allowing the regular NVA main-force units to quickly attack a weakened and demoralized South Vietnam. With their carefully crafted strategy, they were assured of eventual victory, but only as long as they protected their supporting political infrastructure inside South Vietnam, their bases and supply depots in Laos and Cambodia, and their means of moving men and supplies south along the Ho Chi Minh Trail.

If the above was the North Vietnamese strategy, what was the American strategy? Sadly, it was a fatally flawed one, doomed from the very beginning once the United States rejected the idea of invading the panhandle of Laos and cutting the Ho Chi Minh Trail. Despite warnings from the South Vietnamese military and the American Joint Chiefs of Staff as early as 1956, and a very direct and prescient warning from Secretary of State Dean Rusk and Secretary of Defense Robert McNamara to President Kennedy in 1961, this key strategic decision not to deal with the North Vietnamese use of the trail and road system in eastern Laos did not appear to deter President Kennedy from confronting the North Vietnamese militarily or President Johnson from escalating the war after he took office. The Rusk-McNamara memorandum in particular should have given pause to the framers of the U.S. strategy for engaging the North Vietnamese. One can only assume that President Kennedy's advisors, many of whom also served President Johnson, thought the danger of not dealing with the road system developed by the French in Laos was minimal or the North Vietnamese would abide by the 1962 Geneva Accords on Laos and not use Laotian territory to move troops and supplies to South Vietnam. In the joint memorandum to President Kennedy, Rusk and McNamara wrote: "It will probably not be possible for the government of [South] Vietnam to win the war as long as the flow of men and supplies from North Vietnam remains unchecked and the guerrillas enjoy a safe sanctuary in neighboring territory."[6] At the time, there were advisors in the Kennedy Administration who recognized the strategic importance of the road-and-trail system in eastern Laos, but their advice was largely dismissed. Advocates for adhering to the 1962 Geneva Accords on Laos, primarily Averell Harriman and Roger Hilsman in the State Department, convinced President Kennedy that it was imperative for the United States to keep U.S. ground troops out of Laos. Their advice was based upon the importance of the United States to keep its international agreements, and the fear that any U.S. military presence in Laos would have an adverse effect on U.S.-Soviet relations and might even result in China's taking military action against the United States in Laos and possibly Korea. While there was no firm intelligence that military action by the United States in southern Laos or Cambodia would trigger a military reaction from either the Soviet Union or China, President Kennedy's advisors assumed the worst and decided to attempt to solve the problem of South Vietnam by treating it as a problem solely restricted to that country and North Vietnam. Many of the president's advisors were rightly worried about the nuclear threat posed by both the Soviet Union and the PRC, and they did not want to precipitate armed conflict with either of these countries, fearing such an escalation could necessitate the use of strategic nuclear weapons. Because of this well-founded fear, they had developed the concept of the "graduated response" to any aggression launched by either of these adversaries. Ironically, one of the principle architects of gradually escalating military action against North Vietnam, primarily through the use of bombing, was Walt Rostow, who recognized the importance of eastern Laos to the North Vietnamese strategy. This strategic concept, often referred to as the "Rostow Thesis," called for a gradual escalation of violence against North Vietnam until the leadership of the Lao Dong Party in Hanoi decided their continued aggression in South Vietnam was not worth the punishment inflicted upon them. It assumed a "rational player" would desist once they saw the continued escalation of the violence was not worth the price. While not abandoning the U.S. strategy of containment of communism, the United States adopted a strategy of "graduated response" to any communist expansion on the periphery of the Eurasian landmass in order to reduce the likelihood that either the Soviet Union or the PRC would use nuclear weapons. Despite some very sound advice from Rostow that warned of the problem of North Vietnamese sanctuaries in Laos, President Johnson continued to adhere to the flawed strategy of "graduated response" developed by President Kennedy's national security staff.

Unfortunately for South Vietnam, the idea of "graduated response" caused the United States to employ a strategy in Southeast Asia that was not based upon any hard intelligence that it would have the desired effect on the leadership of the Lao Dong Party in North Vietnam. The U.S. national security advisors simply *assumed* that the North Vietnamese were "rational players," and they would abandon their goal of unifying Vietnam once they saw that United States will was firm and that the United States could ratchet up the level of violence to a degree that would break their will to resist. It all made very good sense to the president's advisors, who assumed the North Vietnamese thought as "rational players." These presidential advisors thought if the United States showed resolve and escalated the violence in a gradual and sustained manner, the North Vietnamese would come to their senses and reach a settlement that allowed the pro–Western GVN to remain in power in South Vietnam. By telling the world that the United States had no interest in overthrowing the regime in North Vietnam, had no interest in territorial acquisition in Southeast Asia, and had no intention of "expanding" the war into Laos and Cambodia, the U.S. national security advisors thought this benign and reasonable approach would be accepted by America's allies and the American people. As for the North Vietnamese and their allies, such a statement of U.S. goals only served to convince them that U.S. interests were limited to South Vietnam alone, and therefore there would be no tangible threat to their strategy of using the Ho Chi Minh Trail and their bases in Laos and Cambodia.

Many commentators have offered a wide variety of reasons for our failure to win the Vietnam War. There are those who say we should have mined the harbor of Haiphong, we should have unleashed the full might of our air power against North Vietnam, we should have pursued a more enlightened or more aggressive pacification program inside South Vietnam, or we should have tried to turn South Vietnam into a Jeffersonian democracy by a combination of political, social, and economic reforms. While we will never know if any of these proposals would have brought victory, none of them address the central reason for our failure to win the war—our inability to prevent North Vietnam from moving troops and equipment to South Vietnam using the Ho Chi Minh Trail. Our political and military leaders failed to ask the most critical question affecting their strategy: What if the enemy's will is stronger than ours and, if so, what can we do that will thwart their ability to carry on the war in South Vietnam regardless of their will to do so?

The only plausible answer to the question above is the one that General Westmoreland and his staff came to in 1967 when they began to plan for the occupation of the panhandle of Laos. Instead of relying on air power and indigenous special operations teams, which failed to stem the flow of troops and equipment to South Vietnam through Laos, Gen. Westmoreland finally saw the necessity to use U.S. ground troops to block and hold the terrain between Dong Ha in South Vietnam and Savannahkhet on the Mekong River in Laos. This obvious plan, which was studied as early as 1964, was delayed initially by the U.S. State Department, which did not want to threaten the neutrality of Laos or give up their primary role for management of American affairs in that country. Later the implementation of the plan was thwarted by the CIA, which did not want to give up its mission of conducting the "Secret War" in Laos, or to diminish the importance of their responsibility for pacification programs in South Vietnam. Even the U.S. military tried to kill the plan by asserting that it was logistically infeasible or the North Vietnamese would simply go farther west to get around it. A leading opponent of the plan was the U.S. Marine Corps, which did not like the idea of any barrier defense inside South Vietnam, let alone stretching across Laos to the Mekong River. In fact, the U.S. Marine Corps did everything possible to prevent their forces in I Corps from being used for any form of static defense, a position that often put them at odds with Gen. Westmoreland and the MACV headquarters. The Marine Corps' insistence on the primacy of mobile defense and their attachment to an "ink spot" counterinsurgency strategy, along with their dislike for any form of warfare that involved occupying static positions, delayed the implementation of the attack into Laos until the Tet Offensive of 1968 made such an attack by U.S. ground forces politically impossible.[7]

Of all the possible strategies proposed for an American victory in Vietnam, the strategy of cutting the Ho Chi Minh Trail in southern Laos offered the best chance for success, for the following reasons:

First, the use of U.S. ground troops along the Dong Ha-Savannakhet axis would cut the Ho Chi Minh Trail, making it impossible for North Vietnamese troops and equipment to move into South Vietnam. U.S. and ARVN forces would no longer need to protect a border with North Vietnam, Laos, and Cambodia that stretched for nearly 1,400 miles, but could concentrate their forces along a frontage of only 225 miles, the distance from the East China Sea to Savannakhet. In order for North Vietnamese supply columns to move south, the North Vietnamese would need to breach this barrier using large numbers of conventional forces fighting in terrain that heavily favors the defense. Even if they broke free, they would have to maintain the breach continuously or face isolation of their forces moving south through mountainous terrain. If, as some unsophisticated commentators have asserted, the North Vietnamese chose to attempt to go around the barrier, they would be forced to cross the Mekong River, a significant physical obstacle easily covered by U.S. air and riverine forces and screened by a force like the U.S. 1st Air Cavalry Division using bases on the Thai side of the river. What's more, if the North Vietnamese were able to move their troops and supplies across the Mekong River into Thailand, they would be confronted with a hostile population and without the political infrastructure needed to create a system of bases and sanctuaries, not to mention adding nearly 500 more miles to any trip south. Also, unlike the terrain in eastern Laos, which is mountainous and jungle-clad, the terrain the North Vietnamese would have to transit in Thailand is flat and open, making it relatively easy to find and attack them. Furthermore, any North Vietnamese units that were able to get to the Mekong River would have to abandon their vehicles on the Laos side, and they would not be able to maintain any petroleum pipelines once they were in Thailand. It is hard to imagine that the North Viet-

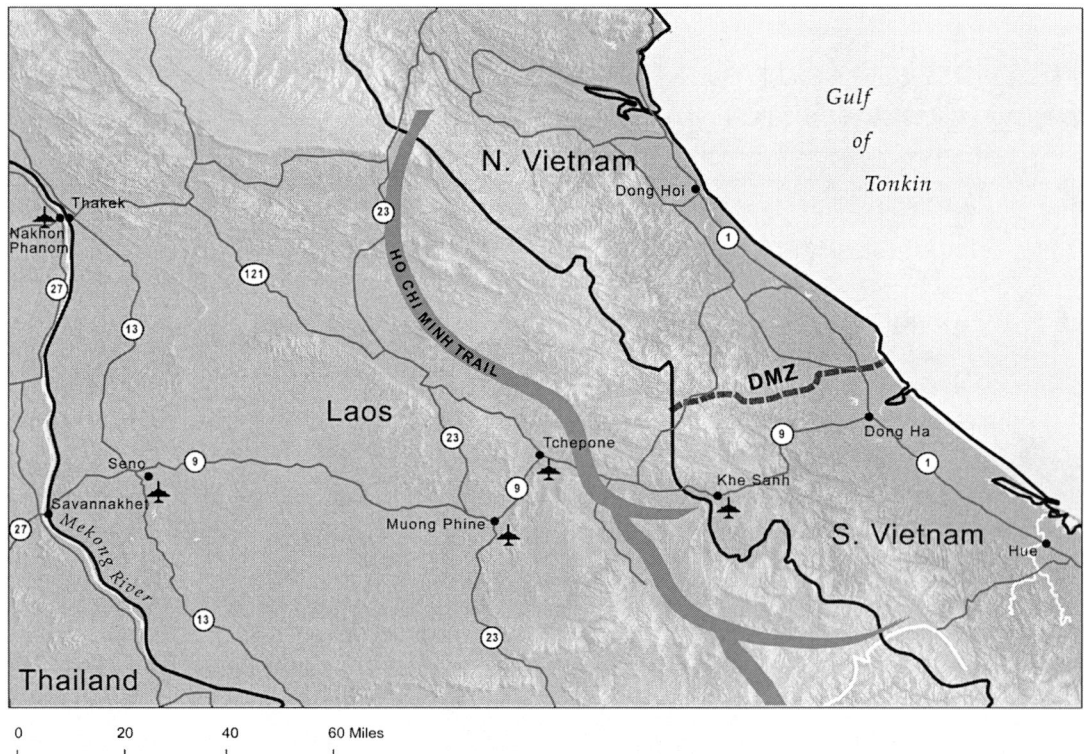

Map 6

namese would be able to maintain their required infiltration figure of 8,000 men and 500 tons of equipment and ammunition per month if U.S. forces were occupying defensive positions from Dong Ha to Savannakhet.

Second, the force levels needed to defend the Dong Ha–Savannakhet axis would have been less than those that were employed by the United States pursuing their attrition-based strategy in South Vietnam. By 1969, the United States employed eleven divisions in South Vietnam with over 500,000 troops. The plan to establish the Dong Ha–Savannakhet defensive barrier would require only two U.S. Marine divisions in Quang Tri Province, South Vietnam, and four U.S. Army divisions in southern Laos, with an additional U.S. Army division positioned in the vicinity of Paksane, Laos, where it could screen the Mekong River north of Savannakhet and threaten the right flank of any North Vietnamese force moving against the barrier to the south. As a Southeast Asia Treaty Organization (SEATO) ally, Thailand could be called upon to employ their military and border police units along the Mekong River and in-depth along any potential infiltration routes the North Vietnamese might try to establish in Thailand. South Vietnamese units, such as the Rangers and the elite 1st ARVN Division, could serve as a second line of defense for the barrier and used to hunt down any NVA units that penetrated the barrier. Such an alignment of forces would require the North Vietnamese to fight a conventional battle against an American, South Vietnamese, and Thai force that enjoyed a considerable advantage in terms of firepower, mobility, logistics, and terrain.

Third, by concentrating the U.S. military in only one province of South Vietnam—Quang Tri—and southern Laos, the bulk of the South Vietnamese forces could be devoted to dealing with the VC military units and the VCI in the remaining forty-three provinces of South Vietnam, thus allowing them to concentrate on pacification and nation-building, two tasks better suited to indigenous forces. In addition to using both the U.S. and ARVN forces in a more appropriate manner, it would effectively remove the presence of American forces from the South Vietnamese countryside, where their presence often took on the appearance of an occupying army. It would also end the sometimes profligate use of excessive American supporting arms in the populated areas of South Vietnam and concentrate that immense destructive power against the North Vietnamese inside North Vietnam and Laos. By reducing South Vietnamese civilian casualties from American supporting arms and employing American military forces in the largely uninhabited regions of southern Laos and the DMZ of South Vietnam, a far more humane and moral military strategy would be employed.

Fourth, while logistically challenging, the Dong Ha–Savannakhet defensive barrier was far easier to establish and maintain than its detractors claimed at the time, and still claim today. The port of Da Nang in northern I Corps could easily support two U.S. Marine Divisions, while the ports of Thailand and the road system running from those ports to Savannakhet and along the Thai side of the Mekong River are adequate to support five U.S. divisions, with only modest improvements. U.S. Air Force bases already existed in eastern Thailand and would only need some expansion to support the U.S. forces in Laos. An argument made by military planners on the Joint Chiefs of Staff for the need to activate the reserves to support the engineering requirements for the barrier does not stand up to scrutiny. Private U.S. and other Western engineering contractors, already active in both Thailand and South Vietnam using local labor, could have handled this requirement easily without the political cost in the United States incurred by calling up Reserve military engineer units. If the North Vietnamese could build and maintain roads under the pressure of constant bombing by U.S. aircraft using coolie labor, it is safe to assume that South Vietnamese and Laotian laborers could do it under the threat of North Vietnamese attack. Using local labor to build roads and defensive positions would be cheaper than using U.S. military engineers and would help the local rural economies by providing a large number of peasants with better wages than they would have received tilling the land. Such road-building jobs would also reduce the demand for farmland redistribution, a key communist propaganda theme.

Finally, with the U.S. strategy of fighting the North Vietnamese along the DMZ in South Vietnam and in the panhandle of southern Laos, U.S. aircraft and U.S. airfields would no longer be spread out all over South Vietnam and vulnerable to attack. Instead, U.S. air power could be concentrated at just a few airfields in South Vietnam, such as the one at Da Nang, with the bulk of our aircraft stationed in eastern Thailand or at sea on U.S. Navy aircraft carriers, thus obviating the need for tying down so many U.S. infantry units protecting airfields in South Vietnam.

Many Western critics of the "barrier defense" explained above point to the failure of the electronic defense system in southern Laos that was employed as part of the McNamara Line as proof that a barrier would prove ineffective in stemming the flow of men and supplies from North Vietnam. These critics point out, quite correctly, that the North Vietnamese were able to adapt to the system of intrusion devices used to monitor foot and vehicle traffic along the Ho Chi Minh Trail and still move sufficient men and tonnage to support the insurgency in South Vietnam. While the electronic intrusion devices made the North Vietnamese pay a high price for their continued use of the Ho Chi Minh Trail, they did not pose a significant enough obstacle to them, and they overcame this technological system through ingenuity and perseverance. The barrier system explained above is entirely different from the electronic one devised by the "whiz kids" in the Pentagon that relied on technology to stem the flow of North Vietnamese troops and equipment moving down the Ho Chi Minh Trail. This barrier would be one permanently manned by U.S. troops occupying strong defensive positions similar to those found along the DMZ in Korea and defended in-depth. It would not rely on technology and air power to attack traffic on the Ho Chi Minh Trail, but instead would use a system of strong points manned by infantry at key choke points for the trail and backed up with artillery in hardened fire-support bases and mobile reaction forces. The infantry and artillery units employed along the barrier would also have concentrated U.S. air power available to counter any NVA attempt to breach the barrier. It would also entail ground and aerial reconnaissance units prowling the terrain north of the barrier to give advance warning of any enemy movement toward it. The efficacy of such an arrangement could be found in the defensive system that was used along the DMZ in South Vietnam from Dong Ha to Khe Sanh near the Laos border. This barrier system effectively stopped the North Vietnamese from moving men and supplies into South Vietnam through the DMZ after 1965 and forced them to use the Ho Chi Minh Trail system in eastern Laos to infiltrate into South Vietnam.

Some critics accept the fact that a barrier from Dong Ha to Savannakhet would have prevented North Vietnamese infiltration into South Vietnam using a land route, but argue the North Vietnamese would only increase seaborne infiltration using the East China Sea and the port of Sihanoukville in Cambodia. The U.S. and South Vietnamese navies were able to prevent the use of the South Vietnamese coast for infiltration after 1965, and the

North Vietnamese never considered this avenue a serious means of moving the quantities of men and supplies needed to sustain their military operations in South Vietnam. Most of their seaborne attempts at infiltration were quite small and many met with disaster since the movement of their infiltration vessels could be easily observed using U.S. surveillance means. Even if they reached the coast of South Vietnam, they had very few places where they could safely land and unload before they were observed. They would constantly have to change their offload sites, storage sites, and transport units using a seaborne system of resupply and reinforcement, thus complicating their logistics to the point of absurdity. As for the use of Sihanoukville, they did use third-country shipping and their Hak Lee Shipping Company in Cambodia to supply their divisions in eastern Cambodia, but this route was only viable as long as Prince Sihanouk agreed to its use, and it would never be capable of bringing the 8,000 or more North Vietnamese troops needed each month to maintain their force levels inside South Vietnam. It was out of the question to bring over 90,000 NVA troops each year through Sihanoukville, since Prince Sihanouk had an agreement with the North Vietnamese not to use his ports for this purpose. He was sensitive to the issue of sovereignty, and he had to maintain the fiction of neutrality for both international and internal political reasons. He knew the use of Sihanoukville for the infiltration of North Vietnamese troops would be an open and easily verifiable violation of his country's neutrality and would give the United States an excuse to invade his country. In any event, his regime was overthrown in 1970, putting to rest any idea of using a seaborne infiltration route in Cambodia.

Perhaps the best response to the critics of the Dong Ha–Savannakhet defensive barrier can be found in the statement of Colonel Bui Bin, the North Vietnamese officer who accepted the surrender of the South Vietnamese government in 1975 with the fall of Saigon, and went on to fill several high-level positions in the new communist government. In 1995, he was interviewed by Stephen Young, an American attorney and peace activist, who asked him several questions about how the North Vietnamese viewed the conduct of the Vietnam War. The following should dismiss any lingering doubts as to the efficacy of the Dong Ha–Savannakhet barrier plan:

Stephen Young: "How could the Americans have won the war?"

Bui Tin: "Cut the Ho Chi Minh trail inside Laos. If Johnson had granted Westmoreland's requests to enter Laos and block the Ho Chi Minh Trail, Hanoi could not win the war."

When I read Bui Tin's answer to the question posed by his American interviewer, I began to think back on my own experiences during the Vietnam War and how they tended to reinforce his assertion. I thought about how, as a reconnaissance platoon commander and infantry company commander in Quang Nam Province, I saw the North Vietnamese continuing to use the same infiltration routes and the same base areas in 1969 that they were using in 1967, undeterred by the efforts of covert operations and air power in Laos to restrict their movement down the Ho Chi Minh Trail. I thought of the comments of the former VC, Tran Van Qua, when he spoke of the greatest vulnerability of the VC—their supply system—which he contended was almost entirely dependent upon supplies of weapons and ammunition from North Vietnam. I thought about the comments made by numerous captured VC political cadres and North Vietnamese soldiers I spoke with who clearly identified the Ho Chi Minh Trail as the most critical and vulnerable aspect of the Lao Dong Party's strategy and how reliant they were on the troop replacement drafts and the arms and ammunition stocks sent down the trail. And finally, I thought about the analysis the COSVN staff had done after the Tet Offensive of 1968 that the Tay Ninh Source had provided to our CIA, which identified the fear of an invasion of southern Laos as the main cause for their decision to attack the U.S. Marine base at Khe Sanh and launch the Tet Offensive.

From the very beginning of the U.S. involvement in South Vietnam, the evidence was readily available to justify an invasion and occupation of the panhandle of Laos. The United States had the experience, engineering expertise, construction assets, and military forces needed to conduct such an invasion, but the U.S. government decided against it until it was too late. Because the Americans failed to deal with this essential and vulnerable aspect of the North Vietnamese strategy, they allowed the North Vietnamese to continue to send men and supplies south and to maintain sanctuaries inside Laos and Cambodia, which in turn allowed them to modulate the level of violence inside South Vietnam while minimizing their own losses. Without the Ho Chi Minh Trail, the North Vietnamese would never have been able to execute the third phase of their revolutionary war strategy, that of mobile warfare using conventional units and tactics. In sum, the American failure to cut the Ho Chi Minh Trail *on the ground* was the key to our failure to win the war.

Glossary

AK-47: The standard weapon carried by communist forces. This assault rifle was ideal for combat in Vietnam since it was simple to operate, easy to maintain in the harsh tropical environment, and capable of providing both semiautomatic and automatic fire. Most NVA troops were equipped with this reliable and effective infantry assault rifle.

AO: Aerial Observer. The AO was trained to control artillery and air strikes while flying as the observer in the back seat of a single-engine prop-driven aircraft.

Ao Dai: The traditional two-piece formal dress worn by Vietnamese women.

Arc Light: The code name given for a B-52 bombing raid.

ARVN: Army of the Republic of Vietnam.

CAP: Combined Action Platoon. A village defense platoon made up of three squads of Popular Forces and one squad of U.S. Marines.

CAS: Close Air Support.

CHICOM: Chinese Communist.

Chieu Hoi: The Vietnamese term for "open arms." A GVN program by this name attempted to induce Viet Cong to defect to the government.

CIA: Central Intelligence Agency.

CIDG: Civilian Irregular Defense Group. South Vietnamese military units made up of ethnic minorities, such as Montagnards and Cambodians, and initially organized by the CIA and commanded by U.S. Special Forces, but later turned over to the South Vietnamese Special Forces.

CO: Commanding Officer.

COC: Combat Operations Center.

CORDS: Civil Operations and Revolutionary Development Support. A program established in 1967 to manage all U.S. pacification activities in South Vietnam.

COSVN: Central Office for South Vietnam. This organization served as the headquarters of the Lao Dong Party in South Vietnam. It directed the military and political activities of the communist insurgency. Until 1967 it was located inside South Vietnam but was driven into eastern Cambodia by U.S. military forces.

CRIP: Combined Reconnaissance and Intelligence Platoon. A unit that consists of a squad of American soldiers and a platoon of PFs.

Dau tranh: A term used by the Vietnamese communists that is roughly translated into English as "struggle," but it far more complex and profound than that. To a Vietnamese communist it represents both political and military struggle to achieve the party's aims and defines his very existence and purpose in life.

Deep Reconnaissance: The insertion of Marine Corps reconnaissance teams outside the range of friendly artillery and deep into enemy-controlled territory. These missions were the most dangerous missions assigned to Marine Corps reconnaissance units during the Vietnam War.

DIOCC: District Intelligence and Operations Coordinating Center.

DRV: Democratic Republic of Vietnam, the name of the communist state of North Vietnam.

DZ: Drop Zone (for parachutists).

Embassy House: A leased residential house that was used by the CIA to billet their personnel in a South Vietnamese province. For security reasons these leased facilities were often located close to the provincial headquarters or the MACV provincial compounds in a province, with mercenary guards hired by the CIA to protect them.

FAC: Forward Air Controller.

FO: Forward Observer.

FOB: Forward Operating Base.

GVN: Government of Vietnam. The name of the South Vietnamese government.

H&I: Harassment and Interdiction. This term applies to artillery fire that is unobserved and used to harass or disrupt the enemy.

Hamlet: The smallest administrative entity in South Vietnam, usually a small grouping of houses within the larger entity of a village. Hamlets varied in size from 100 to 1,000 people. Within the various South Vietnamese villages, hamlets are normally named after the parent village but designated by number. For instance, in the village of Phuoc Ly, there might be four hamlets identified as Phuoc Ly (1), Phuoc Ly (2), and so on.

Hoi Chanh: The name given to a communist who defects to the South Vietnamese government.

JUSPAO: Joint United States Public Affairs Office.

KIA: Killed in Action.

Lao Dong Party: The name of the communist party of Vietnam. It literally means "Workers Party." All communist forces and political organizations in South Vietnam were commanded and controlled by the Lao Dong Party, but the communists often tried to hide this reality by creating front organizations, such as the National Liberation Front, or bogus governmental organizations, such as the Provisional Revolutionary Government, to make it appear there were non-communists in leadership positions within the insurgency.

LP: Listening Post.

LZ: Landing Zone (for helicopters).

M-16: The assault rifle used by U.S. and South Vietnamese forces after 1967. Initially, there were many problems with this rifle due to deficiencies in design, lack of training, and faulty ammunition.

M-26: The standard U.S. antipersonnel fragmentation grenade.

M-60: The standard U.S. machine gun.

M-79: A 40 mm grenade launcher that had a maximum effective range of approximately 250 meters.

MACV: Military Assistance Command Vietnam.

MAF: Marine Amphibious Force, a corps-level U.S. Marine command.

MEDCAP: Medical Civic Action Program.

MR: Military Region. There were four South Vietnamese military regions. Military Region 1 consisted of the five northern provinces in South Vietnam. Military Region 2 consisted of the next twelve provinces. Military Region 3 consisted of the ten provinces surrounding Saigon. The remaining southernmost sixteen provinces were in Military Region 4.

NFZ: No Fire Zone.

NLF: National Liberation Front.

Nuoc Mam: A Vietnamese fish sauce used as a condiment.

NVA: North Vietnamese Army. Sometimes referred to as the People's Army of Vietnam, or PAVN.

OP: Observation Post. An OP can be either overt or covert.

PF: Popular Forces. Lightly armed South Vietnamese village militia organized in squad and platoon strength.

Phoenix: The American name for the South Vietnamese pacification program called Phung Hoang. This was a program, which began in 1967, aimed at defeating the communist political infrastructure in the villages of South Vietnam, by forcing all of the American and South Vietnamese organizations involved with defeating the VCI to cooperate and coordinate their efforts at every administrative level of the South Vietnamese government. The Phoenix Committees at the national and regional level addressed policy, while the Phoenix Committees at the province and district level dealt with operational matters.

Phung Hoang: The South Vietnamese organization that paralleled Phoenix, with committees at each administrative level of the South Vietnamese government down to district level.

PIOCC: Provincial Intelligence and Operations Coordinating Center.

POIC: Provincial Officer in Charge. The senior CIA officer in a province.

Police Special Branch: The main intelligence branch of the South Vietnamese National Police.

POSREP: Position Report. A report used by American forces to give their location using grid coordinates.

PRG: Peoples' Revolutionary Government.

Province: A grouping of districts. There were forty-four provinces in South Vietnam.

PRU: Provincial Reconnaissance Unit. This was the primary action arm of the CIA's war against the Viet Cong political infrastructure.

PSDF: People's Self-Defense Force. A local anti-communist militia made up of rural villagers.

Punji stakes: Wooden or metal spikes that are emplaced so anyone stepping on them would suffer a severe foot injury.

R&R: Rest & Recuperation. A five-day holiday that allowed U.S. servicemen to travel at the

U.S. government's expense to various locations in Asia and Hawaii.

Radio Relay Site: A location, usually on a prominent terrain feature, that allowed for the retransmission of radio traffic. Such sites were frequently employed by U.S. Marine reconnaissance units since many of their patrols were conducted in areas of steep mountainous terrain where line-of-sight radio transmissions were masked.

RF: Regional Forces. These were South Vietnamese company-size light infantry militia units at district level. They were used by district chiefs to reinforce PF units who were under attack by communist forces.

RPD: Light machine gun used by communist forces.

RPG: Rocket Propelled Grenade launcher. Used by communist forces, the earliest version was often called the B-40, and the later improved version the RPG-7.

RVN: Republic of Vietnam. The name for South Vietnam.

RVNAF: Republic of Vietnam Armed Forces.

S-1/G-1: The administrative staff section for a military unit.

S-2/G-2: The intelligence staff section for a military unit.

S-3/G-3: The operations staff section for a military unit.

S-4G-4: The logistics staff section for a military unit.

SALUTE Report: A report used by American forces to identify and describe enemy activity.

SEA Hut: Southeast Asia Hut. A wood-framed structure with a corrugated steel roof and screened siding, which was commonly constructed by U.S. engineer units for rear-area cantonments and bases.

782 Gear: Individual field equipment issued to Marines, such as cartridge belt, ammunition pouches, canteens, packs, etc. Also called deuce gear or web gear.

SITREP: Situation Report.

SKS: A semiautomatic rifle used by communist forces.

Snake and Nape: A combination of fin-stabilized bombs and napalm canisters used by fixed-wing aircraft in support of ground troops.

Snap-in patrol: A patrol where an individual accompanies the patrol as an observer so they can gain the experience necessary to qualify as a patrol leader.

SNCO: Staff Noncommissioned Officer.

Stingray: A Marine Corps reconnaissance tactic that used small reconnaissance teams to call in supporting arms on the enemy, often far from friendly lines.

TAOR: Tactical Area of Responsibility. This term applies to the geographical area assigned to a combat unit and for which that unit is responsible for security and operational control.

VC: Viet Cong. The name used to identify southern communists. In actuality, all communist forces in both North and South Vietnam were either military or civilian organizations controlled by the Lao Dong Party headquartered in Hanoi.

VCI: Viet Cong Infrastructure. The term used to describe the Lao Dong Party's political organization in South Vietnam.

Village: A grouping of hamlets that constituted the basic rural administrative entity in South Vietnam. They ranged in size from 1,000 to 10,000 people and often were spread over significant terrain due to dispersed land holdings and rice fields separating hamlets within the village structure.

VNQDD: Viet Nam Quoc Dan Dang, a South Vietnamese political party that opposed the communists.

VR: Visual Reconnaissance. A term used to describe a helicopter flight over a projected reconnaissance patrol area.

XO: Executive Officer. The second in command of a unit who normally was given the responsibility of managing the staff of a unit.

Chapter Notes

Chapter 2

1. 1st Force Recon Company CC, Pickwick Paper Patrol Report, December 15, 1968.
2. 1st Force Recon Company CC, Hunt Club Patrol Report, December 16, 1968.
3. 1st Force Recon Company CC, Steel Rim Patrol Report, December 21, 1968.
4. 1st Force Recon Company CC, Steel Rim Patrol Report, December 21, 1968.
5. 1st Force Recon Company CC, Crazy Bone Patrol Report, December 29, 1968.
6. 1st Force Recon Company CC, Scandinavia Patrol Report, December 31, 1968.

Chapter 3

1. 1st Force Recon Company CC, Team Forefather Patrol Report, January 12, 1969.
2. 1st Force Recon Company CC, Team Icebound Patrol Report, January 14, 1969.
3. 1st Force Recon Company CC, Scandinavia Patrol Report, January 12, 1969.
4. 1st Force Recon Company CC, Team Crazy Bone Patrol Report, January 15, 1969.
5. 1st Force Recon Company CC, Icebound Patrol Report, January 23, 1969.
6. 1st Force Recon Company CC, Paddle Boat II Patrol Report, January 23, 1969.
7. 1st Force Recon Company CC, Penny Wise Patrol Report, January 26, 1969.
8. 1st Force Recon Company CC, Night Scholar 5 Patrol Report, January 27, 1969.
9. 1st Force Recon Company CC, Saddle Bag Patrol Report, January 29, 1969.

Chapter 4

1. Letter to parents, February 17, 1969.
2. 1st Force Recon Company CC, Screen Test Patrol Report, February 18, 1969.
3. 1st Force Recon Company CC, May Fly Patrol Report, February 25, 1969.
4. 1st Force Recon Company CC, Pony Team Patrol Report, February 20, 1969.
5. 1st Force Recon Company, Off Spring Patrol Report, February 20, 1969.
6. Letter to parents, February 25, 1969.
7. 1st Force Recon Company CC, Off Spring Patrol Report, February 28, 1969.

Chapter 5

1. 1st Force Recon Company CC, Trailer Park Patrol Report, March 5, 1969.
2. 1st Force Recon Company CC, Report Card Patrol Report, March 2, 1969.
3. 1st Force Recon Company CC, Puppet Show Patrol Report, March 3, 1969.
4. Letter to parents, March 16, 1969.
5. Col. James B. Ord, Jr., the CO of the 5th Marines, and Lt. Col. John A. Dowd, the S-2 of Task Force Yankee, two very intelligent and thoughtful officers, spent several hours with me one night in the 5th Marines COC at An Hoa discussing our war strategy and their belief that no amount of attrition would convince the North Vietnamese communists of the futility of continuing the war. They told me the NVA were like the Chinese communists and other Asian people who were inured to heavy casualties. Both officers often referred to the horrendous casualties suffered by the Japanese during World War II and the Chinese communists during the Korean War as proof that any Asian war strategy based upon attrition was doomed to fail. Lt. Col. Dowd was killed in action a few months later on August 13, 1969, in the Arizona Territory and was posthumously awarded the Navy Cross for his valor.
6. 1st Force Recon Company CC, Crazy Bone Patrol Report, March 19, 1969.
7. 1st Force Recon Company CC, Off Spring Patrol Report, March 24, 1969.
8. 1st Force Recon Company CC, Report Card Patrol Report, March 27, 1969.
9. 1st Force Recon Company CC, Third Round "A" Patrol Report, March 28, 1969.
10. 1st Force Recon Company, Recline Patrol Report, April 4, 1969.
11. 1st Force Recon Company, Hireling Patrol Report, April 3, 1969.
12. 1st Force Recon Company, Impressive Patrol Report, April 4, 1969.

13. 1st Force Recon Company CC, Crazy Bone Patrol Report, April 7, 1969; Serviceman II Patrol Report, April 7, 1969.
14. 1st Force Recon Company CC, Serviceman II Patrol Report, April 17, 1969.
15. Letter to parents, April 6, 1969.
16. Letter to parents, April 20, 1969.
17. Letter to parents, April 29, 1969.

Chapter 6

1. 2/5 May 1969 CC, p. 5.
2. 2/5 May 1969 CC, pp. 10 and 13; letter to parents, May 19, 1969.
3. 2/5 May 1969 CC, pp. 25–27.
4. 2/5 May 1969 CC, p. 35.
5. Letter to parents, May 25, 1969.

Chapter 7

1. 2/5 CC, June 1969, p.17.
2. 2/5 CC, June 1969, p. 21.
3. 2/5 CC, June 1969, pp. 23–24.
4. Letter to parents, June 27, 1969.
5. 2/5 CC June 1969, p. 36.
6. 2/5 CC, July 1969, pp. 10–11.
7. 2/5 CC, July 1969, p. 20.
8. 2/5 CC, July 1969, p. 23; letter to parents, July 14, 1969.

Chapter 8

1. 2/5 August 1969 CC, pp. 2–3.
2. 2/5 August 1969 CC, p. 4.
3. 2/5 August 1969 CC, pp. 7–9.
4. 2/5 August 1969 CC, p. 13.

Chapter 9

1. Letter to parents, August 13, 1969.
2. 2/5 August 1969 CC, pp. 33–34.
3. 2/5 August 1969 CC, p. 35.
4. 2/5 August 1969 CC, p. 40.

Chapter 10

1. Qua's unit was part of the VC force that supported the NVA's 2nd Division in the Que Son Valley during Operations Union I and II, from April to November 1967.

Chapter 12

1. In 1985, Mr. Tho was interviewed by the author in Jacksonville, North Carolina, and he revealed what happened to many of the Tay Ninh PRU soldiers after the communists took control of South Vietnam. Mr. Tho was arrested in 1975 by the communists and sent to a re-education camp for two years. After his release, he was again arrested and imprisoned for "counter-revolutionary crimes." After his second release from prison, he escaped on foot to Thailand, where he remained in a refugee camp until 1985, when he was allowed to emigrate to the United States.

Chapter 13

1. Tay Ninh Province PRU Monthly Report for October 1969.
2. POIC Tay Ninh memorandum to ROIC III, October 15, 1969.
3. For detailed information on Pham Xuan An and his contribution to the communist cause, see Larry Berman, *Perfect Spy* (New York: Smithsonian Books, 2007), and Thomas A. Bass, *The Spy Who Loved Us* (New York: Perseus Book Group, 2009).

Chapter 14

1. POIC memorandum to ROIC Region III, November 7, 1969. Also, see Tay Ninh PRU Monthly Report for November 1969.
2. POIC Tay Ninh memorandum, Subject: Mission Aborted Due to Operational Restrictions Placed on PRU Advisors in Tay Ninh Province, November 20, 1969.

Chapter 16

1. Merle E. Pribbenow, *The Most Famous Unknown Spies of the Vietnam War: HUMINT Operations in Vietnam*, unpublished manuscript presented at Texas Tech University Vietnam Center, March 2007, pp. 2–14.
2. Although the agent did not name the new pacification plan, he was referring to the Phoenix Program, which was put into effect in late 1967.
3. Peter Braestrup, *Big Story: How the American Press and Television Reported and Interpreted the Crises of Tet 1968 in Vietnam and Washington* (Garden City, NY: Anchor Books, 1978).
4. "The Fate of a Mole," *People's Army Newspaper* (*Quan Doi Nhan*), July 22, 1995, p. 7.
5. The most detailed and accurate information on "the Tay Ninh Source" can be found in the unpublished work of Merle L. Pribbenow, the former CIA officer and Vietnamese linguist, cited above. However, the "source" is also mentioned to a far lesser degree in Frank Snepp, *Decent Interval* (New York: Vintage, 1978), pp. 122–123; John F. Sullivan, *Of Spies and Lies* (Lawrence: University Press of Kansas, 2002), pp. 229–230; and David Corn, *Blond Ghost: Ted Shackley and the CIA's Crusades* (New York: Simon and Schuster, 1994), pp. 201–203, 271, 289, and 308.
6. The results of this discussion and the new plan for the PRU to concentrate on finance-economy cadres are explained in greater detail in the narrative portion of the Tay Ninh PRU Monthly Report, January 1970.

Chapter 17

1. Tay Ninh PRU Monthly Report, January 1970.
2. Tay Ninh PRU Monthly Report, February 1970.

3. Ibid.
4. Ibid.
5. Tay Ninh PRU Monthly Report, March 1970.
6. Ibid.
7. Ibid.
8. Tay Ninh Province VC/VCI Classification Report, March 1970, and the author's U.S. Marine Corps History Division Occasional Paper, *Marine Advisors with the Vietnamese Provincial Reconnaissance Units, 1966–1970*, pages 47–52.
9. POIC Tay Ninh memorandum, Subject: PRU Information Report Concerning Cambodia, April 9, 1970.

Chapter 18

1. Tay Ninh VCI Classification Report, April 1970.
2. Tay Ninh PRU Monthly Report, April 1970.
3. Tay Ninh POIC memo, Subject: Request Station Decision Regarding Use of PRU Teams in Cambodia, May 5, 1970.
4. This POW's comments are not verbatim since I did not have a recording device when I interviewed him, but I have recreated the substance of his comments based upon notes I took during my interview with him.

Chapter 19

1. Tay Ninh PRU Monthly Report, May 1970.
2. Enclosure to Tay Ninh PRU Monthly Report, May 1970. Since I left Tay Ninh Province on June 12, 1970, these figures cover only the eight months ending on May 31, 1970, and do not reflect the data for these last twelve days of my tour of duty with the Tay Ninh PRU.
3. Felix I. Rodriguez and John Weisman, *Shadow Warrior: The CIA Hero of a Hundred Unknown Battles* (New York: Simon and Schuster, 1989), pp. 127–172.

Epilogue

1. Andrew R. Finlayson, "Vietnam Strategies," *Marine Corps Gazette* (August 1988): pp. 90–94.
2. For excellent works that describe the strategic failure of the United States, the author suggests two books: Larry Summers, *On Strategy: A Critical Analysis of the Vietnam War* (Novato, CA: Presidio Press, 1982); and Norman Hannah, *The Key to Failure: Laos and the Vietnam War* (Lanham, MD: Madison Books, 1987).
3. Merle Pribbenow, *Victory in Vietnam: The Official History of the People's Army of Vietnam 1954–1975* (Lawrence: University of Kansas Press, 2002), pp. 3–20. This translation of the official history of the PAVN by the People's Army Publishing House provides an excellent perspective on how the Lao Dong Party planned and executed its strategy for the conquest of South Vietnam.
4. For a concise explanation of how the Chinese Communist three-stage model for revolutionary warfare was used in China, see Samuel Griffin, *Mao Tse-tung on Guerrilla Warfare* (New York: Praeger Publishers, 1961), pp. 20–34.
5. "How North Vietnam Won the War," *Wall Street Journal*, August 3, 1995, A8; also see Pribbenow, *Victory in Vietnam*, pp. 3–90, which provides the details of the North Vietnamese overall strategy and the importance of the Ho Chi Minh Trail. Also, see Bui Tin, *From Enemy to Friend: A North Vietnamese Perspective on the War* (Annapolis, MD: Naval Institute Press, 2002), pp. 74–75.
6. Memorandum for the President, November 11, 1961. *Pentagon Papers*, Vol. II, 110.
7. Nguyen, Lien-Hang T. *Hanoi's War: An International History of the War for Peace in Vietnam* (Chapel Hill: University of North Carolina Press, 2012), pp. 200–203. Nguyen confirms Hanoi's conviction that the Ho Chi Minh Trail was the "linchpin of Hanoi's ability to wage war in the south." She also explains the American plan for the 1971 invasion of southern Laos, Lam Son 719, and the reasons for its failure.

Bibliography

The primary sources for this book were the official unit histories of the U.S. Marine Corps Command Chronologies (in the Chapter Notes they are referred to as "CC") on file with the History Division at HeadquarterMarine Corps, Quantico, Virginia, and my personal letters to my parents, written on a weekly basis during my entire Marine Corps career. Additionally, I retained original copies of the patrol reports for the period of my assignment in South Vietnam with the 1st Force Reconnaissance Company, along with several original maps and documents from that period. For the time I spent with the CIA in Tay Ninh Province, I retained many of my original files, which I took with me when I left South Vietnam in 1970. I relied heavily on these U.S. Marine Corps and CIA official documents and my letters home because they provided a solid, factual basis for the events I describe, and I wanted to avoid the tendency of relying on a fading memory of events and any personal prejudice I might have developed over the years. In this regard, the reader will note that I have tried to rely almost exclusively on primary sources. While the bulk of my notes refer to the above sources, the following books and articles helped to form my thinking on the war and, in part, pertain to aspects addressed in the book.

Ahern, Thomas L., Jr. *CIA and Rural Pacification in South Vietnam*. Langley, VA: Center for the Study of Intelligence, Central Intelligence Agency, 2001.

Andrade, Dale. *Ashes to Ashes: The Phoenix Program and the Vietnam War*. Lexington, MA: Lexington Books, 1990.

Andrade, Dale, and James H. Willbanks. "CORDS/Phoenix: Counterinsurgency Lessons from Vietnam for the Future." *Military Review* (March-April 2006): 9–23.

Andrews, Robert. *The Village War: Vietnamese Communist Revolutionary War in Dinh Tuong Province, 1960–1964*. Columbia: University of Missouri Press, 1973.

Asprey, Robert B. *War in the Shadows: The Guerrilla in History*. 2 vols. Garden City, NY: Doubleday, 1975.

Bass, Thomas A. *The Spy Who Loved Us*. New York: Perseus Book Group, 2009.

Berman, Larry. *Perfect Spy*. New York: Smithsonian Books, 2007.

Braestrup, Peter. *Big Story: How the American Press and Television Reported and Interpreted the Crises of Tet 1968 in Vietnam and Washington*. Garden City, NY: Anchor Books, 1978.

Clausewitz, Carl von. *On War*. Princeton, NJ: Princeton University Press, 1976.

Colby, William, with James McCargar. *Lost Victory: A Firsthand Account of America's Sixteen-Year Involvement in Vietnam*. Chicago: Contemporary Books, 1989.

Colby, William, and Peter Forbath. *Honorable Men: My Life in the CIA*. New York: Simon and Schuster, 1978.

Collins, John M. "Going to Tchepone: OpPlan El Paso." *Joint Forces Quarterly* (Autumn/Winter 1997–98): 1–13.

Corn, David. *Blond Ghost: Ted Shackley and the CIA's Crusades*. New York: Simon and Schuster, 1994.

Corson, William R. *The Betrayal*. New York: W.W. Norton, 1968.

Davidson, Phillip B. *Vietnam at War: The History: 1946–1975*. Novato, CA: Presidio Press, 1988.

Donovan, David. *War of a Kind: Reflections on Counterinsurgency and Those Who Do It*. Minneapolis: Publish Green, 2012.

Fall, Bernard B. *Street Without Joy: From the Indochina War to the War in Vietnam*. Harrisburg, PA: Stackpole Books, 1964.

_____. *The Two Vietnams*. New York: Frederick Praeger, 1967.

Finlayson, Andrew R. *Killer Kane: A Marine Long-Range Recon Team Leader in Vietnam, 1968–1970*. Jefferson, NC: McFarland, 2013.

_____. *Marine Advisors with the Vietnamese Provincial Reconnaissance Units, 1966–1970.* Quantico, VA: Marine Corps History Division, U.S. Marine Corps, 2009.

_____. "The Tay Ninh Provincial Reconnaissance Unit and Its Role in the Phoenix Program, 1969–70." *Studies in Intelligence* 51-2 (2007): 59–69.

_____. "Vietnam Strategies." *Marine Corps Gazette* (August 1988): 90–94.

Giap, General Nguyen Vo. *People's War People's Army: The Viet Cong Insurrection Manual for Underdeveloped Countries.* New York: Frederick A. Praeger, 1962.

Grant, Zalin. *Facing the Phoenix: The CIA and the Political Defeat of the United States in Vietnam.* New York: W.W. Norton, 1991.

Gravel, Mike, ed. *The Pentagon Papers.* 5 vols. Boston: Beacon Press, 1971.

Griffith, Brig. Gen. Samuel B. *Mao Tse-Tung on Guerrilla Warfare.* New York: Frederick A. Praeger, 1967.

Hannah, Norman B. *The Key to Failure: Laos and the Vietnam War.* Lanham, MD: Madison Books, 1987.

Herring, George C. *America's Longest War: The United States and Vietnam: 1950–1975.* New York: John Wiley, 1979.

Herrington, Stuart A. *Silence Was a Weapon: The Vietnam War in the Villages.* Novato, CA: Presidio Press, 1982.

Hickey, Gerald C. *Village in Vietnam.* New Haven, CT.: Yale University Press, 1964.

Karnow, Stanley. *Vietnam: A History.* New York: Viking Press, 1983.

Kissinger, Henry. National Security Council Memorandum 3173-X (Declassified), Subject: "Lessons of Vietnam," May 12, 1975.

_____. *White House Years.* Boston: Little, Brown, 1979.

Lanning, Michael Lee, and Dan Cregg. *Inside the VC and NVA: The Real Story of North Vietnam's Armed Forces.* College Station: Texas A&M University Press, 2008.

Lansdale, MGen. Edward G. *In the Midst of Wars: An American's Mission in Southeast Asia.* New York: Harper & Row, 1972.

Lehrack, Otto J. *Road of 10,000 Pains: The Destruction of the 2nd NVA Division by the U.S. Marines, 1967.* Minneapolis: Zenith Press, 2010.

Mao Tse-Tung. *Selected Military Writings of Mao Tse-Tung.* Beijing: Foreign Languages Press, 1963.

McNamara, Robert S. *Argument without End: In Search of Answers to the Vietnam Tragedy.* New York: Public Affairs, 1999.

Metzner, Edward P. *More Than a Soldier's War: Pacification in Vietnam.* College Station: Texas A&M University Press, 1995.

Moyar, Mark. *Phoenix and the Birds of Prey: The CIA's Secret Campaign to Destroy the Viet Cong.* Annapolis, MD: Naval Institute Press, 1997.

Nguyen, Lien-Hang P. *Hanoi's War: An International History of the War for Peace in Vietnam.* Chapel Hill: University of North Carolina Press, 2012.

Norton, Bruce H. *Stingray.* New York: Ballantine, 2000.

Palmer, Gen. Bruce, Jr. *The 25-Year War: America's Military Role in Vietnam.* New York: Touchstone, 1984.

Pike, Douglas B. *PAVN: People's Army of Vietnam.* Novato, CA: Presidio Press, 1986.

_____. *Viet Cong: The Organization and Techniques of the National Liberation Front of South Vietnam.* Cambridge: MIT Press, 1966.

Prados, John. *The Blood Road: The Ho Chi Minh Trail and the Vietnam War.* New York: John Wiley, 1999.

Pribbenow, Merle L., trans. *The Most Famous Unknown Spies of the Vietnam War: HUMINT Operations in Vietnam.* Unpublished paper, 2007.

_____. *Victory in Vietnam: The Official History of the People's Army of Vietnam, 1954–1975.* Lawrence: University Press of Kansas, 2002.

Race, Jeffrey. *War Comes to Long An: Revolutionary Conflict in a Vietnamese Province.* Berkeley: University of California Press, 1972.

Robbins, James S. *This Time We Win: Revisiting the Tet Offensive.* New York: Encounter Books, 2010.

Rodriguez, Felix I., and John Weisman. *Shadow Warrior: The CIA Hero of a Hundred Unknown Battles.* New York: Simon and Shuster, 1989.

Snepp, Frank. *Decent Interval.* New York: Vintage, 1978.

Sorley, Lewis. *A Better War: The Unexamined Victories and Final Tragedy of America's Last Years in Vietnam.* New York: Harcourt Brace, 1999.

_____. *The Vietnam War: An Assessment by South Vietnamese Generals.* Lubbock: Texas Tech University Press, 2010.

_____. *Westmoreland: The General Who Lost Vietnam.* New York: Houghton Mifflin Harcourt, 2011.

Stubbe, Ray W., and Michael L. Lanning. *Inside Force Recon: Recon Marines in Vietnam.* New York: Ivy Books, 1989.

Sullivan, John F. *Of Spies and Lies: A CIA Lie Detector Remembers Vietnam.* Lawrence: University Press of Kansas, 2002.

Summers, Col. Harry G. *On Strategy: A Critical Analysis of the Vietnam War.* Novato, CA: Presidio Press, 1982.

Tang, Truong Nhu. *A Vietcong Memoir: An Inside Account of the Vietnam War and Its Aftermath.* New York: Harcourt Brace Jovanovich, 1985.

Taylor, K.W. *A History of the Vietnamese.* Cambridge: Cambridge University Press, 2011.

Thompson, W. Scott, and Donald D. Frizzell, eds. *The Lessons of Vietnam.* New York: Crane, Russak & Company, 1977.

Tin, Bui. *From Enemy to Friend: A North Vietnamese Perspective on the War.* Annapolis, MD: Naval Institute Press, 2002.

Turner, Robert F. *Vietnamese Communism: Its Origins and Development.* Stanford, CA: Hoover Institution Press, 1975.

Westmoreland, Gen. William C. *A Soldier Reports.* Garden City, NY: Doubleday, 1976.

Woods, Randall B. *Shadow Warrior: William Egan Colby and the CIA.* New York: Basic Books, 2013.

Young, Stephen. "How North Vietnam Won the War." *Wall Street Journal*, August 3, 1995, A8.

Index

A Shau Valley 42–43, 48, 70
A Vuong River 70
Able, Bess 7
Adams, Capt. Laurence 45
Air Cavalry Division 292
Allen, Lt. Col. Terence M. 165, 167, 172, 175–176, 178–179, 183, 201–204, 208–210, 212, 229, 274
An Bang (1) hamlet 99
Annamite Mountain Range 5, 45, 48, 280
Antenna Valley 79–81, 84, 159
Antenna Valley Pass 117
Ap Ba (2) hamlet 81
Ap Ba (3) hamlet 79
Ap Phuoc Thuan hamlet 139–142
Arc Light B-52 bombing 34, 51, 256, 297
Arizona Territory 22–23, 38, 47–48, 72, 76–77, 90, 92–96, 101, 103, 128–129, 132–134, 136, 138, 228–229, 300
Asprey, Robert 226, 228–229, 303
atrocities, VC 77, 108, 186
award system, problems with 100–101

B-52 strike (also Arc Light) 51, 234, 256, 264, 297
Barnes, Capt. Eric M. 26, 79, 280
Base Area 112 17, 19, 21, 23–24, 29, 33–34, 41–46, 49–54, 60–62, 65, 67–72, 75–77, 84, 92–93
Base Area 116 63, 71, 114
The Basic School 277
Bau Anh hamlet 206
Beach Nut (team) 67
Beck, Lt. Larry 57–60, 67
Ben Dau (3) hamlet 97, 101
Ben Giang village 70
Bien Hoa 172, 180, 190, 192, 209, 218, 231–232, 260
Bisaha, Sgt. M.T. 105

Blankenship, Sgt. Godfred 79
bombing halts (also truces) 37, 71
Brady, Lt. Col. Eugene R. 99–101
Browder, Lt. Ed 67, 74–75, 79–80, 84
Buda, Robert 45
Burns, Capt. 84

Cambodian Invasion 261–263
Camp Reasoner 14–16, 20–21, 24–26, 28, 35, 40, 42, 65, 76, 82–83, 88, 103–105
Cao Dai Holy See 240–242, 249
Cao Dai religion 167–168, 171, 202, 213–215, 238–240, 279
Champe, Lt. Randy 67
Charlie Ridge 22, 24, 126, 128–130, 132
China Beach 103
Civilian Irregular Defense Group (CIDG) 42, 171, 173, 185, 221, 233, 251–252, 297
Coffer, GySgt John T. 105–106, 109, 114–115, 117, 122, 126–127, 129, 141, 158
Combined Action Platoon (CAP) 73, 113, 205, 297
Commo-Liaison Cadre (VCI) 239, 245, 254
Company B, 1st Battalion, 3rd Marine Regiment (B/1/3) 54
Company C, 1st Battalion, 5th Marine Regiment (C/1/5) 64
Company E, 2nd Battalion, 5th Marine Regiment (E.2/5) 99–100, 105, 114, 123, 133, 136
Company F, 2nd Battalion, 5th Marine Regiment (F/2/5) 90, 92–95, 101, 114, 126
Company G, 2nd Battalion, 5th Marine Regiment (G/2/5) 96, 99, 101–102, 105, 107–109, 114, 119, 122, 124, 134, 139–141, 145, 148
Company H, 2nd Battalion, 5th Marine Regiment (H/2/5) 114

Company K, 3rd Battalion, 5th Marine Regiment (K/3/5) 54
Company M, 3rd Battalion, 5th Marine Regiment (M/3/5) 94
Conti, Lt. Robert 105, 145
Continental Hotel 203
COSVN 161, 167–168, 174, 185, 212, 233–239, 244–245, 261, 265, 296, 297
counter-recon teams 17, 19, 33, 51, 61, 64–65, 67, 74–75
Crazy Bone (team) 38, 42, 51–53, 79, 84
Crouch, Sgt. 84–86
CS gas grenades, use of 44, 59, 80
Cu Ban (2) 108

Da Nang 2, 5, 10, 12–20, 25, 33–35, 44, 45, 63, 70–78, 83, 88–89, 99, 103, 106, 111, 125, 128, 139–147, 155, 157, 160, 163, 165–166, 204, 213–215, 274–275, 277, 279–280, 293, 294
Dai Hiep (4) hamlet 46, 54
Dai Khung (7) hamlet 96
Dai Viet political party 20, 155, 215
Davis, Angela 109
deep reconnaissance patrol 70, 279
Deo Le Mountain 79
Dien 20, 147, 165, 277, 280
Dixon, Albert K., II 12
Dogpatch (also Phuoc Tuong Village) 10–11, 275, 279
Dorris, Sgt. Ron 27, 66
Dowd, John 122
Dowd, Lt. Thomas B. 82, 280
Dowd family 82, 122
Duc Duc District 29, 78, 93, 111
Duc Hotel 146, 163–164, 166, 171, 176, 202, 204, 274–275
Dung, Ngo Van 196, 216–217, 240, 242–245, 252–254, 269, 277–279
Durham Peak (Operation) 114, 116, 123, 125, 128

Duy Xuyen District 107
Dwyer, Brig. Gen. Ross T., Jr. 11, 14

Eddy, Cpl. 81
Elephant Valley 70
Emergency extraction 31, 33–34, 41, 51, 59, 62, 64, 71, 73, 79–82, 86–87
Essential Elements of Information 29
Estabrook, HN 37

Fegan, Col. Joseph 8, 13
Finance-Economy Cadre, VCI 153, 155–156, 158–159, 193, 218–219, 221, 239, 240, 246–248, 251, 254, 257–258, 262, 265, 271
Finkle, Cpl. 51
Fifth Marine Regiment (5th Marines) 14, 22, 26, 29, 35, 37, 60, 62–64, 76–77, 80–84, 87–90, 103, 111, 139, 300
1st ARVN Division 13, 293
1st Force Reconnaissance Company 11–13, 48, 79, 81, 87, 103
1st Marine Air Wing 21, 24, 28, 75, 99
1st Marine Division 8, 10–11, 13, 20, 28, 73, 87, 103, 114, 129–130, 139, 144, 163
First Marine Regiment (1st Marines) 82
1st Medical Battalion (Charlie Med) 10, 77, 103
1st Reconnaissance Battalion 14, 17, 42, 65, 87, 103
1st Viet Cong Regiment 22, 41, 63, 65, 71, 76, 79, 81, 152, 155, 160
Forefather (team) 43–45, 53–54, 56
40th NVA Regiment 97
402nd VC Sapper Battalion 12
Fulbright, Sen. William 66, 109

Gell, Pfc. 86
Glenn, Sgt. 48, 61
Go Noi Island 21–22
Group 44 (Quan Da Provincial Unit) 23, 49

Ham An (5) hamlet 94
Hansen, Lt. Bob 15, 49, 62, 82
Happy Valley 12, 70–71
Harper, SSgt. Travis 105
Harriman, Averill 290
Henderson Hill 105, 109
Henry, Michael C. 82
Hiep Duc, town and district headquarters 22, 63, 76, 78, 80
Hiep Duc Valley 76

Hieu Duc district 70
Higgins, Lt. Col. James H. 91–96, 99, 107, 114, 117, 121–123, 127, 130–132
Highway 1 142, 213–214, 260
Hill 31 110, 111
Hill 34 103
Hill 65 95, 128–134, 138–139, 145, 148, 158
Hill 132 72
Hill 204 33
Hill 232 39
Hill 327 10, 13, 24, 76–77, 103, 139–141, 147, 277, 279
Hill 332 84
Hill 344 81
Hill 350 79
Hill 374 70
Hill 375 74
Hill 381 (Nui Khuc Son Mountain) 117–118, 122–123
Hill 406 60
Hill 452 56, 62, 80, 85
Hill 481 38
Hill 485 (An Chau Dao Mountain) 74
Hill 551 58
Hill 734 77
Hill 845 (Nui Mat Rang Mountain) 76
Hill 1026 (An Bang Mountain) 49, 83
Hill 1031 (Ba Co Mountain) 72
Hill 1143 (Yang Brai Mountain) 49–50, 58–59, 67, 71
Hilsman, Roger 290
Hireling (team) 83
HMM-364 "Purple Foxes" 99
Ho Chi Minh Trail 38, 41–42, 65, 69–70, 78, 81, 128, 224, 235, 256, 264, 288–289, 291, 294–296
Hoi An 83, 213
Hoi Chanh (rallier) 38, 70, 106–107, 133–135, 154, 178, 212, 215–216, 247, 250, 298
Hopgood, Capt. Marvin 115
Hundley, Capt. "Hot Rod" 69
Hunt Club (team) 33
Huth, Lt. Phillip N. 105, 110–112, 117

I Corps 1–2, 13, 23, 41–42, 167, 179, 201, 218, 291, 293
Icebound (team) 45, 47, 51, 53–54, 56, 65, 77
Impressive (team) 84
infiltration, enemy 29, 38, 42, 47, 51, 60, 67, 70–72, 77, 80, 85, 96, 288, 293–295

Jarnolinski, Pfc. 86
Jaskilka, MGen. Samuel B. 60, 100

Johnson, Pres. Lyndon Baines 7, 71, 234–236, 289–290, 295
Jones, LCpl. 33
jungle penetrator 21, 31, 33, 45, 49, 118, 120

Karkos, Sgt. Norman 42, 58–60
Kennedy, Pres. John F. 289–290
Kennedy, Sen. Robert 109
Kham Duc Special Forces Camp 42
Khe Dienne Stream 60–62
Khmer Serey 195, 232–233, 251, 255
Killen, Sgt. James 27
Killer Kane (team) 1, 5, 12–14, 70, 79–80
King, Martin Luther, Jr. 7–8, 109
Kingrey, Capt. Robert 92–95
Kit Carson Scouts 96, 105, 107, 111, 118, 125, 129, 136–138, 148–149, 162

ladder extraction device (Simmons Rig) 20–21, 24–25, 33, 45, 59, 62, 84
Lam, Nguyen Hoang 183, 185–186, 189–190, 195, 198, 200–203, 206, 215–217, 220–222, 225–226, 232, 240, 244, 249, 252–254, 257–258, 260–262, 267, 273–275, 280
Landing Zone Barnes 26, 39, 45, 49, 59, 65, 69, 84
Landing Zone Finch 24–25, 105
Lanh An (3) hamlet 123
Lao Dong Party 49, 133, 148, 152–156, 212, 233–238, 282–284, 286–290, 295, 297–298
Laos, strategic importance of 224, 234–236, 256, 261, 264, 266, 282–296
La Thap (1) hamlet 108
Lawder, Lt. Lynn 67, 71
Liberty Bridge 91, 94, 105–112, 128, 138, 148
Ly Thi Lan 88–89, 103

Mackerel, PFC 105
Madeleine, Sister Marie 35, 83, 278–280
Mai Ly 20, 83, 147, 165, 275–277, 280
Marble Mountain 2, 19, 21, 69, 86
Marine Barracks, Washington, D.C. 7–8, 13, 115
Mathis, SSgt. Jack 27, 40, 48, 53, 63, 69–71, 75, 82
Mau Chan (2) 64
Mau Chung (1) 37
McCarthy, Sen. Gene 65–66
McDaniel, LCpl. 34

Index

McDonough, Sgt. 53–54
McNamara, Robert 66, 78, 202, 289
"McNamara Line" 294
Meade River (Operation) 22
MEDCAP 111, 132, 298
Meiners, Lt. Gene 15, 27, 40–41
Merchantville, NJ 3, 7, 122, 226
Miller, Lt. Rick 67
Miller, Maj. "Rip" 100
Minh Tan (1) hamlet 95
Montagnard tribesmen 38
Murphy, Lt. Kevin J. 96–98, 100–101, 105
Muskogee Meadow (Operation) 84
My Dong Village 94–95, 133, 136
My Hiep (1) hamlet 132, 134–136
My Hiep (2) hamlet 136–137
My Hiep (4) hamlet 132, 135–136
My Hoa (1) hamlet 133
My Hoa (2) hamlet 132
My Hoa (3) hamlet 132
My Le (1) hamlet 99
My Le (3) hamlet 96–97, 99–100
My Loc (2) hamlet 110
My Loc (4) hamlet 108
My Loc (6) hamlet 109
My Phu hamlet 132, 138

New Life Hamlet 107
Ngo Dung 35–36, 83, 277–279
Ngo Hue 35–36, 83, 277–279
Nhgi Thuong (1) hamlet 123
Nickerson, Maj. Gen. Herman, Jr. 11–13
Night Scholar (team) 62
90th NVA Regiment 95
Ninh Long (2) hamlet 80, 85
Nixon, Pres. Richard M. 211, 256
Nong Son Coal Mine 161
Nui Ba Den Mountain 172, 175, 193–197, 200, 231, 236, 248
Nui Do Mountain 63–64
Nui Duong Thong ridgeline 64
Nui Hon Sai Mountain 29, 31
Nui Mo Cam Mountain 63–64
Nui Ro Mountain 70
NVA base areas 23–24

Off Spring (team) 72, 74–75, 79
Ong Thu Slope 17, 19, 22–23, 29, 31, 34, 45, 47–50, 54, 56, 65, 67, 69, 71–72, 74–75, 83–84, 92, 139
Ord, Col. James B. 81–82
Ott, Sgt. Theodore 45–46, 53–54, 56, 65

Pace, SSgt. Robert C. 99, 105
Paddle Boat II (team) 42, 57–60

Pate, Sgt. 83–84
patrol leader seminars 42, 65
patrol order 28
Pearce, HN 59–60
Pelham, Lt. 105, 115–116, 125, 135, 137
Penny Wise (team) 60
Peppin, PFC David D. 110–112, 117
Phoenix Program 63, 78, 167–168, 185–186, 188–189, 191, 195, 197, 208, 210–212, 218–219, 223, 238, 245, 249–250, 254–255, 265, 271, 298; see also Phung Hoang
Phu Bac Village 93–94
Phu Loi (2) hamlet 92–94
Phu Nhuan (3) hamlet 110
Phu Nhuan (4) hamlet 106, 110–111
Phu Nhuan (7) hamlet 109
Phu Phong (3) hamlet 94
Phuoc Hoi Village 34, 37, 50
Phuoc Ly hamlet 15, 107
Pickwick Paper (team) 29, 31
"Pony" Fire Support Base 114
Pony Team (team) 72
Poolaw, Capt. R.W. 96
Popular Forces (PF) 25, 63, 73, 107, 113, 123, 134, 141, 161, 205, 247, 253, 298
Porpotage, Lt. 42
Powell, Lt. G.E. 101–102, 111
Prisoner Grab 38, 58, 79–80
propaganda, enemy 65–66, 108–109, 150, 155, 157, 166, 256, 265, 287, 294
Provincial Reconnaissance Unit Program 133–136, 144–147, 163, 165–168, 179, 195, 208–210, 212–213, 298
Puppet Show (team) 77

Qua, Tran Van Kit Carson Scout 105, 107, 111, 125, 129, 135, 138, 148–162, 218, 280, 295
Quang Nam Province 5, 8, 20, 23, 25, 27, 40–41, 46–47, 49–50, 63, 65, 69, 70, 73–74, 77–78, 81–83, 92, 107, 114, 128, 130, 132–133, 140, 148, 152, 157, 160–163, 166, 213–215, 277, 295
Quang Tin Province 5, 27, 41, 50, 71, 159–160
Que Son Mountains 63, 65, 76, 83, 114–127, 161
Que Son Valley 63, 71, 79–80, 84, 114, 117, 121, 148, 159–160
Quyen, Phung Thi (also Ba Quyen; Chi Tam) 187–189, 258–260, 273–274, 280

racial tensions 8, 104
Radio Battalion 46
Ralston, Sgt. John 105
rappelling 20–21, 25, 44, 48–49, 53, 60, 69, 84
Recline (team) 83
Regional Forces (RF) 299, 25, 253, 299
Report Card (team) 77, 80
Richie, Lt. Jim 67, 76
Rivera, PFC 61
Robertson, Maj. Gen. Donn J. 12
Rollings, Lt. Wayne 67, 72, 80–81, 84
Rose, PFC 59–60

Sacred Heart Orphanage 34
Saddle Bag (team) 63–64
Saigon 73–74, 144–147, 163–168, 201–204
Scandinavia (team) 39, 48–49
Screen Test (team) 70–71
2nd North Vietnamese Army Division 13–14, 17, 22–24, 33–34, 37–39, 41–43, 46, 50, 53, 56–57, 65, 67, 71, 75, 77, 80, 84, 159–161
Sen, Nguyen van 195
Serviceman II (team) 84–85
7th Marine Regiment (7th Marines) 128
Shoemake, Cpl. G.L. 105
Shultz, Cpl. 27
Siem, Nguyen van 186, 200, 269
Simmons, Roger 13–15, 17, 19, 22–24, 26, 28, 41–43, 45, 47, 54, 58–60, 62, 64–65, 77, 81, 86–87, 103
Simpson, Maj. Gen. Ormond R. 11–13, 130
SITREP report 299
Slater, Lt. John E. 29, 31, 33, 67
Smart, Mr. 20, 83, 165, 277, 280
Song Cai River 29, 34, 38–39, 43–47, 49–51, 54, 58–59, 65, 67, 69–71, 75
Song Ky Lam River 22
Song Thien Yen River 22
Song Thu Bon River 22–23, 33–34, 37–38, 50, 72, 77, 79–80, 84–85, 90, 93–94, 99, 101, 108–109
Song Vam Dong River 172
Song Vu Gia River 22, 94–95, 128, 132, 138–139
Sparks, SSgt. Henry E. 110–112, 117
Staging Battalion 8
Stainback, Charles O. 172–174, 196, 212, 244
Steel Rim (team) 34, 37, 42
STINGRAY 63, 299

Index

Storm, Lt. Dennis 98–101, 105, 145
Studies and Observation Group (SOG) 19–21, 24, 43, 45

Tan Phuoc (1) hamlet 90
Task Force Yankee 11, 14, 28–29, 41, 43, 45–46, 48–49, 51, 54, 58, 60, 64–65, 69, 75–76, 87
Tat Lay Mountain 70
Tay Ninh City 168, 170, 172–173, 180, 182, 184, 186, 190–191, 198, 200, 203, 206, 217, 225, 247
Tay Ninh East Airfield 172, 190–191, 198–199, 206, 211, 222, 231
Tay Ninh Source 231–238
Tay Ninh West Airfield Base and Airfield 184, 191, 195, 198, 216–218, 248–249, 258
Taylor Common (Operation) 11, 14, 34, 43, 54, 65, 67, 70–71, 76–77, 81, 83–84, 87, 92
Tet Offensive (1968) 7, 13, 20, 25, 37, 41, 63, 73, 78, 83, 132, 141, 160, 162, 168, 185, 212, 229, 234–236, 245, 247, 264, 291, 296
Thach Bich hamlet 80, 84–85

Thanh Hai (1) hamlet 123
Thanh Xuyen (3) Refugee Camp 101, 103
The, Trinh Minh 171, 175
III MAF 19, 43, 103, 144, 165, 275
Third Marine Regiment (3rd Marines) 14, 28, 65, 67
3rd NVA Sapper Battalion 109–110
Third Reconnaissance Battalion 28, 33
Third Round "A" (team) 81
38th NVA Regiment 118, 121
31st NVA Regiment 161
Tho, Tran Quoc 183–186, 188, 190, 192, 196–198, 200, 205–207, 210, 215, 222, 239–242, 244–245, 250–254, 262–263, 267, 280
Thomas, Lt. John R. 98, 105, 112
Thompson, Sgt. David 43
Thon Ba (2) hamlet 123
368B NVA Artillery Regiment 24, 33–34, 71
Thu Bon (3) hamlet 107
Thua Thien Province 23, 70
Thuong Duc District and Special Forces Camp 28–29, 46, 70
Trailer Park (team) 76

Treseloni, Sgt. 62
Trevathan, GySgt Bruce D. 40, 85–87
Tu Pho (5) hamlet 85
25th Infantry Division 184, 188, 191–192, 197, 231, 261
21st NVA Regiment 23, 71

Ulstad, Sgt. 60–61
Urenovich, Lt. Michael C. 108–109, 125

Vallese, Maj. A.L. 91–92, 99, 114, 122, 132–133
Viet Cong Infrastructure Phoenix categories 185
Viet Cong mass organizations 152
VNQDD political party 155, 215, 299
Vogel, Frederick J. 133, 135

Wallis, LCpl. 76
Westmoreland, Gen. William 235–236, 291, 295
Williams, Dell Capt. 62

Zaro, Col. William 82, 90, 100
Zia Rong (2) hamlet 58